The Limited Raj

The Limited Raj
*Agrarian Relations in Colonial India,
Saran District, 1793–1920*

Anand A. Yang

UNIVERSITY OF CALIFORNIA PRESS
Berkeley • Los Angeles • London

University of California Press
Berkeley and Los Angeles, California
University of California Press, Ltd.
London, England
© 1989 by
The Regents of the University of California

1 2 3 4 5 6 7 8 9

Library of Congress Cataloging-in-Publication Data

Yang, Anand A.
 The limited Raj.

 Bibliography: p.
 Includes index.
 1. Saran (India)—Politics and government. 2. Saran
(India)—Rural conditions. 3. Local government—India—
Bihar—History—Case studies. 4. Elite (Social sciences)
—India—Saran—History. 5. Great Britain—Colonies—
Asia—Administration—History—Case studies. 6. India—
History—British occupation, 1765-1947. I. Title.
JS7025.S27Y36   1989   320.8'0954'12   87-5658
ISBN 0-520-05711-2 (alk. paper)

Contents

Acknowledgments	ix
List of Abbreviations	xi
Introduction	1

PART ONE: The Setting of Control

1 Metaphors of Control: The View from Sonepur Mela and Meet	13
2 The Agrarian Landscape of Control	31

PART TWO: The Limited Raj System

3 The Initial Encounter: The British Establishment of Connections, 1765–1793	55
4 Government and Its Allies: The System of Control and Collaboration	70
5 The Limited Raj: The British Development of Local Control Institutions	90

PART THREE: Estate Control and Management Systems

6 Between Raja and Raiyat: The Structures of Control in the Great Estate of Hathwa	115
7 The Dynamics of Hathwa Control: Two Case Studies	139
8 Zamindars and Maliks: Structure and Strategies of Control	155

PART FOUR: Peasant Options in a Colonial Society

9 Desertion and Migration as Peasant Options	181
10 Resistance, Violence, and Collective Action as Peasant Options	206
Conclusions	225
Glossary	241
Bibliography	245
Index	267

Tables

1. Population Growth in Saran District, 1872–1961 — 33
2. Population Density in Saran's Thanas, 1872–1921 — 35
3. Agricultural Seasons, Principal Crops, and Cultivated Areas under Different Harvests — 37
4. Percentage of Saran's Crops by Order of Importance, 1873–1921 — 38
5. Percentage of Major Caste Groups in Saran, 1872–1921 — 45
6. Average Annual Wholesale Price of Rice in Seers per Rupee, 1861–1901 — 51
7. Hathwa Raj's Property, 1873–1874 — 117
8. Indirect and Direct Management Systems in the Hathwa Raj, 1874–1898 — 127
9. Tahsildars in the Hathwa Raj, 1872 — 128
10. Origins of Hathwa's *Thikadars*, 1898 — 130
11. *Khas* System in Hathwa Raj Circles, 1905 — 136
12. Transfer of Raiyati Rights, 1891–1901 and 1911–1921 — 174
13. Categories of Transferees, 1891–1901 and 1911–1921 — 175
14. Outmigration from Saran, 1881–1921 — 191
15. Principal Destinations of Saran's Outmigrants, 1881–1921 — 192
16. Average Daily Wages in Saran, Dacca, and 24-Parganas — 196
17. Number of Riots in Saran, 1862–1920 — 214

Illustrations

Figures

1. The Sonepur Mela — 16
2. The Role of the Dutt Family in Hathwa Management — 125
3. The Structure of Hathwa Management — 126

Maps

1. Saran District in 1901 — 10
2. The Location of the Sonepur Mela and Meet — 24
3. The Parganas of Saran District — 32
4. Hathwa Raj Parganas — 118
5. The Core Villages of Hathwa Estate — 120

Acknowledgments

The generosity of teachers, friends, colleagues, and organizations has greatly benefited the completion of this study.

Over its many lives, this book has incurred many debts. At the doctoral dissertation stage, Walter Hauserji shared with me his extensive knowledge of the world of peasants and the region of Bihar, and I am deeply grateful to him for his constant encouragement, enthusiasm, and support over the years. Tom Kessinger has also guided my thinking, especially in directing me toward appreciating the vistas of the "new" social history. C. A. Bayly, Richard Barnett, and Ravinder Khare assisted me in many ways on different versions of this manuscript. I also owe much, personally and intellectually, to the friendship and discussion I have shared with James R. Hagen, Philip E. McEldowney, and Ann Waltner.

My debts abroad begin with the ordinary people of Saran—too many to list here—who shared their experiences with me. To the working people of libraries and repositories, I also owe deep gratitude: Maqbool Alam and the staff of the Saran District Record Office, Tara Saran Sinha, Rafiq Babu, and the staff of the Bihar State Archives, and the India Office Library and Records in London. I am also grateful to the library staffs of the British Museum, the School of Oriental and African Studies, the South Asia Centre of Cambridge University, and the Bodleian at Oxford.

As a graduate student fresh in the field, R. S. Sharma of Delhi University was my wise and knowledgeable guide. K. S. Singh, Q. A. Ahmad, and the History Department of Patna University were gracious hosts and sources of intellectual stimulation. S. H. Askari, the grand old man of Bihar studies, patiently answered all my questions. R. K. Chopra, his son, Ashok, and the rest of that remarkable family taught me the meaning of Indian hospitality. Tan Chung and I-Ssu were my kind family in Delhi.

Maharaja Kumars Mrigendra Pratap Sahi and Brajeshwar Prasad Sahi of Hathwa not only gave me access to their rich zamindari records, but also welcomed me to their homes. I must also acknowledge the many ex-zamindars who gave freely of their time and records: the Hathwa branch family, Chainpur, Manjha-Rusi, and Bagoura. Equally forthcoming were Sir Eric Cecil Ansorge, V. E. Davies, Arthur Hugh Kemp, the late P. T. Mansfield, and other former Bihar civil servants.

For permission to include here, in altered form, material from previous publications, I am grateful to *Modern Asian Studies, Journal of Interdisciplinary History, Journal of Social History*, and Peter Robb, the editor of *Rural India*.

I record my indebtedness as well to my history colleagues at the University of Utah who have been willing listeners and encouraging critics. So many incarnations has this work undergone, that in the course of typing and retyping this manuscript, Tony Scott, Roxann Dickson, Betty Sedgley, Carroll Gillmor, and Barbara Evans have seen the coming of the word processor. Barbara Metcalf of the University of California Press has shown confidence in this work from the start. To Phyllis Killen, the senior editor at that press, and Nancy A. Blumenstock, a professional editor, as well as to the referees of an earlier version of this manuscript, I owe many thanks for their contributions.

Financial assistance to conduct research for this study in India and England in 1972–1974 came from a Fulbright-Hays Doctoral Dissertation Research Abroad grant and an American Institute of Indian Studies Junior Research grant. Thanks to University of Utah Research Committee awards in 1975–1976 and 1976–1977 and an American Council of Learned Societies Grants-in-Aid for Recent Recipients of the Ph.D. in 1977, I was able to complete additional research. Appreciation is also happily acknowledged to the University of Utah College of Humanities and its career development committee for their financial assistance in defraying the production costs of this work.

To Christiane Fauron, merci beaucoup, for helping me keep this work in proper perspective. Above all, I am grateful to my parents, Yun Yuan and Loheng, for giving me a head start in the field of South Asian studies and for their continuing support, encouragement, and love.

Abbreviations

AGRPD	Annual General Report, Patna Division
B&O	Bihar and Orissa
BOR	Board of Revenue
Colltn.	Collection
Colltr.	Collector
Commr.	Commissioner
Consltns.	Consultations
Cr.	Criminal
EPW	*Economic and Political Weekly*
Gen.	General
G.G.	Governor General
GOB	Government of Bengal
GOB&O	Government of Bihar and Orissa
GOI	Government of India
H.R.	Hathwa Raj
IESHR	*Indian Economic and Social History Review*
JAS	*Journal of Asian Studies*
Jdcl.	Judicial
Magte.	Magistrate
MAS	*Modern Asian Studies*
Offg.	Officiating
P.C.	Patna Commissioner's
Polit.	Political
Procs.	Proceedings
Rev.	Revenue
S.C.	Saran Collectorate
Secy.	Secretary
SDG, 1908	*Bengal District Gazetteers: Saran*, by L.S.S. O'Malley. Calcutta, 1908.

SDG, 1930	*Bihar and Orissa District Gazetteers: Saran,* rev. ed. by A. P. Middleton. Patna, 1930.
SDG, 1960	*Bihar District Gazetteers: Saran,* by P. C. Roy Chaudhury. Patna, 1960.
SDO	Subdivisional officer
SR	*Final Report on the Survey and Settlement Operations in Saran District, 1893 to 1901,* by J. H. Kerr. Calcutta, 1903.
SRR	*Final Report on the Survey and Settlement Operations (Revision) in the District of Saran, 1915 to 1921,* by Phanindra Nath Gupta. Patna, 1923.
Supr.	Supervisor
SVN	Saran District Village Notes.
U.P.	Uttar Pradesh

Introduction

Man's control by man is a central theme in human history. Who controlled whom, how, why, and with what consequences? These questions inform my historical study of the structures and effects of colonial rule in rural South Asia. I will examine mechanisms of control, whether those designed by the formal apparatus of the British government or the informal networks of landholders and village notables operating in local society, and their ramifications for the peasant population of Saran District in north Bihar between 1793 and 1920. My concern with control is to illuminate the pattern of agrarian relations and its changes in a local society over more than a century of colonial rule.

The concept of control in this book refers to behavior that aims at establishing and maintaining unequal relationships. Control means the exercise of power by a superordinate over a subordinate's resources—economical, political, and social—and person.[1]

My use of the idea of control is not to be equated with the classic sociological term "social control," defined recently by Morris Janowitz as "the capacity of a society to regulate itself according to desired principles and values."[2] In this formulation, the focus is on the normative mechanisms, such as custom, tradition, morality, family, school, and religion, that contribute to order in society. This concept has a long tradition in American sociology, beginning with Edward A. Ross's work at the turn of the twentieth century and developed thereafter by such scholars as Robert E. Park, Robert M. MacIver, and Talcott Parsons.[3] In viewing it as the key to understanding order in society, these scholars came to reject "economic self-interest theories," asserting instead that "the individualistic pursuit of economic self-interest" explains "neither collective social behavior nor the existence of a social order and does not supply an adequate basis for the achievement of 'higher ethical goals.' "[4]

Precisely this aspect of the notion of social control, with its emphases on the "capacity of a social organization to regulate itself" and "acknowledged moral and collective goals," has led some Marxist scholars, pace Gareth Stedman Jones, to reject its usefulness in historical analysis. Correctly identifying the sociological tradition of functionalism as the source of the concept, Jones takes issue with its preoccupation with the relationship between the individual and

---

1. For a general discussion of the terms "control" and "social control," see Jonowitz (1978: 27–52); Gibbs (1982); and Watkins (1975).
2. Janowitz 1978: 28.
3. Ibid.: 27–52; Coser 1982: 13–22.
4. Janowitz 1978: 29.

society in terms of commonly accepted norms. Largely absent, therefore, in the standard sociological usage of this theoretical framework is the idea of class struggle.[5]

Although the critics of social control have justifiably questioned the consensus and equilibrium models of society implicit in the works of many "social control" sociologists, they have not convinced all historians that the concept does not provide a useful perspective. On the contrary—and it is in this respect that my notion of control resembles the recent reworkings of "social control" theories—some scholars have not only rejected its "functionalist approach," but view it as the key to comprehending the "power arising from economic inequalities and from control of the state apparatus."[6] In this enlarged concept, social control has been borrowed by one group of historians to investigate the "relationships between rich and poor in nineteenth-century British society ... for whom social order is maintained not only, or even mainly by legal systems, police forces and prisons, but is expressed through a wide range of social institutions, from religion to family life, and including, for example, leisure and recreation, education, charity and philanthropy, social work and poor relief."[7]

As with these reformulations of the idea of social control, I do not assume an absence of coercion or conflict. Indeed, my concept of control is linked directly to conflict because it refers to the manipulation of behavior in relationships that entail conflict of interests. *Control is the basis of power in society.*

Where I diverge from both the old and new scholarship on social control is in their emphasis on normative mechanisms. My concerns center more on the institutional and processual arrangements of power—the arrangements that enabled the British to dominate an indigenous society and, within that society, Indian local controllers to command its resources. In this conception, there is much more of a direct, intentional quality to the institutions of control that reinforced and enhanced the relations of inequality existing among different actors in the agrarian setting of Saran.

My social control perspective adds another dimension to the study of power relations in a colonial society by highlighting the normative aspects of relations. As some radical historians have done by combining this perspective with the concept of "hegemony," power is not always expressed in forms of "overt physical coercion."[8] In the words of Tom Nairn, the "hegemony of one social class over subordinate classes in society may be extremely complex, a cultural tissue of great variety and subtlety, extending all the way from the education of infants to the naming of streets, present in people's inhibitions and mental blocks as well as in what they profess to believe."[9] Although not explicitly

5. G. S. Jones 1976: 304 and 1977: 162–70.
6. Moorhouse 1979: 484–85. Also see Moorhouse (1978: 61–82) and Reid (1978: 347–61).
7. Donajgrodzki, ed. 1977: 9. See also Muraskin (1976: 561).
8. Moorehouse 1979: 485.
9. Nairn 1964: 19. Also see Guha, ed. (1982a, 1982b, 1984) and Guha (1983)

concentrating on social control as expressed in forms of ideological control or hegemony, my discussion of the mechanisms of colonial and landholder control seeks to trace the extent to which the state and local controllers intruded into the lives of ordinary people. This perspective is in sharp contrast to the scholarship on the British Raj, which continues to mine the exhausted vein of British policies in South Asia—the policies themselves or the effects of the policies as measured against the ideals of the blueprint or the conditions of the target population.[10]

Recently, some scholars have shifted this line of inquiry "to deal with two hitherto unexplored areas: the internal operation of government with emphasis on the process of rule, and British administration and administrators as part of a broader political system."[11] Nevertheless, the actual workings and machinery of the colonial system at the local level remain largely neglected. As D.A. Low noted in 1973, "we still remain abysmally ignorant about how the Raj's political domination was articulated beneath the British district officer through various networks of locally prominent families, subordinate Indian bureaucracies and rural dominant castes."[12] In converging on the structures of rule at levels below the formal administrative apparatus, these scholars have also turned to the crucial ties between the alien intruders and the indigenous elites. Both John Gallagher and Ronald Robinson, concerned with the politics and processes of collaboration, have propounded theories about the non-European sources of imperialism that attach key significance to the centrality of the arrangements for collaboration between Europeans and non-European elites in shaping the workings of colonial systems.[13] By coopting local notables, the colonial administration could control vast territories and populations with only a handful of administrators and troops. As a growing body of intensive investigations on colonial settings shows, European regimes maintained and enhanced their authority by winning the support of powerful local individuals and groups who became the recipients of their patronage and enjoyed favorable agrarian and commercial policies.[14]

The processes and structures of collaboration were crucial determinants in the British framework of rule in South Asia. In urban centers and rural hinterlands (*mofussil*), the Raj was anchored at the local level by alliances with powerful men—identified in north India as rais (respectable persons), rajas, taluqdars (holder of an estate, or taluqa) and zamindars (landholders).[15] These connections were so central to the workings of the colonial system that they also defined the nature of indigenous resistance to alien rule. Eric Stokes's pioneering work on the Mutiny/Rebellion of 1857 illustrates this relationship when he notes that the "critical factor . . . for the promotion or suppression of

10. See Stokes (1959) and Ray (1979).
11. Barrier 1981: 199.
12. Low 1973: 9. See also Bayly (1979: 21–54).
13. See Louis, ed. (1976: 53–151).
14. See, e.g., Munholland (1981).
15. Bayly 1971 and F. C. R. Robinson 1971: 289–311, 313–36.

revolt . . . was the action of magnate elements."[16] Coopting these men, to whom I refer as local controllers, also enabled the Raj to enhance its own legitimacy.

In analyzing the structures and processes of British control, I will highlight the actual workings of this collaborative system of rule in Saran in the late eighteenth to early twentieth centuries. The previous body of scholarship focused exclusively on the development of the so-called "steel frame" of colonial administration in India (the Indian Civil Service), but my interest here is on uncovering the deep extensions of the colonial state into the countryside in order to delineate the contact points at which government impinged on the lives of the majority of the population—the peasants (raiyats). The arrangements that this system of rule effected with local controllers are reconstructed to present a model of a "Limited Raj," which operated at the level of local society.

My focus on the system of collaboration and the Limited Raj may shift attention away from the earlier preoccupation with Western impact and indigenous response to tracing "the locus of historical initiative"[17] within the indigenous society itself, but I do not seek to neglect other props of the imperial edifice that European regimes constructed in Asia and Africa. In seizing territory as well as in maintaining power over its possessions, colonial rule also relied on superior military technology and organization.[18] And colonial takeover and expansion in South Asia entailed the disarming of the subject population as well as the assumption and consolidation of repressive force in the hands of the government. Indeed, the colonial system drew its strength from its monopoly of the apparatus of armed power, epitomized in its ability to overwhelm and contain resistance through its control and deployment of military and paramilitary institutions, such as the police.[19]

Ultimately, however, the institutional advantages that relatively small armies and groups of European administrators and settlers were able to acquire over vast territories and populations rested on Europe's domination of the world economy. Ever since Karl Marx formulated his theory about the nature and effect of the linkages between colonies and the world capitalist economy,[20] scholars have sought to understand the effects of the integration of a "traditional" economy into the world capitalist network of production and exchange. But what processes accompanied this development remain vexing and controversial in the historiography of colonial societies, especially.

The tenor of the debate has been set by the writings of a pre-Independence generation of nationalists bent on producing an "advocacy history," designed to question the benefits of British rule in India by highlighting its destructive effects on the indigenous economy and society. Running counter to this interpretation is

16. 1978: 189   17. Ibid.: 19–45.   18. Ness and Stahl 1977: 5–9.
19. Arnold 1977 and Yang, forthcoming.   20. Marx and Engels, n.d.

a theory, supported largely by Western scholars, that there was little disruption.[21] The essential questions raised by these two schools, as well as by interpretations straddling these two points of view, are ably sketched by Frank Perlin:

> Did colonial rule lead to a successful development of Indian economy . . . or did it instead lead to the underdevelopment of that economy, thereby destroying already advanced manufacturing industries (partly through direct administrative and mercantilist intervention, partly through the open door available for England's newly industrializing production of yarn and cloth)? Or was colonial rule too temporary and impotent a phenomenon to have any profound effects on a resilient, profoundly conservative, alien society?[22]

The former view, associated with the work of R. C. Dutt and subsequently developed principally by Indian scholars, argues that the relatively non-monetized rural economy of traditional India and its flourishing handicrafts industry were shattered by the advent of market forces unleashed by Western commercial and industrial penetration. Not only did agriculture stagnate under deleterious colonial revenue policies, but it had to shoulder the additional burden of supporting a labor force displaced from the handicrafts industry, which was unable to keep pace with European competition.[23] Recently this debate, centering on the question of deindustrialization, has been revived by the writings of A. K. Bagchi, and, as before, the "classical" view has not gone unchallenged. The debate continues to rage within a familiar framework, with no conclusive interpretation apparently in sight. A major problem is the sketchy nature of the available data.[24]

An important outcome of the debate, however, has been a sharpened focus on the question of the ties between the wider capitalist network and the colonial economy. Although scholars differ on their choice of the exogenous or indigenous system as the activating force in the relationship, they at least agree that these links generated vital changes in the Indian economy and society during the Raj. And with the rising interest in the "modern world-system" approach of Immanuel Wallerstein,[25] the quest for better answers about the nature of links between the world capitalist network and colonial societies is likely to continue.

Already these trends have drawn attention to the precolonial period as researchers begin to explore the earlier phase of interaction between European expansion and Indian society to uncover clues about the later encounter. Thus, the argument of Irfan Habib regarding the parasitical "commercial" capitalism of the Mughal Empire, which declined with the passing of its political power, supplies a crucial variable in understanding the subsequent

---

21. The different views are argued in Morris et al. (1969). An influential interpretation in this debate is the work of Bipan Chandra (1966, 1979).   22. 1983: 52.
23. Dutt 1960. See also the essays in "Review of the Cambridge Economic History of India and Beyond," *MAS* 19 (1985): 353–698.
24. Bagchi 1976a: 135–64, 1976b: 499–522. Also see Vicziany (1979) and Bagchi (1979: 105–46, 147–61).   25. 1974: 1979

colonial takeover.[26] Other writers discuss the late Mughal economy in terms of the world economy, focusing specifically on the growing European demand for Asian luxury goods or the effects on the Mughal political economy of the inflow of European bullion.[27]

Although much of this research is still tentative in its conclusions, it establishes the significance of the conjunction of external and internal forces that enabled the European powers, first, to gain a foothold in the South Asian subcontinent in the eighteenth century, when a weakened economic and political system made it vulnerable, and, then for the British to fill the vacuum and gain dominance by virtue of their wider network of ties to the world economic system.[28] Although not concerned with these linkages, I recognize the decisive influence of this conjunction of forces in shaping economy and society at the local level. In this context, as well as that of the collaborative system, the Limited Raj operated effortlessly and economically.

Another major focus of mine is on the level of society where the power of the colonial state tapered off and the landholders' system of control took over. In focusing on the actual workings of zamindari control—both the mechanisms and their operations—the nature and structure of the Limited Raj and the ways in which peasants were subordinated into the pattern of agrarian relations in the district are further delineated.

The configurations of the two control systems were related. The lack of penetrating state institutions at the local level restricted the British presence to an administrative apparatus that focused on districts (at best, subdivisions) with British personnel largely confined to towns and urban centers. In this system of rule, partly by design and partly by benign neglect, much of the countryside was abandoned, thus placing the overwhelming majority of the rural population in the grip of devices fashioned by zamindari networks.

Ranging in size from the land of the Maharaja of Hathwa who commanded the resources of over a thousand villages to that of the petty proprietor (malik) who claimed only a few acres (usually shares in a village or several villages), most of the district's landholdings were carved out into fiscal units called estates (mahals). In this book, the term "estate" refers to the entire holdings of a zamindar; the focus here is on the estate both as a territorial unit and as a map of human relationships. With the state largely absent at this level of society (except for estates devolving on minors, females, and persons of known incapacity, in the form of the institution of the Court of Wards), the estate's organization and network of control defined the political, social, and economic relations between zamindar and peasant.[29]

By highlighting the control that mediated the relationships between land-

26. 1969: 32–78. 27. Ali 1975; Richards 1981.
28. Ali 1975; Richards 1981. Also see Perlin (1980) and Bayly (1983).
29. The advantages of focusing on the estate as an analytical unit can be seen in the work of Musgrave (1972) and Metcalf (1979).

holder and peasant, I will seek a dynamic presentation of the strengths and weaknesses of the different actors in the agrarian system of the district. Control in the agrarian society ultimately rested on the extractive capacities of the zamindars who monopolized the production and distribution of the resources of the land. As Marxist writers note, the key lies in the relations structured by the agrarian economy. While not isolating class relations in society as the principal variable, as do the Marxists, I will look at the ways in which interrelations of control were shaped by the forces and relations of production. In not using class as an analytical tool, however, I am not turning to caste—a concept generally set up as its polar opposite—as providing any more accurate a model for comprehending the nature of power in rural society. Both class and caste features form the basis of the "native categories" used here, formulations that the anthropologist André Beteille believes represent the terms in which the Indian villager "thinks and acts."[30]

An examination of the indigenous categories of agrarian society reveal that they centered around the manipulation of the forces and relations of production. From the "native" perspective, two distinctly functional groups existed: zamindars and raiyats (landholders and peasants). The indigenous society made further distinctions among the district's leading landholder, Hathwa, who was recognized as a raja (or maharaja); lesser landholders who were lumped together in the category of zamindar; and the small landholders who were usually labelled petty maliks. Likewise, in terms of both their roles in the modes of production and the systems of zamindari control, the raiyats occupied a range of positions, from the big raiyat whose holdings of several acres and privileged access to external resources made them the equivalent of the petty malik to the cultivator whose primary identification was as laborer (mazdur) rather than a tenant.[31] The crucial roles were played not by those who lived in mud huts or *garhs* (mud forts) and, later, palaces, but by those in a village who had power, wealth, and prestige and who were integrated in networks of supravillage authority, power, and systems of control.

At the level of village society stood another category of controller. These village-level controllers dominated their locality's economy and society, in their roles as petty maliks and substantial raiyats, and by virtue of their command over credit and marketing networks. Links to the larger society through their quasi-official positions as village headmen and accountants (patwaris) or as intermediaries for local controllers (zamindars) legitimized their mastery over village-level society.

Colonial rule in the form of the Limited Raj penetrated into local society and affected the relationships in the multilayered agrarian society. I will show how the colonial state enhanced the control and, thus, the power and dominance of the district's zamindars. I will also reconstruct the experiences of the district's

30. 1974: 49.
31. Indigenous terminology and its local variants are described in Grierson (1975).

peasants, framing their actions and behaviors within the context of state and zamindari systems of control. This perspective is a useful corrective to the studies of peasant societies that fail to account for the other components in the agrarian system by seeing the peasantry as self-contained and integrated. As a result, peasants are portrayed as enjoying a degree of decision-making power over their own lives, but with limited options because they comprise a component distinctly subordinate to the larger agrarian system. From this angle, the real locus of control in the agrarian society of Saran becomes apparent.

Peasants in this work are, to use Wolf's characterization, "populations that are existentially involved in cultivation and make autonomous decisions regarding the processes of cultivation."[32] However, unlike Wolf, I do not exclude agricultural or landless laborers from this definition because they share many of the characteristics of peasants; nor is the distinction made in the indigenous vocabulary. Wolf's emphasis on the occupation of peasants as autonomous cultivators, furthermore, ignores the occupational diversity of Indian rural society, including Saran, where peasants may engage in several occupations at the same time.

In viewing peasant actions within the context of control, I will also relate peasant behavior to its social, political, and moral contexts. And by viewing local control in terms of agrarian relations, groups on the land are seen as operating with corporate identities fashioned by both caste and class aspects. Such an analysis also shows economic relations mediated and modified by social relations with an explicitly "moral" or normative edge to them—one where rights, duties, and obligations determined a dharma (code of right conduct or behavior) for both landholders and peasants. My purpose in adopting this framework is not to validate James C. Scott's theory about the moral premises on which peasant action is based and his detailed ideas regarding their rootedness in a "minimal culturally defined subsistence level."[33] Nor is it my intention to take the opposing view identifying the peasant as a "rational actor" who is committed to decisions prompted solely by economic considerations. Such precise divisions of peasant actions cannot be made from the data on Saran peasant behavior and *mentalités*. Instead much more on the mark is the observation made in a current debate about these two contending schools of thought regarding peasant action:

For those interested in the actions of rural peoples within the political-economic settings in which they live, it seems essential to recognize that, although some action is the consequence of calculated intent on the part of individuals to maintain or improve their lot and that of their families, such calculation takes place within a social space structured with reference to moral premises that are meaningful to these individuals.[34]

Within this framework, actors in Saran's agrarian society clearly followed rational strategies. For superordinates the moral imperative necessitated that

32. 1971: xviii. See also Mintz (1973) and Shanin (1979). 33. 1976.
34. Keyes 1983: 755–56: Popkin 1979.

their appropriations be restricted to guarantee an expected subsistence minimum to peasants. This did not inhibit the latter's seeking strategies designed to maximize subsistence, but the risk of losing the minimum level was generally avoided. Ultimately though, because peasant choices were made within the parameters of the landholders' control systems, their choices entailed a limited range of possibilities. Thus, the limits of control modified, mediated, and truncated relations among the British Raj, zamindars, and raiyats alike. When and where the colonial state was weak, the local landholders increasingly held sway, jeopardizing the delicate balance that insured basic subsistence for the peasants.

The methodological usefulness of a delimited social and economic setting as a convenient focus of analysis is now a valued approach in many disciplines. In this book, the questions centering on control are related to the specific experience of the old Bihar district of Saran between 1793 and 1920. Extending over 2,600 square miles, this district—before its division into Saran, Siwan, and Gopalganj districts in 1973—was shaped like an isosceles triangle. Rivers formed the natural boundaries on two sides: the Ganges divided it in the south from the districts of Patna and Shahabad, the Gandak from Muzaffarpur and Champaran, and the Gogra formed its southwestern boundary with Shahabad and Ballia in Uttar Pradesh (U.P., formerly United Provinces; and before that, the North-Western Provinces and Oudh). The base of this triangle was shaped by the administrative line demarcating the northwestern border with Gorakhpur District in U.P. (See map 1.)

In applying the magnifying glass to manageable and delimited settings, historians have begun to reap the benefits that anthropologists have had in pursuing "community studies."[35] For South Asia the possibilities for intensive investigations of a locality over a fixed period of time are indicated by Robert Eric Frykenberg's account of localizing and centralizing forces in one South Indian district and by Tom G. Kessinger's examination of one village in Punjab.[36] Whether yielding a detailed picture of the interrelationships and interactions between rulers and ruled or the structure and functioning of society at its fundamental levels, such grassroots perspectives have brought the historical experience of India and Indians into sharper focus. A promising aspect of this line of inquiry has been the realization that source materials exist to reconstruct the rich, subtle pasts of local societies.[37]

35. Bell and Newby 1972; Macfarlane 1977. 36. 1965; 1974.
37. Yang 1979c; Diehl, comp. 1971; Gustafson and Jones, eds. 1975; Ludden 1985.

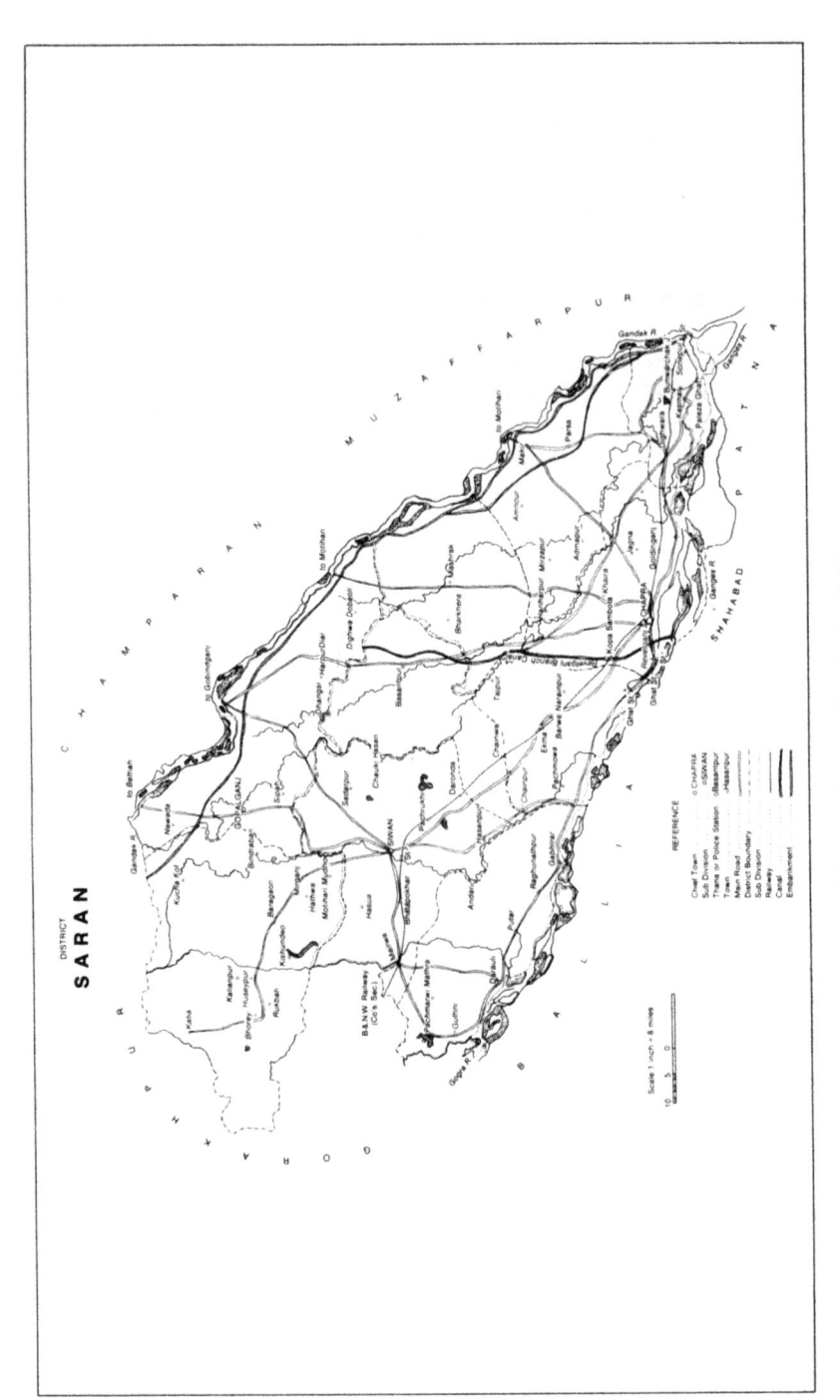

Map 1. Saran District in 1901.

PART I

The Setting of Control

1

Metaphors of Control: The View from Sonepur Mela and Meet

I

Who thinks Sonepore
An awful bore—
Dislikes the Fair's *gol gopra* [disorder]
Who'll nothing know
Of indigo—
He's not the man for Chupra!

II

Who little cares
For drills nor wears
Behar Light Horseman's *kapra* [clothes]—
Of sticking pig—
Recks not a fig—
He's not the man for Chupra!

III

Who shuns the sweets
Of social meets;
The dances and the supp'r—ah!—
Who thinks small beer
Of Hutwa's cheer—
He's not the man for Chupra!

IV

We can but sigh
For days gone by
When Forbes' hand was upprer—
Oh! Mister Clay
I grieve to say
You're not the man for Chupra![1]

Thus wagged the doggerel bards in 1886 when A. L. Clay replaced the popular Arthur Forbes as the district magistrate of Saran. Such inkslinging in the

---

1. Cited in Abbott (1896: 174–75). Unfortunately, "Mister Clay" is silent about his Sonepur years (1896).

Indigo Planter's Gazette, the tabloid of the planting community in north India, was prompted by Clay's reluctance to support the Sonepur Meet in the manner expected of Saran administrators. As one of the "guardians" of the Sonepur tradition lamented, Clay did not want to be the "open-handed, genial sportsman to boss our show"—a transgression that he inadequately redressed by finally accepting to serve as a "cypher Secretary."[2]

No doubt, Clay's indifference aroused the ire of the resident European community because the Sonepur Meet was the premier social event of the year. An 1884 guide dedicated to "young men who are thinking of devoting themselves to a professional career in India" singled it out as an example of the kind of social life available to new India hands. It described the Meet as the "oldest established meeting . . . larger and more cosmopolitan . . . than other race-meetings, and . . . the trysting place where the planters of several districts can assemble."[3] Throughout the late nineteenth and early twentieth centuries, British officials and nonofficials converged on Sonepur from all over north India to enjoy its "three days [horse] racing, and three balls, and cricket, tennis, polo, golf, and other fun."[4]

The meet's origins date back to the turn of the nineteenth century, when horse races were held at Hajipur, in the neighboring district of Muzaffarpur. In 1839 the site was shifted across the river to Sonepur, ostensibly because of the poor condition of the Hajipur track. However, a more important consideration was to coincide its staging with the "great" Sonepur Mela, "probably the oldest . . . in Bihar and . . . one of the largest annual fairs in the world."[5]

The most dramatic way in which government maintained its presence at Sonepur was by its "unofficial" staging of the annual meet. The foisting of the British gathering on the Hindu mela and its encroachment on the latter's sacred space and time represent metaphorically the processes whereby the Raj extended its control into local society. However, the rituals and symbols encompassed by each event evoked different models of religious, social, and political order.

Indian Traditions at Sonepur

The mela celebrated Sonepur's significance as a place of pilgrimage and puja (worship).[6] Located at the confluence of the sacred Ganges and Gandak rivers, its sanctity is embodied in the belief that a ritual dip at the junction of the rivers is tantamount to giving away a thousand cows as a gift. Such ceremonial bathing in the Ganges (*ganga-asnan*) is considered especially efficacious on Kartika Purnima (the day of the full moon in Kartik [October-

2. Abbott 1896: 177. 3. Buckland 1884: 62. 4. Abbott 1896: v.
5. *SDG, 1930*: 155.
6. *Harihar Kshetra Mahatamya* 1924; Chaudhury 1965: 116. See also Ostor for a discussion of the meaning and forms of puja, which is a person's "expression of respect for the gods—an event, an idiom of action, and a symbol" (1980: 6).

November]). In Hinduism the very concept of pilgrimage (*tirtha-yatra*) refers to "undertaking journey to river fords."[7]

Sonepur is also enshrined in legends as the setting of the story of Gajendramoksha—the liberation of the king of the forests, the elephant, from the jaws of the king of the waters, the crocodile, because of the timely intervention of the god Hari (Vishnu). Further religious significance is endowed by its association with Vishnu's incarnation, Rama, who is said to have traveled through here enroute to Janakpur to win the hand of Sita in marriage.

The proliferation of temples reflects the growing prominence of a holy place. Local tradition credits Rama with the founding of Sonepur's first temple, perhaps a precursor of the principal place of worship today, the Harihar Nath Mahadeo Temple. Its existence in the Mughal period is verified by contemporary accounts. The temple is unusual for its statue combining the images of Hari (Vishnu) and Har (Shiva) together, thus the association of the name *Harihar Kshetra* with Sonepur. Temples to other deities were subsequently established, including the Kali *Asthan* and the Panch Devata *Mandir*, widening Sonepur's range of devotees.[8] Sonepur's long-standing historical significance as a pilgrimage center is confirmed by recent excavations that unearthed a stone pillar of the Sunga period (184–75 B.C.) and statues from the later Gupta and Pala dynasties.[9]

The beginnings of the mela are traditionally ascribed to the legendary period of Rama. The emergence of Sonepur as a pilgrimage center must have led to the establishment of the Harihar Kshetra Mela, also known as the Sonepur Mela, its founding reflecting the fact that the traffic of pilgrims had become so heavy that new sacred domains were annexed and additional facilities installed to cater to rising nonspiritual demands. Small wonder then that the fair was synchronized to the same calendar that most devotees followed in timing their visit to this junction of rivers. Extending over a fortnight, the climaxes of the mela came in the period two days before, and two days after, Kartika Purnima.[10]

In the sixteenth century the venue of the fair was shifted, apparently due to political considerations, to the other side of the Gandak, to Hajipur, which was then the district headquarters of local Muslim rulers. The erosion of this fairground by the fluvial action of the river, however, prompted its return to Sonepur. In its everyday character, Sonepur formed part of a cluster of several villages that constituted a "minor marketing area" focusing on the periodic marketplace (*hat*) of Dudhaila, which convened every Tuesday, Thursday, and Sunday. In 1919 this area extended over forty-three villages inhabited by over 7,300 people.[11]

7. Bharadwaj 1973: 2.
8. *SDG, 1930*: 156–57; Chowdhary 1917: 130–32.
9. *SDG, 1960*: 498.
10. *SDG, 1930*: 156–57. Also, Turner and Turner (1978: 1–39).
11. Hunter 1877: 262; SVN, 1915–1921, Sonepur thana nos. 1–100, 106–159. See also Skinner (1964).

Fig. 1. The Sonepur Mela.

The mela transformed about four square miles of the area centering on Sonepur into a canvas town and market. Some tents housed people, others shops, which offered many products not commonly available in local markets, including European goods by the late nineteenth century. The mela was also the occasion of the most important cattle fair in north India.[12]

These developments ensured that Sonepur as a pilgrimage center and the site of the Kartika mela appealed to a wide constituency. The English traveler, John Marshall, wrote in the late seventeenth century that people had "come thither from the remotest parts of India" and from as far away as "Tartary Central Asia." According to his estimate, the crowd numbered as many as fifty thousand people.[13] Participation from nearby districts was so extensive that entire towns seemed deserted. In Patna city "in the great days of bathing," Hamilton Buchanan observed, "most people cross the junction of the Gandaki."[14] He also reckoned that "Harihar Chhatra" was the "most fashionable pilgrimage" from Patna and Gaya districts, attracting as many as one-quarter of the entire population of Patna and a sizable number from Gaya. In the late nineteenth and early twentieth centuries, official enumerations regularly returned counts of over a quarter of a million visitors.[15]

Sonepur's attraction lay in, to use the language of its devotees, "the greatness of Harihar Kshetra as a place of pilgrimage."[16] At the appropriate time in the religious calendar of the region, pilgrims performed rituals at this sacred site, which defined their common religious identity. Although colored by ethnocentric notions, the following description by a veteran British official suggests the powerful sentiments that Harihar Kshetra aroused:

The mystic "sungum," or junction of the holy river, so sacred in the mind of the superstitious Hindoo, yearly attracts a vast concourse of religious bathers, who, at the full of the moon, rush at a given signal, with the force of a torrent and the roar of a cataract, into the confluent waters, each human wave struggling for preeminence of submersion, and each individual maddened with fanatic excitement.[17]

"Those who reach the water, exactly at the second calculated, are supposed to be cleansed of all sin."[18]

The act of devotion at Sonepur brought together pilgrims who were of high and low castes, sadhus (holy men), and saints. And as at other pilgrimage sites, the religious experience, located in sacred time and space, did "away with . . . most of the distinctions of caste, and the separation of the sex."[19] The evocation of such a sense of community is also noted in the anthropological literature. As McKim Marriott's study of the north Indian village of Kishan

12. *SDG, 1960*: 501; Wilson 1908: 171.   13. Khan, ed. 1927: 141–42, 158.
14. Buchanan 1925: 183.
15. Buchanan 1928: 365–66; *SDG, 1930*: 168. For annual figures, see, e.g., AGRPD, 1888–89; for a 1961 estimate of 3 million visitors, see S. D. Prasad 1964: 69 (GOI).
16. *Harihar Kshetra Mahatamya* 1924. See also *Abha* (May 1956).
17. Tayler 1881, 1: 492.   18. M. Wilson 1908: 155.
19. Rankine 1839: 27; *Harihar Kshetra Mahatamya* 1924: 6.

Garhi shows, "many festival observances cut significantly across the routine barriers of social structure."[20]

In the late nineteenth century, it was precisely this community identity that leaders of the Hindu "revivalist" organization, the Cow Protection Movement, sought to press into their service when they convened the first meeting of the Indian Association of Cow Protection (*Gauraksha*) lecturers at Sonepur. In 1888 lectures were held near the Hariharnath temple about the evils of cow slaughter and "the wretched condition to which the peasantry had been reduced by cow-slaughter."[21] The fair was an especially important recruiting ground for the movement not only because its message was assured of being heard by many people, but also because, as the venue of a major cattle fair, the mela vividly dramatized the urgency of cow protection.[22]

The major resistance movement against the British in Bihar in the Mutiny/Rebellion of 1857, organized by Kunwar Singh, is said to have been hatched at a gathering held at the Sonepur Mela. The fair also provided a cover for a political meeting convened in 1845 by Hindu and Muslim notables who were up in arms against British violations of their cultural and religious beliefs and practices. Secret invitations were issued to many prominent Biharis, and a plot organized to win the support of sepoys and the assistance of the Mughal emperor and the king of Nepal.[23] Nor were the advantages of mobilizing people at Sonepur lost on the leaders of the nationalist movement in the twentieth century. As early as 1908, regional supporters of the Indian National Congress held a meeting at this site and established the Bihar Provincial Congress Committee. In later years recruiters for Congress returned often to seek new adherents. The Bihar Provincial Peasant Association (*Kisan Sabha*) was another organization that sought to tap into the popular dimensions of the Sonepur Mela: an early attempt to establish a peasant association in 1922 convened there, and it was also the venue of the founding meeting in 1929. The mela was chosen, as Walter Hauser explains, because it "attracts peasants from all parts of Bihar and provides a logical and convenient forum for the airing of agrarian problems."[24]

Religious celebrations, the market, and the fair also attracted the British to Sonepur, although for different reasons. Because pilgrimages "are an expression of the communitas dimension of any society ... from the point of view of those who control and maintain social structure, all manifestations of communitas, sacred or profane, are potentially subversive."[25] Moreover, a common assumption in contemporary British thinking was the belief that fairs posed a

20. Marriott, ed. (1955: 193); Singer 1972: 228–40. See also Turner (1974: 166–229) for a discussion of such experiences as generating "liminality" and "communitas."
21. GOB, app. E, II, "Saran," with A. Forbes, Commr. of Patna to Chief Secy., Oct. 27, 1893, L/P&J/6/365, encl. 7.   22. Yang 1980: 587.
23. K. K. Datta [1970: 21–30, and 1957.
24. 1961: 35. See also K. K. Datta (1957b, 1: 150, 279, 309).
25. Turner and Turner 1978: 32. 250–51.

threat to law and order because they were "a nursery of crime and a hotbed of vice."[26] Such concerns underlay the official patronage of the Meets, if not the actual superimposition of the British-created event, the Sonepur Meet, on the mela. As the "official" history of the meets states, "the raison d'être of the yearly European gatherings... is of course the fair, which local officials have to attend to keep order, and see to the sanitary arrangements. In the olden days planters visited it to buy horses, and gradually it became one of the most popular and enjoyable social gatherings of the country."[27]

Thus, the barbs aimed at Clay because of his reluctance to support the meet were not without political overtones. The presence of the "man for Chupra" was imperative because he understood the significant roles that the European indigo planters, the paramilitary Bihar Light Horse, and the Maharaja of Hathwa (the district's leading landholder) played in the system of British control in the locality. These actors embodied the basic props of Pax Britannica: the "man for Chupra" was the epitome of the district administrator, the local representative of the Raj; and the local European residents (primarily indigo planters) and government's Indian supporters (the major local landholders) comprised his network of allies. Together they constituted the formal and informal structures on which the rule of the Raj rested. Therefore, to reconstruct the activities of the Sonepur Mela and Meet and the arenas in which they intersected, particularly as manifested in rituals that abound in metaphors and "are a series of performative acts creating the imagery of the metaphor,"[28] is to identify the parameters of official control in local society. The activities at Sonepur offer an opportunity not only to observe Indian and British societies behaving in systems that were condensed in space and time, but also to extract the striking metaphorical statements that mela and meet make about the limits of British control in Saran in the nineteenth and early twentieth centuries.

The British Meet

Unlike the Sonepur Mela, the British-organized meet clocked the passage of a different kind of time. In his autobiography, William Tayler, an old Bihar hand, described it as

a social gathering of... supreme and unrivalled attractions. Taking place at the close of the enervating six months during which the hot season, from April to June, and then the rains from June to September, have combined to stupefy and enfeeble the unhappy British sojourners, it forms the auspicious entrance upon the fresh and invigorating delight of the cold weather, when for at least three months, the climate of India is, perhaps, the finest in the world.[29]

The opportunity to interact in a social setting was also highly treasured by the "sojourners" because such gatherings alleviated one of the chronic com-

26. Cunningham 1977: 163.
28. Bastien and Bromley 1980: 50.
27. Abbott 1896: 1.
29. 1881, 1: 494.

plaints of British existence in the rural interior. In a candid discussion about better leave privileges for its civil servants, the Bengal government acknowledged that "the depressing effects of life of small stations in Lower Bengal from the deficiency of European companionship is undoubtedly a serious fact." Other testimonies submitted on this occasion mention that this "serious fact" afflicted the lives of large numbers of administrators stationed in desolate towns and unhealthy weather. So "lonely and deadly [had] life [become] in many stations," according to one official, "that an officer on leaving office, cannot even look forward to the creation of a game of tennis or whist. He must take a solitary walk or drive." Furthermore, he concluded that the "lonely and dull life in an unhealthy climate must act prejudicially on the mental and physical powers of even the strongest man."[30] No wonder that, for a community that considered itself "exiled" in India, the Sonepur Meet was, as a "man for Chupra" put it, "what Christmas is to home folks."[31]

The beginnings of the Sonepur "Christmas" date back to the late eighteenth century when British authority was extended into the countryside. Ostensibly in keeping with long-standing tradition, the local judge deputed officials to proceed to the fair in person "to prevent ryots gambling and drunkeness, and to be particularly careful that the zemindars did not levy any taxes or contributions."[32] Official interest in Sonepur heightened thereafter, especially when the government sought to build up the fair as a horse market in 1801. Not only was this intended to be an inducement for native horse and cattle dealers from the nearby towns and the city of Patna to ply their trade, but it was also designed to facilitate the recurring government need to purchase horses for its cavalry. To build Sonepur into the premier horse fair of the region, the government withdrew its patronage from the competing Duddry Fair—also held in Kartik, but at the confluence of the Ganges and Sarju rivers in the Banaras region—which had been operating since 1770 with the support of the raja of Banaras.[33]

By 1807 the official presence at Sonepur had already acquired the proportions of a tradition. As Charles Boddam, the Saran judge and magistrate acknowledged, district officials annually received orders to attend the mela. This participation had become so incorporated into official calendar by the late nineteenth century that every district officer began his cold weather tour with "the necessary annual halt at Sonepur."[34] It was also a regular stop in the itineraries of administrators from other districts and their senior divisional

30. GOB, Bengal Jdcl. Procs., Aug.–Dec. 1889, Aug., 25–41.
31. Abbott 1896: v.
32. C. Boddam, Judge, to Hon. Sir John Shore, G.G., Apr. 8, 1796, GOB, Bengal Cr. Jdcl. Consltns., Mar. 3–17, 1809, Mar. 10, no. 2, encl.
33. Jacob Rider, Colltr., Govt. Customs, Banaras, to Marquis Wellesley, G.G., Nov. 6, 1803, GOB, Bengal Cr. Jdcl. Consltns., July 12 to Aug. 30, 1804, July 19, no. 13.
34. Boddam to G. Dowdeswell, Secy., Jdcl. Dept., GOB, Bengal Cr. Jdcl. Consltns., Nov. 6 to Dec. 24, 1807, Nov. 6, no. 1; AGRPD, 1878–79.

and provincial officials. For attendance at the meet, as a newly appointed head of Patna Division realized, "is a duty of the Commissioner, especially in his first year.... He there has an opportunity not only of meeting subordinates, but of making the acquaintance of many of the non-official gentlemen of the division, and his presence in some small degree assists in encouraging this very important 'meet'."[35] And it was also a featured attraction in the local tours of the lieutenant governors, whether they came from Calcutta when Bihar was part of Bengal, or from the new capital of Patna, when Bihar and Orissa became a separate province in 1912. Even the highest officials of the land, the governor-general, the Earl of Mayo, and Viceroy Lord Northbrook, came to Sonepur on different occasions to join the "men of Chupra."[36]

Thus, Sonepur was a "family" gathering of Europeans from all over north India in the late nineteenth century. In the words of a contemporary observer:

The whole of Bahar society now makes holiday in that week.... Men rejoice in the annual opportunity of renewing ... friendships with old companions from whom they have been separated throughout the remainder of the year by vast distances and vile roads. The complicated family connexions, so general in the Civil Service, render this periodical gathering particularly pleasant. The wife of the Judge of Boglipore looks forward for months to meeting her sister, the Collectrix of Gya; and the Commissioner of Benares, like a good cousin, has promised to bring her brother in his train.... The desirable young ladies come ... already engaged to local partners for every dance during the meeting—a circumstance extremely discouraging to casual swells who may have been attracted from Calcutta by the glowing accounts of the doings at the races.[37]

The convergence of such large numbers of the local populace as well as of administrators prompted one enterprising magistrate in 1825 to convene his court on the "high road" to Sonepur where he could, as he put it, intercept the "mela-bound litigious natives."[38] Although no one followed his unusual lead, official representation in the meets continued to soar, reaching such numbers in the late nineteenth century that many criminal courts and revenue offices in Bihar districts had to be kept closed during the days of Sonepur. When the lieutenant-governor sought to prevent this unauthorized closing in 1892— objecting particularly to its occurrence on the heels of the long Durga Puja holidays—he was persuaded to tone down his criticism and leave the matter to the discretion of the local officials. Although differing in their opinions about the requisite duration of the Sonepur "Christmas," Bihar administrators spoke in unison about the "holidays ... as a time-honoured institution which should not be lightly interfered with."[39]

35. AGRPD, 1891–92.
36. AGRPD, 1890–91; *An Account of the Tours of His Honour the Lieutenant-Governor of Bihar and Orissa* 1914: 33; *SDG, 1930*: 500.   37. Trevelyan 1866: 351.
38. W. Lowther, Magte., to W. H. Macnaghten, Registrar, Nizmat Adawlat, n.d., Bengal Cr. Jdcl. Consltns., Aug. 4–25, 1825, no. 44.
39. Commr, C. F. Worsley to GOB, June 2, 1892; GOB to Commr., Feb. 15, 1892; GOB to Secy., Aug. 18, 1892, Bengal Jdcl. Procs., July–Sept. 1892, Aug., 141–47.

In addition to the routine presence of administrators, government was also represented at the mela by the police. Already in the late eighteenth century, apparently in response to a request by zamindars, the judge of the district had ordered the darogha (local police inspector) and several peons to Sonepur to maintain law and order. By the late nineteenth century, this police presence had grown to a special force drawn from the reserves of several districts.[40]

Sonepur was also woven into the fabric of British rule in other ways. By the late nineteenth century, all roads led to this sacred site as it was increasingly drawn into the "geometry of colonialism,"[41] a process facilitated by its long-standing centrality in the district's communications network and its significance as a focal point of pilgrimage devotion. And its location at the junction of rivers endowed it with a strategic geographical position in relation to the waterways, the premier city of the region, Patna, and the important district town of Hajipur. In the late eighteenth century, there were only three major roads in the district, and none of them extended to Sonepur, but by 1830 a road described as "in excellent repair" and usable nearly all year round by wheeled carriages had been constructed between Sonepur and Chapra, the district headquarters town thirty miles away. But this was characterized by local authorities as "more in the light of military roads."[42] From Chapra, other roads radiated to different corners of the district, to the northern district of Champaran, and to the west and northwestern districts in neighboring U.P.

The completion of the Bengal and North-Western railways in the 1880s further enhanced Sonepur's ties to the rest of the region, linking it to Mairwa in the northwest, from where it continued into Gorakhpur District. And from Sonepur it reached over a bridge link, inaugurated by Viceroy Lord Dufferin in 1887 to north Bihar and the Tirhut State railways, which in turn led into Bengal proper. The development of these links led to the rise of various service facilities in the late nineteenth century. As a railway junction, Sonepur became the headquarters of the District Traffic and Locomotive departments. Thereafter, railway workshops were established there, as well as quarters for railway employees, a subregistry office, a dak (post station) bungalow, a post and telegraph office, and a police station.[43]

British involvement in Sonepur also extended to the lands on which the great fair was held. At the time of the Permanent Settlement of 1793, the proprietors of Sonepur and its neighboring villages were unwilling to accept the revenue rate established by government because they considered it excessive. The lands were therefore placed under official management, and their farming

---

40. R. P. Jenkins, Offg. Commr., Patna, to GOB, no. 178, June 30, 1868, Bengal Jdcl. Procs., July-Aug. 1868, July, no. 161. The police presence is also noted in *Harihar Kshetra Mahatamya* (1924: 5).
41. The phrase is from Robinson, ed. (1979: 18).
42. Rankine, 1839: 9.
43. *SDG, 1908*: 109; *SDG, 1930*: 155-57, *SDG, 1960*: 497-501.

rights leased out. Much to the consternation of local officials, the collector's assistant, McArty, using a pseudonym, illegally sought to assume the lease (*patta*) of Sonepur. He was attracted by the "considerable advantage" and "considerable benefit" that could be secured from the rents and cesses levied on merchants and pilgrims patronizing the mela.[44]

In the late nineteenth century, after the problem of the lands was settled, the government sought to obtain the space needed for the meet on a lease in perpetuity at fixed rates (*mokarrari*). They offered Rs. 3-2 per *bigha* (two-fifths of an acre). The maliks felt that this rate was too low and, rather than be bound to an unfavorable lease, chose not to press for rents for several years in the 1880s and 1890s. When the proprietors were finally assembled in 1892, they still refused to give a lease to the British and also refused an offer of back rent. One government administrator suggested that the lands be acquired under the Land Acquisitions Act, but this move was voted down because of the costs of compensation. Thus, the makeshift agreement between government and the maliks persisted, with government retaining the upper hand by offering only a minimum rent.[45]

Official supervision over the lands used by the mela and meet was also exercised by control of the ghats (landing places) at which boats carrying passengers from across the rivers docked. In the 1850s the governmental lease, which returned handsome profits because of the income from tolls on the boats mooring there, was given to Behari Singh. He continued to hold this lease until he was removed by the magistrate of Patna in 1895. According to a "man for Chupra," this action was taken "much to the disgust of old Soneporeans ... for Behari had done yeoman service to the Sonepore Stewards, as well as the thousands of native pilgrims.... There was nothing one fell short of he could not supply at the shortest notice, from an elephant to take ladies to see the fair, down to a dhurry [mattress] or chicks [blinds] for one's tents."[46] The new lessee of the ghats, however, continued to support the meet. In 1896, for instance, he donated Rs. 2,000 for the improvement of the grandstand, the ballroom, and the supper rooms.[47]

Income from the ghats also contributed directly to the official presence at Sonepur by subsidizing, in part, the costs of official arrangements for conservancy measures at the Fair. The local ferry fund exacted this by levying assessments on the ghat contractors. Government found this plan convenient because it did not require much coordination or expense. Nor was it disruptive. The official presence at Sonepur was thus maintained at a minimal cost, its conservancy arrangements being the only extraordinary expense. And, with ghat owners assuming most of these charges, government's special expenses at

---

44. Boddam to Dowdeswell, Oct. 24, 1807, and C. Buller, Secy., BOR to J. R. Elphinstone, Colltr., Saran, Dec. 10, 1807, Bengal Cr. Jdcl. Consltns., Nov. 6 to Dec. 24, 1807, Nov. 6, nos. 1 and 2.
45. "Diary (and correspondence) ... Sonepore Fair," P.C. Gen. *Basta* no. 308, 1894.
46. Abbott 1896: 30, 263–64.   47. Ibid.: 298–99.

the mela remained small. In 1894 they amounted to only Rs. 3,632, of which Rs. 1,572 was covered by its income.[48]

The mela has traditionally been held in a cluster of villages centering on Sonepur. As many as nine *mauzas* (revenue villages) have been involved: Rampur Madho Sonepur, Sonepur Kesho, Sawaich, Bagh Mirza Adil, Bangali Bagh, Sonepur Kesho Rampur Madho, Bagh Raja Man Singh, Akharpur, and Sonepur Adam (thana nos. 102–9, 111, see map 2). This area is the site of the major shrines, the sacred topography, the fair itself, and also the place of congregation for pilgrims.[49]

The British meet expanded into this area in the nineteenth century. As one local resident reminisced, the "space occupied by English visitors . . . was annually enlarged, that allotted to Orientalism proportionately contracted."[50]

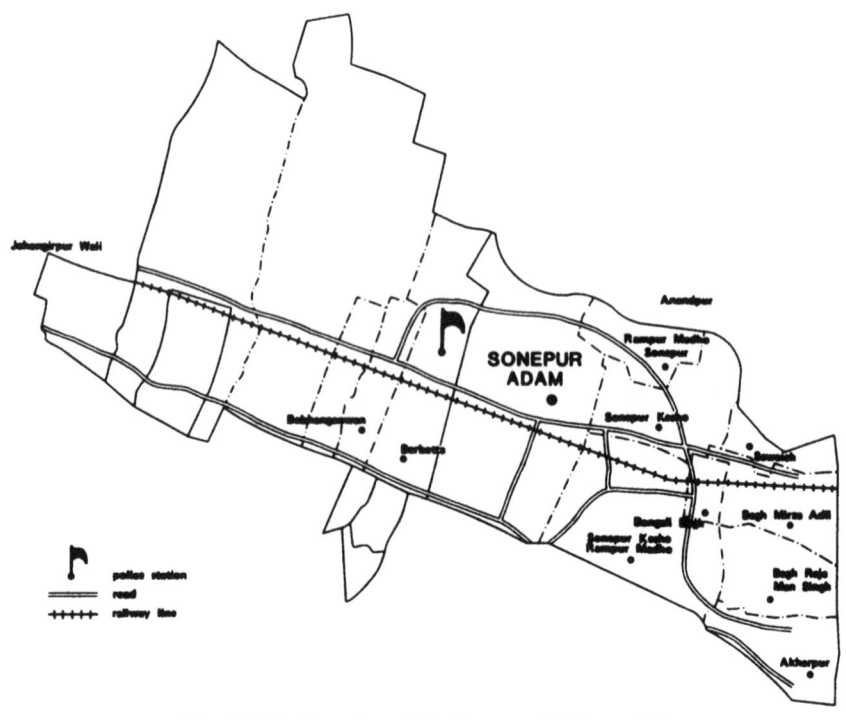

Map 2. The Location of the Sonepur Mela and Meet.

48. AGRPD, 1894–95.
49. Prasad 1964: xxxii–xxxiv (GOI); "Diary (and correspondence)."
50. Tayler 1881, 1: 501–4.

By the late nineteenth century, the "camps of European gentlemen and native noblemen and race stables" extended over much of the traditional mela site of Rampur Madho, Sonepur Kesho, and Sonepur Adam, as well as into the village of Anandpur (thana no. 106); horse race courses were laid out in the villages of Jehangirpur Wali, Babhanganwan, Barabatta, and Sonepur Adam (nos. 91, 98, 99, and 111); a polo ground was laid out in Sonepur Adam (nos. 111–12); and a ballroom and a supper room were constructed in Sonepur Adam.[51]

The extensive mango groves that grow in these villages provided the setting for the "canvas town," erected annually for the Sonepur Meet. A frequent visitor to this event described the European encampment: "The whole society live in tents which are sent beforehand, with furniture, servants, and all the paraphernalia requisite for a gigantic picnic of fourteen or fifteen days. Carriages, saddle-horses, and buggies are all brought over, and some of the visitors form large parties. We generally mustered ten or twelve ourselves."[52] The "whole society" of 1895 included many indigo planters, the collector and judge of Muzaffarpur, the commissioner of Patna Division, and the officials of Saran ("Chupra camp"). The military was represented by the Manchester regiment, which had a "well filled camp." Women served as the presiding hostesses in most of these camps, but the "biggest camp" had a Mr. Mills playing "sole host." A number of individuals also established quarters, and each of these groups and individuals entertained many guests.[53]

All the accoutrements of "Anglo-Indian" life were displayed in this canvas town. The tents were "handsomely carpeted and furnished; while . . . the dining tents, down the centre of which are placed long tables, indicate that a luxurious and comfortable style of hospitality will soon be dispensed." And within each tent, "all the necessary articles of furniture duly arranged, forms the principal sitting-room; while the sleeping tents, bathing-rooms, and other accessories . . . are pitched around it."[54]

As a meet, horse races were, of course, a premier feature. They were generally scheduled for Tuesdays, Thursdays, and Saturdays of the Sonepur fortnight (later shortened to ten days). The day before the races, lotteries were held. On the day of the races, the canvas town awoke at daylight to a cannon fired from the racecourse. The band of the regiment from Danapur, the military cantonment west of Patna city, played and marched between the encampment and the racecourse. The festive crowd then made their way to the racestand by "carriages, dog-carts, and conveyances of all kind." The races began at 8 A.M. The verandah of the ballroom served as the grandstand and the area behind it as a promenade. The races were over by 11 A.M., and people returned to their camps for breakfast followed by an afternoon of social calls. In the evening everyone drove around the racecourse, making for "a very gay

51. "Diary (and correspondence)."
52. Tayler 1881, 1: 494.
53. Abbott 1896: 270–73.
54. Tayler 1881, 1: 494; Wilson 1908: 156.

appearance." At the center of the course, the paramilitary force of European residents put on shows of horsemanship, replaced by polo matches in the late nineteenth century.[55]

At 9 in the evening, the bugle sounded to announce the commencement of the ball within half an hour:

> The ballroom is a most brilliant scene. The elegant dress of the ladies and the varied and many-coloured uniforms of the military men, mixed with the sombre evening dress of the civilians, give the assemblage a gay and gaudy appearance. At midnight the band strikes up "The Roast Beef of Old England," and at this signal there is great rushing about of gentlemen in search of ladies they are to take in to supper.[56]

The day after the races and the balls was usually taken up with playing tennis, luncheon parties, and riding. On Sundays the chaplain from Patna officiated over a "Divine Service." These were the kinds of festivities that made the "men for Chupra" declare that they had "sworn by Sonepore."[57]

In the late nineteenth century, however, regular "sojourners" at Meets noted with regret the passing of an era. As one observer fondly recalled, "the Sonepur Fair, which had for years been in fact a 'family gathering,' with no foreign intermixture, and no elements of swelldom, self-exultation, or officialism, has to some extent degenerated into an everyday 'party,' and the rare excellence of informal rare-hearted sociability has been impaired."[58] This change came with the development of better transportation, i.e., the railways, which brought in an influx of people who did not stay for the entire meet and were not part of the "family gathering." According to George Graham, the last "great Sonepore fair" was in the 1870s; thereafter, it was no longer "sacred to the enjoyment of the European inhabitants ... for in succeeding years the railway was open, and the European society was quadrupled."[59] Equally nostalgic was the "man for Chupra" who, writing at the turn of the century, lamented the disappearance of "Sonepore as a place for races and gaiety.... The scream of the locomotive, as it rushes past on its way to the North-West, warns us that Sonepore is doomed and the end is at hand. The charm of Sonepore was the large picnic it represented; that gone, a visit to Sonepore resolves itself into a matter of business to purchase horses or other cattle."[60]

Mela-Meet Interactions

"Mister Clay" notwithstanding, the British organizers of the Sonepur Meet did not think "small beer of Hutwa's cheer" or those of other regional notables. As early as 1840, the Maharajas of Hathwa, Dumraon, Bettiah, and Darbhanga—the major zamindars of Bihar—contributed trophies to the horse races. Their participation was subsequently enlarged to include representation

55. M. Wilson 1908: 156–57.   56. Ibid.: 158.   57. Ibid.: 139, 157–58.
58. Tayler 1881, 1: 508.   59. 1878, 1: 178.   60. M. Wilson 1908: 159–60.

in the races and donations to assist in the building and maintenance of various facilities.[61] The camps of many local notables were also a standard feature of the meets. The maharaja of Darbhanga was singled out by one British source as "the chief supporter of the races," and he was said to have occupied "two camps, one for his native friends, and one for his English friends."[62]

Indian involvement in the British-created event also provided an opportunity for local notables to reaffirm their ties to government. Their routine participation in the meets was reinforced by their staging of other acts of loyalty. The festivities at Sonepur in 1878 included a meeting of about a hundred landholders who had convened to establish the Bihar Landholders Association, an organization created "to lay before the authorities from time to time, the view of those whom it will represent as also of the general public, in questions affecting public interest."[63] The suppliant tone at the founding meeting mirrored the fact that the British were acknowledged as the political authority of the realm. And, if public pronouncements by local notables did not make that recognition sufficiently plain, such ritual occasions as the durbars did. As Bernard S. Cohn points out, these "rituals of authority" stamped Indian notables with the "marking of subordination."[64] At the Sonepur durbar of 1877, the highest-ranking official, the lieutenant-governor, presided and distributed the insignia and dress of honor (*khilluts*). Elaborate ritual rules were followed whereby local and regional "gentry" were seated in order of precedence to the right of the main dais where the lieutenant-governor sat, and government officials to the left, according to their rank. To reach the durbar tent, participants traversed a road lined by the police and a guard of honor of native troops.[65]

For the rest of local society gathered at Sonepur for the mela and puja, though the authority of the Raj was considered paramount, its presence was of interest only because it ensured law and order at the fair. From the British perspective, the religious ceremonies and the ritual bathing, which occurred away from their encampment, aroused little interest. To cite one statement of social geography, "We Europeans further inland, in our pleasant canvas town . . . took little notice of these things, but devoted ourselves to Anglo-Saxon pleasure with very remarkable energy."[66] Another contemporary observer noted, in even stronger ethnocentric terms, that the mela was an occasion that assembled

not only the ornamental and useful, but the sacred and religious, the strange and picturesque, the beautiful and the hideous; the whole scene, in short, is ultra-Asiatic and sensational.

. . . although there is a certain proportion of Asiatic elements, and a partial admixture

61. Abbott 1896. 62. Buckland 1884: 63.
63. "Proceedings of an inaugural meeting of the Behar Landholders Association." P.C. Rev. *Basta* no. 329, 1878–1879. 64. 1979.
65. "Instructions re: . . . the Lieutenant-Governor's Durbar at Sonepore, 19 November 1877." P.C. Rev. *Basta* no. 329. 66. Graham 1878, 1: 181.

of religious enthusiasm, that proportion and that admixture is exceedingly small and insignificant.... At Sonepore, the large assemblage of Englishmen with their wives, families, and attendants, monopolize the ground, with its race-course and cricket-fields, while the picturesque, though unmeaning, exhibition of bears, monkeys, mendicants, and other half-disgusting, half-horrible objects are in the background.[67]

Perhaps nowhere is the British disdain toward the mela more apparent than in Harry Abbott's reminiscences of the years from 1840 to 1896. He was a resident of north Bihar and a major organizer of the annual meets, and his account has many details about the meet festivities but contains little about the mela. He notes the "average" nature of the "native fair... and the usual variety of booths.... A brisk business seemed to be done in native wares." He also devotes a few lines to the "good" horse and elephant fairs. Typically, though, he writes, as for 1892, that the "native fair was dirty and crowded as it always is."[68]

However, the mela was an event that transformed the locality of Sonepur from an ordinary periodic marketing area into a major marketplace for the region and an outlet for locally produced wares. It was, as one late nineteenth-century visitor noticed, a fair at which "everything from a pin to an elephant was offered for sale."[69]

Immediately surrounding the camps of the British and Indian meet- and mela-goers was the English Bazaar with shops catering to European tastes: European toys, groceries, brandy, beer, soda water, furniture, and various kinds of carriages and conveyances.[70] Beyond this lay the activities that gave Sonepur its reputation of holding "one of the biggest fairs in the world ... [where] every type of big or small ... birds and animals are available for sale."[71] And where the English Bazaar ended, the horse mart began, with an open space where prospective buyers could ride the animals. The cattle mart, historically linked with the mela, formed another important sector. Bullocks, cows, goats, sheep, and other domesticated animals made this area the focal point for buyers from all over Bihar and the neighboring provinces. A camel fair occupied the next grounds, followed by an elephant bazaar, which always drew crowds because of its circus atmosphere, and past this lay the bird fair.[72]

A late nineteenth-century mela-goer estimated that "cows and calves, ploughing oxen, cart-bullock, and buffaloes sell to the number of some thirty thousand. Not less than ten thousand horses change their masters. The number of elephants bought for sale sometimes amounts to two thousand."[73] According to another source, from 1920 to 1930, 7,180 horses and ponies were sold, 2,030 cows, 1,510 buffaloes, 363,300 bullocks and calves, and 735 elephants.[74]

67. Tayler 1881, 1: 501–4.
68. 1896: 231.
69. Ashby with Whately 1938: 103.
70. "Diary (and correspondence)"; M. Wilson 1908: 167–71; Aggarwala 1922: 134–35; *Harihar Kshetra Mahatamya* 1924: 5–7.
71. Prasad 1964: xxxiii (GOI).
72. Ibid.; Buckland 1884: 72–73.
73. Chunder 1869: 122.
74. *SDG, 1960*: 501

Beyond the livestock area was the Mina Bazaar, which was usually the most crowded because it contained shops "where you can buy almost anything," which, to the eyes of a British observer meant, "goods from Manchester, Birmingham, Delhi, Cawnpore, the Punjab, Cashmere, or Afghanistan, and . . . rather neat Indian-made curios."[75] An Indian traveler of the late nineteenth century found this bazaar the "attractive part of the fair." His attention was drawn to the "rows of booths extending in several streets, and displaying copper and brass wares, European and native goods, toys, ornaments, jewelry, and all that would meet the necessity or luxury of a large part of the neighboring population. Numerous are the shops for the sale of grain and sweetmeats."[76]

The fair was also a center of popular entertainment. Bholanauth Chunder, who visited Sonepur in the late nineteenth century, recalled seeing "parties of strolling actors, dressed fantastically, ply to and fro, dancing and singing."[77] An English resident of the district remembered encountering

all sorts of amusements calculated to please youth, toys of every description are exposed for sale, dolls, the squeaking trumpet, the tinsel sword and gun; kings and queens innumerable may be bought decked in gorgeous array. . . . At one place a bear or other wild beast become domesticated is to be seen, whilst the facetious and mischievous monkey, riding on a goat by way of a charger, is always present where fun is to be looked for; jugglers, nautches, puppet shows, and the attractive ups and downs, and round abouts, filled with boys and girls laughing, as they ascend the air, in their little swinging boxes, are met with on all sides.[78]

But, as he quickly added, these scenes were "a very good sample of the manners and amusements of the lower orders, and in some respects resemble similar sights in England."[79]

No less unusual was the fact that the mela, to use the language of the official district gazetteer, was also "a notorious place for prostitution."[80] But, as seen through the wonder-struck eyes of a late nineteenth-century Indian traveler, the fair was "open to all descriptions of visitors. Much money is expended on the nautch-girls, whose dancing and songs form the great source of Indian entertainment."[81]

At the end of the markets stood the main temple of Baba Hariharnath. For a visitor approaching from the river, this "lofty white temple that glistens from afar, and greets the eyes across the immense expanse of the waters"[82] was the initial sight that alerted pilgrims that they were in the presence of a sacred tradition vast in space and time. Rituals and celebration at Sonepur fostered a community that resonated with elements of a society beyond the reach of the

---

75. M. Wilson 1908: 171.   76. Chunder 1869: 122–23.   77. Ibid.: 123.
78. Rankine 1839: 27–28.
79. Ibid.: 27. See also Cunningham (1977: 163–84).
80. *SDG, 1960*: 500.   81. Chunder 1869: 122.
82. Ibid. Three-fourths of the fair-goers went to Sonepur by the river (Offg. Commr., Patna, to Secy., GOB, no. 10, Jan. 13, 1868; Bengal Sanitation Procs., April 1869, no. 18).

"Europeans further inland" but that was kept contained by the authority and power of the British Raj.

Indeed, government was never entirely oblivious to the religious aspects of such fairs, especially in the aftermath of the Mutiny/Rebellion of 1857. Thus, in the wake of an international medical conference in Constantinople in 1866, which concluded that cholera emanated from India and, most probably, from the gatherings at fairs and pilgrimage centers, it sought to impose restrictions on such travel, but to no avail. In Bengal almost all local administrators argued, as did the commissioner of Patna, that such prohibitions "would at once be considered as an attempt to interfere with religious freedom, and would give rise to all kinds of rumours, and thus open a door to the disaffected to work on the feelings of the people and create a discontent and dislike to our Government, which in time might grow into open rebellion as serious and dangerous as was the Indian Mutiny of 1857."[83]

As the metaphor of the Sonepur Meet reveals, the colonial state increasingly superimposed itself on Indian society in the nineteenth century. However, its apparatus of control, its personnel and collaborators remained only bit players in the larger drama of worship and the mela, which followed the imperatives of a sacred place and a sacred time. Except for a handful of local notables, most Indians stood far removed from the mental and physical spaces staked out by the colonial system of control.

In the twentieth century, when the traditions of the mela were fused with the ideas and actions of nationalist leaders, the new agenda of creating a nation-state superseded the prerogatives claimed by the Raj. This new agenda drew as much upon the wellsprings of the Hindu and Muslim Sonepurs, which transformed the struggle for independence into a defense of a sacred landscape, as upon the streams of new ideas from across the "black waters," i.e., from the West. Thus, the rising tides of nationalism swept away the British claims to authority and power. And as the sun set on the British Empire in India, indigenous identities transcending caste, class, religion, locality, and province endured long enough to emerge triumphant. Sonepur would no longer serve as the site of "Christmas pleasures" and "family gatherings" but instead became a place unsafe for the "man for Chupra."

83. Commr. to GOB, no. 10, Jan. 13, 1868, Bengal Sanitation Procs., April 1869, no. 18.

2

The Agrarian Landscape of Control

Saran has "since the earliest time of settlement . . . been the home of a sedentary agricultural society."[1] During Akbar's reign (1556–1605), it already contained much of its present day area. As a district (*sarkar*) of the province (*subah*) of Bihar, it was divided into seventeen parganas (units of revenue administration).[2] Except for minor territorial changes, the British retained these fiscal divisions.

Under the East India Company, Saran District included Champaran until 1837 when the latter was made a separate criminal jurisdiction, and in 1866, a separate district. Within Saran District, two subdivisions were formed in 1848 when Siwan and the headquarters (*sadr*) subdivision of Chapra were established. A third subdivision, Gopalganj, was created in 1875. The district was further organized into ten thanas (police circles), which became the grassroots level of administration in the late nineteenth century, with the parganas enduring only for revenue purposes.[3] (See map 3.)

Population and Agriculture

For the last two centuries, a high population density has been the most important characteristic of the district's human ecology. As early as 1793, the collector observed its "state of high cultivation, and . . . [its] numerous population throughout."[4] The district had by then recovered from the demographic crisis caused by the disastrous famine of 1769–1770, in which some areas in the region lost 50 percent of their inhabitants. Raja Sitab Rai, the

---

1. Ahmad 1961: 268.
3. Chaudhury 1956: i; Mishra 1978: 1.

2. Habib 1982: 10A, 39–40.
4. Cited in *SR*: 103.

Map 3. The Parganas of Saran District.

deputy governor of Bihar, encountered villages where only 10 or 20 out of 100 inhabitants had survived.[5]

Until the advent of official census in the late nineteenth century, figures on population sizes are largely guesswork. An enumeration made in 1800 estimated a total population of 1,104,000, but this figure included the inhabitants of Champaran. In 1843 another estimate of Saran alone placed the number at 1,476,215; another in 1860 at 1,271,729. These rough calculations were drawn up by multiplying the estimated number of houses by a figure considered to be the approximate number of inhabitants per house. In 1800 the multiplier used was 6; in 1843, 5.5.[6]

5. GOB, "Copy of a Translation from Raja Sitabroy," Jas. Jekyll, Geo. Vansittart, Robt. Palk, to Comptrolling Committee of Rev., June 4, 1771, Calcutta Rev. Committee Consltns., April 1 to Dec. 31, 1771, June.   6. Hunter 1877: 238.

The first census, taken in 1872, showed a total population of 2,075,527 (table 1). A considerable increase of 10.6 percent was registered by the census of 1881. In 1891 a rise of 7.4 percent was recorded. This trend was reversed in 1891 to 1901 when the district's numbers declined by 2.3 percent, caused by so-called "Malthusian positive" checks: a "famine, a consequent reduction in birth rate and plague."[7] From 1901 to 1911, the population again declined by 5 percent, with plague and "fever" accounting for most of the higher mortality rate.[8] But, as the birthrate for this decade was also extraordinarily high, averaging 40.1 per 1,000, the difference between the two rates was only 9,000 deaths over births. Migration is said to have caused the remaining decrease in numbers.[9]

Table 1.
Population Growth in Saran District, 1872–1961

	Population	Variation	Saran (%)	Bihar (%)
1872	2,075,527			
1881	2,295,001	+219,474	+10.6	+15.6
1891	2,464,830	+169,829	+ 7.4	+ 5.9
1901	2,409,365	− 55,465	− 2.3	+ 0.2
1911	2,289,699	−119,666	− 5.0	+ 3.7
1921	2,340,222	+ 50,523	+ 2.2	− 0.7
1931	2.486,737	+146,515	+ 6.2	+11.5
1941	2,860,537	+373,800	+15.0	+12.2
1951	3,155,144	+294,607	+10.3	+10.3
1961	3,584,918	+429,774	+13.6	+19.8

Source: S.D. Prasad 1966.
Note: Population figures may vary from source to source, depending on whether adjustments have been made for territorial changes.

Population rose dramatically in the early twentieth century. After 1911 the expansion was initially gradual and then increased in leaps and bounds (table 1). Although the surge between 1872 and 1881 may be explained by better enumeration, the overall tendency in the nineteenth and early twentieth centuries has been of growth. Notwithstanding the guesswork involved in arriving at the early nineteenth-century figures, all the estimates, when compared to the more reliable census figures, indicate this steady increase in population. Compared to the all-India increase of 0.4 percent per year in the nineteenth century, Saran's growth for the same period is much more

---

7. The famine of 1897 was followed by a plague epidemic in 1899–1900 (SDG, 1908: 32).
8. O'Malley 1913: 123–25, 69. "Fever" usually meant malaria (Klein 1973: 642; 1972: 132–60).
9. O'Malley 1913: 123–25.

spectacular—0.9 percent per year (calculated on the basis of a highly inflated figure of 1 million for 1800).[10]

These figures by themselves, however, do not indicate the extent to which Saran District was characterized by overcrowding. The seventh most congested district in India in 1921, its density of 872 persons per square mile was surpassed only by Howrah (1,911), Dacca (1,164), Tippera (1,057), Noakhali (970), Hooghly (909), and Muzaffarpur (907). With similarly high numbers—774, 855, and 919 persons per square mile in 1872, 1881, and 1891—Saran's population density was even higher in the late nineteenth century in relation to other areas.[11]

Unlike Howrah and Hooghly, which included large urban populations, Saran was an overwhelmingly rural area. As late as 1921, over 90 percent of the district's population worked in agricultural occupations. In 1930 more than 97 percent of the inhabitants lived in villages (numbering 4,341 in 1921). In 1891 only twelve settlements were defined as towns, that is, having 5,000 or more inhabitants: Chapra (57,352), Siwan (17,700), Revelganj (13,473), Parsa (7,123), Manjhi (6,723), Mashrak (5,098), Mirganj (5,053), Chainpur (5,017), and Guthni (5,008). But among these, only Chapra, Siwan, and Revelganj deserved to be classified as towns, the first two because of their administrative importance, and all three because of their commercial significance. The remaining settlements, as one report noted, "are merely large villages or collections of tolas [hamlets], in the midst of which are conducted all the operations of rural life."[12]

Within the district, the population was fairly evenly distributed (table 2). The least crowded area was the northeastern corner forming Gopalganj subdivision, presumably because it contained a good deal of *diara* lands and numerous rice swamps.[13] But it is also the area in which the most noticeable growth took place.

To support the enormous population, little land remained uncultivated. No doubt, this process began slowly at the outset of the British Raj in Saran, when the increase in cultivated lands had to keep step with the gradual emergence of society from the demographic crisis of the famine of 1769–1770. But by the 1790s and the initial years of the 1800s, local officials were already commenting on the high state of cultivation in the district; both "surplus lands" and wastelands were scarce. The only forested area in the territory was a thin strip of jungle straddling Saran and Gorakhpur: "[W]here 60 bighas in 100 were cultivated formerly," wrote one administrator in 1801, "80 or more are now in that state."[14]

---

10. Gupta 1972: 419–35; Morris 1974: 303–313. See also *SDG, 1908*: 32, on inaccuracies of early censuses.
11. *Census of India, 1931*, table 20; O'Malley 1913: 116.
12. Hunter 1877: 257; Bourdillon 1898: 6–7; *SDG, 1930*: 36, 87.
13. Bourdillon 1898: 6.
14. Cited in *SR*: 103.

Table 2.
Population Density in Saran's Thanas, 1872–1921

Thana	Number of persons per square mile					
	1872	*1881*	*1891*	*1901*	*1911*	*1921*
Chapra	767	848	1,144	907	939	969
Manjhi	901	1,047	1,100	931	814	859
Parsa	839	889	878	843	804	808
Mashrak	984	1,240	819	822	772	780
Sonepur	925	1,134	1,037	868	809	810
Subtotal	872	988	1,001	906	846	864
Siwan	830	928	1,013	1,023	959	989
Darauli	718	834	893	903	815	827
Basantpur	801	860	977	988	926	944
Subtotal	786	879	966	975	905	925
Gopalganj	605	727	768	786	758	769
Mirganj	620	689	827	820	849	871
Subtotal	611	707	800	804	808	825
District total	778	870	930	898	853	872

Sources: Bourdillon 1898: 5; Tallents 1923, 7, pt. 2: iv.

Throughout the nineteenth century, the extension of cultivation continued as the primary means by which the growing population was accommodated. Probably 60 percent of the district was under the plow at the outset of the century. Thereafter, the pace of this expansion quickened, with the sharpest gains being made earlier in the century rather than later. One indication of this process is the data relating to 64 villages scattered across the district's ten thanas. The registers of the resumption proceedings of 1828–1838 recorded an uncultivated area of 28.7 percent of these villages, but the survey and settlement records of 1893–1901 for the same sample showed an uncultivated margin of only 17.1 percent. The largest expansion of cultivation had occurred in Mirganj and Gopalganj, the least densely populated areas of the district. A similar trend is evident from the revenue survey records of 1845 and those of the 1893–1901 settlement; 19.9 percent was uncultivated in 1845 in a cross section of 124 villages; but, by the later date, only 18.4 percent remained.[15]

A more rounded picture can be obtained from the data of the survey and

[15]. *SR*: 104–6. MacDonnell (1876: 28–30) estimates that 88.3 percent was cultivated by 1873–1874.

settlement operations. In the initial survey of 1893–1901, 78.6 percent was returned as cultivated area. By thanas, Mirganj and Siwan had the highest percentage of cultivated area; Darauli and Sonepur, the lowest. Sonepur had the lowest proportion of wasteland available for cultivation; over 16 percent of its total area was sand and water in the *diara*. And of the district's 21.4 percent uncultivated area, 0.9 current was fallow, 11.4 percent cultivable, and 9.1 percent not cultivable. In other words, approximately 12 percent of the total area was "available for the expansion of cultivation, and of this more than one third is covered with mango groves, and most of the rest is absolutely necessary for pasturage for the cattle."[16]

According to the revision settlement of 1915–1921, an increase of only 14,224 acres (1.0 percent) in the total cultivated area had occurred since the previous settlement. Even in the twice-cropped area, there was relatively little shift, from 477,495 (37 percent) of the net cropped area to 510,234 (39.3 percent).[17] But this expansion, according to the revision settlement officer, was incurred at the expense of pastureland, "another evidence of the imprudence of the people who are prone to kill the goose that lays the golden egg.... The inevitable result is that the breed of cattle has deteriorated."[18]

Clearly, any extension of cultivation was diminished because virtually all arable lands were occupied by the close of the nineteenth century. Further expansion, therefore, entailed recovering marginal lands. In other words, Saran had "reached the optimal natural limit or 'margin' of cultivation," a margin that compelled rural society to be even "more firmly reliant on the products of agriculture itself."[19]

Prior to reaching this final margin of cultivation, Saran's population, though large from the outset of the British Raj, had been adequately supported by time-honored ways of farming. Proverbially skillful, the district's cultivators[20] were fortunate in having unusually fertile land of uniformly rich alluvial soil replenished by the deposition of silt from frequent floods. And with a well-distributed rainfall, the land yielded a wide variety of crops in close succession and in a sequence that favored high population density. Saran's crops were produced by three harvests, fairly evenly divided among all three, which provided some insurance against famine (table 3). Thus, the experiences of the five severe famines in the district's recent past—1769–1770, 1783, 1866, 1873–1874 and 1897—show that it required the failure of two or three harvests to cause a famine.[21]

The imperative of supporting an enormous population also clearly shaped

16. *SR*: 103. Ninety-five percent (1,633,435 of 1,711,142 acres) of the district was cadastrally surveyed.   17. *SRR*: 43, app. 1.
18. *SRR*: 43. The livestock sector has typically played a limited role in Indian agriculture (Charlesworth 1982: 20–21).
19. Richards, Hagen, and Haynes 1985: 726, 708–10.
20. *SDG, 1930*: 66, describes them as "among the most advanced agriculturists of the Province."
21. Ibid.: 68–71.

Table 3.
Agricultural Seasons, Principal Crops, and Cultivated Areas under Different Harvests

	Bhadoi (Autumn) August–September	*Aghani* (Winter) November–December	*Rabi* (Spring) March–April
	Indigo Indian corn Marua rice Millet Rice	Rice Sugarcane	Barley Oats Pulses Wheat
	Area (%)	Area (%)	Area (%)
1893–1901	525,118 (41)	445,099 (34)	791,288 (62)
1915–1921	503,031 (39)	477,390 (37)	762,002 (59)

Sources: Compiled from *SR*: 110, app. I; *SRR*: app. I.
Note: Areas in acres; percentages are of net cultivated area.

the primacy given to food crops in the district. According to an 1875 estimate, less than 11.9 percent of Saran's cultivated area was taken up by nonfood crops. A more comprehensive study carried out by the survey and settlement of 1893–1901 showed a proportion of 85.2 food to 14.8 percent nonfood crop area. By the time of the settlement of 1915–1921, only 10.1 percent of the gross cropped area was considered nonfood.[22]

Rice has long occupied the largest acreage among the food crops. Covering 415,932 acres in 1872, it had, by the 1893–1901 survey, been extended to 440,172 acres, or 24.9 percent of the whole cropped area and 34.3 percent of the net cropped area (table 4). But, compared to other north Bihar districts, Saran's area under rice was relatively small: in Champaran, Muzaffarpur, and Darbhanga, it covered 54.1, 49.4, and 47.0 percent of the net cropped area. Rice, maize, barley, and other food grains—especially for the ordinary people of the district—were the staple items of diet.[23]

Although the area under nonfood crops declined slightly, some conspicuous shifts in the cropping patterns of nonfood crops occurred (table 4). Indigo, cultivated in less than 9,000 acres in the early 1860s, was extended to over 50,000 acres by the 1870s, but then steadily declined due to the competition from German synthetic dyes.[24] Even at its height, indigo constituted only a

---
22. *SRR*: app. 2.
23. Other crops did not exceed 10 percent of the net cropped area (*SR*: 115–17; MacDonnell 1876: 32).
24. Fisher 1976: 122.

Table 4.

Percentage of Saran's Crops by Order of Importance, 1873–1921

	Gross cropped area			Net cropped area		
	1873–74	1893–1901	1915–21	1873–74[a]	1893–1901	1915–21
Food Crops						
Rice	20.1	24.9	24.9	34.3	34.7	
Barley	9.0	14.7	12.7	20.3	17.7	
Maize	17.9	12.1	14.2	16.6	19.8	
Grains[b]	—	11.4	11.0	15.7	15.3	
Kodo	—	6.1	5.1	8.4	7.1	
Wheat	4.0	4.6	4.9	6.0	6.8	
Arhar	—	3.7	3.5	5.0	4.9	
Gram	4.5	3.3	5.2	4.6	7.3	
Marua	—	2.3	1.8	3.1	2.5	
Miscellaneous[c]	—	2.1	2.9	2.9	4.1	
Subtotal		85.2	86.2	116.9	120.0	
Nonfood						
Oilseeds	6.0	5.2	5.4	7.2	7.5	
Indigo	2.2	2.6	0.4	3.5	0.6	
Opium	2.4	2.3	—	3.1	—	
Sugarcane	0.9	2.1	3.4	2.8	4.7	
Kharhaul	—	1.1	—	1.5	—	
Fibers	0.6	1.0	0.9	1.3	1.2	
Others[d]	—	0.6	0.01	0.8	0.01	
Tobacco	0.02	0.02	0.03	0.04	0.04	
Subtotal		14.9	10.1	20.3	14.1	
Total		100.0	96.3	137.2	134.1	
Deduct twice-cropped area	—	—		37.2	34.1	

Sources: Compiled from MacDonnell 1876: 29; *SR*: 155; *SRR*: app. II. The figures for 1873–74 and 1915–21 are incomplete.

[a] No breakdown given.
[b] Includes pulses.
[c] Includes potatoes.
[d] Includes dyes other than indigo.

small fraction of the district's cropped area: in 1893–1901 it covered only 3.5 percent of the net cropped area (table 4). Consequently, the argument that the commercialization of agriculture and the labor-intensive nature of "commercial" crops resulted in advantages for an area's economy by creating new employment prospects is not pertinent to Saran.[25]

The commercialization of agriculture did not become a significant trend in the district. In fact, the area planted to nonfood (cash) crops declined in the late nineteenth and early twentieth centuries (see table 4). As elsewhere in north Bihar, the reduction was caused by the growing population pressures and the fact that cash crops displaced one another rather than encroach on land used for food crops. Thus, indigo, which had replaced sugar in the nineteenth century, was supplanted by sugar in the early twentieth century when the cultivation of indigo (and opium) was abandoned.[26]

Cash crops also failed to gain ground on food crops because they offered virtually no inducements to the ordinary cultivator. With prices for food crops rising steadily in the late nineteenth and early twentieth centuries, there was little appreciable advantage in switching to cash crops. Figures for 1915-1921 of net profit per acre for a variety of crops partially explain this fact: Rs. 50 for tobacco, Rs. 35 for sugarcane, Rs. 23-8 for mustard and oilseed, Rs. 13-8 for linseed, Rs. 10 for indigo, Rs. 24 for winter rice, Rs. 19-4 for rice, and Rs. 15 for maize. And while such crops as indigo and opium held out the attraction of providing cash liquidity for raiyats in a district where cash rents were widely prevalent—opium and indigo pumped two, and one and a half million rupees, respectively, into the district in the 1880s—the actual benefits accruing to cash crops were substantially minimized by the production and marketing systems that typically characterized commercial agriculture in the region. For example, as a government monopoly, opium was grown by cultivators under a contract-and-advance system by which prices were set by administrative fiat, but these prices were rarely on a par with market rates. Even less popular was indigo because its profits were largely pocketed by the planters themselves.

Therefore, for the peasant the disadvantages of cultivating opium or indigo heavily outweighed other considerations. As Fisher states: "The cultivation of both crops was based on the bait and snare of advances and political control, and the price received for both was less than the market price. The similarity between the two was enhanced by the fact that at the village level both the indigo and opium systems were operated by the same class of men ... recruited from amongst local village controllers."[27] Nor was there much incentive to grow oilseeds and sugarcane, because both crops required cultivators to deal with traders who were generally monopsonists and were popularly regarded as the mahajan's (moneylender's) crops because they had to be financed by a

---

25. See McAlpin (1975: 289–302), who suggests the positive effects of the expansion of commercial agriculture; and Fisher (1976: 121–24), who argues that the expansion of indigo cultivation was not at the expense of agricultural production. Chowdhury (1964) asserts that the growth of commercial agriculture heightened tensions in the agrarian society by strengthening the hand of the landholders.   26. Fisher 1976: 136–37.
27. Ibid.: 145; AGRPD, 1884–85; *SRR*: 49.

moneylender. Traders were the prime beneficiaries of commercial agriculture because they intercepted most of the value of the cash crops.[28]

Sugarcane was a crop better suited to the resources of well-to-do villagers because it required a year or more to mature, a commitment few ordinary cultivators could afford to make. Saran peasants, faced with the prospect of choosing between food and nonfood crops, regarded the option through the lens of their ethic of "safety-first," which steered them toward food crops for consumption. This attitude informed the pervasive peasant distrust of indigo, "a notion," which a local administrator found "very deeply engrained in the native mind, that indigo by occupying land which would otherwise grow cereals, diminishes the available food-supply of the village."[29]

Other alternatives for enhancing agricultural production did not arise. For example, no systematic irrigation existed until, at the insistence of the indigo planters, the "Saran canals" were constructed between 1877 and 1880, but their overall impact was minimal.[30] Even less substantive change occurred in farming technology in the nineteenth and early twentieth centuries. The *hal* (a wooden plow with an iron shoe) remained the main agricultural implement. Although more sophisticated implements and new varieties of seeds were experimented with, they were never accessible to the ordinary cultivator.[31] Nor was the district's agricultural production enhanced by the use of fertilizer. Systematic manuring was unknown; cattle dung, although sometimes applied to the fields, was considered more important as a source of fuel.[32]

With virtually no changes in agricultural technology or farming techniques, it is not surprising to find few significant fluctuations in yields per acre over time. Although new lands were being brought under the plow, their contribution to the district's total cultivated area was minimal because they were more likely to be less fertile. These lands were not enough to offset the steady growth in the population. In short, the imbalance between agriculture and population in Saran, as elsewhere in Bihar, reached the proportions of a crisis in the late nineteenth and early twentieth centuries, giving rise to rumors that the resources of the land were exhausted.[33]

As early as the 1870s—in the aftermath of the famine of 1873–1874—government had publicly expressed its fears regarding overpopulation and recommended immediate emigration to alleviate rural crowding. The 1921 census noted: "Signs of overpopulation are apparent. The most densely populated subdivisions (Chapra and Siwan) are decadent, and the Gopal-

28. Fisher 1976: 140; Amin 1984: 102.
29. Cited in AGRPD, 1874–75. On sugarcane, see AGRPD, 1882–83.
30. *SDG, 1930*: 57.
31. The indigenous agricultural implements were, however, considered well suited to the local soils (Gibbon 1838: 221).
32. D. N. Reid, Suddowah, Sarun, "Answers to the Enquiries in Chapter I of the Famine Commissioner Circular," 1878, H.R. *Bastas*, 1890, colltn. no. 12.
33. Blyn 1966; 98–107; Yang 1987.

ganj subdivision where the pressure on the soil is not so heavy is practically stationary."[34]

Statistical data add further details to this portrait of a district in agricultural crisis. While population rose dramatically (12.7 percent between 1872 and 1921), the gains in agricultural production were minimal. Food grain cultivation per capita stabilized from 0.59 acre per capita in the 1870s to 0.57 in 1891–1892 to slight increments later on and stabilized at 0.73—in 1901–1902, in 1911–1912, and again between 1915–1921.[35] The slight expansion of cultivation in the last quarter of the nineteenth and the first two decades of the twentieth century occurred primarily in the double-cropped areas, that is, in areas where a second crop was produced on the same piece of land in the same year, a process that tended to decrease the yield per acre. The burden of accommodating larger numbers was also realized at the expense of the customary practice of maintaining the fertility of the soil by keeping lands untilled for a year or more. By the turn of the twentieth century, only 1.1 percent of the cultivated land was left fallow.[36]

Another distinct indicator of the declining agricultural system of Saran was the fact that its production was unable to provide for the local population. According to MacDonnell's report of 1876, the district's food crops annually yielded 671,385 tons; the inhabitants (2,063,860), consumed food at the rate of three-fourths of a seer (kilogram) per day per individual and needed 504,430 tons. Of the surplus production of 166,955 tons, 43,000 tons were used for seed, and another 51,340 tons were sold in the market to generate cash to pay rents. Of the remaining 72,615 tons, he subtracted another portion due to wastage and concluded that in an average year a surplus of 40,000 tons existed. But this amount was sufficient only to tide the population over for a month. Saran, therefore, had to import rice and other grains, by his reckoning as much as 60,000 tons.[37]

This trend increased in the early twentieth century. Data for the years between 1902 and 1919 reveal that the average annual import of food crops amounted to almost 100,000 tons by railway alone.[38] So massive was this pattern of traffic that the gazetteer of 1930 noted that the "distinguishing feature of Saran . . . is the extent to which the balance of trade is against it. It

---

34. Tallents 1923: 123–24; *SR*: 13.
35. MacDonnell 1876: 32–33; *Agricultural Statistics of British India, 1890–91*; 128–29, 138–39; *SDG, B Vol., Statistics, 1900–1901 to 1910–11*: 8–9; *SRR*: app. II.
36. *SR*: 107, app. 3; *SRR*: app. 2.
37. MacDonnell 1876: 33, 35; GOB, *Report of Enquiries made Regarding Food-Stocks in Bengal, 1896–97*, 1897: 135–38. Between 1890 and 1900 the average annual import of food grains into Saran was 94,558 tons; the export, 8,737 tons. For earlier years, see, e.g., GOB, *Report on the Internal Trade of Bengal for the year 1877–78* (1879: 216), which shows that the imports that year exceeded 60,000 tons, and the exports, 20,000 tons.
38. GOB, *Enquiries regarding Food-Stocks*, 1897: 281–82; *SRR*: 7. Export of food crops in this same period added up to a little over 14,000 tons per year.

never produces sufficient food for its own consumption, and imports consequently exceed exports, the cost of surplus imports being met largely from the earnings of natives... employed elsewhere."[39]

Under these circumstances, the well-known annual exodus of Saran's poorer peasants for employment "abroad" during the slack period of their agricultural calendar assumes a different meaning. Although migration is usually considered an economic choice that people make for better income opportunities, in the case of Saran, the compelling factor was the conditions at home. In other words, the district's seasonal migration was precipitated primarily by "push" factors.

Clearly, the relationship between population and agriculture in Saran between 1793 and 1920 had developed into a crisis of stagnation. Although an important variable in this equation was the steady growth of population, my concern here is not on settling the debate between the classical view associated with Malthus that such changes in numbers can only have adverse effects and the interpretation of Ester Boserup that rising population density is the major source of agricultural change.[40] Instead, I will address the issues provocatively expounded by Robert Brenner in two recent articles. His observations, although they concern preindustrial Europe, are useful in understanding the social context of agricultural conditions in colonial British India:

> The feudal social-property system established certain distinctive mechanisms for distributing income and, in particular, certain limited methods for developing production, which led to economic stagnation and involution. It did so, most crudely, because it imposed upon the members of the major social classes—feudal lords and possessing peasants—strategies for reproducing themselves which, when applied on an economy-wide basis, were incompatible with the requirements of growth. In particular, reproduction by the lords through surplus extraction by means of extra-economic compulsion and by peasants through production for subsistence precluded any widespread tendencies to thorough specialization of productive units, systematic reinvestment of surpluses, or to regular technical innovation. The system-wide consequence of this structure of reproduction—especially given the tendency to long-term demographic increase—was a built-in secular trend towards declining productivity of labour and ultimately to large-scale socio-economic crisis.[41]

In other words, the relationship between population growth and food supply cannot be viewed exclusively in terms of one another but in their interdependence on, to use Brenner's vocabulary, "historically developed systems of social-property relations and given balances of class forces."[42] However, studies of agricultural performance frequently skirt the "issue of the social distribution of the products of agriculture."[43] For my study of control, this aspect is a basic concern.

39. *SDG, 1930*: 91.
40. Boserup 1965. The basic debate revolves around the issue of whether population growth is the source of change in the means of subsistence or is a function of the latter.
41. Brenner 1982: 17.
42. Ibid.: 16.
43. Charlesworth 1979b: 131–32. For a similar omission, see Blyn (1966: 93).

Land, Caste, and Community

At the root of Saran's "social-property relations" lay the fact that the district's inhabitants had differential access to land and its resources. The fundamental division existed between people who enjoyed proprietary rights in the land and were recognized by government as its owners and revenue-payers and those who did not have such rights. No less crucial, however, were the distinctions within these categories. The range of rights subsumed under the category of landholders is evident from the striking disparity between the maharaja of Hathwa, the district's leading zamindar whose writ extended over a thousand villages, and the petty malik whose control was felt in a village or two or in partial shares of them. Likewise, among raiyats, sharp differences were defined by the nature of their cultivating rights, from the peasant who was recognized as an occupancy raiyat with tenure in a plot of land to the landless laborer who had no legal stake at all in land and lived by hiring out his labor.

"Territory, power, village dominance result from the possession of the land."[44] So writes the French anthropologist Louis Dumont, who then goes on to note that the economic and political domains in India are closely intertwined, and these are in turn encompassed by the caste system. For him, caste equated with the indigenous term *jati* and "social class are phenomena of the same nature."[45] Three characteristics of the caste system are crucial and organize

> the whole society into a large number of hereditary groups distinguished from one another and connected together by . . . *separation* in matters of marriage and contact, whether direct or indirect (food); *division* of labour, each group having, in theory or by tradition, a profession from which their members can depart only within certain limits; and finally *hierarchy*, which ranks the groups as relatively superior or inferior to one another.[46]

And ultimately this system is anchored in a "system of ideas and values."[47]

Not all scholars of South Asia agree with Dumont in assigning caste priority as the basic structural variable defining hierarchy in society; they note instead the autonomous role of class or economic power in ordering society. One framework in which such analyses have been played out is the competing models of dominant caste and rich peasant set up by those who see power in contemporary rural India either along caste lines or located in economic factors.[48] In both interpretations, however, the close correlation between the two is inescapable. As a recent attempt to merge the key features of both models proposes:

> For the purposes of analysing power structures and the long-run trends in the political economy, caste should be seen as one of the most important overt groupings through which subgroups (such as economic strata or factions) attain a group identity and

---

44. Dumont 1970: 153.   45. Ibid.: 36.   46. Ibid.: 21.   47. Ibid.: 35.
48. MacDougall 1980: 77–94; Beteille 1974: 35–55. See also Leonard (1978: 285) for an argument that "families, kin groups, and marriage networks were the characteristic social units."

mobilize for political action. Moreover, the processes whereby one caste exercises dominance in a village are major tactical and ideological mechanisms whereby the rich peasants maintain their power and cohesiveness as a class.[49]

My concern is not to isolate caste or class as the basic source of cleavage in the agrarian society, but to emphasize that land, economic power, and caste were closely tied together in the agrarian setting of Saran[50] and defined a hierarchy that was manifested in the relationships of control.

A striking feature of Saran's caste composition in the nineteenth and early twentieth centuries was the large percentage of "twice-born" castes (table 5). A common explanation for this high representation is that the district "lay on the line of the Ayran march eastwards, thus Brahmins, Rajputs, Babhans [Bhumihar Brahmins], Kayasths and Goalas [Ahirs] accounting for more than one-third of the entire population."[51] As elsewhere in India, Brahmins ranked foremost in social precedence. Local-level caste research, carried out for the 1901 census, found Brahmins, Bhumihars, and Rajputs "universally entitled to the distinction of the sacred thread (Janeo) . . . the claim of these three is . . . regarded as indisputable."[52]

A close correspondence existed between ritual rankings and economic status (table 5). In landholding and tenanted holdings, the predominance of higher castes was overwhelming and grossly disproportionate to their numbers in the district. Indeed, they appeared so all-powerful to one district official that he reported that Brahmins, Rajputs, and Bhumihars were the only castes that figured in the "actual life" of the district.[53] Their domination was acknowledged from the outset of the British Raj when they were recognized as the major landholders of the district. By the Permanent Settlement of 1793, "made entirely with old landed proprietors of the country,"[54] they accumulated landholding rights in 57 percent of the district's area. Kayasthas, Muslims, and Banias accounted for another sizable portion with 23, 15, and 4 percent, respectively; agricultural castes (0.3 percent) and low castes (0.7 percent) controlled the remaining 1 percent. Nor did this pattern change significantly in the next century. In 1872–1873, Brahmins, Rajputs, and Bhumihars remained in control of 54 percent of the district's landholding rights, followed by Kayasths, Muslims, and Banias with 19, 17, and 6 percent, respectively. The so-called agricultural and lower castes accounted for the remaining 4 percent.[55]

---

49. MacDougall 1980: 92.
50. Studies of the contemporary agrarian scene in the region tend to emphasize the cumulative effects of caste and class, usually noting the "caste base of . . . classes" (P. H. Prasad 1979: 481; Das 1982). A caste-centered approach is taken by Blair (1979).
51. *SDG, 1930*: 44.
52. Risley Collection, Notes of A. P. Muddiman, SDO of Gopalganj, with Magte. of Saran to Supt. of Census Operations, Beng., Dec. 26, 1901: Reports on Castes and Sub-castes of Bengal (hereafter cited as Risley Collection, Muddiman Report); Bourdillon 1898: 13.
53. Risley Collection, Muddiman Report. 54. *SR*: 23.
55. GOB, "District Report, Saran," in *Selections from Divisional and District Annual Administration Reports, 1872–73*, 1874: 397–98.

THE AGRARIAN LANDSCAPE OF CONTROL 45

Table 5.
Percentage of Major Caste Groups in Saran, 1872–1921

Category	Caste	1872	1881	1891	1901	1911	1921
"Twice-born" Castes	Brahmin	7.7	7.6	6.7	7.6	7.3	7.4
	Bhumihar	4.3	3.7	5.2	4.4	4.4	3.9
	Rajput	10.9	10.7	10.8	10.8	10.6	10.3
	Kayastha	2.3	2.2	2.1	2.0	1.8	1.7
	Banias[a]						
Subtotal		25.2	24.2	24.8	24.8	24.1	23.3
Upper Shudras	Ahirs	11.6	11.2	12.5	12.0	12.8	13.2
	Kurmi	4.9	4.9	5.1	4.8	4.7	4.5
	Koeri	6.8	6.6	6.9	7.0	7.3	7.0
Subtotal		23.3	22.7	24.5	23.8	24.8	24.7
Lower Shudras[b]	Kandu	5.4	5.3	3.9	3.8	3.7	3.5
	Nuniya	3.2	3.0	3.2	3.3	3.3	3.7
	Teli	2.7	2.8	2.9	2.9	2.8	2.8
	Lohar	1.9	1.8	1.9	2.0	2.0	2.0
	Hajam	1.4	—	1.4	1.4	1.5	1.4
	Kahar	1.3	1.6	1.7	1.4	1.5	1.3
	Kumhar	1.1	1.1	1.1	1.3	1.1	1.4
	Barhi	0.8	0.7	0.7	0.8	0.7	0.8
	Dhanuk	0.8	0.8	0.8	0.8	0.8	0.8
Scheduled Castes[c]	Chamar	4.6	4.9	5.1	5.0	5.2	5.5
	Dusadh	3.5	3.5	3.4	3.3	3.3	3.4
Muslims		11.7	11.8	11.8	11.8	11.5	11.8

Sources: Report on the Census of Bengal, 1872, pp. 155–79; Bourdillon 1883: 260–281; Bourdillon 1898, 5: 72–81; Gait 1913, 6A: 192–265; O'Malley 1913, 5, pt. 3; and Tallents 1923, 7, pt. 2: 93–99.
[a] Banias usually about 0.1 percent.
[b] About 25 percent, including "Other Shudras."
[c] About 11 percent, including "Other Scheduled Castes."

A similar picture can be painted from statistics regarding tenant holdings by caste. According to data compiled by the survey and settlement of 1893 to 1901, Brahmins (11 percent), Rajputs (24.1), Bhumihars (2.9), and Kayasths (3.5) together accounted for 41.5 percent of the total cultivated area. Other castes cultivating significant amounts of land were the "Upper Shudras": Ahirs occupied 9.9 percent, Kurmis 4.8, and Koeris 9.1. Muslims took up 6.5

percent, "Lower Shudras," 5.7. Of the remaining area, 4.9 percent was rented out to Scheduled Castes, and 17 percent by "Others" (no caste breakdown).[56]

These correlations between social and economic status are not, however, precise equations. Viewed from the perspective of the district's agrarian structure, Bhumihar Brahmins clearly held a special position in the social and economic hierarchy. A contemporary observer attributed it to "their numbering amongst their caste nearly all the leading zamindars in the district."[57] To name the major zamindars in Saran, with one or two exceptions, is to identify the prominent Bhumihar families: the maharaja of Hathwa and the babus of Manjha, Chainpur, Parsa, Rusi, Khaira, Sadwa, and Bal. But, as a 1891 report pointed out, not all Bhumihars were "landlords and well-to-do. They are also occupancy raiyats, and serve as peons and constables."[58]

Although accorded the highest ritual status, Brahmins were not among the district's major landholders. Late nineteenth-century accounts describe them as primarily maintaining their traditional occupation of priesthood. Many were also said to "have taken to cultivation as a means of livelihood."[59] Rajputs, the single largest caste group next to the Ahirs, mostly subsisted by cultivation, "as occupancy raiyats, a few only being tenure-holders and zamindars. From their ranks, peons, constables and sepoys are recruited, and some of them have taken to horse-breeding and dealing."[60] With an income of over Rs. 50,000, the babu of Amnour, a Rajput, was considered a leading zamindar in the late nineteenth century.[61]

The Kayasths also rank among the "twice-born" castes. In the nineteenth century, they were frequently portrayed as a caste in economic and social decline. Such a picture, however, only contrasted their contemporary position to the Mughal period when they were said to have virtually monopolized government office. It did not take into consideration the fact that Kayasths held 19 percent of the land in Saran.[62] Indeed, in both economic and social status, Kayasths were a prominent caste group in the late nineteenth century. The most literate caste in Bihar, many of them were record-keepers, estate managers, and teachers. Although not immediately successful in their attempts to gain recognition as ksatriyas (warriors) and, thus, second only to the Brahmins, such acceptance appeared forthcoming because of their "education and wealth." According to the 1891 census, they were considered "to stand on equal footing with Rajputs and Babhans."[63]

"Bania," an umbrella term extending to all members of the Vaishya varna

---

56. *SR*: 16.   57. Risley Collection, Muddiman Report.
58. Bourdillon 1898: 14. Nineteenth-century reports frequently refer to Bhumihars as "zamindar Babhans." See, e.g., Offg. Mgte. C. B. Garrett to Commr. of Patna, no. 130, Aug. 1, 1870, S.C. *Faujdari Bastas*, 1870.
59. Bourdillon 1898: 13.   60. Ibid.   61. Ibid.
62. Hunter 1877: 248; GOB, "District Report, Saran," *Selections* 1874: 397–98.
63. Risley Collection, Muddiman Report; Hagen 1981: 84, 441; Bourdillon 1898: 14.

(term used to designate the four ranks of Brahmin, Ksatriya, Vaishya, and Shudra), includes Agarwalas, Banwars, Kasarwanis, Khatris, Rastogis, Rauniars, and Sindurias. Although constituting only 0.1 percent of the district population, they deserve to be ranked just below the "twice-born" category because of their political and social prominence. Not only did this tiny fraction control as much as 4 percent of the district's land, but they also were the important bankers, traders, and shopkeepers. Khatris managed shops in the biggest markets of the district: Chapra, Siwan, Gopalganj, Mirganj, Baniapur, Mashrak, Doriganj, Muhammadpur, and Parsa. Marwaris, on the other hand, were the cloth dealers in the big markets and were "generally speaking wealthy."[64]

Castes in the Shudra varna represented a majority of the district's population. Their division (table 5) into "upper" and "lower" Shudras is on the basis of economic and social status; thus, Ahirs, Kurmis, and Koeris occupied the next most important level in the agrarian hierarchy after the twice-born castes, Banias and some Muslim castes. Ahirs, formerly called Goalas, were the single largest caste group in the district. Traditionally cattle-herders who once congregated along the banks of the Sarju and Gandak rivers for its good grazing, they later took to cultivation. Koeris and Kurmis were widely regarded throughout Bihar as the major, as well as the most efficacious, "cultivating class." Fourth in numerical strength among the district's castes, Koeris were represented in almost every village. Among the more important Kurmi caste clusters—the Ayodhiya, Saithwar and Jaiswar—the Ayodhias were particularly singled out as the "substantial farmers and . . . the most influential sub-caste."[65]

Kandus, the single largest caste in the "lower Shudra" category, were inhabitants of almost every village in the district. Mostly grainparchers, many were also engaged in selling rice, salt, and other essentials. Some of their wealthier members were even moneylenders. Similarly, Nuniyas, formerly makers of saltpeter, turned to other kinds of labor once the saltpeter industry declined in Saran. And Telis, who traditionally monopolized the making and selling of oil, were also grain merchants, frequently combined with moneylending. Others, such as the Kahars, who were formerly palanquin bearers, and the Dhanuks, who were archers, found employment as under-raiyats or field laborers and menial servants, respectively. Other castes in the lower Shudra category were mostly artisans. Kamars or Lohars were the ironworkers; Hajjams, also known as Nais or Thakurs, were barbers by tradition; the Kumhars, potters; the Barhis, carpenters. All these castes were also under-raiyats and cultivators.[66]

64. Bourdillon 1898: 15. Gait (1913, 6, pt. 1: 373) ranks Banias of Agarwal and Khatri caste as 'on a par with twice-born castes."
65. Hunter 1877: 250; Bourdillon 1898: 15; Risley Collection, Muddiman Report.
66. Bourdillon 1898: 15; *SDG, 1930*: 46.

In contrast to the large number of high castes in Saran, the Scheduled Castes (formerly known as Untouchables) comprised only one-tenth of the district's population. In this category, Chamars were the predominant caste, ranking fifth among all castes. In addition to their traditional occupations of tanning hides and working in leather, they were primarily agricultural laborers. Dusadhs, the other large Scheduled Caste, were the "ordinary laboring class of Bihar" and often the village watchmen. Dhobis (washermen) were the only other caste in this category with any significant numbers.[67]

Muslims comprised approximately 12 percent of the district's population—11.7 percent in 1872 and 11.8 in 1921. Siwan contained the highest number of Muslims with 19.4 percent, followed by Gopalganj with 13.9 percent. As in the case of the Hindu community, Muslims were divided into several "castes": Sayyids being regarded as the most respectable, followed by Sheikh, Mughal, Pathan, and lower-caste Muslims. Most Muslims in Saran were Shias. Only a few Muslims were zamindars; the rest followed a variety of agricultural and urban occupations.[68]

Peasants and Subsistence

Ninety percent of the total occupied area of the district (which constituted 86 percent of the total area) was held by tenants who were categorized in the official language as "occupancy tenants," rent-free (and other) tenants, or "tenants at will or non-occupancy tenants." Of the remaining 10 percent, 0.6 percent was privately cultivated by landholders (i.e., *ziraat*), 5.7 occupied by landholders, but not held privately, and 3.7 was in the cultivation possession of tenureholders (generally *thikadars* [rent collectors for zamindars]).[69]

Evidence from the turn of the twentieth century indicates that approximately 2 million or 84 percent of the total population were fully engaged in agriculture. A majority were apparently self-sustaining peasant cultivators: 1.5 million people had average holdings extending over 3.8 acres, well above the 2 acres that official administrators deemed necessary to support an agricultural family of five persons. In contrast to these relatively well-off people were 250,000 who had no lands at all or minute plots—cultivators who had to eke out an existence by the wages of labor. Another 250,000 had holdings below the subsistence minimum of 2 acres. Together they comprised the agricultural laborers of the district and constituted 20 percent of the total population. One-half of them—or 10 percent of the inhabitants—were said to be landless laborers.[70] These numbers are verified by other contemporary observers, one late nineteenth-century official estimating that up to 15 percent of the inhabitants of every village were landless laborers. Comparable figures can also

---

67. Hunter 1877: 250–52; Risley Collection, Muddiman Report; Bourdillon 1898: 16.
68. Bourdillon 1898: 18; Risley Collection, Muddiman Report.
69. *SR*: 124–26.   70. Ibid.: 133–36, 156–57.

be ascertained by estimates of caste composition because most of this category of peasants was drawn from the lowest rungs of the social and ritual order.[71] In Saran the Scheduled Castes comprised 11 percent of the population—roughly equal to the number of landless laborers computed in official sources.[72]

Whether landless laborers were people who had been transformed into rural proletariats by the economic factors unleashed by the establishment of British rule[73] is not my concern here, although qualitative evidence suggests that this process may have been heightened in the nineteenth century. Invariably, this category of people was the hardest hit by agricultural crises, such as the bad years of harvest and high prices, which characterized the period between 1892–1893 and 1901–1902. Because wages remained low and even fell in some areas, "the agricultural labourer of Bihar... suffered most of all."[74] For many, a major escape out of these conditions was seasonal migration to make ends meet. What can also be clearly gauged from a number of sources is the worsening plight of the poorest raiyats under the impact of the growing agricultural crisis in Saran. Rent and price statistics in the nineteenth and early twentieth centuries further underscore this trend.

The average rent was higher in Saran than any of the other north Bihar or neighboring U.P. districts. In 0.7 percent of the total occupied area where raiyats held land at "fixed rates," the average rent was Rs. 3-4-9 per acre; "settled or occupancy raiyats," who held the lion's share of the land (84.6 percent) paid an average rate of Rs. 4-5-4; nonoccupancy raiyats whose plots added up to 1.1 percent paid Rs. 5-0-6. "Under-raiyats," the category of tenants with the least rights in the land, whose tenures extended to 2.6 percent of the occupied area, paid the highest rate—Rs. 5-2-8 per acre.[75]

Official reports estimate that the average rent per acre in the late eighteenth century (when cash rents were already widely prevalent) varied between 0-9-1 and Re. 1-8. One study, based on figures from 64 villages situated in all but one of the district's ten thanas, found that the rates compiled in the resumption proceedings of 1833 to 1841 compared with those of the survey and settlement proceedings of 1893 to 1901 showed an average increase of 98 percent, running as high as 266.6 percent in Chapra thana and as low as 74.8 percent in Gopalganj.[76] The enormous surge in rent rates is also corroborated by the well-preserved records of the Hathwa estate whose rent rolls indicate that an increase of 100 percent occurred between 1800 and 1852. Subsequently, three increases followed in quick succession—the first a 25 percent raise in 1854; 12.5 percent a few years later; and 6.2 to 12.5 percent in the 1870s.[77]

71. D. Kumar 1965. For Saran, see AGRPD, 1878–79.
72. Hagen (1981: 93–95) notes that status considerations separated people who used a plow and actually worked in the fields (mostly lower and laboring castes) and those who rarely, if ever, soiled their hands. The latter (mostly upper castes) supervised cultivation.
73. See Rankine (1839: 37) for an early nineteenth-century view regarding the paucity of laborers in the district; and AGRPD, 1879–80, regarding the steady increase of the "landless class ... owing to the fecundity of the people and ejectments by petty zamindars and indigo factories."
74. Shirres 1902: 14.   75. *SR*: 137.   76. Ibid.: 140, 145.   77. Ibid.: 141.

A special investigation of rent rates in 1872 confirms the widespread increases. According to the Saran magistrate, the increases were prompted by a competition for land, made scarce by the extension of indigo cultivation. His report also noted that a differential rent system existed that demanded less from the higher castes—Brahmin, Rajput, and Bhumihar raiyats—even though they occupied the best lands in a village, but 40 to 50 percent more from such low-caste cultivators as Nuniyas, Chamars, and Dusadhs, who presumably held less fertile plots.[78]

Rents continued to soar in the early twentieth century; the revision settlement of 1915 to 1921 computed a total cash rental for the district of Rs. 5,133,021, a raise of 5.2 percent over the previous settlement. A similar trend can be charted from the year-by-year record of gross rental between 1890–1891 and 1910–1911. In the case of Saran, the increase from Rs. 5,975,000 to 6,529,000 represented an increase of 9.2 percent for this period.[79]

The rent history of the district can also be reconstructed on a village-by-village basis from the village notes compiled in the survey and settlement proceedings of 1893–1901. In Saran Khas, a raise of 2 annas in the rupee (a 12.5 percent increase) was imposed by one malik who had recently become a purchaser there. In Pindari village raiyats complained of several enhancements; in other villages, such as Jahangirpur, raises "now and then." In Kanhia no record of increases was found, but it was common knowledge that maliks had made them "from time to time."[80]

Data gathered for the revision settlement of 1915 to 1921 make comparisons with the conditions existing during the earlier settlement. In Khaguria the change was from Rs. 3-7 an acre to 3-8-9; in Barahima from 2-12-6 to 3-12-9; in Mathia from 3-9-3 to 5-3-3; in Kalyanpur Mathia from 4 to 6-1-6; in Pipra from 2-14-3 to 3-3-9; and, in other cases, the village notes simply report that "rents have been enhanced in some holdings."[81] The registers of rent disputes (*fard tanaza*) reveal in still greater detail the rent increases because they identify by village and landholder.[82]

In both survey and settlements, nine out of ten rent settlement cases resulted in increases. A major factor in the official sanction of increases in rent was the rise in food grain prices, which were calculated by comparing prices in the 1900s with the 1910s. But because prices had skyrocketed, especially in the 1910s, the official formula of allowing a 4 annas 6 pies per rupee enhancement (over 25 percent) was not strictly followed. Instead, the "normal enhancement"

78. GOB, J. S. Drummond, Offg. Colltr. to Secy., GOB, no. 190, Aug. 18, 1870, P.C. *Basta* no. 228, Important Bundles, Rev. Dept., Alphabet T & U.
79. K. L. Datta 1914: 461.
80. Saran Khas, Pindari, Jahangirpur, and Kanhia villages, Chapra thana nos. 5, 49, 51, and 132, SVN, 1893–1901.
81. Khaguria, Barahima, Mathia, Kalyanpur Mathia, Pipra, and Sarfara villages, Gopalganj thana nos. 401, 408, 410, 413, 418, and 449, SVN, 1915–1921.
82. See, e.g., Pachpatia village, Basantpur thana no. 16, Saran *Fard Tanaza*, 1915–1921.

was 3 annas on the rupee (a little more than 18 percent).[83] Nevertheless, such a blanket legal endorsement of enhancements completely overlooked the relation of prices to the agrarian structure because the boom in food grain prices did not affect *all* peasants and landholders evenly.

The steady rise of rent was accompanied by an equally constant growth in prices, especially in the late nineteenth and early twentieth centuries, and both trends were particularly felt by poor peasants. As a touring magistrate observed in 1892 that "the landless labourers, the widow, the orphan, and the infirm; in other words, the 'submerged tenth' . . . must have felt keenly the tightening grip of poverty and the rise of prices of food."[84]

The great surge in prices in the nineteenth and early twentieth centuries can be traced by following the cost of the staple crop of the district: rice. In 1790 one rupee purchased 74.25 seers; by 1872–1873 it could only secure 16.6 seers.[85] Additional details (table 6) on the average annual price of rice in seers per rupee for the period between 1861 and 1901 show that rice prices continued to climb. In famine years the prices especially soared, as is evident in the

Table 6.

Average Annual Wholesale Price of Rice in Seers per Rupee, 1861–1901

Year	Price	Year	Price
1861	26.35	1881	22.33
1862	25.37	1882	21.31
1863	25.37	1883	17.67
1864	20.49	1884	12.96
1865	15.85	1885	16.80
1866	17.56	1886	19.32
1867	18.54	1887	21.00
1868	17.56	1888	17.60
1869	18.54	1889	12.72
1870	16.59	1890	14.77
1871	21.32	1891	14.36
1872	20.04	1892	12.26
1873	17.16	1893	14.14
1874	15.01	1894	14.06
1875	22.21	1895	16.52
1876	20.50	1896	13.75
1877	15.62	1897	9.97
1878	11.67	1898	13.78
1879	14.45	1899	14.42
1880	17.86	1900	12.55
		1901	12.19

Source: *Prices and Wages in India, 1901*, 19th issue, pp. 4–5.
Note: One seer equals one kilogram. Wholesale prices include transportation and other operating costs but nevertheless provide a good indication of trends.

83. P. T. Mansfield, 1933, S.C. Library.
84. Cited in AGRPD, 1891–92.
85. AGRPD, 1872–73.

mid-1860s, 1873–1874 and 1897–1898; enormously high prices are also recorded for 1883 to 1885 and for 1889 to 1901, except for 1895. In the first two decades of the twentieth century, prices continued to rise. Although prices went down briefly in 1902–1905, increases beginning in 1906 shot the price well above the highest price recorded, that in 1897, with only 1910 and 1911 offering a respite from the upward movement of prices.[86]

More important, increases in prices were not accompanied by comparable increases in wages for agricultural laborers. On the contrary, as in the 1890s, when bad harvests caused food shortages and enormously high prices, there was no corresponding increase in wages. One-tenth of the district's population were landless laborers, who were unable to take advantage of soaring prices. And another tenth, who, together with the landless, made up the category of agricultural laborers, were also at a disadvantage because their holdings were barely sufficient to support a minimal existence. Local administrators acknowledged this relationship when they reported the differential effects of higher prices on various categories of peasants during the difficult years of 1905–1906 to 1910. In the words of the official report: "The rise in the prices of food-grains, though causing distress among the landless and labouring classes, has considerably benefited the well-to-do cultivators in the profits received for their excess supply of produce."[87]

That the heavy outmigration of seasonal workers coincided with peaks in agricultural prices further reinforces this analysis of the disproportionate burden that the growing agricultural crisis of the late nineteenth and early twentieth centuries placed on the lives and livelihood of the poorest of Saran's peasants. On the other hand, landholders continued to thrive. The extent to which they made gains is indicated by their growing incomes, reflected in the widening gulf between the sums they owed as revenue to the state and the amounts they collected as rent. Revenue, pegged at the time of the Permanent Settlement of 1793 at a level high enough to intercept nine-tenths of their gross rental, was, in the early twentieth century, taking up less than one-fifth. Because the revenue demand was permanently set—rising only minimally from Rs. 1,027,110 in 1793 to 1,270,737 in 1920 (23.7 percent)[88]—their real income (gross rental less revenue) at the turn of the twentieth century was much larger than the amount that would have been appropriate under the terms of the Permanent Settlement: according to one source, "a thirty-fold increase over what was considered fair a century ago." The conclusion of this report was inescapable: "Truly the Saran landlord has no cause to deplore his fate under British rule."[89] The social and economic dimensions of the agrarian landscape of Saran between 1793 and 1920 defined the configuration of local control.

86. Prices for this period are of the retail level of the average annual price of common rice in rupees and decimal of rupees per maund (82.2 lbs.), e.g., 1897, 4.0; 1902, 3.1; 1907, 4.5; 1912, 4.0; 1917, 4.1; 1920, 8.0. (GOI, *Prices and Wages in India, 1921*, 1923: 73–74).
87. Cited in GOB, "Report on ... Tirhut Division for the Quinquennial Period from 1905–06 to 1909–10," Bengal Gen. (Misc.) Procs., April 1911: 224; *SR*: 133–36, 156–57.
88. *SR*: 30–36; *SRR*: 38. Most of the increase in revenue came from the increase in revenue-assessed lands.
89. *SR*: 146.

PART II

The Limited Raj System

3

The Initial Encounter: The British Establishment of Connections, 1765–1793

Mughal emperors and regional nawabs never ruled alone in India, and neither did the British. These regimes governed with the collaboration of powerful allies who served as "connections" to the indigenous society. By the late nineteenth century, the British had developed a system of support based on local allies with whom they maintained a relationship of "consultation and control."[1] These were men whose "cheer" was not to be considered "small beer" by the "man for Chupra" because they were the local controllers. Their cooptation as intermediaries provided a solid foundation for Pax Britannica, extending its reach into levels of society that lay outside the grasp of its formal structures of rule. Thus, the overarching authority of the Raj was able to encapsulate even the most distant hinterlands in its political system.

The edifice of consultation and control was erected in the Permanent Settlement of 1793, which defined the "legal and administrative framework within which agrarian relations were determined . . . until the zamindari abolition acts of the 1950s."[2] Based on the Decennial Settlement, concluded in 1791, the 1793 settlement recognized 353 Saran zamindars whose claims were aggregated in 959 estates extending over twelve parganas. In the parganas of Kalyanpur Kuari, Sipah, and Chaubara, two zamindars held most of the lands—the raja of Huseypur in the first two, the raja of Majhauli in the third—but a settlement was deferred because of their rebellion against the British East India Company. Instead, their lands were leased out to revenue farmers: Jagmohan Mukherji leased Huseypur for a revenue of Rs. 139,209

1. F. C. R. Robinson 1971: 313–36.
2. Ratnalekha Ray 1979: 1. The best statements on British intentions in instituting the Permanent Settlement are Stokes (1959) and Guha (1963).

(almost 15 percent of the district's total revenue); the farmer of Chaubara paid Rs. 40,000.[3]

None of the 353 zamindars controlled an entire pargana; most interests were scattered across several administrative units. There were, however, several large revenue payers among them: the Narayans, the ancestors of the Chainpur family, were collectively liable for a revenue of Rs. 94,098; the Muslim family of Taque Ali Khan of Manjhi for Rs. 75,525; the Goolera zamindars of Chirand for Rs. 57,318; and the Siwan family of sheikhs Muhammad Ali and Miramal Ali for Rs. 43,751. Four other individuals were identified as paying revenue of over Rs. 20,000: Sheikh Abdullah of Barharia, Hargovind Shah of Bagoura, Parmeshwar Sahi of Manjha, and Sheowan and Bonesar Singh.[4]

The Permanent Settlement offered these zamindars a significant role in the evolving system of British rule in Saran by recognizing them as local controllers with long-standing anchorage in the indigenous society.[5] In this respect, they were considered different from those encountered in many other parts of the Raj's eighteenth-century domain. An early version of this belief, subsequently enshrined in the official records, was pronounced by the Patna Council in 1774:

> The several divisions of Sarun are not like most of the other Pergunnahs in the hands of foreign renters, unconnected with the country they govern and removeable at pleasure but held by zemindars, inhabitants and proprietors of the spot they farm, on whose local influence depends the cultivation or desolation of the lands and if carried away into imprisonment the Talook must be sold to some other zemindar, a practise seldom found to answer, or remain neglected till necessity obliges you to bring forth and reinstate the former zemindar.
>
> The zemindars of Sarun comparatively with others of the province are esteemed . men of some substance.[6]

Local Controllers Before the Raj

The last centralized empire in north India before the spread of Muslim rule ended with the demise of Harsha in the mid-seventh century. In its wake, non-Aryan aboriginal groups, the Cheros and the Bhars, carved out principalities in Saran. The Cheros settled along the banks of the Gogra, Gandak, and Ganges rivers, clearing forests to establish a swath of territory along an east-west grid. The Bhars occupied the northwestern edge of the district. From the original settlements founded by aboriginal chieftains, kinsmen, organized in clans, worked cooperatively to secure villages in the sparsely inhabited and thickly forested areas away from the rivers.[7]

3. *SR*: 23–25; A. Montgomerie to John Shore, Pres. and Members of BOR, July 23, 1789, Bengal Rev. Consltns., Sept. 18, 1789.
4. *SR*: 23–25; Montgomerie to Shore, July 23, 1789, Bengal Rev. Consltns., Sept. 18, 1789.
5. In England too it was "an axiom of government policy that the 'respectable' inhabitants and men of property should stand forward and protect their localities" (Stevenson 1977: 36).
6. Patna Council to Bengal Rev. Council, Nov. 24, 1774, Bengal Rev. Consltns., March 1 to April 4, 1775, March 9, no. 164.
7. R. P. B. Singh 1977: 32–43; Diwakar 1959: 527.

Oral legends and British accounts suggest that Rajput inmigration followed next, a movement extending all across north India and coinciding with the Muslim conquests in the northwest in the eleventh and twelfth centuries. In Saran a coalition of Muslims and Rajputs were instrumental in driving the Cheros out.[8] Bhumihar Brahmins also joined the inmigration into the region, and the influx of these groups eventually displaced the Cheros and Bhars. As a "frontier area," Bihar lay between the spheres of influence of the sultans of Delhi and of the independent kingdoms of Jaunpur in U.P. and Lakhnauti in Bengal, and was caught in a constant pushing and pulling. Following the decline of the Tughlaq Empire in the late fifteenth century, the Sharqi rulers of Jaunpur moved into Bihar.

Not until the fifteenth century was there effective and complete "external" control. Only then were the local rajas subjugated. Muslim penetration into the local society, however, remained incomplete:

> The ruling class lived in military stations and cities. It was only very slowly that rural areas were penetrated by non-military Muslims except for the missionaries. Contact between the non-Muslims and the ruling race was not frequent. But by the end of the period, Muslim settlements in villages (e.g., Siwan sub-division of Saran) became common. The village was left undisturbed so long as it did not create trouble by recalcitrance in paying the revenue.[9]

In other words, local rajas persisted in power as local tributaries. The Saran situation, therefore, resembled that of neighboring Gorakhpur where "the facts appear to be that the district was one of those in which the Muslims really interfered very little. Its Hindus Rajas remained independent in all but name."[10]

Saran was integrated into the Mughal Empire when the Afghan King of Bengal, Daud Khan, was defeated and Patna captured in 1574. The 1582 settlement described the district as covering seventeen parganas assessed at 16,172,004 *dams* (Rs. 404,300). The general contours of the district were known, but the area measured only 415 square miles (about a fifth of the district).[11]

Before the advent of, and during, Mughal rule, Rajputs, Muslims, and, especially, Bhumihar Brahmins, gained predominance at the village and pargana levels. The family records of the Harihobans Rajputs of Haldi, Ballia district, illustrate this history: their forefathers settled in Manjhi after a protracted struggle with the Cheros. On the eastern edge, along the Gandak, the Karamwar Rajputs founded the Amnour zamindari in the late sixteenth century. Formerly, as the Gaharwar branch, they had been a leading clan in the Banaras area.[12]

8. Interview with Dr. S. H. Askari, May 21–22, 1974.
9. Diwakar 1959: 407.
10. Atkinson 1881: 438, 466; Diwakar 1959: 391.
11. Beames 1885: 162–82; Habib 1982: 10A, 39–42.
12. Nevill 1909: 110; Atkinson 1881: 401–412.

Arabic and Persian inscriptions, the earliest one dating to 1373 and others to 1501 (from village Ismailpur) and 1503-1504 (from village Chirand and Narhan), record the long-standing Muslim presence in the district. According to popular legend, Muslim interests clustered particularly in the locality of Siwan because of land grants given to two Muslim mercenaries by the Majhauli raj in return for their services in rescuing this Rajput zamindari from the clutches of another Rajput landholder. In the town of Siwan, Raja Ali Bakhsh held sway in the mid-eighteenth century; his memory is preserved by an extant ruined fort associated with him, an inscription in the town mosque, which mentions him as its sponsor, and by the fact that the town is also called Aliganj after him.[13]

The Rajput Majhauli raj also figures in the history of the Hathwa raj. This Bhumihar Brahmin lineage of Baghochias acquired territory in the northwest corner at the expense of the aboriginal settlers. In contrast to other Bhumihar Brahmin lineages that acquired considerable land, the Baghochia Hathwas rose to the rank of raja, although not in the manner of the "typical eighteenth-century story" of the Bhumihar rajas of Banaras.[14]

Hathwa myths and legends claim an incredible genealogical depth stretching back to a hundred generations from the early twentieth century. Their myth of origin ties their beginnings closely to those of the Rajput rajas of Majhauli, with the latter being ascribed a longer ancestry; it ranks accurately the order in which the Rajputs and Bhumihars appear to have gained predominance in Saran.[15] In addition, the two families are traditionally supposed to be linked by kinship ties, a relationship that explains their salience in both Saran and Gorakhpur.

Majhauli tradition features a founder named Mayyur, who has been identified variously as a Brahmin, Rajput, or even a Bhat. After an initial stay in Banaras where he studied Sanskrit and astrology, he settled in Azamgarh district where he gradually acquired pargana Sikandarpur. From Gorakhpur where he moved next, he also established himself in Saran. His son seized pargana Salempur Majhauli and established a fort.[16]

Majhauli myth associates Mayyur with three wives and a Kurmi concubine. From each he had sons who established major estates from their inheritances. The offspring of his first marriage to a Brahmin initiated the line of Misra Brahmins; from his second wife, a Surajbans Rajput, came the founder of the Majhauli estate; and the son of his Bhumihar Brahmin wife received the

13. Q. Ahmad 1973: 102-3; 107-9; *SDG, 1960*: 496.
14. Cohn (1962: 314) has an account of the rise of a Bhumihar family in the eighteenth century from controller of a few hundred bighas in a village to a successful revenue farmer, and, finally, to becoming the raja of Banaras and a zamindar of three districts.
15. Atkinson 1881: 401-412; Nevill 1909: 111; G. N. Dutt 1905: 2-3. The founding of the Majhauli family is said to be ca. A.D. 1100, but the family chronicles claim a hundred generations between the founder and the mid-fourteenth century.
16. Majhauli 1881: 1-2; Nevill 1909: 110; G. N. Dutt 1905: 2-3.

portion of his kingdom that later constituted the Hathwa and Tamkuhi estates. His Kurmi concubine produced an heir who established the Kakradih estate.[17]

The descendants of the Bhumihar Brahmin line established themselves in the northwestern corner, in Kalyanpur Kuari pargana, in the late sixteenth century. By the early seventeenth century, according to Hathwa accounts, the family had become prominent enough for the eighty-seventh raja to receive both the title of "Maharaja Bahadur" and "Shahi" from the Mughal Emperor Jahangir (1605-1627). Attached to this story of attainment of authority is also that of increasing power and prosperity of the raj. The eighty-seventh raja shifted his headquarters from the little fortress of Kalyanpur to a larger one at Huseypur, which remained the seat of the raj until the advent of the British. The preceding raja, Kalyan Mal, had already established a reputation for the family by acquiring the title of maharaja and by having his capital named after him, an appellation also passed on to the pargana of Kalyanpur Kuari.[18] The growing might of this family was also enhanced by the ninety-fifth raja, Maharaja Jubraj Sahi Bahadur, who seized pargana Sipah from an Afghan chief named Kabul Mohammad of Barharia. The latter had "set himself up as a semi-independent chief in North Behar [and], had been constantly encroaching on the Hathwa [Huseypur] Raj."[19] A similar "success" story is told about the ninety-eighth Raja, Sirdar Sahi, who is said to have invaded the Majhauli raj and destroyed its fortress. Thus, Huseypur gained ascendancy over its "founding" line.

South of the Huseypur raj, the Eksaria Bhumihar Brahmins gained a foothold at the end of the sixteenth century. The pivotal figure was Jagarnath Dikshit who settled in the village of Eksar in the early sixteenth century. Although successful in staking out territory, Dikshit's descendants were not able to form a unified lineage and rise to the rank of raja by the late eighteenth century. They did not follow "the developmental cycle of the Rajput lineage" that Richard Fox has identified for U.P. Eksaria Bhumihar histories and genealogies, while tending to collapse chronology and ignore historical conditions, suggest, however, that the pioneering Eksarias reached the first stage of the cycle. In the case of Jagarnath's immediate descendants, the initial expansion appears to have occurred because of the inability of the state to restrict such territorial dispersion. And the abundance of male heirs in the lineage meant that expansion was necessary to prevent complex stratification.[20]

The two youngest of Jagarnath's four sons moved to other parganas, while the two oldest remained behind. The eldest, Saran Rai, also had four sons,

17. A fourth marriage is not mentioned in Majhauli 1881: 2; Atkinson 1881: 517.
18. D. N. Dutt 1909: 7; G. N. Dutt 1905: 5.
19. D. N. Dutt 1909: 9; *SDG, 1908*: 21.
20. Discrepancies exist regarding the genealogical depth of the Eksarias and the seniority of the different brothers who established the major houses. See Chapra, Private Holding, "History of Manjha"; Lala 1894. Also Fox (1971).

each of whom settled new villages and founded zamindaris; the second oldest had no issue. The first son created the Manjha line; the second, Nath Rai, went to Parsa from where his descendants subsequently established themselves in Chainpur; the third son produced the line eventuating in the Rusi and Khaira zamindaris. The youngest became the pioneer of the Bagoura zamindari.[21] Thus, in a span of four generations the foundations of several major zamindaris had been laid.

But this outmigration was confined to a limited area. The new nodal points lay within a mean distance of eleven miles from the parent settlement, within a day or two of walking distance.[22] Progress along the "developmental cycle" was thwarted, no doubt, by the growing encroachment of the state as manifested in the centralizing tendencies of the Mughal Empire. If the early sixteenth century marks the beginnings of Jagarnath's arrival in the district, the rise of the various branches of his heirs must have coincided with the zenith of the Mughal Empire in the late sixteenth and early seventeenth centuries. Furthermore, a factor that Fox ignores but that had a considerable effect on the fortunes of the Eksarias was the internecine fighting that frequently erupted among the heirs because none of the families of this lineage followed the practice of primogeniture and estate impartibility.[23]

The rise of Rajput and Bhumihar Brahmin zamindars in terms of Fox's "developmental cycle" also needs another more fundamental qualification. Fox's "speculative" analysis insightfully notes the close relationship between the power of the state and of dominant landed families organized by kinship, but it fails to account for the growth of clan or lineage power vis-à-vis other groups, both competing and subordinate ones. Nor is attention paid to clan formation as a function of control over the resources of the land and its distribution—both the modes of production and the marketing and trade systems. Frank Perlin's critique of Fox notes precisely these gaps in arguing that the structures of dominance in the fifteenth to the eighteenth centuries in western India were organized by territorial structures of rule in which "the emerging structure of properties—peasant-held and lordly—was of a widespread precapitalist kind."[24] Coupled with recent findings about the agrarian expansion in the late Mughal period, 1600 to 1800, in diverse areas, including Bihar, the emphasis on the rise of territorial rule characterized by "the growth of a ruling class and its private interests" explains more convincingly the process of consolidation in local society that produced the landed groups of the eighteenth century.[25]

21. Chapra, Private Holding, "History of Manjha"; Lala 1894.
22. R. P. B. Singh 1977: 106–9. See also Hagen (1981: 71–72) regarding the ordering of society according to "the *effective living circle* based on distance, roughly half a day's walk out from one's house (a four-mile radius)."
23. Interview with Gouri Shanker Prasad Sahi, June 10, 1974.
24. Perlin 1981: 281.
25. Ibid.: 288. See also Perlin (1978).

By the late eighteenth century, Rajput, Muslim, and Bhumihar Brahmin zamindars in Saran stood at different stages of the "developmental cycle" in their relation to the state, with the Huseypur rajas clearly furthest along in this "cycle." Most of them enjoyed high caste status and legitimacy, acquired through titles sanctioned either by the imperial or regional authorities. Furthermore, the dominance of this well-established configuration of Rajput and, especially, Bhumihar Brahmin lineages, as their spirited resistance to the initial British penetration into the district reveals, also rested on their control over territory as well as its peasants.

The Initial British Penetration

The British victory at the battle of Plassey in 1757 opened the door for the East India Company to become complete masters of Bengal, Bihar, and Orissa. The economic boom that ensued expanded internal trade throughout the region and extended British influence far beyond the confines of Calcutta and the upcountry factories to the rural interior. These developments further undermined the authority of the nawab of Bengal, Mir Kasim, and forced him to confront the growing power of the British. Eventually, the conflict also drew in the nawab of Awadh and the Mughal emperor. Their collective defeat at Buxar in October 1764 by the Company's forces installed British military primacy in northeastern India and extended its western frontier from Bihar into Awadh. Acknowledgment of the changed political realities in the region came in 1765 when the Mughal emperor transferred the right of revenue administration and collection (diwani) of Bengal, Bihar, and Orissa from the nawab to the British.[26]

The acquisition of diwani elevated the Company to the status of a regional political authority. Devolution of authority in the eighteenth century, however, did not necessarily ensure the effective exercise of local control. Indeed, in the absence of a supreme authority, victories on the battlefield merely provided entry into local arenas where additional military or political contests had to be won to secure the prized economic resource in society: revenue from control of the land. Thus, the diwani of Bihar brought the Company into confrontation with locally dominant groups.

The Company's new power was exercised in Bihar by enlarging the responsibilities of the chief of the Patna factory to include the task of collecting revenue, an assignment in which he was to be assisted by Shitab Rai and Dhiraj Narayan, two former diwans; together these three men comprised the Patna Council. Almost immediately, contentiousness set in between the British and the Indian officers involved in the collection, as well as between the two groups. The actual collection was carried out by subordinate Indian agencies.

26. Marshall 1976: 106–28; S. G. Misra 1970: 52–121; Barnett 1980: 42–66.

In 1770 British officers, called supervisors, were appointed to take charge of each of the districts.[27]

Effective control over the hinterlands was more shadow than substance in the early years of British rule. Troops, while mustered easily from headquarter towns to suppress uprisings even in the remote corners of the Company's domain, were not available to curtail more routine disturbances. Because of the costs of maintaining military units, permanent military stations were usually not established in rural localities. In their absence, raids by marauding bands of mercenaries, who had detached themselves from the shifting military alliances of the late eighteenth century, were not uncommon. In a "frontier area" like Saran, incursions occurred frequently, as in 1771, when 4,000 Nagas marched through the district, or in 1773, when Sannyasis plundered several villages.[28]

The most significant challenge to the initial British penetration into Bihar as a regional political authority came, however, from local magnates. Nor was such resistance to centralizing forces novel. The Bettiah rajas of Champaran, for example, functioned as independent chiefs in the early eighteenth century, refusing to acknowledge the suzerainty of either the imperial authority or the dominion of the regional Mughal authorities. This antipathy had to be broken down anew by the Company: three military expeditions were launched against Bettiah before the raja accepted British authority.[29]

Opposition to the British also issued from other parts of the region. Some zamindars took up arms and resisted openly; others resorted to recalcitrance in paying revenue and to attempts to defraud local collections. Revenue collection, therefore, frequently required the use of force, a task that a battalion posted at Patna and "pargana battalions" stationed in different parts of the province were organized to discharge.[30] Most uprisings and recalcitrant zamindars were brought under control quickly, but the rebellion of the ninety-ninth Huseypur raja, Fateh Sahi, was a long, protracted affair that kept Saran in turmoil for most of the last three decades of the eighteenth century.

The Revenue Rebellions

In 1767 Fateh Sahi challenged the British diwani over his "district" of Huseypur, in the northwestern corner of Saran, comprising the parganas of Kalyanpur Kuari and Sipah. In this area, far removed from the British

27. S. G. Misra 1970: 137–53.
28. Edwd. Golding, Supr. Sircar Saran, to George Hurst, Acting Chief, Council of Rev., Patna, Procs. of the Controlling Council of Rev. at Patna (hereafter Patna Rev. Procs.), Feb. to Dec. 1773, Apr. 12; Golding to Richd. Barwell, Chief, Patna, Rev. Council, Dec. 20, 1771, Patna Rev. Procs., Aug. 3 to Dec. 30, 1771, Dec. 23. Also Barnett (1980: 56–57) on the "stark naked, ash-smeared Naga *sannyasis*" who formed an "unusual contingent of Shaivite warriors" in the forces of the nawab of Awadh.
29. GOB & O, Swanzy 1938: 135; Husain Khan 1902: 2.
30. Raye 1927: 284–317. Also see L. Prasad (1981) on resistance in different parts of the region.

headquarters at Patna (which lay across an unbridged river), he must have felt confident of his power and influence. Furthermore, his control extended beyond the frontiers of the Company's domains into Gorakhpur (then part of the kingdom of Awadh).

The initial act of defiance occurred precisely when the representative of the new political authority, the *amil* (revenue collector), sought to collect an outstanding balance. Fateh Sahi refused to pay up, mobilized his supporters, and took to his fort, where he kept local authorities at bay. Only when troops were sent in from Patna was he dislodged. Eventually defeated, he fled into the jungles of Gorakhpur. British attempts to capitalize on this victory, however, met with numerous obstacles:

> The unsettled state of the country, his easy access to the territories of an independent prince, where British troops were unable to pursue him, and the impenetrable forest which surrounded his retreat, the collusion of the agents of the Vizier of Oudh, and above all, the attachment of the people to their expelled Raja and their dislike of a Government farmer, all contributed to favor his designs; and he kept the country in a state of terror and the British authorities constantly on the alert.[31]

The Gorakhpur sanctuary also served the raja well because of his family ties to the leading Gorakhpur notable, the Majhauli raja. His presence in the area, moreover, was welcomed as a "powerful bulwark against Banjara raids."[32] Power and influence, connections, and the "foreign" territory explain why Fateh Sahi retreated to the area of pargana Sidhua Jobna and established himself there in the fort of Tamkuhi. By 1808 he held 100 villages.[33]

Nor was the Company's attention solely confined to Fateh Sahi. Consolidating the incipient Raj in Saran also required campaigns against other zamindari forts and the disarming of local forces. An early target was the "independent" fort of the Muslim zamindars of Barharia. In 1771 the private ownership of the fort was deemed an "indignity offered to the Government; in case of Disturbance it would become a Station of Importance in the hands of an Enemy; situated towards the Borders of the Company's possessions, and open to Shuja Dowla's Country."[34] The family, moreover, resided in Awadh and refused to turn over charge of their fort, a rebuff that local administrators sought to overcome cautiously for fear of driving Barharia into the camp of Fateh Sahi. But in May, the Company's forces besieged the fort and compelled its zamindars, Sheikh Abdullah and Imam Baksh, to surrender.[35]

Although dislodged from Huseypur, Fateh Sahi continued to harass the collection of revenue in his former territory by launching raids from the safety

---

31. *SDG, 1908:* 30.
32. Nevill 1909: 117; S. G. Misra 1970: 13–14.
33. Nevill 1909: 117–18. Jobna was transferred from Saran to Gorakhpur in 1730.
34. Golding to George Vansittart, Patna Council, Jan. 23, 1771, Patna Rev. Procs., Nov. 13, 1770 to May 28, 1771, 45.
35. See Copy-book of letters issued by Chief of Factory at Patna, April 1771 to March 1773, passim.

of Gorakhpur. In 1772 he marched into Huseypur and killed Govind Ram, the Company-appointed revenue farmer of that district, but the British persisted in their efforts to bring him back into their fold because his forays had completely disrupted revenue collection. Even after this incident, the district collector recommended that he be pardoned because the "disadvantage of his being out of the province in case of disturbances or an incursion of the Marhattas would be very forcibly felt, for Huseypur being a large frontier district and Fateh Sahi himself related in some degree to most of the zamindars of Sircar Sarun."[36] Following a brief period of two months when the Patna Council allowed him to return to his former stronghold, as part of a compromise, he broke the terms of the agreement and returned to his Gorakhpur hideout. Mir Jamal was then designated as the superintendent of the Huseypur revenue, and the estate farmed out to Basant Sahi, a cousin of Fateh Sahi. To strengthen his hand, Basant Sahi sought a marriage alliance in 1773 with the family of Raja Chait Singh of Banaras, who also became his financial guarantor for the Company's share of revenue. But he was also aware, as he candidly admitted to Supervisor Edward Golding, that he would always be regarded as a "usurper." And, notwithstanding Golding's attempts to effect a reconciliation with Fateh Sahi, such efforts were bound to fail because Fateh Sahi was unwilling to set aside his claims to Huseypur.[37]

The Company Raj was also challenged in 1773 by the "Narrowney zemindars," Rajput landholders who held villages in pargana Pachlakh, adjoining Gorakhpur. Like Fateh Sahi, they too rebelled against the new regime when it sought to recover revenue arrears and attacked the local representatives of the state; in their case, they killed a *gomastah* (agent, steward) and several of his servants and then fled to Awadh.[38]

Disaffection in the region continued to escalate in 1774 when Ajit Mal, raja of Majhauli, although not as yet in arms against the British, openly resisted the attempts by the *amil* of Gorakhpur to collect revenues. So did Fateh Sahi and the zamindar of Perrouna, Gennoo Rai; all three resorted to the familiar tactic of crossing over to the Bihar side whenever Awadh's local officials approached them for revenue payments. Meanwhile, the Narrowneys continued to harass the Company's administration, marching into Saran in 1774 with 500 "matchlockmen," killing several petty officials and demanding financial contributions from local zamindars. They were now also linked to the raja of Majhauli who allowed them to camp in his Gorakhpur territories, and to Fateh Sahi.[39]

Biding his time, Fateh Sahi marched into Saran in 1775 and killed both

36. Golding to Patna Council, Oct. 11, 1772, Patna Rev. Procs., April 1772–Jan. 1773, Oct. 12.
37. Golding to Patna Council, n.d., Golding to Patna Council, n.d., Patna Rev. Procs., Feb.–Dec. 1773, March 4 and July 24.
38. Golding to Patna Council, Jan. 8 and 26, 1773, Patna Rev. Procs., 1772 to 1773, Feb. 1, 1773.
39. *Arzees* (petitions) of Mahommed Ashruff Khan, Diwan of Saran to Patna Council, n.d., and encl. from amil of Gorakhpur, n.d., Patna Rev. Procs., 1774, May 12, 19, 26.

Basant Sahi and Mir Jamal. His ability to strike at will showed the considerable support he still enjoyed in Huseypur and the weakness of British control in the locality. And his repeated incursions invariably crippled revenue collection, making it virtually impossible for newly appointed farmers of the Huseypur zamindari to collect rent, let alone establish alternative networks of control. Prospective farmers, wishing to tap the riches of this large estate, were also frightened away by the ever-present threat of assassination. Unable to stop his raids, the British took the precautionary measure of relocating the late Basant Sahi's minor heir to Patna.[40]

His growing string of successes and the widening circle of disaffection emboldened Fateh Sahi, in early 1777, to march on the Company's Barragaon military station, which had been established especially to suppress his rebellion. There, he tore down the officers' quarters and *kachcheri* (office) and placed his own men in charge of the buildings. He then undertook the daring feat of rebuilding his Huseypur fort and openly reasserting his right of rent collection. A frantic message from the Company's farmer at Huseypur reported that "the malguzars [rent collectors] of every Tuppeh having appeared before him engaged for one-fourth of the produce to him and are now accordingly paying his people in specie."[41]

To this growing list of troubles for the British, the raja of Majhauli added another in 1777 by also refusing to pay revenue in the Bihar portion of his holdings. Not wishing to force his hand, the Company treated his case gingerly, even going so far as refusing to assist the Gorakhpur authorities in their efforts to compel his return to their territory. The Patna Council, ever aware of the Huseypur rebellion, refused to see any similarities in the actions of Fateh Sahi and Ajit Mal and instead pronounced the former "guilty of the atrocious crime of premeditated murder and rebellion" and the latter guilty of "no offence" because he had merely "relinquished his lands in Gorakhpur on being unable to pay the rent charged on them."[42] Nor were they eager to apprehend Gennoo Rai, the zamindar of Perrouna, who had absconded into Saran. The Patna authorities believed, however, that an invitation into the district to the pursuing nawabi forces, as well as their own attempts to mobilize and send troops into battle, would disrupt "the peace and obstruct the collections of a large district."[43]

Passivity was quickly transformed into accommodation, however, when a nawabi detachment arrived in Company territory in pursuit of the Majhauli raja. In an about-face of its earlier position, the Patna Council asked Saran

40. Patna Council to G.G. Warren Hastings and Council, June 17, 1776, Bengal Rev. Consltns., Oct. 25 to Nov. 12, 1776, Nov. 5, no. 776.
41. *Arzees* from Mahmud Moshruff, renter of Huseypur, Patna Rev. Procs., Aug. 4 to Dec. 31, 1777, Nov. 17 and 24.
42. Patna Rev. Procs., Jan. 2 to Dec. 28, 1775, Sept. 21.
43. Nathaniel Middleton, Resident, Vizier's Court, Lucknow, to Ewan Law, Chief of Patna, March 15, 1777, Patna Rev. Procs., Jan. 2 to July 31, 1777, March 27. Majhauli paid Rs. 32,000 revenue for the Saran portion of his holdings.

officials and the local military commanders to assist the nawabi forces. because the Gorakhpur authorities had agreed to join in the fight against Fateh Sahi once the expedition against Ajit Mal was successful.[44]

From the outset the Patna Council had sought the cooperation of the Awadh authorities because of Fateh Sahi's tactic of retreating to Gorakhpur whenever he was confronted by a superior force. Furthermore, the Company did not have an administrative infrastructure to supplant the networks of control and support that Fateh Sahi had constructed in Huseypur. The special official report into the "original causes of Futtee Saw's rebellion" spelled out his many advantages:

> the aid and protection afforded . . . by some frontier zemindars in Gorakhpur, as well as by the inhabitants of Housseypore . . . an apparent attachment of the inhabitants to his person and interests . . . it may arise greatly from a fear of his power, since they have seen him maintain his situation so long and have such frequent opportunity of punishing those who may have shewn attachment to Government, which he always has done with rigour; the circumstances of his being a Bramin may also be a cause which restrains the inhabitants from taking part against him.[45]

The alliance of convenience proved to be short-lived, however. The nawabi-Company force was unsuccessful against both rajas. But pressure from the highest levels of government continued to be placed on the nawab, and while the nawab seemingly complied, little changed to upset the balance of the seesaw contest. Rather than wage war against Fateh Sahi, the nawab's representatives in Gorakhpur found it more expedient to compromise with him.[46] Even Major Alexander Hannay, the revenue farmer of Gorakhpur by a secret agreement signed between Warren Hastings and the nawab in 1779, was unwilling or unable to displace Fateh Sahi. To the Calcutta Council, he attributed his failure to the fact that the rebel evaded the Awadh forces by crossing into the Huseypur side where he enjoyed the support of the Company's Indian coadjutors.[47]

Clearly, both the nawab and the Company recognized the advantages that "rebels" had in seeking the safety of "foreign" soil, but neither party was willing to renounce the politically expedient strategy of collecting revenue at the minimal costs possible. Neither government, consequently, committed itself fully to expelling fugitives from the other side. Cooperation was therefore, at best, transient, because just as Company officials weighed questions of joint efforts against the potential damage to their primary goal of extracting revenue,

---

44. J. Harding, Lt., Commanding at Barragong, to Simeon Droz, Chief of Rev. Council, Jan. 8 and Jan. 15, 1777, Patna Rev. Consltns., Jan. 2 to July 31, 1777, Jan. 20.

45. Samuel Charters to Hon. Warren Hastings, G.G., no. 233, June 25, 1782, Bengal Rev. Consltns., Apr. 16 to June 28, 1782, June (hereafter cited as Charters Report).

46. T. Harding, Lt., 5th Battalion, Sepoys, to Simeon Droz, Chief of Patna Council, June 29, 1777, Bengal Rev. Consltns., May 21 to July 1777, July 1.

47. From Alexander Hannay, Lt. Col., Nugger, March 15, 1781, Bengal Rev. Consltns., Sept. 1 to Oct. 23, 1781, Sept. 6. On Hannay's role in Awadh politics, see Barnett (1980: 184–85).

so did the nawabi officials. Therefore, neither side could win against enemies who availed themselves of the escape option.

Political and financial considerations also explain why the British were not willing to take action against Fateh Sahi's followers in Huseypur even after his rout in a pitched battle in 1781 was followed up with a detailed investigation of his rebellion and his supporters. An arrest of his Saran supporters, it was feared, "might extend almost to every man in the District, or that the seizure of particular persons would so much alarm the inhabitants that they would again desert to Futtee Saw."[48] In the raja of Huseypur the Company had acquired an adversary who was firmly anchored in local society as a territorial magnate with control over both land and its inhabitants.

These rebellions showed that the British did not have a well-developed local system of control to supersede existing zamindari networks. Furthermore, by straddling the frontiers of two political systems, which were, in this period, moving toward a new relationship, Fateh Sahi, as well as the Majhauli raja and the Perrouna and Narrowney zamindars, were able to persist in the face of seemingly superior forces. On the other hand, these "rebels and outlaws" remained beyond the reach of the regional authorities precisely because their resistance was confined to localized areas where they enjoyed popular support. For the Company, already a formidable regional power, such local challenges did not constitute a serious enough threat to warrant commitment of unlimited resources. Nor did the British have the capability to make their full power felt expeditiously and inexpensively at the local level. Thus, the loyalty of rebels had to be frequently reinvited, despite their contravention of authority.

Increasingly, though, zamindari resistance was beginning to place a heavy burden on Company administration and finances: revenue collections were falling sharply and the expenses of beating back local rebels was rising rapidly. This new situation demanded decisive action, a determination apparent in the Company's willingness to double the reward for Fateh Sahi's capture (to Rs. 20,000) in 1781.[49] Events in the 1780s further undermined the delicate balance that characterized the uneasy standoff prevailing between the emerging colonial state and contentious local zamindars.

The New Balance of Power: The Emergence of Hathwa

The uprising of Raja Chait Singh of Banaras in August 1781 added a new dimension to the rebellions against Company rule in Bihar because it threatened to link up with the recurring uprisings at the local levels and erupt into a major

48. Charters Report.
49. Macpherson 1927: 390; Chas. Graeme, Colltr., Saran, to Bengal, Rev. Council, no. 563, Bengal Rev. Consltns., Aug. 10 to Oct. 12, 1779, Oct. 5. Military expenditures and the disruptions caused by Fateh Sahi affected revenue collections in Huseypur adversely; by 1768 Rs. 900,000 had been lost on account of Fateh Sahi's rebellion (S. G. Mishra 1970: 140).

regional conflagration. That contingency loomed large because Chait Singh was related to many Bihar zamindars by kinship and/or caste ties, and because he actively sought their assistance. Fateh Sahi not only received Banaras money, but also letters from Chait Singh encouraging him to kill Europeans and their sepoys (Indian soldiers). And within the district resistance to local authorities increased as many more landholders refused to cooperate, some even assaulting the emissaries of the Company. "Every day," the Saran collector encountered "fresh instances of a determined disposition in the inhabitants . . . to throw off all subjection of my authority."[50]

In the wake of the Banaras uprising, a full-fledged alliance was forged between the rajas of Huseypur and Majhauli, the Perrouna zamindar, and the Narrowneys. Together they fielded an army of 8,000 troops and six cannons. Other Saran zamindars, including Sheikh Muhammad Ali of Siwan, and the Bhumihar Brahmin landholders of Bagoura and Chainpur, although they did not actually take up arms against the British, at least supported the rebel cause by creating obstacles for the Company forces or by secretly assisting Fateh Sahi.[51]

In October 1781 Fateh Sahi and his allies assembled a sizable force of 12,000 men at Munjoora, six miles away from the Company military station at Barragaon, and fought a pitched battle with the British troops. But he was "defeated, and having lost everything which was in his camp, he fled to the jungles and his troops disappeared."[52] Thereafter, the Huseypur raja never regained his ability to strike into the district at will or to mount other major campaigns, but his periodic incursions continued, although after 1785, they had essentially subsided. In the last reported raid in official records, in 1795, he marched into Champaran and carried away 1,600 head of cattle.[53] His subsequent career, narrated by a Hathwa family chronicle, notes that he turned away from "his predatory life," eventually becoming a fakir (ascetic) in 1808, "perhaps finding in despair all his attempts to gain independence."[54]

The reverses Fateh Sahi suffered in the 1780s were indicative of the overwhelming military supremacy in the region that the British had acquired as well as its growing willingness to dispatch troops to defuse threats to its authority. British successes on the battlefield were accompanied by their rising advantages on the political and diplomatic fronts. Rebels in the interior, tenacious adversaries to overcome in their strongholds in the initial years after diwani, were becoming less formidable opponents as the Company developed its revenue collection machinery and backed it up with enough firepower to deprive recalcitrant zamindars of their major source of funds—their lands.

This change in balance of power between the regional authority and local

50. Charles Grome, Colltr., to Bengal Rev. Council, Sept. 15, 1781, Bengal Rev. Consltns., Sept. 1 to Oct. 23, 1781, Sept. 28, no. 582.
51. Charters Report. 52. Ibid.
53. W. R. Amherst, Acting Colltr., to Capt. John Archdeacon, Commander at Barragaon, Sept. 4, 1788, Bengal Rev. Consltns., Oct. 1 to 10, 1788, Oct. 10.
54. G. N. Dutt 1905: 16.

controllers is epitomized in the different strategies the Company used to suppress Fateh Sahi's rebellions in the 1770s and 1780s. In the earlier decade, although he virtually crippled revenue collection on a number of occasions, his "loyalty" was still sought. In the 1780s no effort was made to reinvite his support. On the contrary, local officials were increasingly drawn to the possibility of bypassing his customary claims by acknowledging Mahesh Dutt, the son of his murdered cousin (Basant Sahi) as the proprietor of the estate. After Mahesh Dutt personally approached Warren Hastings at Banaras in 1782 and accompanied him to Patna, the governor-general recommended the Dutt claim to the Patna Council.[55] Although this right was not granted at the Decennial Settlement when the estate was leased out to revenue farmers, Company officials by then approved of his designation as the "next heir." Only the fear of inciting Fateh Sahi into taking drastic action against revenue collection and the life of the sole male survivor of the loyal cadet line of the Huseypur family deferred the immediate enactment of this recognition.[56] Meanwhile, Fateh Sahi continued to press for his right of rajaship through the intercessions of his wife whose petitions appealed to the "unequal liberality of an English government" to consider the plight of her and her daughters "left destitute of a resource or even the means of a poor subsistence."[57]

Although Mahesh Dutt died before his claim was accepted, in 1790, his four-year-old son, Chatterdhari Sahi, was "made proprietor."[58] Being a minor, he was placed under the guardianship of a Company-appointed manager until he attained his majority in 1802. Symbolic of the new beginning was Chatterdhari Sahi's decision to relocate the estate headquarters to Hathwa where he built his palaces and a fort. The cadet line ascended to the rajaship, but the senior line remained in Gorakhpur and became the Tamkohi rajas.[59]

Thus, the triumph of British authority in Saran was accompanied by the transformation of the rebellious Huseypur zamindari into a loyal and "captive" Hathwa estate. "Hutwa's cheer" thus became an important political imperative of the system of colonial rule in Saran. And, although other zamindars also became incorporated into the system as permanent "connections," they were more likely to be considered "small beer" by the "man for Chupra." In the nineteenth and early twentieth centuries, these relationships served as the foundation of the developing pattern of collaboration between the British Raj and the district's local controllers.

55. *Arzee* of Baboo Maheiss Dut Sah, Zemindar of Pergunnah Hoouseepoor &c. and Nephew of Futteh Sah, n.d., Bengal Rev. Consltns., April 21 to July 20, 1784, May 26.
56. Grome to Sir John Shore, Acting Pres., July 6, 1784, with Montgomerie to Hon. Chas. Stuart, Pres. and members of BOR, June 16, 1790, Bengal Rev. Consltns., July 28 to 30, 1790, July 28, no. 63.
57. Translation of *arzee* of Ranee of Rajah Futtay Saw, n.d., Bengal Rev Consltns., June 23 to July 9, 1790, June 23, no. 52.
58. Montgomerie to Stuart, BOR, Nov. 18, 1790, Bengal Rev. Consltns., Jan. 7 to Feb. 25, 1791, Feb. 21, nos. 11 and 12.
59. See Yang (1979a: 247–64) on official support in shoring up great estates.

4

Government and Its Allies: The System of Control and Collaboration

Collaboration between European regimes and influential local allies in Asia and Africa was a basic prop of the colonial systems of rule.[1] In Saran the British alliance with local controllers developed out of the arrangements created by the Permanent Settlement and their initial encounter in the late eighteenth century. The new regime held the reins of power and authority not only by virtue of its superior economic and military resources, but also because of its ability to serve as protector of its allies. Especially in the case of Hathwa, this led to the development of a close and mutually beneficial relationship—central to the pattern of British interactions with local society. Although lesser zamindars were not consistently singled out to receive official largess, they too were granted special concessions.

Fluctuations in the fortunes of individual families notwithstanding, there were relatively few substantive changes in the pattern of landholding. Not only had the Permanent Settlement been made with the "old landed proprietors," but this original group remained largely intact as the major allies of the Raj. Because there were relatively few changes in the social background of the district's zamindars, the major alterations, as the family histories of local controllers indicate, were in the form of substitution of landholders from particular families, lineages, and caste for those of similar social backgrounds. In other words, land—the basic resource of the agrarian society—remained in the hands of the local controllers singled out as "permanent" connections of the Raj in the late eighteenth century.

The working of the system of control and collaboration are further delineated

1. The classic statement of this relationship is the work of Robinson and Gallagher (Louis, ed. 1976: 53–72, 128–51).

by a study of the British institution of the Court of Wards. Although this mechanism enabled government to manage "captive" estates directly, its efforts were not directed at gaining greater control over landholders. It did seek to ensure the loyalty of its wards by supervising their education, but the primary result of this institution's efforts on behalf of landholders was to shelter them from financial woes and deleterious social encumbrances.

The Context of Collaboration

That the Permanent Settlement provided a solid foundation for the British system of rule is evident from the Mutiny/Rebellion in 1857, when Saran's local controllers-cum-connections and the administrative machinery together served to maintain the British Raj in the district. Precisely these two supports were used by the deputy magistrate of Siwan to elude rebels approaching from neighboring Champaran: in his flight, he was helped by landholders and by petty police officers.[2] Such bulwarks further guaranteed, even in the absence of British officials, that "the general tone of the people was for peace and order." Other than "two or three cases of Riot and boat plundering," as the district magistrate reported on his return, not "one single offence [was] committed... which can be said to have arisen out of the disturbed state of the district."[3] As Eric Stokes's district-level analyses of 1857 reveal, the "critical factor in rural reactions was the presence or absence of a thriving magnate element heavily committed by interest to British rule."[4] Thus, the year 1857 was relatively quiescent in Saran because landholders "as a body behaved well since the commencement of the disturbance."[5]

For most loyal landholders, the roots of cooperation with the government in 1857 were established during the initial penetration of British rule into the local society. Although the Rajput maliks who had lost all their estates did "kick up a row" (the only local outburst in 1857), it was "not so much to fight Government as against the men who have bought up their estate."[6]

Saran's landholders also served as vital links in other crises that the British faced in the nineteenth and early twentieth centuries. In the Cow Riots of 1893, for instance, the lieutenant governor's telegram to the maharaja of Hathwa is particularly telling about government expectations: "Lieutenant Governor has heard with much regret of the riot.... He relies on you to afford active assistance to the authorities in restoring order and bringing offenders to

2. Deputy Magte. Lynch to Magte. W. F. McDonnell, no. 2, Sept. 9, 1857, S.C., Letters received from 1854 to 1859 from Deputy Magte. of Sewan.
3. McDonnell to Commr., no. 37, Feb. 18, 1858, S.C., Letters from the Magte. of Saran to the Commr. of Patna, March 1857 to March 1858.   4. 1978: 188.
5. McDonnell to Commr., n.d., S.C., Letters from Saran to Patna, March 1857 to March 1858.
6. McDonnell to Commr. W. Tayler, demi-official, Aug. 13, 1857, P.C. *Basta* no. 105, Monthly Bundles, Gen. Dept. from 1854 on, from Magte. of Saran.

justice."[7] When famine threatened the district, the relief committees, the centers of relief, and the grain storage depots were all organized around these "respectable gentlemen."[8] In less critical times, in the routine operations of the governmental machinery, these connections were also used, at least symbolically, for example, when their opinions were sought on new legislation.[9]

From the perspective of the local notables, the interaction with the British can also be seen socially at *Dashara* (religious festival at the beginning of the agricultural year) festivities, which was an "old institution of the [Hathwa] Raj ... [where] a large European party ... [was] entertained ... with a gymkhana, dances, polo, tennis and golf,"[10] and at the much-celebrated Sonepur meets. Informally, they worked as members of various ad hoc organizations and committees, of which the "Committee to Reduce Marriage Expenses" is one example.[11] Formally, they served on such provincial bodies as the Bihar Landholders' Association, at whose inaugural meeting in November 1878, the maharaja of Hathwa, bábus Ram Saran Sinha, Achabar Prasad Narain Sinha of Parsa, Parsid Narain Sinha of Chainpur, and Raghubans Sahai of Chapra represented Saran. In its formation and its activities, it resembled the "loyalist" British Indian Association, a similarity that the Bihar organizers consciously tried to cultivate.[12]

The Raj's intermediaries were also tied to it by the patronage and honors disbursed to them. Notables could be exempted from the provisions of restrictive laws like the Indian Arms Act.[13] Some, like the maharaja of Hathwa, were exempted even from the necessity of personal attendance in civil courts. They were also named to institutions of "local government," for example, the district road committee, the district education committee, municipal committees, and benches of honorary magistrates.[14]

This collaborative relationship of British consultation with, as well as control of, their landed allies was also manifested in durbars, meetings at which honors and rewards were presented to Indian notables. As Cohn shows, these audiences constituted "a ritual idiom, which the British rulers ... developed as part of a system by which they sought to control their Indian

7. Telegram from L.G. to Maharaja of Hathwa, Sept. 7, 1893, Bengal Jdcl. Procs., Police, Oct. to Dec. 1894, Nov., no. 26.
8. Secy. to Central Relief Committee to Commr. of Patna, June 16, 1866, S.C., Misc. File Book of Letters re: Late Scarcity, 1866.
9. "Government Resolution dated 28 Aug. 1873 ... [on] zamindars of Saran, who were consulted on the subject of the joint management of estates," Bengal Rev. Procs., 1873 to 1875, Branch Land Rev., B, Oct. 1874, nos. 165 to 167.
10. D. N. Dutt 1909: 54.
11. See Peyare Lal to Colltr. of Saran, Nov. 29, 1876, S.C. *Faujdari Basta*, 1876; *Jagopakarak* 1871. Also S. Prasad (1969).
12. "Proceedings of the Inaugural Meeting of the Behar Landholders Association," Dec. 19, 1878, P.C. Rev. *Basta* no. 329, 1878 to 1879.
13. Bengal Polit. Dept., Police Branch B Procs., Jan. 1875, nos. 167/68.
14. Bengal Jdcl. B Procs., June 1875, nos. 272–282; AGRPD, 1872–73.

subjects."[15] Individuals singled out for inclusion in the durbari lists, maintained in every locality, represented the people whom the government repeatedly aided, supported, honored, and consulted: in short, the group recognized as its local connections. To quote an official source, the durbar lists were drawn up "to enable local officials and their superior officers to see at a glance who are the leading men of the district, and what claim they have to consideration."[16]

The Sonepur Durbar of 1877 listed twenty-seven persons in order of precedence. Members of the Hathwa family occupied positions ranging from number one and two to four through seven. The third rank was held by the maharaja of Bettiah whose property lay primarily in Champaran but also extended into Saran. Others, in rank order, were the landholders of Goldinganj (Chirand), Manjha, Chainpur (this family placed eleven people on the list), Chapra, Samha, Amnour, Parsa, Khajhua, Husseinganj, and Mashrak.[17]

Of the twelve families represented by the twenty-seven durbaris of 1877, four—Hathwa, Chainpur, Chirand, and Manjha—were among the nine leading zamindars with whom the Permanent Settlement had been concluded in 1793. Of the other five permanent connections, the zamindars of Manjhi, Siwan, and Bagoura show up in durbar lists compiled in 1874 and 1904; only Majhauli whose estate lay largely in the Northwest Provinces and Barharia do not appear in any of these records.[18] Thus, there was considerable continuity in the nineteenth and early twentieth centuries in the personnel of the group tapped as government's permanent allies in 1793.

The Consolidation of Local Allies

Government's role in consolidating local allies is best illustrated by its involvement in the affairs of Hathwa. Not only was its intervention a significant factor in the emergence of Hathwa from the ashes of the rebellious Huseypur zamindari, but also in the subsequent development of Hathwa as the great estate of the district.

The first century of British rule in Saran "legally established" primogenitural succession and proprietary impartibility of the Hathwa estate, developments identified as the "important diagnostics of the rise of the raja."[19] Before his death in 1858, Chatterdhari had announced to his kinsmen and the district officials his intention to pass on the estate to his great-grandson.[20] His two sons

15. 1979: 14–15.
16. Private Secy. of L.G. of Bengal to Commrs. of Division, no. 97P-D, April 18, 1904, S.C. *Faujdari Basta*, 1904.
17. "List of Maharajas, Rajahs and Zamindars prepared in order of precedence for local Durbar in Saran, Oct. 1877," ibid., 1877.
18. "List of Native Gentlemen presented to the Lieutenant Governor at Chupra, October 1874," Richard Temple Collection, Native Opinion, Vernacular Press, 1867–1873, Mss. Eur. F. 86/214; "Recognized List of Local Notables, Saran District," S.C. *Faujdari Basta*, 1904.
19. Fox 1971: 81.
20. "Judgement of the Judicial Committee... delivered March 4, 1868," in D. N. Dutt (1909: xliv-lv).

had died before him and his eldest grandson, Ugra Pratap, waived his claim in favor of his son, Rajendra Pratap. His contestants were the sons of Chatterdhari's younger son, Tilakdhari and Birpratap, and their claim was that the estate was an ordinary zamindari and could be partitioned "in accordance with the ordinary rule of Hindu Law, (and was not) . . . an Estate which is a Raj."[21] In their interpretation, Fateh Sahi's rebellion had led to the estate's confiscation; therefore, the "family custom" of primogeniture no longer applied to the resettled estate.

Tilakdhari and Birpratap first pressed their claims in the district court, which dismissed their suit but awarded them Rs. 2,000 per month as maintenance. While their appeal was being decided in the Calcutta High Court, Tilakdhari withdrew from litigation and accepted a compromise granting him several villages as maintenance. The High Court eventually dismissed the case and halved the maintenance awarded by the district court.[22] In the Privy Council, where Birpratap sought a hearing next, the rules of inheritance of family usage were finally settled for Hathwa, and the appeal dismissed. The estate was defined as an impartible Raj, which "descended on the death of each successive Raja to his eldest male heir according to the rule of primogeniture, who took the whole, subject to the obligation of making to the junior members of the family certain allowances by way of maintenance." This allowance could be either in cash or landed property which reverted to the parent estate if a recipient died without issue.[23]

In a statement resounding with confidence in its perceptions of the early British power and authority, the Privy Council declared that "he [Chatterdhari] derived his title by grant from the East India Company, which had full dominion over the Estates and therefore the power to grant it."[24] This was the so-called "great Hathwa case," great not only because it took ten years and some two million rupees to settle, but also because it ensured the continuity of the largest estate in Saran.[25] Thus, by the end of the first century of British rule, the process of making the great estate of Hathwa had been completed under the guidance and supporting hand of the colonial regime. The Huseypur rajas had been transformed into a "success story" as the Hathwa maharajas.

The story of most other estates in the district, though also illustrative of the effects of British rule on local society, highlights the different experiences faced by most zamindars in staying on as local controllers under the new regime. Representative of the "majority story" are the histories of zamindaris descended from Jagarnath Dikshit, the pioneer of the Eksaria Bhumihar fortunes in

---

21. See Calcutta High Court judgment, Aug. 24, 1860, ibid: app. 39, xxxvi. Legal documentation was said to have been carried away by Fateh Sahi (p. xxxii). See also Rajendra Prasad (1957: 2) about the strong sentiments that this litigation aroused among the different claimants. While the case was in the courts, Prasad's grand-uncle (the diwan of Hathwa) slept near his raja's bed and "afraid of the young ruler being poisoned, would even taste his food first."
22. D. N. Dutt 1909: xxxiv.   23. Ibid.: xliv, 30.   24. Ibid.: app. 40, liii.
25. Ibid.: 40.

Saran. In the nineteenth and early twentieth centuries, these families—Bagoura, Chainpur, Khaira, Manjha, Parsa, and Rusi—continued to occupy prominent intermediary positions between government and local society but were never accorded the status and privilege allowed the Hathwas. In part, these estates figured less significantly in the political limelight of the Raj because they did not match the phenomenal growth of Hathwa into a great estate and were therefore secondary allies; in part, some paid the price of reluctance in a partnership with the Raj.

From the outset, the Chainpur family, second only to Hathwa at the time of the Permanent Settlement, remained at odds with government. A twentieth-century official adjudged them as showing "the same recusancy in meeting Government dues (in 1787) which characterize their descendants at the present day."[26] Nor was their reputation enhanced by the fact that their family was directly implicated on the rebel side in Fateh Sahi's uprising.[27] And during the Mutiny/Rebellion of 1857, the entire family was regarded with suspicion because "whenever any rebels entered the district, they seemed to consider Chynepoor and its neighbourhood as a safe place of refuge." Thus, although the Chainpur zamindars did provide elephants, carts, and other supplies, their petition for "Government's commendations for service rendered" was denied.[28] Unlike the Hathwas, the Chainpur babus never successfully came to terms with the state.

However, not only was the family at odds with the emerging Company Raj and thus did not enjoy the protective umbrella of the state, but its fortunes suffered from a strict application of revenue laws and their inherently fissiparous tendencies. Without primogenitural security and complete impartibility, the estate split up into smaller and smaller pieces. Under the threat of constant dissolution, Chainpur faced perennial intrafamily squabbles that frequently erupted into bitter lawsuits and acts of violence.[29]

The recurring squabbles among the Chainpur babus led many contemporary observers in the early nineteenth century to predict the imminent demise of the estate. A report in the 1840s wrote off the Chainpur family as the "Bhoonya Bhumihar baboos who formerly exercised great influence over the inhabitants of the pargana Bal."[30] But the prognostications proved to be premature. Although the proliferation of heirs always threatened to complicate their financial fortunes, it never quite reached the level where the family was no longer considered among the district's prominent landed notables. Their failure to institute the custom of primogeniture in their joint undivided estate simply meant that family members constantly battled one another for each other's possessions as well as the property of others.

26. *SR*: 22.   27. Charters Report.
28. Magte., Saran, to Commr., Patna, no. 341, July 1, 1859, P.C. Monthly Bundles, Gen. Dept., from Colltr. of Saran to Patna Commr., 1854 on, *Basta* no. 103.
29. Interview with Gouri Shanker Prasad Sahi; *SR*: 22.
30. Wyatt 1847(?): 6.

Furthermore, in the late nineteenth century, a good measure of security was added to the Chainpur fortunes by strategic marriage alliances. Gajadhar Prasad Narain Singh, one of the Chainpur babus, married the daughter of the Maksudpur raja, a prominent estateholder in Gaya District, and when his wife's father died without a male heir in 1856, she inherited the estate. Through her the estate was passed on to their son when he attained his majority in 1859, and in 1891 he received the title of raja.[31] Thus a Chainpur babu became the raja of Maksudpur.

Another landholding family whose experiences typify the fate of most local controllers during the long haul of British rule was the Bhumihar Brahmin zamindars of Manjha. Representing this family at the Decennial Settlement was Parmeshwar Sahi who was succeeded by two sons: the eldest died without issue, the younger, Sundar, had one heir, Sridhar, who sided with the British in 1857 and was a loyal ally of the Raj. Following Sridhar's death, his two sons proceeded to divide up the estate because they were not "on very friendly terms."[32] A few years later a district official referred to them as "practically a cipher. One is an absentee and the other is almost an imbecile."[33] A presentday descendant of this family, described the younger of these two, Hariharendra Sahi, as the "creator of the family." His remark, no doubt, refers to the fact that the Manjha family enhanced its zamindari in this generation through strategic marriages. The elder brother married into the family of the great estate of Bettiah. Hariharendra was married twice, first to the daughter of the Sursund zamindar and subsequently to the daughter of the Baraon raja of Allahabad District. The next generation also made good marriage alliances: Hariharendra's first son, a product of his Sursund marriage, linked up with the Hathwa family by marrying the only daughter of the raja; his second and third sons, from his Baraon marriage, also established prominent alliances. The second son not only married the daughter of the Sheohar zamindar but also became the adopted heir of the childless Rusi zamindar. His daughter became the wife of the present maharaja of Banaras. Unlike Bagoura, the Manjha zamindars weathered the first century of British rule and, through the strategies of marriage and adoption, emerged in the second century as the Manjha-Rusi zamindari.[34]

The majority story is also reflected in the declining fortunes of the Muslim zamindari of Manjhi. Taque Ali Khan of Manjhi was the third highest revenue-payer at the time of the Permanent Settlement. His holdings, extending over 144 villages, were aggregated in four estates situated in parganas Manjhi,

31. India, Privy Council, no. 1401, Appeal from Calcutta, 1906, Rani Sunder Koer vs. Chandreshwar Narain Prasad Singh; Lister 1907.
32. "Exemption . . . from . . . Indian Arms Act," Bengal Police B Procs., Jan. 1888, 167/68.
33. AGRPD, 1891–92.
34. Interview with Hari Surendra Sahi, descendant of Manjha family, May 1974; Chapra, Private Holding, "History of the Manjha Family."

Bal, Narhan, and Chirand. On his death in 1794, his eldest son Shahamat Ali Khan inherited the estate. After selling off 31 villages by 1798, he agreed to a private partition with his younger brother Ghulam Nadjif Khan, whereby they divided up the remaining 113 villages, as well as the responsibility of paying the total revenue of Rs. 56,594. But this arrangement failed to arrest the gradual dissolution of the property, because each brother began to dispose of his own portion. An official report attributed this turn of events to the fact that both were "men aswell of mean capacity," squandering away their wealth or falling prey to "every designing and artful knave who could manage to insinuate himself into their confidence."[35]

The Manjhi fortunes received a further blow after the death of Ghulam Nadjif, when his wife and heir, Bibi Manick Jan, became embroiled in disputes with her brother-in-law Shahamat Ali. With both sides inciting their followers, the conflict erupted into serious breaches of the peace in the vicinity of Manjhi. In 1813 the district magistrate recommended that provincial authorities place the estate under the Court of Wards in order to preserve the peace and halt the "fighting, Parties in serious number and shameless perjuries."[36] Although government assumed the estate, Bibi Manick Jan died in 1814, childless, and her estate heavily in debt. Once again the estate passed into the hands of one branch of the family; her share went to Hussein Ali Khan, one of the three sons of her brother-in-law.[37]

When Shahamat Ali died in 1823, he left his three sons with only fifty-two villages. In other words, since the initial partition in 1798, another sixty-one villages had been sold.[38] By 1835 the three sons together held a mere thirty-five and one-half villages, assessed at a revenue of Rs. 18,030, while Hussein Ali Khan, the heir of Bibi Manick Jan's share, occupied sixteen villages assessed at a revenue of Rs. 7,370. The government sought to consolidate these two shares in order to safeguard the collection of revenue, but it was unable to act because many of the villages had already fallen into the hands of purchasers or were in the process of being sold.[39] This downward spiral apparently continued: by the mid-nineteenth century, the Muslim zamindars of Manjhi no longer show up in the rolls of the district's prominent families.

Another "very long established and important family" also experienced the majority pattern of decline. Deo Kumar Singh, the late nineteenth-century descendant of this line, traced his forefathers, who came to Saran in the late

---

35. "Correspondence re... Shahamut Ally Khan," Bengal Rev. Consltns., Oct. 9 to 16, 1823, Oct. 16, nos. 15–19.
36. W. Leycester, Magte., to Secy. Dowdeswell, Oct. 15, 1813, Bengal Cr. Jdcl. Consltns., Oct. 16 to Nov. 20, 1813, Oct. 13, no. 9.
37. Acting Colltr. H. Middleton to R. Rocke, Acting Pres., Feb. 27, 1815, Bengal BOR Consltns., Wards, 1815, March 31, no. 1.
38. "Correspondence re... Shahamut Ally Khan," Bengal Rev. Consltns., Oct. 16, 1823, nos. 15–19.
39. C. Tucker, Commr., to BOR no. 84, April 26, 1836, Bengal Rev. Consltns., June 14 to July 26, 1836, June 14, no. 30.

seventeenth century, back to Bhagnagar in Thatha, Sind. Called the Goolera zamindars after the name of their caste, they controlled fifty-two villages in Thatha until they were forced to flee in the wake of an abortive rebellion against the newly emergent Muslim rulers of their locality. After an initial stopover in Rajasthan, they arrived in Saran where they acquired a large estate.[40] At the Permanent Settlement, the Goolera zamindar Mul Chand held five mahals at a revenue of Rs. 57,318. Less than a century later, the revenue paid by this estate amounted to only Rs. 10,000, and the total income was only Rs. 40,000. After the death of his great-grandfather, Deo Kumar recounted: "disunion and quarrel began among the brothers and this contention lasted for a long time in which estates yielding an income of lacs of rupees were squandered away and when the properties were placed in the hands of their widows who on account of the dishonesty and infidelity of their servants sold their entire estates."[41]

However, even though Deo Kumar was not a "very wealthy zamindar," he was warmly supported by the British. Despite his limited holdings, he was, for instance, exempted from the provisions of the Indian Arms Act, a privilege generally reserved for "great zamindars." He was treated "as a special case on the ground of the active part which he takes in local affairs." As Deo Kumar described his own contributions, he served seventeen years as a municipal commissioner and ten years as an honorary magistrate, in addition to being a donor to various causes.[42]

Thus, the British apparatus of collaboration in Saran relied on the crucial connection provided by the Hathwa zamindars. This relationship had grown out of the fact that government had subsidized and developed the cadet line of the Huseypur family into becoming the major raja of the district. Other notables, though treated favorably, were largely left to their own devices. The exception was when estates fell under the jurisdiction of the Court of Wards.

The Court of Wards: An Institutional Shelter

As early as 1782 the British established an office to supervise the estates of minors, females, and persons of known incapacity.[43] At the Decennial Settlement, consideration was given to appointing a manager to deal with such estates, with preference to be shown, first, to a near relation of the assumed estate-holder, second, "a credible servant of the family and in the last resort a person unconnected." This same statement also noted that "lunacy, contumacy and notorious profligacy of character" were grounds for official takeover.[44] By

40. Commr. to GOB, no. 352G, May 10, 1833, Bengal Police B Consltns., June 1883, no. 159.
41. Deo Coomar Singh to Commr., June 23, 1883, and Commr. to GOB, no. 352G, May 10, 1833, ibid., nos. 160 and 159.   42. Singh to Commr., June 23, 1883, ibid., no. 160.
43. Firminger 1962: 302; B. B. Misra 1959: 139.
44. Montgomerie to Shore, Pres. &c. BOR, July 23, 1789, Bengal Rev. Consltns., Sept. 18, 1789, encl.

its founding legislation, Regulation X of 1793, the basic purposes of the Court of Wards were "to prevent disqualified proprietors from being reduced to ruin by the misconduct of the agents entrusted with the management of their concerns. To provide an adequate superintendence of their estates for the benefit of the proprietors. To ensure to minors an education suitable to their rank, and such as might qualify them for the future management of their own concerns."[45]

The idea of the Court of Wards drew its sustenance from the same theory regarding the sanctity of private property that informed the Permanent Settlement. And, as with the rationale of securing permanent connections with local society, this mechanism too was geared toward propping up the Raj by enabling government "to strike its roots deeply into the loyalty of its beneficiaries, the new (sic) landowning class."[46] Zamindars fortunate enough to be assumed by government, especially in the late nineteenth and early twentieth centuries, found the Court of Wards an institutional shelter that not only rescued their ailing and tottering estates, but also enhanced their power and privilege as local allies and controllers. By rescuing such estates from financial ruin, government also stabilized the flow of revenues.

The initial years of the operations of the Court of Wards were beset by problems. Although it successfully averted, on behalf of most of its clients, the fall of their estates under the hammer of the auctioneer, it was less effective in improving the management of their lands. Nor did it come close to attaining the ideal of overseeing the education of minors, resigning itself instead to the fact that that aspect of wardship would remain in the hands "of the minor's nearest relatives and friends." Official sentiment located the defects of the Court of Wards not in its "rules," but in the people to whom it was applied.

The early experiments with the Court of Wards in Bihar also revealed other shortcomings. Many estates requested government takeover in order to avert ruin, some landholders even resorting to the legal maneuver of transferring their financially troubled lands to minors so as to receive the benefits of official management. Before the enactment of Regulation III of 1793, which disallowed such transfers, some zamindars had taken this step to prevent their indebted estates being sold for arrears of revenue. Additional legislation (Regulation VII of 1822) empowered the Court of Wards to employ discretionary judgment in selecting estates for takeover, with the right to refrain from assumption in cases where profits were unlikely or where the property was of little value.[47]

The failures in the initial years of the operations of the Court of Wards resulted in financial losses to the government. An 1804 estimate for Bengal put

45. Cited in R. W. Cox and Members, Rev. Bd., to G.G. Marquis Wellesley, June 8, 1802, Bengal BOR Consltns., Wards, Jan. 5, 1798 to May 23, 1805, June 17, 1802, no. 1.
46. Guha 1963: 18.
47. C. Buller, Board of Commrs., Behar & Benares, to Rev. Board, Jan. 23, 1821, and Court of Wards, Lower Provinces, to Lord Amherst, G.G., June 6, 1826, Bengal Rev. Consltns.. Aug. 31 to Sept. 7, 1826, Sept. 7, no. 7.

the figure at over a million rupees. But, weighed against the alarm over the deficit was the consideration, expressed by one governor general, that a willingness "to considerable sacrifice (if they are unavoidable) for the preservation of the rights and interests of the numerous body of helpless proprietors ... must always exist in the country."[48]

Once additional regulations were effected to curb the loopholes in the original act, landholder interest in seeking government takeover of their estates seemed to decline. Some estates, however, continued to reap immense benefits from government tenure. The Hathwa family, who inherited the Huseypur zamindari with the support of government and assumed their newly acquired status in 1791 under official management, was perhaps the principal beneficiary in the first half-century of the institution's existence. Until the estate's release in 1802, when Chatterdhari Sahi attained his majority, government management provided the care and nourishment that enabled it to emerge as one of the great estates of the nineteenth and early twentieth centuries. Government supervision ranged from monitoring the activities of the estate managers, such as replacing Lalsaram as the manager for not overseeing the minor's education and communicating clandestinely with the rebel branch of the family, to protecting the ward from the threatening designs of Fateh Sahi's family and from "farmers" on his estate who took up with the Huseypur branch.[49]

Although an elaborate administrative establishment did not exist at this time, government remained ever-vigilant in protecting the estate from the machinations of its appointed managers. Lalsaram was only the first of several managers removed from office. His successor, Khaujah Mahommed Shah, was approved by the Court of Wards in July 1793, investigated for misconduct in 1794, and formally discharged in December of that year.[50] His replacement, Radhakishen Mahto, remained in office for the longest tenure. Although he had wished to resign in 1797, his request was not granted. An altogether different step was taken in 1798, however, when the Court of Wards removed him for "mismanagement," citing large arrears in revenues and his acquisition of a village under a pseudonym. His successor was "an old and creditable servant of the family."[51]

The attention lavished on Hathwa was also apparent in government's interest in manipulating the investments of the estate. Its guiding philosophy

48. G. Dowdeswell, Secy. to.Govt., to Thos. Graham, July 19, 1804, Bengal BOR Consltns., Wards, July 19, 1804, no. 3.
49. F. Hawkins, Colltr., to Wm. Cowper, Dec. 16, 1796, Bengal BOR Consltns., Jan. 8 to Aug. 11, 1797, Jan. 6, no. 9; T. Hawkins, Colltr., Saran, to Cowper, Pres. & Members, BOR, Feb. 28, 1794, Beng. BOR Consltns., Wards, Jan. 3 to June 12, 1794, April 17.
50. T. Hawkins to Cowper, Oct. 31, 1793, Bengal BOR Consltns., Wards, Jan. 3 to June 12, 1794, Jan. 8; F. Hawkins, to Cowper, Dec. 20, 1794, ibid., 1795, Jan. 6.
51. G. Fordyce, Colltr., to Charles Buller, Acting Sub Secy. to BOR, Sept. 25, 1797, ibid., Sept. 5 to Dec. 20, 1797, Oct. 10, no. 4; N. Stuart, Colltr., to Cowper, Sept. 26, 1798, ibid., May 1 to Nov. 30, 1798, Oct. 5, no. 3.

in this matter, as summed up by one district collector, was "that no other mode can be half so secure or advantageous . . . as that of laying it out ["profits"] in the further purchase of lands at public outlay."[52] In 1794, for instance, the estate purchased, at public auctions, twelve villages in June for Rs. 7,435 and four in August for Rs. 320.[53]

On the whole, few major Saran estates devolved on the Court of Wards in the early nineteenth century. One that did was the large Goolera zamindari, which accounted for a revenue of Rs. 57,318 in 1793. Subsequently, however, disputes between members of the family over rights of inheritance were dragged through the courts in long and costly battles lasting two successive generations. Initial attempts by the court to assume charge of this joint undivided property were rebuffed, but the estate was finally made a ward in 1834. Almost immediately, several persons claiming large chunks of the property as mortgage stepped forward, but the court succeeded in turning back their attempts to assume possession, although not to continue to hold them in lease.[54] Wardship also embroiled government in arduous and vexing battles with the estate's rent collectors (*thikadars*) who sought to carve up the property into their own private parcels. With the zamindar's resources rapidly dissipating in legal and factional fighting between rival claimants, the estate appeared on the brink of financial collapse. Although the Court of Wards was unable to arrest its decline, which stemmed largely from internecine family squabbles, it did manage to salvage the Goolera zamindari from complete ruin. In 1844 management of the estate reverted into the hands of a new generation of heirs.[55]

Thus, in its conception, as well as in its operations in the early nineteenth century, the Court of Wards acted as an institutional shelter for some zamindaris. Increasingly, it was this aspect of its activities in Saran that became its characteristic feature. As perceptively observed by Sir George Campbell in 1871, it had evolved into an institution concentrating on the development of the resources and control of its wards:

According to the theory of the law we assume the management in order to secure the Government revenue. But it is now notorious that there is no risk whatever of the revenue, and that with this object Government management is wholly unnecessary. The more modern idea seems to be that the object is to rescue the estate from debt, difficulty and danger, and the triumph of management is considered to be to accumulate large sums for the minor which are made over to him when he comes of age. . . .

We do for them all the unpopular things which their fathers never dared to do for

---

52. F. Hawkins to BOR, Nov. 17, 1794, ibid., July 4 to Dec. 11, 1794, Dec. 11, no. 3.
53. Encl. with F. Hawkins, to Cowper, April 29, 1795, ibid., 1795, May 14, no. 10.
54. Offg. Commr. C. Tucker to BOR, Nov. 15, 1836, Tucker to Offg. Colltr. W. Luke, Oct. 25, 1836, no. 125, ibid., 1837, April, nos. 14 & 15; Commr. E. C. Ravenshaw to BOR, no. 342, June 11, 1840, ibid., July, nos. 8 & 9.
55. Ravenshaw to Sadr Rev. Board, March 29, 1844; Ravenshaw to Colltr., March 9, 1844; Ravenshaw to BOR, May 2, 1844; Offg. Secy. G. Plowden, BOR, to Ravenshaw, no. 148, n.d.; Bengal BOR Consltns., Wards, 1844, May, nos. 2–15.

themselves: dismiss their dependents, reform their establishments, resume the rent-free lands, enhance the rents, and let out the estates to speculators who give large sums for the farms.[56]

Under the new circumstances, many more estates came under the wardship of government. Hathwa was assumed by the Court of Wards between 1871 and 1874, and again between 1896 to 1911. In 1872–1873, for instance, the nineteen estates under wardship accounted for as much as 16 percent of the district's total land revenue. Most wards were minors, others were females, idiots, and lunatics, and some held estates taken over by order of the civil court because of disputes among the co-heirs.[57]

Precisely because the Court of Wards ushered in a wide range of governmental imposition, from increased control and information about the workings and resources of an estate to supervision of the wards' education, many interests on a threatened estate opposed takeover. The occasion of large estates devolving on minor heirs frequently engendered opposition from interested parties in the zamindaris, but the government inevitably gained control.

Such a scenario was enacted at the death of Maharaja Rajendra Pratap Sahi of Hathwa in July 1871, when his wife, relatives, and estate officials combined to thwart government assumption. By producing a forged horoscope, they attempted to establish that the fifteen-year-old heir was already eighteen years old.[58] In the government ranks, too, there was some opposition to takeover because the minority tenure of three years was considered too brief to serve any purpose. Moreover, as one Board of Revenue member put it, the estate was free of revenue arrears, reliably managed, and the minor was a "sharp, intelligent boy, very fairly educated [and] with a considerable knowledge of English."[59] The lieutenant governor, however, insisted on official management. His arguments clearly refer to the important role of the Court of Wards in shaping the British relationship with local controllers:

It may be desirable to take no action in cases of comparatively unimportant estates, where there is little risk of great intrigues being set on foot, and no immediate possibility of dispute or litigation; but in the case of an enormous estate like Hutwah where great intrigues have already been set on foot . . . it seems to His Honour clear that so vast a property and vast an income cannot be left altogether outside the law.[60]

Although the opposition to takeover quickly died away with the disproof of the forged horoscope, government sometimes faced far stiffer resistance on other estates.[61]

56. "The Administration of Wards' Estates," Sir George Campbell, Nov. 23, 1871, Bengal Rev. Procs., Sept.–Dec. 1871, Nov., 157. See also Yang (1979a) for details on its operations in the region; and Baker (1976: 29–34) on its workings in south India.
57. See P.C. *Basta* no. 136.
58. "Management of the Hutwah Raj," Bengal Rev. Procs., Jan.–April 1872, April, no. 149.
59. "Note on . . . age of the Hutwah Rajah," by V. H. Schalch, Bengal Rev. Procs., Sept.–Dec. 1871, Dec., 70.
60. Secy., GOB to Offg. Secy., BOR, no. 4581, Dec. 19, 1871, ibid., 71.
61. E.g., the enormous Darbhanga estate where the family "thwarted and opposed the manager

The tendency, though, was for zamindars to court government management: "[S]o numerous are the applications ... that many have to be refused." This manual also added that "applications are usually refused, when an estate is hopelessly involved; but many an estate has been saved from ruin by the careful management of some district officer."[62] But the estates of "old zamindari families" (the district's important connections) were almost always assumed, regardless of their financial situation.

Increasingly, in the nineteenth century, the attraction to government management was the salutary shelter provided by the Court of Wards, which successfully enhanced the resources of many wards, especially those representing large estates. The income of Triguna Nand Upahdya, whose estate was taken over in August 1863, rose from Rs. 7,301 to Rs. 17,395 in 1878.[63] Although its brief tenure under government from December 1871 to October 1874 did not match the spectacular gains of the Darbhanga estate during its long tenure, substantial growth was also attained for Hathwa. Income during this period increased from Rs. 682,168 to Rs. 687,921, while debts were reduced from Rs. 83,944 to Rs. 67,710, and of the Rs. 271,875 due by the estate, all but Rs. 10,514 was left unadjusted. That there was any gain at all is remarkable because the estate was in sound financial shape to begin with, and, during much of the Court of Wards period, large areas of the estate were hit by a famine.[64]

Hathwa's prosperity had its roots in the initial Court of Wards tenure between 1791 and 1802 when Maharaja Chatterdhari Sahi was a minor. According to one early nineteenth-century source:

From the circumstance of the property having long remained under the management of the Court of Wards during the minority of the present owner, he entered upon the enjoyment of his estates with some degree of affluence. Having no incumbrances on his property, and having been carefully brought up under the protection of the British Government, he is in better circumstances than any of his contemporaries holding larger domains.[65]

Government increased its wards' resources by making safe investments. Wards' monies were generally put into government securities, debentures, and land. The pattern of bidding for villages at auction sales in the late eighteenth century was also continued. In Hathwa's second tenure, in 1873–1874, Rs. 157,369 was spent on landed property, and Rs. 40,000 on government securities. Altogether, during the 1871–1874 tenure, government invested Rs.

and the Commissioner [of Patna] in every possible way for months" (GOB to BOR, no. 1796, April 25, 1872, Bengal Rev. Procs., April 1872, no. 149). See also Graham (1878: 229), who was then the assistant magistrate of Darbhanga.
  62. H. A. D. Phillips 1866: 43.
  63. P.C. *Basta* no. 141, Wards' Dept., Gen. Collections, 1873–1876, 1876–1877, 1870–1882.
  64. Offg. Under-Secy., GOB to Secy. BOR, no. 1796, April 25, 1872, Bengal Rev. Procs., April 1872, no. 150; *Report on Wards and Attached Estates in the Lower Provinces* 1876: 60.
  65. Wyatt 1847(?): 10.

320,765 of Hathwa's funds in the purchase of land.[66] In 1897–1898, again under official direction, Rs. 1,815,513 was expended on government promissory notes, the debentures of the Calcutta Port Trust and Indian Steam Navigation Company, Madras and Calcutta municipal debentures, and land.[67]

In its role as manager, government sought to maximize its wards' resources with little consideration for other interests. Hathwa's acquisitions of land in 1897–1898 came from "occupancy holdings purchased at auction sale in execution of decrees obtained by the [Hathwa] Raj against its raiyats in some of the villages in Shahabad [district]."[68] The large slice of Chapra town that Hathwa assembled in the late nineteenth century stemmed from investments originally made during the Court of Wards tenure. Prior to 1873, the raj had only a few houses in Chapra, but, under government initiative, the purchase of 444 bighas for Rs. 100,000 was negotiated from a smaller estate also under official management. The deal was considered in the best interests of both parties because Hathwa had a large surplus, whereas the estate of Musamat Maracho Kuer "was heavily involved in debt." To this sale, representing only one-half of Ratanpura village in Chapra town, the maharaja of Hathwa later added another three-eighths (333 bighas) in January 1877 (for Rs. 81,000), and the remaining one-eighth (for Rs. 35,000) in September 1878. The last two transactions were concluded when Maracho Kuer's estate was still under the Court of Wards. There are numerous other instances of government juggling the holdings of its wards, such as in 1903–1904, when Hathwa raj bought several villages from the estate of a fellow Saran ward, Mobarak Hossein.[69]

Economic gain was only one of the many important benefits of government management. The Court of Wards also acted as a shelter in another equally significant way. Although the following remarks of a senior revenue official refer to the Darbhanga estate, they have much wider application:

> The truth is that this [income] alone is a most inadequate test of the effects of the management of the Estate by Government officers. The rental, in the time of the late Maharaja and his forefathers, was little more than nominal: it was never realized, and was in fact, not susceptible of realization. The property was assigned away, under fictitious leases to the numerous hangers-on and domestics of the palace, who met all demands for rent with monstrous counter-demands on accounts of supplies and services, which the Maharajas were too ignorant or too indolent to contest, and which were never contested until the Court of Wards appeared on the scene.[70]

66. "Management of the Hutwa Estate during 1873–74," Bengal Rev. Procs., April 1873 to 1875, Aug. 1874, nos. 2–3. The collector deliberately spent large sums of the ward's funds on land so that there would not be surplus cash to tempt the young maharaja to be extravagant when he attained majority (Offg. Colltr. A. Forbes to Secy., BOR, no. 959G, Sept. 24, 1884, P.C. Rev. Basta no. 340, 1884–1885).
67. "Report for 1897–98," P.C. Basta no. 166, Court of Wards, Hathwa Estate.
68. Ibid.
69. Forbes to BOR, no. 959G, Sept. 24, 1884, P.C. Rev. Basta no. 340. "Report for 1903–1904," P.C. Basta no. 166.
70. Secy. BOR to GOB, Jan. 13, 1866, Bengal Rev. A Procs. Bundles, Feb. 1866, no. 52.

Indeed, especially in its extended tenures of the large zamindaris, Court of Wards management disrupted many of the traditional networks of intermediary control on the estate, thus paving the way for a bureaucratic system of management. Often this changeover came at the expense of the wards' relatives, retainers, and tenants. During the 1871–1874 tenure, the power of Hathwa's rent collectors, whose families had in many cases held their leases for several generations, was reduced. In the 1896–1911 period, a more direct system of administration was instituted when the circle system of management replaced the *thikadari* system.

Court of Wards tenures generally also introduced new personnel to the estates' administrative positions. When government assumed Hathwa in 1871, G. J. S. Hodgkinson of the Bengal Civil Service, a former assistant magistrate of Saran between 1865 and 1867, became manager. He recruited his subordinates mostly from the staff of his former collectorates, retaining only a few of the old estate hands. For the top post of superintendent of the Hathwa administration, he tried unsuccessfully to entice the head clerk of the Tirhut Collectorate. Except for the important managerial position of diwan (head officer), which was then a sinecure, he filled his Hathwa office, consisting of a treasurer and a *sarishtadar* (head ministerial officer), *mohurrirs* (writers), and clerks, with former members of the Saran, Tirhut, and Muzaffarpur collectorates.[71]

The Bengali domination of the Hathwa administration also began during the 1870s tenure of the Court of Wards. So did the infiltration of other "outside" groups, such as Europeans, into the managerial ranks. The career of Angus Ogilvy, who worked as manager of both the sizable Tikari zamindari and the Hathwa raj reflects this changing pattern of recruitment.[72]

Unlike the former estate managers who were powerful men in their own right, with their own networks of control and patronage, the new administrators had little anchorage in local society and were closely allied to the proprietor, but their close official connections allowed their estates easier access to government, perhaps even endowing their estates with some vestiges of official power and authority.

For the bulk of the population on captive estates, however, the Court of Wards was hardly a shelter. On the contrary, it often acted as a legitimizing channel for its wards' informal control mechanisms. The following observations on the long government management of the Darbhanga estate by a senior British official is a familiar refrain on wards' estates:

While the Court of Wards has done so much for the proprietor of the estate, it is frankly admitted by the Manager that the condition of the Raj tenants is not generally

---

71. In 1878, four years after Hathwa's release, he returned to Saran as magistrate. (GOB, *Appointments in Bengal and Their Holders* 1912: 454–55). "Management of Hutwa Raj," Bengal Rev. Procs., April 1872, no. 149.

72. See Metcalf (1979: 253, 258–59) on similar developments in other north Indian estates.

prosperous.... There has been in years gone by, under the Court of Wards, the same kind of rack-renting, the same ignoring of ryot-right, the same unwillingness to recognise occupancy tenures, the same resort to illegal distraint, that have been found and condemned in every district of Behar. The traditions of the Court of Wards have from the time of its institution been essentially proprietary.[73]

Charles James O'Donnell, an outspoken Bengal civil servant, echoed similar criticisms when he blamed government management in Hathwa for the "wholesale desertions" from the estate in 1879.[74] The report of the official investigation into the desertions offers a remarkable insight into tenants' perceptions of the Court of Wards. Tenants had paid the enhanced rents willingly to the government administrators of the estate but resisted the demands of the maharaja of Hathwa after he resumed control: "It may be that the ryots paid the increased rent more resignedly to the Court of Wards (as being identified with the Government) than they pay to their landlord."[75]

Clearly, such an extraordinary shelter existed for local controllers because of the government's efforts to maintain its allies. The Court of Wards also functioned as a channel for British control of its allies. Through this institution, government actively interfered with and directed the resources of its wards, thereby strengthening its own hand. For instance, as manager, government was in a position to regulate the flow of charitable donations from its wards' estates. During the famine in Bihar in 1873–1874, government control over Hathwa enabled it to expend wards' monies for relief measures.[76]

But as long as there was no state-ward conflict of interest, the coercive aspects of the Court of Wards were subtle, and the government concerned itself with mobilizing its resources to manage its wardships successfully. The option to use this institution as a mechanism for direct state control, however, was always a possibility. During the 1893–1894 Cow Riots, this possibility almost persuaded the members of the viceroy's council to propose the assumption of the maharaja of Dumraon's estate in Shahabad because of its turbulent peasantry and the cow-protection sympathies of its manager.[77]

The most important and systematic way in which the Court of Wards acted as a support for British rule was through its supervision of its wards' education. As early as 1830, both a Hindu and a Muslim college were opened in Calcutta for wards' education. But, until Act XXVI of 1854 was promulgated, wards' institutions were little developed because no provisions existed for the com-

73. Cited in Jata Shankar Jha (1962: 81). 74. 1880: 25.
75. A. P. MacDonnell to Commr., Jan. 1, 1880, P.C. Rev. *Basta* no. 331, 1879–1880.
76. One-half of a year's rental was spent on importing grain and additional sums on relief works (GOB, *Report on the Administration of Bengal, 1873–74* 1875: 43). During the 1896–1911 Hathwa tenure, the Court of Wards spent Rs. 751,155 on charities and donations (GOB&O, *Reports on Wards' Encumbered, Trust and Attached Estates* 1912: 43).
77. MacDonnell to Earl of Elgin, May 9, 1884, no. 178, Elgin Papers, Mss. Eur. F. 84/34. MacDonnell urged takeover because "it would give Government, for some years, a great position of control and advantage in the heart of the tract in which the Cow Protection movement is strongest."

pulsory attendance of wards. In 1854 a wards' institution was opened in Calcutta, and in 1863 another in Banaras (which thereafter served most Bihar Hindu wards).[78]

Throughout its existence, the British expressed much doubt about the quality of the Banaras Wards Institution. The Saran collector echoed the view of many administrators who believed that their wards were better off at home than at Banaras because the boys were not sufficiently disciplined. As illustration, reference was made to the case of the Saran minor of average intelligence whose eight years in Banaras did not result in any real familiarity with the English language or the literature. A common complaint was that the Banaras training did not have "any real lasting or good effect on the nature and character of the wards." Also many boys took extended leaves for illnesses and family religious ceremonies. But there was praise, too, especially for the kind of "equality which exists among English boys at a public school."[79]

Measured against government's expectations, the education of wards was seldom deemed satisfactory. Some wards were so troublesome that it welcomed their attainment of majority.[80] In most cases, government exerted itself in order to educate its wards to become faithful allies. A notable government protege in Saran was Triguna Nand Upadhya who became a ward in 1863 when he was only two years old. During its long tenure, government enhanced his income and defended his rights against all comers, including his great-uncle who the collector thought was trying to seize his nephew's holdings by litigation. Government also scrutinized his upbringing closely. When the collector expressed dissatisfaction with Upadhya's conduct in 1865, the commissioner of Patna not only denied the ward's petition for Rs. 600 but reduced the collector's proposed Rs. 300 allowance to Rs. 200.[81] The boy's record at the Banaras Wards Institution was also carefully monitored. In 1878 the official report noted with considerable satisfaction Upadhya's ability to speak English and his marriage to a daughter of a respectable Brahmin family. Government was also encouraged by the prospect that "he would turn out to be one of the most enlightened landholders of his time."[82]

Wards from major estates were even more closely supervised, often by being placed under the care of a European tutor. The official directive to the tutor of

78. The 1854 Act empowered collectors to make suitable arrangements for their wards' education. Act IV (Bengal Code) of 1870 established specific rules entrusting the education of minors to the Court of Wards. See BOR to GOB, March 31, 1871, Bengal Rev. Procs., May to Aug. 1871, July, 23; Offg. Secy. BOR to Secy. GOB, no. 220A, June 14, 1872, ibid., May–June 1872, July, 28.
79. "Education of Minors at the Benares Wards' Institution," Report of Patna Commr., Feb. 20, 1872, Bengal Rev. Procs., Jan. to April 1872, March, 83. See also Offg. Commr. to GOB, no. IW, Aug. 15, 1872, ibid., Aug.–Sept. 1872, Sept., 52.
80. See, e.g., "Return of the Management of the Estate of Jung Bahadoor for year ending 31st March 1870," P.C. *Basta* no. 136. As the collector commented: "He is the most troublesome boy and minds nobody. I'm glad to say that in another year we shall be quit of him."
81. "Return of ... the Estate of Trigunanand Upadhya for year ending 30th Apr. 1865," ibid.
82. "Return for year ending 1878," ibid.

the Darbhanga minors sums up the importance attached to their education: "You will doubtless bear in mind that the happiness of many thousands of persons must largely depend upon your success in this respect, especially with the young Raja. If he grows up such as the Court of Wards would like to see him, his influence for good will be immense."[83] Because the maharaja of Hathwa was already fifteen in 1871 when government assumed charge, he was not sent to Banaras. But, under a Mr. Hickson, he studied accounts of ancient Rome and Greece, modern history, especially of India, and spent as much time as possible discussing estate matters with the manager of the estate.[84]

That the supervision of wards' education was part of a wider strategy of government control is also suggested by a 1910 dispute between the maharani of Hathwa and the government of Bengal. Although the specific issue was the institution at which the Hathwa minor was to be educated, the main question was the extent of state supervision in relation to that of the Hathwa family over the minor maharaja.[85] Until 1909 the young maharaja had attended his district high school. In September 1909, after visiting Hathwa, a senior Board of Revenue official noted that the boy's "upbringing away from companions of his own age and class did not tend to the development of a strong, robust and independent character."[86] On the same grounds, he argued against Patna College and suggested Mayo College in Ajmer. But, due to anticipated opposition from the maharani, the proposal was never implemented, and in October 1909 the lieutenant governor approved the minor's entrance to Patna College. However, when Captain Allanson, the lieutenant-governor's former private secretary, was appointed manager in 1910, the previous arguments were revived. Shortly after taking charge, Allanson reported that the maharani and the Bengali diwan were influencing the boy's mind so that he regarded all officials "from the Lieutenant-Governor downwards with distrust and animosity, and were inspiring him with feelings of hostility towards Government itself."[87]

After the secret police documented the anti-British sentiments of the diwan and pointed out the revolutionary inclinations of the large Bengali staff at Hathwa, the government took immediate action, dismissing the diwan and ordering him not to reside in the district. At the urging of Allanson, government then transferred the minor maharaja to Ajmer. As the boy was soon to gain his majority, this move was considered imperative to prevent his falling "into the ranks of the party of disaffection."[88]

83. BOR to Chester McNaghten, no. 882A, July 28, 1866, Bengal Rev. A Procs. Bundles, 1866, Aug., no. 5.
84. GOB to BOR, no. 1796, April 25, 1872, Bengal Rev. Procs., April 1872, no. 150.
85. "Affairs of Hatwa Zamindari," in GOI, Public and Judicial, L/P&J/6/1038, 1910 (3660–3783), J&P 3660.
86. W. R. Gourlay, Offg. Secy., GOB to J. H. Kerr, Secy. GOB (confidential), no. 2129T-R, Oct. 17, 1910, ibid. 87. Ibid.
88. The diwan was linked with Phanindar Nath Mitter, editor of the "seditious" *Yugantar* and, later, in 1906–1907, of the *Motherland* (ibid.).

Precisely because the Court of Wards was a beneficial shelter for its wards, it also served as a device for turning landholders into allies. That it was successful in producing loyal connections seems to have support in estate histories. The official account of the Hathwa raj makes this point when it lauds the Court of Wards for the estate's improvement in resources and the "sound and liberal education imparted to their protege." This history also praised the government-appointed manager because he "had not only *sown* the seeds of Hutwa's present prosperity but had implanted in the heart of the minor proprietor ... noble ideas and principles which made him *hereafter* so successful."[89]

The normative role of the Court of Wards is also apparent in the larger framework of changing life-styles among zamindars in the nineteenth and early twentieth centuries. As Tapan Raychaudhuri has shown for eastern Bengal, zamindars preferred emulating "the nineteenth-century English gentleman rather than the seventeenth-century Indian raja."[90] A similar orientation developed among Bihar's major landholders in the late nineteenth century, with the initial impetus and certainly the stimulus coming during the Court of Wards tenures. Hathwa, which began the nineteenth century under the Court of Wards, and followed with two further terms, set the pace in this regard. The process is reflected in the architectural changes in Hathwa in the 1870s when the Maharaja introduced to his estate new buildings: parks with marble statues and fountains, an audience hall with crystal chandeliers and mirrors, and oil paintings of the crowned heads of Europe on the walls![91]

The Court of Wards in Saran acted as an extraordinary shelter for government's permanent connections. Along with the British policy of maintaining rural bulwarks, this institution served to consolidate the power and control of government's local allies and, consequently, to reinforce the state's system of control and collaboration. Although it provided an opportunity for the state to enhance its control over local landholders, wardship was generally used to bolster and develop the resources of the major estates especially. Viewed in the context of the apparatus of control that the British developed to administer directly, such as when they attempted to extend their own network of control into local society, the ties between government and zamindar, particularly as manifested in the operations of the Court of Wards, reveal the character of the colonial system as a Limited Raj.

89. D. N. Dutt 1909: 31–32.
91. D. N. Dutt 1909: 33–34.

90. Raychaudhuri 1969: 173

5

The Limited Raj: The British Development of Local Control Institutions

The limits of the British machinery of control in Saran can be reconstructed by a selective examination of the processes and mechanisms by which government extended into local society, particularly down to the grassroots level to impinge on the "little world" of the district's raiyats. Three institutions—the chaukidar (village watchman), the *qanungo* (registrar) and the patwari (village accountant)—that represented government's deepest penetration into local society highlight the undergirdings of Pax Britannica.

In India, as in their other colonial possessions, the British relied on "native organisations [which were] strong enough to deliver large armies, taxes and authorities into their hands, yet weak enough to be cajoled into doing so, rather than unite and resist the invaders."[1] And "like any colonial regime," the British Raj "was perpetually pulled in opposite directions by the need to leave the ruled-over society alone and equally pressing need to deal with it in an effective way."[2] Increasingly in the nineteenth and early twentieth centuries, these countervailing tendencies resulted in efforts to develop a local control infrastructure even while the larger framework of rule rested on a system of collaboration between the British and their local allies. British efforts to forge direct links with local society, therefore, were defined by that system of collaboration, leading, in effect, to a Limited Raj system.

The Context of British Control

The other prop on which British rule rested, along with the support provided by loyal landholders, was the administrative machinery. This apparatus,

1. Robinson 1978: 142.   2. Heesterman 1978: 52.

embodied in the persons of the district's subordinate officials, was pressed into action to regain and maintain order in late July and August of 1857 when the British officials fled to the safety of Patna. In addition to the police, *Qazi* (Judge) Ramzan Ali took charge in Chapra; and, in Siwan, Syed Hussain Ali, the registrar of the subdeputy opium agent and Munsif (Civil judge) Muhammad Wajid.[3]

However, the viability of British rule in Saran was never seriously threatened in the period between 1793 and 1920. The regime's power rested on its superior military force: its coercive capabilities were always sufficient to contain and defeat any local challenges. During crises, the British were quick to impress local populations of their decisive edge. Although hostilities in 1857 were limited, the return of the British administrators, after a brief evacuation, was accompanied by a military force. The presence of a few companies of European and Sikh soldiers was considered necessary to provide "the most beneficial effect on the district."[4] In the wake of the Cow Riots of 1893–1894, similar considerations prompted the Saran magistrate to request that the regiment marching through the district's southern edge also pass through the center. Such a display of force was deemed "conducive to the maintenance of order."[5] An unequivocal expression of this source of state control is the statement by the commissioner of Patna that the "Empire is held together solely by British supremacy, and a declaration of equality between the British and the natives would be nonsense. The Army furnishes the clearest and simplest illustration. The Army in India is the backbone of the Government."[6]

However, the British were more inclined to emphasize the blessings ushered in by their rule than the institutional bases of control or their military prowess. Implicit in such self-congratulations was the notion that control stemmed naturally and inevitably from the prosperity and law and order that the Raj had brought to its subjects. In the late nineteenth century, such beliefs were expressed in the idea that government was a guardian of the peasants against the landed elite. Indeed, the heroic magistrate toiling against innumerable odds to bring the local oppressive zamindar to justice is a standard image in the recollections of British officers.[7] Details regarding the actual structure and functioning of the Raj system rarely figured in such accounts. Instead, they highlighted the positive aspects of British rule in order to commit official memory to the task of creating records that would serve as charters legitimizing the Raj. Big kingdoms as well as little kingdoms operate in a political order

---

3. Magte. W. F. McDonnell to Commr. W. Tayler, no. 314, Oct. 9, 1857 and no. 307, Oct. 7, 1857, S.C., Letters from Magte. of Saran to Commr. of Patna, March 1857 to March 1858.
4. Deputy Magte. to Magte., no. 531, Feb. 12, 1858, S.C., Letters received from 1854 to 1859 from Deputy Magte. of Sewan.
5. AGRPD, 1894–95.
6. Commr. to GOB, May 6, 1883, Beng. Jdcl. Procs., July 1884, no. 143.
7. See, e.g., Muddiman (1930: 24–25); he was Asst. Magte. in Saran in 1899–1900 and Acting Magte. in 1901. Also see Beames (1961: 180) and McLane (1963).

maintained and legitimized through a set of ground rules based on "rituals, traditions, myths and histories."[8]

The ideal for Saran administrators was that of "Revelganj," a local town named after a former collector. The eulogy on his tomb, inscribed in marble in 1883 at the suggestion of the lieutenant-governor of Bengal, sums up this ideal: "In this grave lies Henry Revel, Collector of Customs . . . from whom the town of Revelganj derives its name . . . in 1788, and during a long residence close to the spot he succeeded in gaining the esteem and affection of the surrounding people, who raised the tomb over his remains, and whose descendants still cherish his memory with religious veneration."[9] His tomb remained the object of "posthumous honours" among a populace who regarded him as a "deified hero."[10]

But the Revelganj model was an ideal that could not be easily emulated. Sir Alexander Muddiman, who was in Saran at the turn of the nineteenth century, observed: "I doubt if the tomb of future collectors will be utilized in this way."[11] Indeed, "Revelganj" was a mythic ideal—the "Magistrate of yore," the administrative face of the "man for Chupra"—celebrated in the verses of Thomas Frank Bignold, the poet-laureate of the Indian Civil Service and an old Bihar hand:

> I mourn the rule of the Magistrate of yore,
> A fostering despot o'er his people bore;
> He reigned supreme within his little State,
> His smile shed honour, and his frown was fate.
> Prompt with the rifle, niggard of the pen,
> By manly deeds he won the hearts of men;
> His watchful eye each rival chieftain viewed,
> And oftener calmed than curbed the rising feud.
> He knew the intense devotion that reveres
> Each usage hallowed by a thousand years;
> Nor sought to substitute with ruthless hand
> The alien systems of a distant land.
> Friend of the people, in their midst he moved,
> To all familiar and by all beloved;
> And those who gathered prattling where he came,
> Grey-headed now, still gossip of his name.
>
> . . . . . .
>
> For all good Magistrate, our Rulers say,
> Decides all night, investigates all day;
> The crack Collector, man of equal might,
> Reports all day, and corresponds all night.[12]

Such posturing notwithstanding, an occasional "Magistrate of yore" revealed the considerable ambivalence that underlay the rulers' sense of self-confidence. As one "man for Chupra" declared:

8. Cohn 1962: 313; 1979.
9. Cited in *SDG, 1930*: 150.
10. See "Reports on Hindu Religion," Saran, in Risley Collection.
11. Muddiman 1930: 50.
12. 1888: 6, 9.

It is generally the fashion to describe the feelings of the people as good and loyal; I believe myself that it would be much more correct to describe it as simply acquiescent. I do not think there is any actual discontent with our rule . . . but I cannot say that anything like the active feeling of loyalty exists in the minds of either Hindoos or Mohammedans. . . .
At best we are an alien and, worse than that, an unbending and unsympathetic race, and the race we are called upon to rule is essentially a feeling and impulsive one. The consequence is, that as we never thaw to them, they never open to us; and we must all . . . feel that as we come to the land strangers, so we leave it, and that scarcely any of us penetrate beyond the outward shell of native feeling.[13]

Although couched in cultural terms and focusing on interpersonal relationships, these remarks accurately characterize the limited British interactions with Indian society in all respects. Government institutions simply did not extend into local society, nor was its machinery especially geared to economic or social problem solving. These drawbacks of the state's ruling institutions were evident in its handling of the 1866 famine. In a far more revealing way than the events of 1857, the crisis in 1866 highlighted the weakness of the institutional infrastructure. As in other Bihar districts, administrators in Saran were slow in recognizing the advent of famine conditions and responded with inadequate ameliorative measures. Although there was a series of poor harvests from the autumn of 1864 onward, government did not spring into action until October 1865, when the collector organized a meeting of "native gentlemen" to purchase cheap grain from other districts to sell at cost. In November the Collector reported the failure of two-thirds of the rice crop but still pinned his hopes on the spring harvest. Only after a hailstorm had destroyed a large part of the crops in February 1866 was action taken. Then, as relief works and centers opened up, local officials finally perceived "the depth and distress and misery into which the wretched inhabitants . . . were plunged, or of the extent of relief which would have to be afforded them."[14] As the subsequent inquiry report noted, when people went to obtain food at the relief centers, finally opened in June 1866, they were "already in a moribund state, to whom the first meal gave the death blow."[15] Nor was relief afforded on a scale commensurate with the needs of the people. According to one indigo planter, there were not enough Europeans and trustworthy natives to establish additional centers.[16]

Not surprisingly, the famine inquiry report was highly critical of the lack of official links to local society, particularly the tenuous links to the central government. The report urged that the police be made entirely subordinate to

13. Cited in AGRPD, 1871–72.
14. G. J. S. Hodgkinson, Secy., Relief Committee to Commr. J. R. Dalrymple, no. 32, July 9, 1866, and Colltr. F. M. Halliday to F. R. Cockerell, no. 290, Dec. 29, 1866, S.C., Misc. File Book of Letters re: Late Scarcity, 1866.
15. *Parliamentary Papers* (Commons), *1867*: 16.
16. N. MacDonald, Sereepur Factory to Commr. F. M. Halliday, Feb. 12, 1867, Misc. File Book re: Late Scarcity, 1866.

the district officer and the number of channels between the provincial government and the district officer be reduced. Otherwise, the Bengal district officer was in a weaker position than his counterparts in other provinces because he enjoyed less "influence, knowledge, and executive power." However, in keeping with the British image of the "Oriental people," the magistrate and collector needed to have in his hands, "all live Executive authority of the Government."[17]

District officers were also said to lack "external symbols . . . [and] the Magistrates, who among an alien people maintain no unnecessary private establishments, appear abroad as plain, unpretending men who go to their offices like clerks." Nor were these officers familiar with local conditions because they were transferred so frequently. The report also recommended the development of a subdivisional system organized around an executive establishment at the subdistrict level and headed by a subdivisional officer serving as the link between the "European and native systems of Administration."[18]

The lack of penetrating institutions at the local level, nevertheless, persisted as government efforts to fill this gap were inevitably constrained by its larger imperial aims. In Anil Seal's words:

The British wanted to pull resources out of India, not to put their own into India. Therefore, the administration and military system had to pay for itself with Indian revenues. At the top, this called for a skilled bureaucracy capable of handling large issues bearing upon the economy and the army. But at lower levels this control had to be looser. . . . In the localities the main tasks were to secure the cheap and regular collection of revenue to see to it that the districts remained quiet.[19]

Such considerations—as well as the crucial support provided by local allies—explain why the administrative apparatus was developed languidly and irresolutely. Writing in 1815 (over two decades after the institution of the Permanent Settlement) the Saran magistrate acknowledged that the "interior of this District which is very extensive . . . has never to the best of my Knowledge [been] visited . . . by an European officer of the Government."[20] Nor did the pattern of limited government penetration of the countryside change significantly in the early nineteenth century. In 1839 a touring commissioner of Patna determined that the officially defined links between district magistrates and daroghas (Indian police officers) presiding over thanas—the basic level at which the formal bureaucracy of government was represented—existed only "on paper." Echoing the 1815 finding, he reported: "I believe I am the first person who for nearly 20 years has taken the trouble to visit the Thannahs [the actual police station at the thana level], and inspect the records

17. GOB, *Famine, Bengal and Orissa, 1866*, 1867, 3: 1, 8. From the GOI, the official chain extended through, first, the GOB, then the BOR followed by the commissioner of the division and the collector of the district. 18. Ibid.: 8, 11, 15. 19. 1973: 327–28.
20. J. B. Elliott, Magte., Saran, to W. B. Bayley, Secy., Jdcl., Oct. 25, 1815, Bengal Cr. Jdcl. Procs., Dec. 22 to 29, 1815, Dec. 22, no. 45.

in Zillah Sarun."[21] Typically, in Saran, in the late nineteenth and early twentieth centuries, there were never more than five or six official Europeans stationed there; added to indigo planters, the total was only about one hundred, less than 0.01 percent of the district's population. The mainsprings of control, in other words, were government's relations with its allies.

In such a configuration of control, tensions were inevitable. On the one hand, government needed powerful allies; on the other, it had to keep them from threatening the authority of the state. Because its local connections were landed magnates with their own networks of power and control, it was in the state's best interests to see that the power of its allies remained localized within the framework of the Raj and that their impositions on the rural society were restricted so as not to cause any major peasant outbreaks.

Furthermore, unlike the Mughals, the British quickly overcame or contained secondary or regional powers. Not until the development of the nationalist movement in the twentieth century was there any real challenge at the supralocal level. The absence of opposition meant that government did not have to watch over its allies too closely. Moreover, as the Permanent Settlement had stabilized the vital question of revenue, only a minimal system of official control was sufficient to ensure its flow.[22]

If a localizing influence existed in this system, as has been portrayed for Guntur District, it arose not so much from the fact that the administration was "sometimes only nominally under the control of European officers."[23] Certainly, the Guntur scenario of local coadjutors manipulating their strategic positions under the Raj to reap sizable benefits was not uncommon, reaching (in the late nineteenth century) such alarming proportions that government had to mount a concerted campaign to stamp out the rash of *kachcheri* conspiracies, which had led to enormous defalcations. Government also sought to prevent local combinations of traditional caste and interest groups from forming in its bureaucracy.[24] But the primary localizing force was generated by government's relations with its local allies. Indeed, to view state-local interactions solely from the perspective of the "Gunturs" of colonial India is to focus exclusively on the activities of the headquarters town at the expense of ignoring the vast areas of the interior that lay beyond the control of the Limited Raj.

The context of official control at the local level was defined not only by the administrative structures emanating from Chapra, but also by the networks of power extending outward from zamindari headquarters. Hathwa, as the seat of the district's major landholder, of course, formed the single most important

---

21. R. Brownlow, Offg. Magte., Saran, to C. Tucker, Commr. of Circuit, Patna, April 9, 1837, ibid., April 18 to 25, 1837, April 18, no. 79.
22. Cohn 1960: 430. See also Yang (forthcoming) for how the collaborative framework of rule and financial considerations shaped the structure and functioning of the police.
23. Frykenberg 1965: 233.
24. Colltr. F. A. Slack to Commr., no. 1697G, Aug. 30–31, 1895, Bengal Rev. Procs., Jan.–Feb. 1896, Jan., 15.

zamindari hub, its centrality in the local configuration of control acknowledged by the administrative arrangements made to accommodate its special position. Thus, the official interest in the late nineteenth century was to develop a subdivisional system there in order to have an executive establishment at the subdistrict level linking the "European and native systems of Administration."[25] Such a concern underlay the formation of Gopalganj subdivision in the 1870s; Chapra and Siwan had previously been created in 1848. In part, the reason for this additional administrative unit was to enable government to supervise the great estate of Hathwa, which extended over much of Gopalganj. Naturally, the maharaja of Hathwa strongly opposed its establishment, as an unwelcome intrusion into his affairs.[26]

Although the Hathwa maharaja lost the battle to stop the creation of Gopalganj subdivision, the estate's undisputed primacy in the locality quickly made the continuing need for that subdivision a matter of official debate. Within three years of its establishment in 1878, the Saran magistrate proposed to merge Gopalganj with Siwan because its subdivisional officer had little to do: a workload of only two hours a day, consisting primarily of criminal cases. This officer, formerly a Court of Wards manager of the Hathwa estate, noted, in a recognition of the realities of local power: "Miscellaneous work in the Collectorate is next to none owing mainly to the great part of the subdivision being owned by one zamindar—Hence there are no partition cases; very few land registrations and only some trifling settlements. The treasury work is nominal, confined to receiving money for stamps and excises, and to paying salaries."[27]

Although the efforts to do away with Gopalganj as a separate administrative unit failed, Hathwa's dominating role continued to influence its administrative functioning. This feature of the subdivision was again recognized in 1914 when a recommendation was made to place it under the charge of a provincial civil service officer. But, as the commissioner pointed out, the presence of Hathwa in the locality necessitated that "the Subdivisional officer should be a Civilian. . . . There are certain number of Europeans connected with the estate and at the present time Hathwa is the central meeting place of the district. Chapra itself is tucked away on the south of the district and Hathwa now occupies the place that Siwan formerly did."[28]

Hathwa gained the position it did in the district because the British presence at the local level was limited. Government's ties to local landholders and its attempts to expand its administrative machinery were directly related, each shaping the character of the other. As long as the government lacked penetrating

25. GOB, *Famine, 1866*, 1867, 3: 8, 15.
26. Commr. Halliday to Magte., no. 85J, Oct. 24, 1878, S.C., *Faujdari Bastas*, 1879.
27. Offg. Magte. G. J. S. Hodgkinson to Commr., no. G/1613, n.d. (1878?), P.C. Gen. *Basta* no. 329, 1878–79.
28. Offg. Commr. B. Foley to GOB&O, June 2, 1914, B&O Jdcl. Procs., Appointments, Aug. to Oct. 1914, Aug., 81.

institutions in the interior, its half-hearted efforts to extend control to the subdistrict levels invariably came up against the well-entrenched structures erected on the foundations of zamindari control. In such a contest, as the government attempted to link up with the *qanungo*, the patwari, and the chaukidar, the strengths and weaknesses of the Limited Raj were clearly exposed.

Qanungos and Patwaris

Saran had two *qanungos* in 1924: Maulvi Wali Muhammad in charge of the Chapra subdivision and Shital Prasad in charge of the Siwan and Gopalganj subdivisions. The former had read up to the preliminary standard of Calcutta University and knew surveying; the latter had reached the level of the B.A. examination, passed the *qanungo*ship examination, and received surveying training.

Shital Prasad's duties consisted of: (1) collection of rent from tenants of government estates (seven villages); (2) survey and settlement of petty government estates in diaras (alluvium); (3) measurement of government lands covered by government buildings; (4) crop cutting under section 40, Bengal Tenancy Act; (5) miscellaneous enquiries; (6) pauper suit enquiry; (7) probate enquiry; (8) tuccavi (government loans) distribution enquiry; (9) tuccavi collection; (10) deep stream verification; (11) enquiry into the solvency of sureties; (12) enquiry regarding alluvion and diluvion of government estates; (13) inspection and replacement of boundary marks; (14) demarcation of lands; (15) similar work in Gopalganj subdivision.[29]

In other words, the *qanungo* worked as part of the administrative machinery. He was particularly useful because he carried out the tasks that would otherwise have to be done by a subdeputy collector, who required substantially higher pay.[30]

The patwari, on the other hand, invited few official encomiums. A 1914 report explains why: "(1) that the patwari is in fact the servant of the zamindar and under his control; (2) that his papers, even when their production can be enforced, are of little or no value and are not required at all since the preparation of a record-of-rights; and (3) that his continued presence in the villages as a quasi-government servant is harmful as in many cases he instigates litigation and foments disputes."[31] Despite various regulations, government control over patwaris was tenuous. Figures collected under the provisions of Regulation XII of 1817, by which landlords had to report their appointments, dismissals, and remunerations to the collector, show that they were rarely complied with in Saran. In the five years between 1908–1909 and 1912–1913,

29. Commr. to BOR, June 12, 1924, B&O Rev. Procs., 1924, Oct., 46.
30. Colltr. P. Meerza to Commr., n.d., ibid., Oct. 1924, 49.
31. "Note on Patwaris in Bihar," Annexure A to Offg. Secy. H. K. Briscoe, BOR to Secy., Rev. Dept., 20 June 1914, ibid., Jan.–March 1915, Jan., 39 (hereafter cited as "Note on Patwaris, 1914").

there were only ninety-one cases of appointment, fifty-three of dismissal, and thirty-nine regarding remuneration. The production of patwaris' accounts during the same period was even less, numbering only twenty-four.[32]

Noticeably absent, moreover, in these twentieth-century descriptions is any reference to a working relationship between the *qanungo* and the patwari. In the Mughal administrative system, however, the *qanungo*, considered the state's "permanent repository of information concerning the revenue receipts, area statistics, local revenue rates, and practices and customs" and a "friend of the peasants," was assisted at the village level by the patwari who was an accountant for the peasants and an employee of the village.[33] The effectiveness of this system stemmed from the inherent tensions between the *qanungo* who was the government agent and the patwari who spoke for the village. As part of the Mughal administrative machinery at the pargana level, the former represented the deepest extension of the state into local society. Also present at this level, considered the "hub of rural administration under Muslim rulers . . . [and] as important as the district under the British" were the officials responsible for revenue (*amil*), police and criminal administration (*shiqdar*), and civil justice (*qazi*), but only the *qanungo* stood independently of other local officials and was directly linked to the provincial government.[34]

In the initial years of British rule, the *qanungo*-patwari system was closer to its Mughal predecessor than to its twentieth-century counterpart. Increasingly, however, the *qanungo*'s position of maintaining a balance between the interests of landholders and tenants gave way to an exclusive concern with collecting and registering information to safeguard the revenue demands of government.[35] Writing in 1787, W. A. Brooke, the revenue chief of Patna, stated that there were "canoongoes in every pargana in Bihar whose forefathers originally received their appointments from the [Mughal] King and had sanads [patents] granted them at the time."[36] Another report noted that "their office is not only for life, but hereditary to families" and recorded their importance in gathering "accounts from the mofussil."[37] Without their records, as the chief of the Patna Revenue Council wrote in 1773, "no judgment could be formed of past collections and it would be in the power of every dismissed Aumil by destroying or concealing his Papers to leaving his successor in almost Total Ignorance of the value of the Talooks which composed his District and which it would be the interest of the zemindars to keep from him as much as possible."[38]

32. Similar returns came in from other districts, see Annexure B, ibid., 40.
33. Habib 1963: 125, 289–90; Saran 1972: 274–75.
34. Quereshi 1966: 231; N. A. Siddiqi 1970: 77.
35. "Kanungo Establishment in Bihar and Orissa," J. R. Dain, Rev. Dept. to Secy., BOR, April 5, 1924, B&O Rev. Procs., 1924, Oct., 3. An interpretation attributing the change in the office to British actions is in B. K. Sinha (1961: 11). 36. Cited in Mitra 1944: 18.
37. Controlling Council of Rev. at Patna to Warren Hastings, G.G., Aug. 31, 1775, Patna Factory Records, Jan. 2 to Dec. 28, 1775.
38. Chief of Patna Council to Hon. Warren Hastings, n.d., Patna Rev. Procs., Feb. to Dec. 1773. Aug. 16.

Local officials were also aware of the shortcomings of this institution. Administrative doubts regarding the *qanungo*'s ability to furnish "a true and exact state of the revenue Collections" led to the transformation of his duties into "more those of a surveyor than anything else."[39] After the Permanent Settlement was effected, government considered his information about agricultural statistics and revenue collection even less useful. In this climate of opinion, in the wake of Governor-General Warren Hastings's failure to revive the institution in 1783, the office of *qanungo* was abolished in 1793 in Bengal and Bihar because it was "pernicious."[40] Patwaris were retained, however, in the expectation that their knowledge would be useful in landlord-tenant suits and in partitions of estates. But, without the customary supervisory officer to regulate him, the patwari increasingly became part of the control structure of the zamindar in the nineteenth century. As a result, his "public and impartial village record-of-rights was turned into a private and hostile record under the control of the zamindars."[41] Far better, the logic of this situation seemed to dictate, to strengthen the hand of government's "permanent" connections than to retain an imperfect conduit of information in an agrarian system where the state's share of the revenue had been settled in perpetuity.

Subsequent attempts to reestablish the office of *qanungo* met with little success, nor were full-fledged efforts ever made to restore its former character. The thirty-four *qanungos* appointed in Saran in 1817 were all selected from "the descendants of the former Canongoes," and their annual expense amounted to only Rs. 8,028. This cost was offset, moreover, by the Rs. 42,231 additional revenue government secured as a result of reclaiming lands formerly given to *qanungos* for services rendered (*nankar qanungo*). In short, Saran *qanungos* more than paid for their own revival, and their traditional duties were supplanted by the overriding "information in regard to landed property the want of which has been so long and so severely felt both in the Revenue and in the Judicial Departments."[42]

This experiment proved to be short-lived. With local administrators reporting widespread failure in making use of the office, *qanungos* were once again abolished in 1827. A common complaint was that 'they worked only for local landholders. Consequently, as the Board of Revenue concluded in recommending its abrogation, the "office of kanungo will mislead instead of giving any useful information."[43] Nor were subsequent efforts to revive the *qanungo* any more successful. Without this institution to serve as a counterbalance, however, British attempts to bring the patwari back into the fold of government were nullified by the growing networks of control extending from the estates of their "permanent" allies.

39. Ibid.   40. Stephenson-Moore 1922: 73.   41. Ibid.
42. Holt Mackenzie, Secy. to Govt., to Board of Commrs. in Behar and Benares, March 27, 1818, Beng. Rev. Consltns., Dec. 24 to 31, 1819, Dec. 31, no. 35.
43. Cited in *Muzaffarpur SR*: 77.

A proposal to make the patwari a government-paid servant in 1815 was rejected by the government of India on the grounds that this would make the village accountant even more capable of oppressing the peasantry and defrauding government. By intriguing with the raiyats, he could seriously injure public revenue by bringing ruin on the zamindar. Another objection was the cess that would have to be imposed to pay the patwari, an act said to violate the Permanent Settlement. In looking back at this decision, however, an official report admitted that "the cumulative power of patwaries backed by Government would have been so great that even a well-organized opposition could not have long withstood it."[44]

Rather than incorporate patwaris into its administrative system, government opted to reestablish *qanungo*s to supervise them. Regulation II of 1816 legislated the latter back into existence, and Regulation XII of 1817 endowed government with additional supervisory controls over the former. Section 16 of this regulation described the duties of a patwari: "To keep registers and accounts of his village or circle according as the revenue authorities might appoint; to deliver every half year to the canoongoe a complete copy of such registers and accounts of his village or circle according to custom . . . to deliver every half to the canoongoe a complete copy of the khureff and rubee harvests; to perform other customary duties and services."[45]

These early nineteenth-century deliberations over the "fit" of the patwari in the larger apparatus of official control anticipated a continuing dilemma that would confront government in its attempts to create links to this institution. To wrest control of the patwari away from the zamindar, described as his "natural connection," as the provincial authorities recognized, would be "an irritating innovation . . . an innovation scarcely reconcilable with the condition which the whole of our revenue system is calculated to place the zemindar."[46] The integration of the patwari into a government system of administration also required the existence of an infrastructure that the state had abandoned any intention of even creating because of the arrangements of consultation and control established by the Permanent Settlement. Over village-level officials, therefore, government control was, at best, nominal.

Paid by, and largely responsible to, the zamindar, the patwari was defined by the legislation of 1817 as a "joint agent of the landlords and their Tenants" acting under the supervision of "public officers for the benefit of all parties concerned." A modest aim of this new regulation was to accumulate slowly "a body of records for the most part formed under no immediate temptation to fraud, and becoming authentic in proportion to their uniformity for a continued

44. Ibid.: 73.
45. "A Regulation for the . . . Office of Putwaree in the Province of Behar," A.D. 1817 Regulation, Bengal Board of Commrs. at Behar and Benares, May 17 to June 9, 1817, May 21, no. 270D and encl.
46. Mackenzie, Acting Secy. to Govt., to John Deane, Commr. in Behar and Benares, no. 59, Jan. 31, 1817, ibid.

series of years."[47] Like the *qanungo*, the patwari was to be shaped into an instrument to uphold the system of revenue.

From the outset though, even nominal official supervision over the village accountant was difficult to maintain. When information was sought on estates in Muzaffarpur, patwaris absconded rather than hand over their records. An 1825 report showed that that district's patwaris generally disregarded the rule about filing half-yearly papers with the *qanungo*'s office, and government peons were turned out of villages when they went there to summon patwaris. On another occasion, a village accountant said he was unable to provide his records because his malik would not release them.[48]

An 1827 report of the Board of Revenue described the patwari as completely under the sway of the landholder who acted as his "taskmaster." Occasional attempts to legislate more control over the office produced little change. Although Regulation IX of 1833 required patwaris to file duplicates of their papers in collectors' offices, local enquiries in 1837 showed that the procedure was rarely followed in the region. The incomplete state of their registers was noted again in 1863 by the commissioner of Patna but no remedial action was taken.[49]

The lack of official links to the patwari was clearly visible in Saran where it was not even possible to determine who the recognized accountant of each village was. Zamindars regularly appointed and dismissed patwaris without reference to district authorities, prompting one Saran collector to declare that patwaris, "though nominally public servants . . . [were] really the private servants of zemindars."[50]

The district's patwaris usually received Rs. 2 to 4 per month exclusive of perquisites. Well-to-do patwaris were said to lend money and grain on interest. Most were of a respectable caste, about 97 percent of them Kayasth, and their offices were hereditary.[51] Figures compiled during the 1893 recruitment of patwaris show that the office continued to be filled by members with family ties to that occupation.[52]

The following summary by the commissioner of Patna rounds out the description of the nature and functions of the patwari in Bihar:

Usually there is one putwaree in one village, but sometimes there are many more, each shareholder having one putwaree for his share. . . . It is his duty to keep the biggits, the khusra [field-book] of measurements, and all the various village accounts. He grants receipts for rents collected by the gomastahs [landholder's agent]. As a general rule, the putwaree does not collect the rents, but does so occasionally, especially in villages where there are no gomastahs, and the putwaree is considered sufficiently trustworthy. Putwarees are generally of the Kaiet caste; but sometimes a Koormi or even a Mahomedan putwaree is to be met with. Their office is not absolutely hereditary, but in practice it

47. Ibid.
48. *Muzaffarpur SR*: 76.
49. "Note on Patwaris, 1914," pp. 36–37.
50. Cited in Bengal Government Selections, 1873: 57–58.
51. Ibid. "Chowkidari Papers," S.C. *Faujdari Bastas*, 1884.
52. "Note by W. C. Macpherson, Offg. Director of Dept. of Land Records . . . July 20, 1893," Bengal Rev. Procs., Sept. to Dec. 1893, Nov., 1134.

has generally become so; the zemindar finding it convenient to put in the place of a deceased putwaree his son or some close relation who has undergone a course of apprenticeship under his predecessor, and has thus acquired a knowledge of the estate and its tenants.[53]

Nevertheless, as the sole repository of village accounts, the patwari was also a potential threat to the landholder. The increasing subdivision of landholdings meant that his accounts were often the focus of much jockeying between the different coparceners. As a result, each shareholder preferred to appoint his own accountants. The possibility of patwaris turning against landholders was not unknown, as one Saran collector observed in 1883, when he wrote that they "in cases of disputes between the landlord and his tenants if not partisans of the former are sure to be the partisans of the latter."[54]

No wonder official attempts to revive the patwari were opposed by landholders. It was not to their advantage to have further encroachments by the state or for the anomalous status of the patwari to be better defined. In the words of the Hathwa estate manager:

It is a well-known fact that the patwaris of Bihar are a set of low-paid, unscrupulous men, with a statutory position which enables them to fill their own pockets at the sacrifice of the interests of the raiyats and zamindars alike, particularly in the case of villages owned jointly by several proprietors, where no individual landlord can exercise any effectual control over them, the result being that they become the *de facto* proprietors of the villages.[55]

Such fears were unfounded, though, because government attempts to reorganize the *qanungo*-patwari system consistently failed. Because the Raj neither paid sufficient attention to local conditions nor implemented its legislation effectively, the results were always incomplete. Its various experiments, leading to the appointment of *qanungo*s at the subdivision level, finally produced a decisive rupture of the vital *qanungo*-patwari relationship. Thereafter, the former would have only revenue and statistical functions without any supervisory responsibility over the patwari. Attempts to "revive" the patwari also failed to yield tangible results. Until the lieutenant-governor pointed it out, even the initial "Draft of Rules for the Appointment of Putwaris" was framed in terms of designating patwaris to estates. At his urging, these rules were revised to attach them to villages or circle of villages.[56]

Furthermore, as local officials quickly discovered, their intentions to reorganize the accountant as a village officer of the state clashed with an already

---

53. Bengal Government Selections 1873: 56.
54. Colltr. C. C. Quinn to Commr., no. 127G, April 30, 1883, P.C. Rev. *Basta* no. 338, 1883–1884.
55. Babu Bipin Behari Bose, Mgr., H.R., to Commr., no. 105, Oct. 17, 1893, Bengal Rev. Procs., Jan. to April 1894, Feb., 187.
56. *Qanungo*s originally existed at the *pargana* level (Offg. Secy. GOB to Secy. BOR, no. 2525, Sept. 20, 1873, ibid., July 1873 to 1875, Sept. 1873, 26; Offg. Secy. H. J. S. Cotton, BOR to Secy. GOB, no. 712A, Oct. 21, 1880, ibid., Dec. 1880, 41).

prevailing system. District after district in Bihar reported that patwaris were linked to estates and not to villages, and, where a village was held by several shareholders, each one had his own accountant. Patwaris also adapted to partitions in an estate by farming out new estates to their family members.[57]

Even efforts to gain nominal control over the patwari met with little success. If landholders did register their accountants with district authorities, their return showed nominations made by estates and not by villages. When A. P. MacDonnell took charge of Saran in 1879, the patwari rules of registration had been in effect four years, but legal appointments had only been made in 1,605 of the district's 5,231 villages.[58] Nor did the official drive in the 1870s to have duplicate patwari accounts filed at the collector's office yield results. Papers were not turned in for a single village in Saran.

The 1870s attempt represented government's last sustained and systematic effort to link up with the village accountant. Thereafter, concern over the patwari arose periodically, but only as a question of repealing the patwari regulations. In 1895 the government of India opposed the Bengal authorities' suggestion for repeal. Although the central government conceded that the accountant was not "all that could be wished," it argued for his retention by maintaining the unrealized hope that he was the sole link between the "state and the cultivator." A 1914 proposal for repeal of the "dead letter" that was the Bengal Patwaris Regulation XII of 1817 stirred even less response. Further deliberations were cut short by government's dismissal of the issue by saying that the time was "inopportune."[59] Officially, therefore, the patwari remained identified as a government link on the statute books. But, as the repeated efforts to incorporate him in an administrative apparatus constructed at the subdistrict level reveal, the locus of power resided elsewhere—in the networks emanating from the zamindar's estate. Indeed, the estate was the crucial arena, which provided the framework for the organization of local control systems.

The Chaukidars

In the absence of an extensive police force, especially in the countryside, chaukidars (night watchmen) were significant figures in the maintenance of public order. Even in the late nineteenth century, the police were so thinly stretched across Saran that chaukidars were considered, in effect, "the real police of the country."[60] In 1872, for instance, the district's 408 policemen

57. Commr. Halliday to Secy. BOR, no. 248R, May 4, 1880, Bengal Rev. Procs., Dec. 1880, 49.
58. Ibid.
59. Cotton to Rev. Dept., no. 712A, Oct. 21, 1880, ibid., Dec. 1880, 40. In Madras the role of the patwari diminished while the position of headman rose in significance under British rule (Baker 1979: 26–52).
60. Cited in AGRPD, 1872–73.

meant 1 policeman to every 6.5 square miles or 1 to every 5,058 persons; the 6,067 chaukidars meant 1 watchman to every 0.44 square mile or 1 to every 340 persons. Moreover, the police figures are inflated because at least one-fifth of the entire force was on guard duty over prisons and treasuries, and more than one-fifth on town, municipal, or harbor duty.[61]

Government pronouncements on the watchmen in local administration were therefore effusive in their praise. A typical observation was that made by the lieutenant-governor in 1856, who described "chowkeydars" as not only the "foundation of all possible Police in this country" but also entrusted "upon their renovation, improvement and stability ... the ultimate success of all our measures for the benefit of the country in the prevention, detection, and punishment of crime."[62] No less enthusiastic was the testimony of the inspector-general of police for Bihar and Orissa before the Indian Statutory Commission in 1928, who characterized them as the "reporting agency for all the departments of Government. In other words, they are the pillars of the Constitution; they are the foundations on which everything is laid." They were also said to perform such police tasks as "protecting approaches to a village to catch burglars or dacoits, things that you have not sufficient police to do."[63]

Such praise, however, reflected official aspirations rather than the actual role played by the village watchman. Unlike the patwari whose records were of immediate importance to the British in the effective administration of Bihar, the chaukidar was the repository of information of far less economic or social value. In the late nineteenth century, he was simply charged with communicating information on crime along with the "village headman ... owner or occupier of land, and the agent of any such owner or occupier, and every officer employed in the collection of revenue or rent of land on the part of Government...."[64]

These menial duties suggest the low social status of chaukidars. According to Dewey, chaukidars "were members of economically depressed families and socially-despised castes. Often they became chaukidars because they were too physically infirm to work as labourers, and lacked the capital to set themselves up as tenants. They were illiterate and quasi-numerate." Of the 550 chaukidars in Saran in 1884, 63 percent were Dusadhs, 21 percent were Ahirs, and 2 percent were Chamars.[65]

Their low social status is also illustrated by their petty wages. In 1875 in

61. Hunter 1877: 344–45; GOB, *Twenty Years' Statistics, 1883–84, 1903–04*, vol. B, *Police* 1905(?): 162.
62. "Minute by the Hon'ble the Lieut. Governor of Bengal [on] Police and Criminal Justice in Bengal," April 30, 1856: 8.
63. Evidence of W. Swain, Dec. 14, 1928, Patna, in *Indian Statutory Commission* (1930, 15: 295).
64. See "Obligations of landholders and others in regard to crime," Rules drafted by Col. Skinner, Dist. Supt. of Police, Saran, with no. 569, July 5, 1883, Bengal Jdcl. (Police) Procs., Aug., 1883., no. 4.
65. Dewey 1978: 282; "Chowkidari Papers," S.C. *Faujdari Bastas*, 1884.

Saran, most received an average of Rs. 9-8-3 in cash per year; a small percentage had rentfree land holdings of an average area of 2-5 bighas. Their income was supplemented by perquisites that defined the watchman's ties to the landholder and the village community. He received presents at festivals, such as Diwali (the festival of lights), Holi (the spring festival), and Dashara (the festival at the beginning of the agricultural year), and on other important occasions, such as births and marriages. If there was a bazaar or periodic market, he was allowed to collect a small levy on articles sold. The landholder provided him with a blanket or warm clothing for night duty. Some chaukidars earned small sums for assisting the malik in collecting rents. From all these sources, chaukidars accumulated as much as Rs. 20 to 30 per year.[66]

British attempts to recruit the chaukidars into their network of control were attended to with far less urgency than had been the case with the patwaris. Under the Mughals, chaukidars had played an important role in village policing, though they had no official ties to the state but were instead considered servants of the village community who maintained them by a share of the crops or by rights to some village lands.[67] The initial British policy toward the watchmen was to subordinate them to the newly appointed darogha, legislated by Regulation XXII of 1793, which also removed the police from the control of the zamindars. Chaukidars, on the whole, aroused little official interest. When they were a subject of concern in the early nineteenth century, it was the result of specific events, such as the alarming rise of highway robbery in 1822–1823, which prompted the judge of the then-undivided Saran and Champaran to organize an establishment of 78 chaukidars. These were to be stationed at strategic points on the high roads.[68] This measure was temporary, but a more systematic chaukidari establishment existed in most towns, especially in district headquarters. At Chapra one was set up as early as 1817; by 1829 it had a force of 154 chaukidars and twelve guards subsidized by chaukidari levies on the town's houses. Outside of towns and special cases, however, the office of village watchman was largely ignored.[69]

A special committee, convened in the 1830s to study the "mofussil police" in Bengal, found many administrators who were not even aware of the existence of the watchman. Such was the claim of the joint magistrate of Saran, who believed that there was no village police until a few years ago when chaukidars were appointed to almost every village. Much more on the mark was the testimony of William Adam who called for a more visible police presence in the countryside because magistrates and their assistants lived away from the

---

66. Offg. Magte. G. E. Porter to Commr., no. 505G, April 15, 1875, ibid., May 1875, 142.
67. Sarkar 1963: 13; McNeile 1866: 5–6.
68. H. Lowther, Judge & Magte., to Henry Shakespear, Supt. of Police, Feb. 27, 1823, Bengal Cr. Jdcl. Consltns., Feb. 27 to March 20, 1823, March 20, no. 17.
69. F. C. Smith, Offg. Commr. of Circuit, Saran Div., to Henry Shakespear, Secy., Jdcl., no. 746, n.d., ibid., July 28 to Aug. 25, 1829, Aug. 25, no. 17.

"main part" of most districts in the relative isolation of headquarter towns, such as Chapra.[70]

This committee, however, recommended no change in the chaukidari system. The commissioner of Patna summed up the prevailing view for Bihar when he advocated that the zamindar be responsible for the nomination of the watchman "because, from his [zamindar's] position, he is the person most interested in the welfare of the residents on his estate, and from knowing the tenantry, he can make the most suitable selection." Where the landholder was of "bad repute," he suggested that a "Punch" (panchayet; village council) be formed to make the choice. He did, however, also lash out at chaukidars as "the most debased class of the inhabitants," describing Saran's watchmen in particular as "the leaders of criminal gangs."[71]

The continuing disregard of the chaukidar had led, by the mid-nineteenth century, as the lieutenant-governor acknowledged, to the "lamentable, but unquestionable fact that the rural Police, its position, character and stability as a public institution, have ... deteriorated ... diminished in number, and impaired in efficiency ... and ... unless some speedy measures be taken to save it, it is in danger of perishing altogether from the face of the land."[72] To arrest this decline, a law was proposed empowering magistrates to appoint watchmen in villages without them and to ensure the payment of their customary wages.

No action was taken until 1870 when government strengthened its links to the village watchmen by the Bengal Act VI of 1870, the Village Chaukidari Act. This legislation aimed at correcting what was considered to be the primary reason for the inefficiency of the system: the irregularity of watchmen's pay. By creating chaukidari panchayets of three to five villagers, to control the appointment, dismissal, and maintenance of village watchmen, this act sought to recast him as a servant of the village community rather than of the malik.[73]

Although the importance of incorporating watchmen into the official system was widely recognized, few administrators were able to recruit their services. The touring assistant magistrate of Siwan spoke for several generations of local officers when he commented on the chaukidars of Siswan village as "here as elsewhere all simply useless."[74] But, as in the case of the patwari, there was considerable agreement that ties to the watchmen had to be maintained, regardless of imperfections. Chaukidari reforms, moreover, generated the same problems that the efforts to reorganize the patwari did, that is, structural changes had to be made at a level of local society that lay beyond the reach of

70. W. Luke, Joint Magte., to Commr. T. R. Davidson, Patna, June 1, 1837, and Testimony of Wm. Adam, in Bengal, *Committee on Improvement of Mofussil Police, Bengal, 1838*.
71. Davidson, Commr., to R. D. Mangles, Secy. to GOB, no. 31, June 10, 1837, in ibid.
72. "Minute by the Lieut. Governor of Bengal on Police," April 30, 1856.
73. "Working of the Village Chowkeedaree Act in Patna District," Bengal Jdcl. Procs., April to July 1872, June, 6–19.
74. "Tour Diary of Assistant Magistrate of Sewan from November 1866 to March 1867," P.C. *Basta* no. 107, Letters from Magte. of Saran, 1863–1867.

the government machinery. For the village watchman to function as a government connection, he had to be extricated from his close ties to the local control structure, whether emanating from the estate or the village. And, as in the cases of the *qanungo* and the patwari, official attempts to coopt the chaukidari system revealed the limited penetration of the British Raj into local society.

That implementation of the chaukidari legislation required considerable commitment and effort on government's part was clear from the outset. The initial application of this legislation in thirty select villages in Patna district uncovered many problems. Where the panchayet members were Bhumihar Brahmin or Rajput, they assessed themselves and their friends lightly "and the poorer and more dependent classes with undue severity in order to make up the deficiency; that distraint has been frequently resorted to, and partiality is shown not only in the assessment but even in the collection." Moreover, raiyats were charged twice: they not only paid the levy imposed by the chaukidari panchayet, but also the customary chaukidari cess to the zamindar, which, in many cases, had become consolidated with the rent.[75]

Despite the shortcomings of the Patna experiment, the act was extended to additional districts in Bihar. When Saran's turn came in 1875, the magistrate raised several objections, expressing strong doubts particularly about the effectiveness of the panchayet:

Apart from the difficulties of appointing a punchayet, that it would be sanguine to expect that they will take much interest in the work for which they get no remuneration ... as to the expediency of placing in the hands of an irresponsible committee the power of assessing their fellow villagers, and think that in most villages, even if the Act is introduced and the punchayet is appointed, things will remain much as they are at present, and the malik or zemindar will be held responsible for the regular payment of the chowkeedar, and collect the chowkeedari cess as heretofore from the villages.[76]

He also argued for postponing the introduction of the act because district officers were "fully engrossed by the collection of famine advances, by the introduction of the salt rules, and the emigration scheme, road cess, &c., &c "[77]

Although the lieutenant-governor acknowledged the difficulty of finding "intelligent and literate men to form Panchayets," he overruled the objections of Bihar administrators by suggesting that they recruit the head raiyats of every village. As for the matter of the chaukidari cess already paid by raiyats to zamindars since the Permanent Settlement, he countered by saying, "after the lapse of time it is impossible to say whether this cess, like other cesses, is not part of the rent."[78]

75. Offg. Commr. S. C. Bayley to GOB, April 26, 1872, Bengal Jdcl. Procs., Apr. to June 1872, June, 7.
76. Porter to Commr., no. 505G, April 15, 1875, Bengal Police Procs., May 1875, 143.
77. To which Lieutenant-Governor Richard Temple commented marginally, "Say I do *not* admit this. It looks as if Mr. Porter fears the work which, I am sure, cannot be the case" (ibid).
78. Commr. Bayley to Secy. GOB, Jdcl., May 10, 1875, 168J, and "Marginal Remarks by the Lieutenant-Governor," ibid., 1875, July, 10.

Although Act VI of 1870 was extended to Saran in July 1875, its provisions were not fully applied until the 1890s. As late as 1877, chaukidari panchayets had been appointed in only 1,501 of the district's 4,646 villages.[79] But by 1894 there were 3,205 villages with panchayets and 3,641 chaukidars under Act VI of 1870, with only 543 and 562, respectively, still outside the official provisions. The biggest gains were made in the early 1890s, when the outbreak of the Cow Killing Riots spurred government into action.[80] In their wake, special provisions were introduced into Patna division, whereby in villages under the Chaukidari Act, the district officer was entitled to appoint headmen from the chaukidari councils. These headmen were to be concerned with such activities as the "a. Circulation of letters or notices or signals . . . b. The visits of itinerant lecturers or preachers. c. The collection of funds for any common purpose . . . d. The meeting of *sabhas* or other similar associations. e. The possession of unlicensed arms. f. The passage through or assemblage in the village of a body of persons."[81]

Whereas government found the chaukidari connection useful in matters relating to the security of the state, it continued to encounter all the problems it had hoped to solve with the introduction of the 1870 Act. In the words of one Saran magistrate, the provisions of this act were "distasteful to panchayets, ryots, chaukidars alike."[82] Successive district officers noted that villagers were reluctant to serve on chaukidari councils. As one village headman complained, "my crop was bad, my house was robbed, and now I am made a punch."[83]

The 1883 Chaukidari Committee investigating the workings of the 1870 Act stated that, if service on panchayets was voluntary, they would not exist in a great majority of the villages. Its report cited several reasons why the office was considered "a calamity and not an honour": (1) it was practically compulsory and lengthy; (2) it was unremunerative and therefore not inviting for the well-to-do villager; (3) it was undignified because it involved visits to rate-payers of lower social standing; (4) it aroused the antagonism of fellow villagers, especially toward the collecting member; (5) a panchayet member's property was subject to government confiscation in case of arrears; (6) local officers and police disliked supervision; (7) voluntary regularity of payment was alien to indigenous customs and practices.[84]

79. Of the 4,646 villages, 205 were said to be "non-existent" and the rest supposedly too small for *panches* because they had less than 60 houses. (Commr. E. W. Molony to GOB, July 17, 1877, no. 243J, Bengal Jdcl. Procs., Police, 1876–1877, Aug. 1877, 21).

80. Offg. Commr. H. Luttman Johnson to Chief Secy., GOB, Oct. 17, 1894, no. 60G, Bengal Jdcl. Procs., Oct. to Dec. 1894, Dec., no. 70. In 1892 there were 2,684 chaukidars under Act VI, 3,967 in 1893, and 4,509 in 1894 ("Village Police," *Twenty Years' Statistics, Police* 1905: 159).

81. Luttman-Johnson to Chief Secy., Nov. 2, 1894, no. 637G, and Notification no. 4988J, Dec. 18, 1894, Bengal Jdcl. Procs., Dec. 1894. nos. 72–74.

82. Cited in Molony to GOB, July 17, 1877, no. 243J, ibid., Police, Aug. 1877, 21.

83. Cited in AGRPD, 1879–1880.

84. The usual procedure was for the police to submit a list of five or more suitable men whom the magistrate accepted with little scrutiny ("Report by . . . Committee appointed to enquire into the workings of Act VI of 1870" April 27, 1883, P.C. Gen. *Basta* no. 289, 1884 [hereafter cited as Chaukidari Committee Report]).

Although many of these were cogent arguments, they were not pieced together to gain the larger picture. For Saran the evidence suggests that village-level controllers were generally nominated as council members anyway. And where they were not, such an appointment in itself was not likely to confer power or influence. According to one Saran magistrate, these councils had been inefficient until he reorganized them by recruiting influential raiyats. In another report, this same officer explained that village chiefs were the "class of men from among whom panchayets are usually selected."[85] Such individuals, however, were not likely to carry out their duty assiduously, because it would, in effect, diminish their hold over the chaukidars. Not surprisingly then, the committee encountered many fictitious councils, formed only when accounts had to be submitted.[86]

In 1892 government turned over the power of appointing chaukidars, determining their number, and fixing their salaries to the district magistrate, leaving only the right of nominating to the councils. Nothing, however, was done to ensure the effectiveness of the councils.[87]

Even the long-standing concern with ensuring systematic and timely remuneration of village watchmen produced few results. A. P. MacDonnell, who made the application of the Chaukidari Act his major task during his magisterial tour of 1879, reported finding "that the pay of the chaukidars was in arrears for periods varying from six months to two years."[88] The 1883 Chaukidari Committee arrived at a similar conclusion when it reported that regularity in remuneration was closely tied to executive action. In 60 percent of the cases in Saran, warrants had to be served on the panchayets before they would pay their chaukidars.[89] Furthermore, notwithstanding official efforts to oversee the workings of the village watchmen, they remained bound to the local control system. As one commissioner of Patna noted, they were "so entirely the creatures of the village authorities that they often accept whatever wages the latter choose to pay and acknowledge payment in full for their wages."[90]

In the 1890s government renewed its efforts to establish a strong chaukidari connection. Its new approach was to recruit higher caste, with the expectation that villagers would take a more active role if watchmen were of higher social standing. In the past, administrators had frequently complained that chaukidars were of criminal tribes and often implicated in the crimes committed in their neighborhoods.[91]

85. "Criminal Administration Report for Patna Division, 1879," ibid., no. 281, 1880; AGRPD, 1879–1880.
86. Chaukidari Committee Report.
87. Workings of the new Chaukidari Act, I (Bengal Code) of 1892, Report by Luttman-Johnson, Bengal Jdcl. Procs., Police, Jan. to April 1895, April, 165–69.
88. Cited in "Criminal Report for Patna Division, 1879."
89. Chaukidari Committee Report.
90. "Police Administration Report, Patna Division, 1884," Commr. Halliday to GOB, April 6, 1885, P.C. Gen. *Basta* no. 291, 1885.
91. GOB to GOI, Jan. 9, 1890, Bengal Jdcl. Procs., Jan. to April 1890, Jan., 11; Cox 1911: 47.

Most chaukidars, however, continued to be drawn from the Dusadh caste. As an 1893 report explained, it was "difficult to induce men of good caste to accept owing to past traditions."[92] Subsequent accounts described scattered successes in Bihar: 16 Rajputs recruited in Saran; 1 Rajput in Champaran, 1 Bhumihar Brahmin and 1 Rajput in Muzaffarpur; 50, 16, and 21 men of higher caste in Gaya, Shahabad, and Darbhanga, respectively. Saran's enlistment drive was especially successful. But the 210 higher-caste men recruited in 1895 were only secured after the magistrate ordered that all future vacancies were to be filled by high castes. Where chaukidar panchayets failed to nominate "qualified" candidates, the police had to shoulder the burden. As a result, success was registered in the official report for 1895, which declared that "the traditional objections of Rajputs and others were overcome, until in the end even *Army Pensioners* have come forward and some several disciplined old soldiers wearing medals may be seen in chaukidar's uniform at the weekly muster parades."[93] These were the men on whom government pinned its hopes for a "strong and serviceable village Police system . . . which will go far to break up the old chaukidari thieving organ and be a valuable intelligence and preventive medium."[94]

However, this approach also failed to strengthen British links with the chaukidars. Moreover, there was opposition to such a recruitment strategy at the highest reaches of government: "In Bengal . . . it may undoubtedly be well to secure the services of the more respectable castes and classes. But the menial classes, as village servants, are more amenable to orders and ordinarily maintain better watch and ward than the higher castes. Even members of the criminal classes ought not to be rejected if they are induced to settle down to an honest life. . . ."[95]

Like patwaris, chaukidars were never adequately subordinated to the interests of government. Nevertheless, governmental efforts came much closer to the mark, because they were tied in with its local administration, namely, the police. Better success also stemmed from the fact that chaukidars were primarily menial servants and not crucial links who had to be severed from their already existing roles in networks of power and control. Yet, in spite of repeated reform attempts in the nineteenth and early twentieth centuries, chaukidars served, at best, two masters, because they were never completely detached from the networks of estate and village controls.[96]

The history of *qanungos*, patwaris, and chaukidars in Saran reveals a British Raj with fragile extensions into local society. No doubt, these connections were flimsy because the colonial system of rule relied heavily on local allies and

92. GOB to Commr. of Patna, May 3, 1893, no. 32J-D, P.C. Gen. *Basta* no. 308, 1893.
93. "Police Administration Report for 1895, Patna Division," ibid., no. 313, 1896.
94. Ibid.
95. *Parliamentary Papers* (Commons), 1905, vol. 57, Cmnd. 2478, 1905: 33.
96. Thus, they provided an easy target for the Civil Disobedience Movement of the 1930s (Henningham 1979: 60–77).

because of the state's imperial considerations. Because the Raj enjoyed a monopoly of coercive powers, it could afford to spread its power thinly across rural areas. Therefore, its repeated, but half-hearted, attempts to establish links to the subdistrict levels by reorganizing the *qanungos*, patwaris, and chaukidars consistently failed, and, by the late nineteenth century, it was too late to arrest the tendency of local control institutions to be organized by estate and village systems of control.

Thus, the efforts to revitalize *qanungo*-patwari connections were blocked by an already existing system of informal control emanating from landholders' estates, while the experiments with chaukidars faced not only the network of estates, but also that of village society. Government's inability to incorporate these officials in its own administrative apparatus was proof that local control systems lay beyond its circle of power. Linkages between the British Raj and the Saran raiyat were defined by the networks of estate and village systems of control. Whether viewed from the perspective of government's relations with its allies or from the angle of its control institutions, British rule in Saran was a Limited Raj in the nineteenth and early twentieth centuries.

PART III

Estate Control and Management Systems

6

Between Raja and Raiyat: The Structures of Control in the Great Estate of Hathwa

"Everybody went to Hathwa."[1] Epitomized in this statement by a former district magistrate is an acknowledgment of the maharaja of Hathwa as the leading British connection and the major local controller in Saran. Without "Hutwa's cheer," as generations of Soneporeans knew, one could not be "the man for Chupra." Such appreciation was also intended to lavish praise on what, in the late nineteenth and early twentieth centuries, was widely termed in government records "an admirably managed estate."[2] This acclaim was not aimed, however, at highlighting a model estate of a "great and improving" landholder, but at recognizing its effective system of control and, particularly, its apparatus of rent collection.

Hathwa was a focal point, especially during the religious festival of *Dashara* that marked the beginning of the agricultural year and was celebrated by "the offering of presents and congratulations by the tenants." For the European guests, the occasion included a formal audience with the maharaja and a variety of social events: "The party is wound up with a magnificent elephant [ride] and a reception . . . on the night when the guests are entertained with nautches [dances] and fireworks."[3]

This event mirrored Hathwa's close relations with the British Raj, but it was also intended to manifest its kingly style. As the official history of the Hathwa family observes, Maharaja Sir Krishna Pratap Sahi Bahadur K.C.I.E., who held the estate between 1876 and 1896, wore on these occasions, "a tunic

---

1. Interview with Arthur Hugh Kemp, June 3, 1973.
2. Offg. Secy. E. W. Collin. BOR, to Commr., no. 336W, July 16, 1898, Bengal Rev. Procs., Sept.–Oct. 1899, Sept., no. 92.
3 D. N. Dutt 1909: 53–54.

embroidered with gold and pearls ... a richly ornamental sword ... his tunic and turbans are resplendent with jewels of great value."[4] He built a new palace, which included a durbar hall "glittering with ... crystal chandeliers, with its painted door-panes bearing Shakespearean characters, and its walls hung with oil-paintings of all the crowned heads of Europe and two big life-size portraits—one of the late Queen Empress Victoria and the other of himself attended with his faithful Dewan."[5]

Although the pattern of this conspicuous consumption was embroidered with British motifs in the nineteenth century, *Dashara* remained an event celebrated in Hathwa to signify the raja's primacy over his raiyats because not only did this festival signal the beginning of a new year in the agricultural calendar of the region, but it was also the period in which tenants paid the first installment of their rent. And, as if to stamp upon them from the outset their inferior status in relation to the raja, this initial payment of 6/16 share of the total rent represented the single largest amount for the year; the eight monthly payments that followed demanded shares of only 6/64 each. No rent was tendered in the remaining three months.[6]

As in other great zamindaris, *Dashara* at Hathwa was an occasion that defined the community demarcated by its "little kingdom" and graced by the kingly presence of its raja. By assembling to receive the darshan (blessings) of their raja, tenants articulated the common order to which they all belonged. This ritual performance also included the distribution of turbans to the village headmen (*jeth*-raiyats), a ceremony that identified the hierarchical order of the relationship between raja and raiyats. In authorizing and confirming the headmen's primacy in the smaller domain of the village, the Hathwa raj proclaimed its monopoly over all sources of power in the estate. Along with the insignia, the raja distributed money, generally four to eight rupees, to the village headmen and sweets to the rest of the villagers.[7] Thus, the festivities of *Dashara* defined, on the one hand, as reflected in its rituals of hegemony, the subordination of raiyats to their raja; and, on the other, with its exchanges of presents and honors, the estate structure that bound them together in a single community.[8] The Hathwa-owned newspaper, *The Express*, describes *Dashara*:

Pre-eminently a Kshattrya festival, people of all castes and classes observe the ceremonies and perform the Puja in some way or other. In Bihar, scions of old baronial

4. Ibid.
5. G. N. Dutt 1905: 23. See also Metcalf (1979: 345–75), for a description of the *Dashara* durbar in U.P.
6. G. J. S. Hodgkinson, Mgr., Court of Wards, Hathwa, to J. S. Drummond, Colltr., Saran, May 1, 1872, P.C. *Basta* no. 103, Monthly Bundles, Gen. Dept. from Colltr. of Saran to Patna Commr., 1870–75, no. 80 of 1872–73.
7. F. M. Halliday, Colltr., Tirhut to Commr., Patna, Sept. 2, 1872, ibid., no. 220, Important Bundles, Rev. Dept.; D. N. Dutt 1909: 53–54.
8. Two good general statements on the structure of ritual exchanges are Mauss (1974) and Sahlins (1972). See also Dirks (1979) and Price (1979).

houses and big Zamindars that have the status and position of Rajas ... observe the Puja and perform all the ceremonies in the same way as do the Ruling Chiefs and Princes, and march in state ... with great pomp and splendour.

... the observance of this festival is of great use and value even now to all Hindus, rich or poor, high or low.... It creates a sense of amity, unity and good feeling between the several classes and castes inhabiting a certain place.[9]

This pattern of ritual exchanges on the occasion of *Dashara* lay embedded in an efficient system of estate control and management. That the local representative of the British Raj was joined by the estate's raiyats at Hathwa was thus merely an articulation of the apparatus of control that asserted the primacy of the raja in the locality.

The Estate of Hathwa

Territory, population, and income all endowed the Hathwa raj with the dimensions of a great estate (table 7). Comprising 127 mahals (revenue estates) scattered across several districts, its 1,365 villages grew to 1,443 by 1897–1898. Although its population remained fairly constant in the late nineteenth century (slightly over 390,000), its net income increased substantially from Rs. 689,144 in 1873–1874 to over Rs. 850,000 by 1903–1904.[10]

Despite its enormous size, the Hathwa raj was not a geographically dispersed estate. Its major part, occupied by over 350,000 people, lay entirely in pargana

Table 7.
Hathwa Raj's Property, 1873–1874

	Number of villages	Approximate area (acres)	Estimated population of villages	Gross government revenue (Rs.)	Gross rental (Rs.)
Saran	1,319	360,515	372,500	172,655	817,636
Champaran	23	16,000	10,000	8,372	34,780
Tirhut	5	4,500	3,500	1,356	7,500
Shahabad	15	8,500	5,000	10,241	19,704
Gorakhpur	3	500	350	897	1,592
Patna	—	—	—	—	1,453
Total	1,365	390,015	391,350	193,521	882,665

Source: "Management of the Hutwa Estate during 1873–74," Bengal Rev. Procs., April 1873 to 1875, Aug. 1874, nos. 2–3.

9. Oct. 24, 1915, reprinted in Chowdhary (1920: 89–90).
10. "Return of the Management of the Estate of Hutwa Raj for the year ending 31st March 1904," H.R. *Bastas*, 1904; "Report on Management of Hathwa Raj for 1897–98," P.C. *Basta* no. 166, Court of Wards, Hathwa Estate.

Kalyanpur Kuari, most of which it owned, and in half of Sipah, or, according to thana boundaries, four-fifths of Gopalganj subdivision. This area, a compact block of 550 square miles in the northwest of the district, gained additional geographical coherence from the fact that its holdings in these two parganas were primarily in the form of entire villages.[11] (See map 4.)

Map 4. Hathwa Raj Parganas.

Such compactness was a valuable asset in developing and maintaining an effective system of control. As P. J. Musgrave observes in his study of Uttar Pradesh estates:

The social power of a landlord is likely to be stronger in a tightly knit, coherent geographical unit where he is the sole rais, the sole source of social status ... than where there are a number of alternative sources of glory. But, perhaps more importantly, the economic position of the landlord is likely to be stronger in a situation where he is the

11. In other words, they were sixteen-annas villages; sixteen annas equal 1 rupee, or 100 percent. In other areas, its villages were usually held jointly with other proprietors. See Colltr. W. C. Macpherson to Commr., no. 2495W, March 13, 1898, Bengal Rev. Procs., Sept. to Oct. 1899, Sept., no. 91.

sole supplier over a large area of the basic commodity of rural society, land, than in one in which there are a number of potential suppliers.[12]

Not surprisingly, the weakest links in Hathwa's system of control were to its fifteen villages in Shahabad. These holdings were at a considerable distance from headquarters, and also they were recent acquisitions received as a reward for services rendered during the 1857 Mutiny/Rebellion, and the former property of a "rebel," where the "ryots were . . . disposed to give trouble."[13] Most of the vast estate, however, was closely integrated into the system of control operating out of Hathwa and its contiguous villages.

Hathwa became the hub of the great estate at the turn of the nineteenth century when the zamindari of Huseypur devolved on the cadet line of the family because of Fateh Sahi's rebellion. The shift to Hathwa was initiated by Chatterdhari Sahi in 1802, when, on attaining his majority, he acquired the estate and left Bharathui. At Hathwa he established a fort and a palace, and surrounded them with a moat because the threat of attack from Fateh Sahi and other "banditti" still loomed large.[14]

Under the supportive hand of the British, the Hathwa raj emerged as a great estate. And as the power of the state grew, it adjusted to the new conditions precipitated "by the suppression of open violence and the turning of individual and group struggle into a battle for land rights through the courts. . . ."[15] Indicative of its transition into this new era was its fort, which fell into disrepair and was replaced by the new symbols of its authority—the Hathwa palace and the *kachcheri*.[16] Hathwa and its contiguous villages were also the site of a local market and a sizable temple: together these institutions represented the core of a control complex that extended a variety of formal and informal, social, economic, and religious networks into the farthest reaches of the great estate.

The raj's residential palace, the seat of the maharaja, lay in Hathwa village. Another palace stood in the adjacent village of Gopalpur (map 5), which was also the site of the quarters of the raj hospital's assistant surgeons and the estate *amla* (officials or retainers). Except for the barbers, most of Gopalpur's inhabitants were of high social status. Many were the maharaja's fellow castemen, Bhumihar Brahmins. Others were of social backgrounds that identify the estate's important functionaries: Bengalis, Kayasths, and Muslims.[17] On the other hand, Manni Chapra (no. 1009), where the estate's menial servants came from, had no high-caste inhabitants.[18] A similar compo-

---

12. Musgrave 1972: 261; Metcalf 1979: 270.
13. S. C. Bayley, Offg. Commr., Patna, to Secy., BOR, no. 112W, Aug. 27, 1872, Bengal Rev. Procs., Oct.–Dec. 1872, Oct., no. 155. Similar problems existed in the "periphery" of other great estates (Henningham 1983: 47).   14. D. N. Dutt 1909: 22.   15. Stokes 1978: 35.
16. The towers of the palace and the spires of the temple are clearly visible in the locality of Hathwa. According to D. N. Dutt (1909: 49), they can be seen from three miles away.
17. Hathwa and Gopalpur villages, Mirganj thana nos. 1008 and 1011, SVN.
18. Mirganj thana no. 1009, SVN.

sition of people inhabited Piper Panti (no. 1007) and Rupanchak (no. 1025); they worked as peons and servants of the estate.[19]

To the northeast of Hathwa stood Ratanchak (no. 1012), from where the estate's administrative networks extended out to the raj villages. In addition to the *kachcheri*, the estate manager's bungalow, the diwan's house, the Hathwa Eden School, the post office, the raj dispensary, and the Gopalmandir (a temple consecrated to Radha and Krishna) were situated here.[20] It is also significant that the branch family of Hathwa resided in this village—uncomfortably close to the seat of the maharaja and within reach of scrutiny.[21]

Together the palace and the *kachcheri* epitomized the superstructure of the Hathwa control system, which was embodied in the person of the maharaja, his close relatives and retainers, and the manager of the estate. As far as can be ascertained from government and estate records, all the Hathwa maharajas in the nineteenth and early twentieth centuries, save one, took an active interest

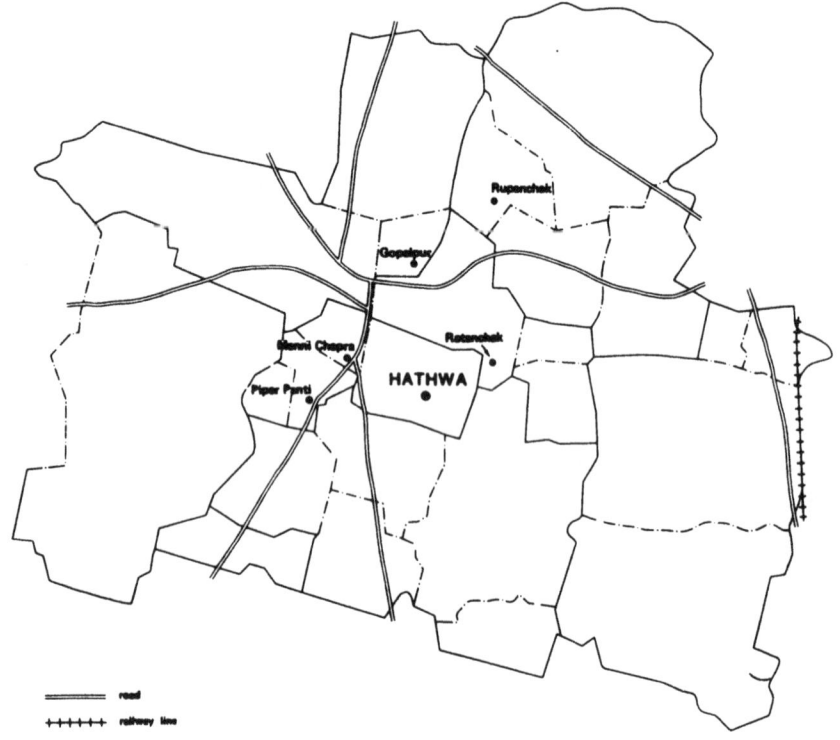

Map 5. The Core Villages of Hathwa Estate.

19. Mirganj thana nos. 1007 and 1025, SVN.
20. Ratanchak village, Mirganj thana no. 1012, SVN.
21. Both branches of the Hathwa family apparently watched each other with some degree of circumspection. One member of the family was said to have expended large amounts of money to keep track of the minor maharaja and the maharani ("Confidential Report of Faujdar Kurmi versus Madan Gopal Sowar," [1900?], H.R. *Bastas*, 1899–1900).

in the operations of the estate. In the case of the exception, the maharaja's mother assumed most of the management responsibilities.[22]

The great estate's presence was not confined to the locality of Hathwa. It also had palaces in the district and regional headquarters towns of Chapra and Patna, respectively, as well as other residences in Banaras, Calcutta, and the hill station of Kurseong in Darjeeling district.[23]

Hathwa and its contiguous villages also formed the economic core of the estate's control system. G. William Skinner's seminal study of rural marketing in China has paved the way to understanding delimited areas of informal control in which "transport, trade, artisan industry, and credit were all structured within it spatially according to the principle of centrality and temporally by the periodicity of its market days."[24] The village of Hathwa was a nodal point for such a marketing cell. Its role in the locality was reflected in its diversified population of four thousand, and its description as one-fourth agriculturalist and three-fourths in the raj's service or retail trade.[25] Again, to follow Skinner's lead, Hathwa was a "standard market," which "provided for the exchange of goods produced within the market's dependent area ... [and] was the starting point for the upward flow of agricultural products and craft items into higher reaches of the marketing system, and also the termination of the downward flow of imported items destined for peasant consumption."[26] The standard market of Hathwa serviced several neighboring villages (see map 5); it had two retail cloth shops, eleven confectioners, three dyers, eight tailors, four betel sellers, twenty-five rope makers, fifteen dealers in grains, and one in hemp and opium. The estate collected Rs. 1,400 per year in professional tax from these traders.[27]

The marketing community of Hathwa was, however, only a subsystem in a larger marketing complex. Although dominant socially, the village was linked to Mirganj, an intermediate market, two and one-half miles away, in a complementary economic relationship (see map 5). Whereas Mirganj's shops were open on Tuesday and Friday, Hathwa's marketing days were Sunday and Thursday.[28] This interrelationship was also manifested by communications links between the two villages. The so-called Hathwa railway station was in

---

22. Maharaja Guru Madhadevasram Prasad Sahi was said to be "inactive" in estate affairs and a "very religious man." Interviews with Maharaja Kumar Brajeshwar Prasad Sahi, Dec. 1973, and Arthur Hugh Kemp. For the "official" history of the family, see D. N. Dutt (1909: 27–48).   23. D. N. Dutt 1909: 63.
24. 1971: 272. Also see Skinner (1964) and Bayly (1983, chap. 3).
25. Hathwa village, Mirganj thana no. 1008, SVN.
26. In Skinner's classification of administrative and economic centers, a hierarchical series exists, ranging from a minor market to a regional city; in between there are the standard, the intermediate and the central markets (1964: 6–9).
27. Hathwa village, SVN. Saran zamindars generally collected *choongee* (a small cess) from persons who used their land for business (Offg. Commr. Bayley to GOB, Jdcl., no. 336R, Aug. 17, 1872, Bengal Jdcl. Procs., 1873–74, June 1873, 80). Zamindari control of markets was also an important means of estate dominance in South India (Baker 1976: 14–15).
28. *SDG, 1930*: app., table 5. Also see Skinner (1964: 10–16).

Mirganj, as were the police station and subregistry office for the locality. Mirganj also offered a greater range of services: its market included seventeen retail cloth shops, nineteen grain stores, three metal dealers, six in spices, twenty in pulses, six confectioners, ten oil shops, seven in miscellaneous commodities, eleven silkmakers, twelve tailors, seven meat butchers, three ghee (clarified butter) shops, four in iron, twelve jewelers, and four betel sellers. Cattle were also sold. In addition, Mirganj was an entrepot for grain from the north and the northwest, which was then exported to Patna and elsewhere. Several Patna merchants had agents here for linseed, cotton, and *gur* (unrefined sugar).[29]

Hathwa was also the focus of the marketing community because of its roads, temples, and schools. The central religious edifice, Gopalmandir, housing the images of Radha and Krishna, was said to be "the largest temple in Behar ... planned and built at a cost of four lacs of rupees."[30] At Thawe, nine miles from Hathwa, a place associated with the legend of an earlier maharaja, the estate supported a temple dedicated to Durga. Another temple, the Sivalaya, was attached to its Banaras residence and consecrated to Shiva. In this holy city, the estate also maintained a shelter where a number of religious mendicants were fed.[31]

Hathwa's religious identity was further expressed in the personal life-style of the family. The authorized history of Hathwa characterized Sir Krishna Pratap Sahi Bahadur, the maharaja between 1874 and 1896:

> He had the heart of an ascetic. Soon after he was installed on the *Gadi*, he set out on a pilgrimage to the shrines of Northern India and travelled through almost the whole of India. Later on he used to pass a portion of the year in travelling and pilgrimage, mostly, in Benares where he had the associations of the Pandits and learned Sadhus, and built palatial buildings, temples, *Chetras* [shelters] endowing in perpetuity suitable sums for their maintenance, and had the reservoir of the image in the Biswanath Temple thickly plated with silver at a great cost.[32]

Hathwa's role as the guardian of orthodoxy was also seen in its major support of traditional education. The village of Machhagarpatti Jagdish (no. 1010) had both a Hathwa school and a Sanskrit *patshala* (school). There were two upper primary and nine lower primary schools sponsored by Hathwa in other parts of its estate. According to one report, there were as many as forty-four schools supported fully or partly by the estate.[33] And just as Hathwa's Durbar Hall and *Dashara* festivities manifested its pivotal role in both British

---

29. Mirganj village, Mirganj thana no. 1021, SVN; *SDG, 1930*: 148.
30. D. N. Dutt 1909: 50. An "estate" of eight villages and a rental of over Rs. 26,000 were set aside to subsidize this temple ("Report on Hathwa Raj for 1897–98").
31. D. N. Dutt 1909: 35–36, 55; G. N. Dutt 1905: 21–22.
32. D. N. Dutt 1909: 35. Rs. 50,000 was spent annually by the estate for religious purposes (ibid.: 63).
33. "Management of the Hutwa Estate during 1873–74," Bengal Rev. Procs., July 1873 to 1875, Aug. 1874, nos. 2–3; Machhagarpatti Jagdish village, Mirganj thana no. 1010, SVN.

and indigenous societies, so too did its patronage of Indian and English education. Its most prominent English school was the Hathwa Eden School in Ratanchak (no. 1012), named after Lieutenant-Governor Sir Ashley Eden, who laid its foundation stone in 1879.[34]

These institutions were not the sole recipients of Hathwa's "politics of charity." Donations and subscriptions extended its largess to a wide range of causes. Typical were its contributions in 1897–1898, to several medical dispensaries and English and vernacular schools in Saran and other districts.[35] The donations of the maharani of Hathwa were so generous that she was awarded a Kaisar-i-Hind Gold Medal. Her contributions included Rs. 100,000 to the Relief Fund of 1902; Rs. 100,000 to the Victoria Memorial; Rs. 50,000 to the Lady Dufferin Victoria Zenana Hospital in Calcutta; Rs. 50,000 to the Victoria Memorial Scholarship Fund for training midwives; Rs. 40,000 to the Ranchi College Fund; and endowments to such varied causes as the war effort in South Africa and the coronations of Edward VII and George V.[36]

These activities reveal the crucial hinge position the Hathwa raj occupied between government and the local society. It was cosseted by the British under whose protective umbrella it flourished, but it also commanded the deference of its raiyats over whom it wielded considerable control and influence. In the nineteenth and early twentieth centuries, this role as the great estate of the district and the region was maintained and enhanced by its skillful fashioning of an effective management system.

The Estate Bureaucracy

Hathwa raj's control complex rested on a solid foundation provided by a management system that closely resembled British administration at the district level. As the district officer was the hub of all activity in the official administration, so was the estate manager in the zamindari bureaucracy. This replication of the government model had been effected during the course of three tenures under the Court of Wards, beginning with an initial term at the turn of the nineteenth century, from 1871 and 1874, and from 1896 to 1911.

In 1791 the great estate was organized in a relatively simple structure consisting of a manager assisted by several petty officials—three writers, one *podar* (cashier), six village clerks, ten peons, and one public pleader. The Hathwa family had recently acquired the zamindari from the "rebel" senior

---

34. Ratanchak village, SVN; "Report on Hathwa Raj for 1897–98." On ties between education and zamindari patronage, see Hagen (1981: 391–99).
35. "Report on Hathwa Raj for 1897–98."
36. *The Hutwa Raj Family* 1914: 7–8. The model of an "enlightened zamindar" who supported a wide range of indigenous and British causes was followed by other great landholders (Jha 1972: 110–48; Metcalf 1979: 352–55).

branch, so they first had to consolidate their hold over the key positions in the estate administration.[37]

Thereafter, the estate's administrative structure grew both in complexity and size. By 1872 the manager presided over a staff of twenty people. It continued to expand as Hathwa assumed a central position in local society. Thus, estate managers, in the words of one Hathwa official, had to take on the additional responsibility of maintaining the symbols of glory, such "important matters other than the management of the landed property, viz., buildings, gardens, stables, charities, religious endowments, etc., etc."[38] By the 1890s the manager received additional support from two assistant and two subassistant managers, and the central management staff, which numbered twenty in 1872, swelled to over one hundred in 1899. This development was the result of both an enlargement of the estate's formal administrative apparatus and an increase in size to accommodate the growing complexities of management. Other changes created specialized departments.[39]

These changes were accompanied by the introduction of new personnel to the estate's key management positions. Impetus came from the Court of Wards tenure of 1871-1874 when professional administration was introduced to Hathwa, and Europeans and Bengalis were recruited to staff the new bureaucracy. These outsiders clearly differed from former estate personnel, who were powerful men in their own right and often used their positions to advance their own networks of control and patronage. The takeover by the Court of Wards in this period led to the removal of Chaudhur Lal, the granduncle of the first president of independent India, Rajendra Prasad, who had been diwan for over a quarter of a century. In part the change in personnel was intended to bring in English-speaking Indians; a more important consideration, though, was to usher in a professional bureaucracy to run the estate.[40]

Hathwa's top officials in the nineteenth and early twentieth centuries were conspicuously lacking in local anchorage, but they enjoyed a close working relationship with the Hathwa family. Under the lead of the Dutt family, who dominated the important administrative positions in the Hathwa ruling machinery, the estate's management often appeared to be largely a Bengali enterprise. (Many of the Hathwa maharajas spoke Bengali.) By the 1890s Bengalis occupied all the major positions below that of the estate manager, A. M. Markham.[41]

37. A. Montgomerie, Colltr., Saran, to BOR, Dec. 8, 1791, Bengal BOR Consltns., Wards, April 3, 1792.
38. M. Buskin, Mgr., H.R., to Colltr., no. 1981, Feb. 21, 1898, Bengal Rev. Procs., Sept. to Oct. 1899, Sept., no. 91 (encl.).
39. A. M. Markham, Mgr., H.R., to Colltr., no. 240, April 26, 1899, ibid., no. 94 (encl.), app. D.
40. Rajendra Prasad 195?: 1-3. Also see Rudolph and Rudolph with Singh (1975: 717-53).
41. See "Report on Management of the Hathwa Raj, 1897-98." See also Lal Behari Basu, "Life of Devendra Nath Dutt" (MS, 1923) and K. W. Jones (1966: 376-95) on the spread of Bengalis to other provinces to take up coadjutor roles.

Between the Dutts and Hathwa family, there was both an official and personal relationship that lasted well into the twentieth century. The beginnings of the Dutt-Hathwa connection can be traced to the Court of Wards tenure of 1871–1874 (fig. 2). A strong relationship developed almost immediately when Maharaja Krishna Pratap Sahi, who was a minor under government charge when the first Dutt entered Hathwa service, came to regard Bhubaneshwar Dutt as his "father."[42] This deep, personal tie also underscored the maharani's support of Devendranath in 1898 when the Court of Wards sought his removal as assistant manager. So did his plea to remain as diwan and head of the maharani's household:

> The varied and conflicting interest existing [in] the Raj, and the Court intrigues and secret conspiracies inseparable in native Rajes like this, especially where the head of the household is only a lady, and above all considering the delicate health of the minor Maharaja.... You are well aware of the nature of work I have done during the last eight months ... I have to get up twice and sometimes thrice in the night to see the minor Maharaja and the guards around him.[43]

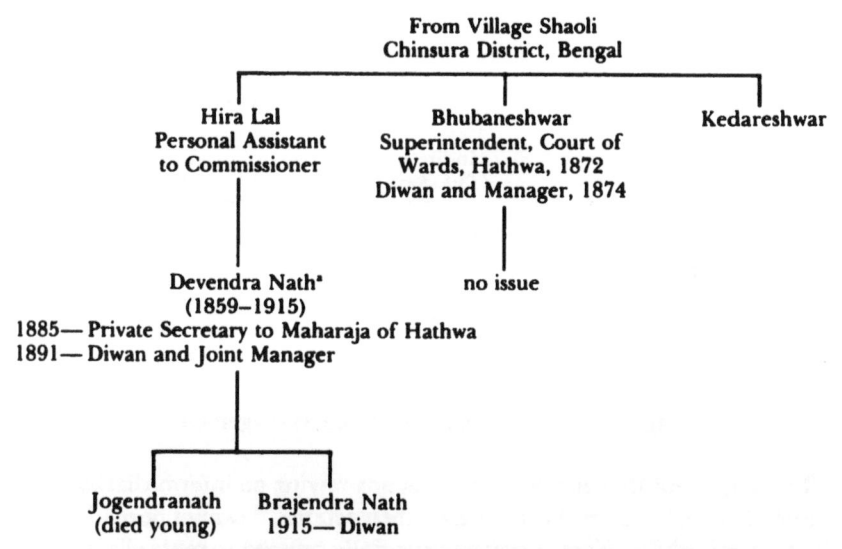

```
                    From Village Shaoli
                    Chinsura District, Bengal
        ┌──────────────────┼──────────────────┐
   Hira Lal            Bhubaneshwar         Kedareshwar
Personal Assistant   Superintendent, Court of
to Commissioner       Wards, Hathwa, 1872
                     Diwan and Manager, 1874
        │                    │
   Devendra Nath*         no issue
    (1859–1915)
1885— Private Secretary to Maharaja of Hathwa
1891— Diwan and Joint Manager
        │
   ┌────┴─────┐
Jogendranath  Brajendra Nath
(died young)  1915— Diwan
```

Fig. 2. The Role of the Dutt Family in Hathwa Management.

Although new people were recruited to fill many staff positions, some posts remained sinecures. The raj's principal officials usually gained rank through their families' long-standing association with Hathwa. The raj's two *sarishtadars*

---

42. Basu MS, 1923. Many Hathwa maharajas thereafter spoke Bengali. Interview with Maharaja Kumar Brajeshwar Prasad Sahi of Hathwa.
43. Devendranath Dutt, Diwan and 2nd Asst. Mgr., to Mgr., H.R., March 4, 1899, Bengal Rev. Procs., April to June 1899, no. 2.

(head ministerial officers), for instance, were described as the "descendants of the formei *dewan* and *naibs* [head and deputy officers] of the Raj and have been in the Raj service for generations."[44] Nevertheless, unlike estates where managers and retainers systematically intercepted much of the proprietor's wealth and power, the central management in the Hathwa raj formed a remarkably effective superstructure.

The Systems of Management

Control over the estate's villages was exercised primarily through two different systems of rent collection: directly (*khas* or *sir*) or indirectly (*thikadari*), through intermediaries (fig. 3 and table 8). Before the introduction of the "circle" system at the turn of the twentieth century, the bulk of the estate was in lease to *thikadars*. As the Hathwa manager stated in 1898, "the thikadari system has all along been the rule, and the direct collection system [*khas*] the exception in this estate."[45]

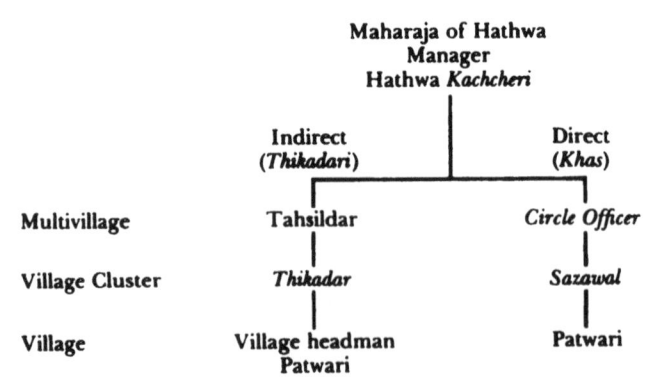

```
                          Maharaja of Hathwa
                              Manager
                          Hathwa Kachcheri
                  Indirect              Direct
                 (Thikadari)            (Khas)

Multivillage      Tahsildar          Circle Officer

Village Cluster   Thikadar              Sazawal

Village        Village headman         Patwari
                  Patwari
```

Fig. 3. The Structure of Hathwa Management.

The argument that management systems relying on intermediaries meant landlords with "little real control over their estates"[46] cannot be made for the Hathwa raj, whose *thikadari* system essentially referred to rent collectors with closely defined powers. The process of subordination of the estate's *thikadars* was initiated by the Court of Wards in the late eighteenth century when it moved to consolidate the power of the new British connection by curbing their

44. Markham to Colltr., no. 240, April 26, 1899, ibid., Sept. 1899, no. 94.
45. Buskin to Colltr., no. 1981, Feb. 21, 1898, ibid., no. 91 (encl.).
46. Musgrave 1972: 267. He also states that "rural power in nineteenth-century India might be seen as being with the estate managers and their cronies" (ibid.: 270). See also Henningham (1983: 49–55) for a view that takes issue with Musgrave; and Musgrave (1983: 56–57). Apposite here are also Metcalf (1979: chaps. 9–10); Palit (1975).

Table 8.
Indirect and Direct Management Systems in the Hathwa Raj, 1874–1898

System	Number of villages (percent)		Gross Receipts in rupees (percent)	
	1874	1898[a]	1874	1898
Thikadari				
Indian	958(70)	729(50)	602,081(68)	471,467(42)
Indigo planters	116 (9)	226(16)	110,616(13)	242,003(21)
Khas (Sir)	204(15)	495(34)	162,145(18)	413,054(37)
Perpetual	60 (4)		7,824 (1)	
Rentfree	27 (2)			
Total	1,365	1,450	882,666	1,126,524

Sources: For 1874 figures, see "Management of the Hathwa Estate during 1873–74," Bengal Rev. Procs., April 1873 to 1875, Aug. 1874, nos. 2–3. For 1898, see M. Buskin, Mgr., H.R. to Colltr., no. 1981, Feb. 21, 1898, Bengal Rev. Procs., Sept. 1899, no. 91 (encl.).
[a] Figures for 1898 do not include villages leased in perpetuity or rentfree.

rights as intermediaries.[47] Some rent collectors were removed because their loyalties were believed to lie with the rebel branch of the family; in other instances, the rents demanded were increased, forcing a few to abscond and others to default and be confined; in still other cases, the estate assumed direct control, turning *thikadari* areas into *khas* property.[48]

The Hathwa *thikadari* system served the interests of the estate effectively. To use the description profferred by one estate manager:

Ticcadars do not hold an independent position in the village, subject only to the payment of rent. The rights of the landlord as regards the tenants are not made over to them absolutely. They have acted in some respects more as servants and tehsildars [rent collectors] of the raj than as ticcadars. They assessed the jumma [rentals] of the village upon the ryots, raising their rent from time to time to meet the beshee or increased demand made by the Rajah upon the village. Cases against ryots were very generally conducted with the permission and pecuniary assistance of the Rajah. His influence was, on the complaint of the ticcadars, brought to bear upon refractory ryots.[49]

Supervised by tahsildars, Hathwa *thikadars* also worked closely with the *kachcheri* staff headed by the superintendent. Tahsildars were expected to submit monthly accounts and report cases of overdue collections. Prior to the

47. Mahtah Radakishen, Mgr., estate of Chatterdary Sah, to BOR, n.d., Bengal BOR Procs., Wards, Jan. 3 to April 20, 1798, March 27, no. 8.
48. N. Stuart, Colltr., Saran, to Thomas Graham, Acting Pres. &c., BOR, Nov. 29, 1800, and Translation of petition presented by Chatterdhary Sahee, n.d., op. cit., Jan. 2 to April 21, 1801, Jan. 20, nos. 4–5.
49. "Management of the Hutwa Raj," no. A, Feb. 20, 1872, Bengal Rev. Procs., April 1872, no. 149.

reorganization of the Hathwa establishment by the Court of Wards, however, the tahsildar's staff depended "rather in the proportion of the favor and influence the tehsildar could obtain with the late superintendent, Chowdhoor Lal, than to the amount of collection or actual work of collection."[50]

The raj, divided into twelve tahsildaris, was in the charge of nine individuals (table 9). But, as the number of thikadari villages decreased and as the control superstructure grew in size and sophistication, the number of tahsildars was reduced. Finally in the 1890s, the tahsildars and *khas* circle superintendent were merged into one person. In 1898 three circles were established: Hathwa, Sripur, and Hajipur.[51]

Table 9.

Tahsildars in the Hathwa Raj, 1872

Tahsildari	Tahsildar	Amount collected (Rs.)	Cost of establishment[a]
Kuryat Nisf	Sitaram Singh	56,955	676
Bhorey	Raghunath Prasad Singh, nephew of Sitaram Singh	39,163	597
Kuryat Nisf	Raghunandan Singh	49,958	499
Sipah Nisf	Raghunandan Singh	39,721	800
Bagahi	Raghunandan Singh	23,650	317
Pachdevri	Nihal Khan	31,638	375
Dhoboul	Nihal Khan	36,621	306
Marhal	Ramdihar Misra	32,907	639
Thawe	Rajkumar Singh	41,958	430
Sipah Nisf	Ganga Prasad Singh	47,482	606
Dhangarhi	Paryag Rai	37,389	370
Afradh	Sheotahal Rai	56,795	529
Total		494,237	6,144

Source: "Management of the Hutwa Raj, 1871–72," Bengal Rev. Procs., April 1872, no. 149.
[a] Costs in 1870–1871.

Tahsildars were of different castes and communities (table 9), but usually recruited from families with long-standing ties to the estate. Udant Rai, for instance, was appointed tahsildar of pargana Sipah at the turn of the eighteenth century as a reward for his services during the internecine fighting between the two branches of the Hathwa family. His successors remained in office until 1857. The petition of Gopal Prasad Sinha in 1899 recounts a similar background: "My ancestors were employed as Tehsildars in the Hathwa Raj under

50. "Management of Hutwa during 1873–74."
51. Buskin to Colltr., no. 1981, Feb. 21, 1898, Bengal Rev. Procs., Sept. 1899, no. 91.

the several managers from several generations past, and as a matter of fact, I inherited this work and tried to carry out the work with as great caution as my predecessors had always done."[52]

Indian *Thikadars*

Indian *thikadars* held the largest responsibility for the raj's villages and rent collection throughout most of the nineteenth century (see table 8). Their income was the difference between the gross amount they collected and the fixed rent they remitted to the raj treasury, plus village expenses. They also gained supplementary amounts from the land they held in cultivating possession (*ziraat*) at nominal rates in their leased villages. Many were also village moneylenders.[53] By the 1890s, their income was fixed as a commission, varying from 8 to 10 percent of their collections. They were required to deposit one-fourth of their annual rental as security.[54]

"Native" *thikadars* were village-level controllers. Their power and influence did not generally range far beyond their village boundaries, extending over the area defined by the periodic marketing system and above the village level (figure 3). In 1899 the lease of 642 villages was held by 328 persons.[55] A similar picture is offered by the village-by-village notes of 1893–1901 and 1916–1921. Details regarding 190 villages in Gopalganj thana belonging to the Hathwa raj show that few *thikadars* appear to have had any considerable supravillage importance.[56]

Most *thikadars* had deep roots in their local communities. Alakh Pandey, the leaseholder of Letaria village, was the descendant of the first settler, who had reclaimed the jungle and founded the village.[57] In the words of an 1874 Hathwa manager, the "great majority of them live in or close to the villages in which they hold in lease, and many of them have been ticcadars—father and son—for several generations. Sometimes a whole family claims shares in the lease in fixed proportions, and look upon it amongst themselves much in light of ancestral property."[58]

These descriptions contrast sharply with Musgrave's characterization of

---

52. Petition of Gopal Prasad Singh, Hajiapur village, to H.R., H.R. *Bastas*, 1899–1900. Tahsildars were apparently quite well off. The descendants of Udant Rai were described as the maliks of several villages and moneylenders; three of them were listed as worth Rs. 400,000 each (Bangra village, Gopalganj thana no. 149, SVN, 1893–1901).
53. "Management of Hutwa during 1873–74." For a similar characterization of *thikadars* in the Bettiah estate, see Mishra (1978: 65–69).
54. See Macpherson to Commr., no. 2495W, March 13, 1898, Bengal Rev. Procs., Sept. 1899, no. 91; "Management of the Hutwa Raj," ibid., April 1872, no. 149.
55. Commr. J. A. Bourdillon to Secy. BOR, no. 363W, Aug. 4, 1899, and Macpherson to Commr., no. 1 C.W., June 18, 1899, Bengal Rev. Procs., Sept. 1899, no. 94 and encl.
56. Gopalganj thana nos. 127–317, SVN, 1893–1901.
57. Letaria village, Mirganj thana no. 15, SVN.
58. "Management of Hathwa during 1873–74." See also Buskin to Colltr., no. 1981, Feb. 21, 1898, Bengal Rev. Procs., Sept. 1899, no. 91.

U.P. *thikadars* as "groups of financiers, frequently coming from the urban money-lending and grain-trading groups, who in return for paying the correct amount of rent in cash, in advance, were allowed a free hand in the management of the estates."[59] On the contrary, many Hathwa *thikadars* were, as estate records reveal, "residents" and "hereditary." Both characterizations correctly emphasize the local anchorage of these rent collectors. Moreover, many of the "nonresident" *thikadars* lived close to, but not within, their leased villages. The different classifications of Hathwa's *thikadars* are given in table 10.

Table 10.
Origins of Hathwa's *Thikadars*, 1898

	Hereditary			Nonhereditary			Total		
	Resident	Nonresident	Total	Resident	Nonresident	Total	Resident	Nonresident	Total
Indian (non-amla)	48	7	55	94	149	243	142	156	298
Amla	9	6	15	1	14	15	10	20	30
Indigo planter	0	0	0	19	0	19	19	0	19

Source: A. M. Markham, Mgr., H.R., to Colltr., no. 240, April 26, 1899, Bengal Rev. Procs., Sept. 1899, no. 94 (encl.), app. 8.

The "hereditary" category requires additional explanation. Although *thikadars* were officially recognized as tenureholders, they enjoyed little legal standing, nor were their rights ensured by time-honored custom. A late nineteenth-century investigation of the estate's records traced the origins of hereditary *thikadars* only as far back as 1835. Although no significance was attached to this date, it probably demarcates the beginning of the nineteenth-century drive that led to the consolidation of the former cadet line as the maharajas of Hathwa. This interpretation is supported by the events leading up to the 1844 disturbances among the appointees of the different Hathwa lines.[60]

As far as the maharaja of Hathwa was concerned, the hereditary status could almost be qualified out of existence. His stance was familiar to the commissioner of Patna who reported that the maharaja opposed any "accrual of rights on his estate, except to himself. . . . My conclusion is that no hereditary rights exist—not even an ancient custom."[61] With no less certitude,

59. 1972: 266–67. Although Henningham (1983: 53–54) takes issue with Musgrave, his argument is based on the fact that bureaucratically managed estates were more centralized than those administered through the *thikadari* system.
60. Markham to Colltr., no. 240, April 24, 1899, Bengal Rev. Procs., Sept. 1899, no. 94 (encl.).
61. Bourdillon to Secy., no. 363W, Aug. 4, 1899, ibid., no. 94.

a Hathwa manager stated that *thikadars* who held leases for more than one generation did "so by reason of their good conduct . . . [and] by no sort of hereditary right whatsoever. Former Maharajas never showed any special consideration to any of these hereditary *thikadars*, except perhaps in the case of some favored amla or musaheb [retainer]."[62]

The subordination of Hathwa's Indian *thikadars* was also apparent in their lack of legal standing. Prior to 1879, only European *thikadars* received stamped and registered leases. When the estate came under government management, this policy was initially called into question,[63] but the Court of Wards explained away the official reservations. To quote the commissioner of Patna's paraphrase of the Hathwa manager: "without legal documents these ticcadars will be practically much more under the control of the Court of Wards."[64]

Similar considerations underlay the short duration of the leases, usually five to nine years:

> Shortness of the terms improves proprietor's disciplinary powers. It enables him to dispense with the services of an unsatisfactory Thikadar without the trouble of proceedings resembling those of a Trial, or the liability to be called to account in the Civil Court and it leaves it open to the proprietor to change the management under a village official into direct management under himself, and gives him the power of exercising this option at short intervals. On the other hand, it would appear that this system equally leaves it in his power to terminate leases capriciously, and to take fines on reappointments and for new appointments.[65]

Amla Thikadars

The thirty *thikadars* described as *amla* (see table 10) were estate officials or retainers who were also rent collectors. As in the case of the other Indian *thikadars*, their leases did not extend over sizable areas, their farming rentals ranging from Rs. 200 to Rs. 15,000. They received better commissions, however, than other *thikadars*; in some cases as much as 13 percent. "This favorable rate," the Hathwa manager reported in 1899, "used to be given them by the late Maharaja not only as an act of favour, but also in consideration of the generally low pay he gave them as amlas."[66]

Local men, *amlas* generally supervised "their native village and other villages around."[67] Since they worked in Hathwa, most were nonresidents. Nine of the thirty were listed as residents because their families lived in the leased villages.

62. Markham to Colltr., no. 240, April 26, 1899, ibid. (encl.).
63. Maharaja Krishna Protab Sahi of Hutwa to Colltr., no. 4A, July 21, 1879, ibid., Dec. 1879, nos. 73–78; Commr. R. P. Jenkins to Colltr., no. 232, March 1, 1872, ibid., Jan. to April 1872, April, no. 149.
64. Offg. Commr. Bayley to Colltr., no. 26, April 18, 1872, Beng. Rev. Procs., May to July 1872, June, no. 93.
65. Offg. Secy. E. M. Konstam, BOR, to Secy., GOB, no. 64, Sept. 28, 1898, ibid., Sept. to Oct. 1899, Sept., no. 90.
66. Buskin to Colltr., no. 1981, Feb. 21, 1898, ibid., no. 91.
67. Hodgkinson to Colltr., no. A, April 2, 1872, P.C. *Basta* no. 103.

In their absence, as one *amla thikadar* noted, their business was handled "by the brothers, nephews and other members of the joint family."[68]

Although Hathwa's *thikadari* system was regarded favorably by government, *amla* rent collectors were not. Therefore, during the Court of Wards tenures of the estate in the late nineteenth and early twentieth centuries, government took advantage of its position to challenge the wisdom of such leases. In 1872 the estate manager successfully averted official action by saying that he did not think that the "mere fact of their being amlah can be held to disqualify them from holding lands and leases from the raj."[69] But, during the next government tenure of the estate, *amla* rent collectors were abolished. The argument against their retention rested on several points:

> The [*amla thikadari*] system gives these men an interest more or less antagonistic to the Raj; and it is impossible for them at the same time to do their duty to their tenants on the spot as *thikadars* and do their work in the office. The anomaly presented itself a few days ago of the sarishttadar of my office appearing as a thikadar, plainly in collusion with other of his relations in a matter concerning his leased villages, contrary to the interests of the Raj. These officials, who are also thikadars, are generally unpunctual in the payment of rent, and by virtue of their position they take, or attempt to take, advantages which have a demoralizing effect on the other thikadars.[70]

Some villages were later inadvertently re-leased to *amla thikadars*. But as *amla thikadars* stated in their complaint, the Court of Wards manager had informed them that he was "determined to put a stop to family parties in the office and in the mofussil staff."[71]

European *Thikadars*

Throughout the late nineteenth century, European indigo planters were rent collectors for a substantial part of the Hathwa estate (see table 10). Their leases typically included both more area and rental than those of their native counterparts. In 1874 eleven different indigo factories held 116 villages[72] (see table 8); in 1900 nineteen factories constituting five or six concerns collected Rs. 235,000 of the estate's rents, an annual average of Rs. 40,000 each.[73]

---

68. Petition of Amla Thikadars of H.R. to Colltr. of Saran, with no. 1966, Jan. 6, 1900, Mgr., H.R. *Bastas*, 1899–1900, colltn. 38, petitions; Markham to Colltr., no. 240, April 26, 1899, Bengal Rev. Procs., Sept. 1899, no. 94, app. B.
69. Hodgkinson to Colltr., no. A, April 2, 1872, P.C. *Basta* no. 103.
70. "Extract ... from Hathwa Manager's no. 1501, 17 Sept. 1898," app. A to Macpherson to Commr., no. 1 C.W., June 18, 1899, Bengal Rev. Procs., Sept. 1899, no. 94 (encl.).
71. Petition of Amla Thikadars, with no. 1966, Jan. 6, 1900, H.R. *Bastas*, 1899–1900; "Report of the Hathwa raj estates under the Court of Wards for the year 1899–1900," P.C. *Basta* no. 166.
72. "Management of Hutwa during 1873–74."
73. That same year 256 Indian *thikadars* paid Rs. 363,333, or an average of Rs. 1,400 ("Note by W. C. Macpherson," June 18, 1900, with Offg. Commr. L. Hare to Secy. BOR, no. 450W, June 14, 1900, H.R. *Bastas*, 1900–1901, colltn. 37).

Furthermore, these villages represented only a factory or concern's lease with one particular landholder, and not its entire holdings.[74]

As in the case of its Indian rent collectors, the raj retained both a legal and extralegal edge over its European *thikadars*. They were, to use the words of an estate manager, "as strictly bound by the conditions of their leases as the native thikadars."[75] In addition, their leases described more closely their relationship to the raj. Whereas Indian *thikadars* were not given formal leases until 1879, lease renewals for indigo planters invariably engendered careful deliberation.[76] Planter *thikadars*, moreover, were not considered to have any hereditary claims.

The extant English records of Hathwa, which cover in great detail the negotiations with indigo planters over contractual conditions and lease renewals, support such an analysis. Consider, for instance, the correspondence in the 1880s between the Jaitpore factory and the estate, particularly the letters relating to the Jaitpore raiyats' demands for certain allowances because of various illegal cesses incorporated into their rent rolls by previous maliks. The factory's dilemma was that it could not realize the entire sum recorded in the rent rolls, nor could it, by the terms of the Hathwa lease, reduce the rent roll on its own initiative.[77]

Above all, the relationship of the estate to its European *thikadars* was defined by their mutually beneficial set of exchanges. As long as indigo remained a highly profitable enterprise, "it did not matter to the planter what he paid for a village. A thousand rupees more or less was of no consequence, so long as he obtained lands for the manufacture of indigo."[78] And for the great estate, an indigo *thikadar* represented a rentpayer who recovered substantial dues with promptness and saved the raj bureaucracy "a great deal of work by conducting all inquiries within his villages, and settling all composable disputes without resort to the law courts."[79] No wonder planters were highly appreciated, especially by Maharaja Krishna Pratap Sahi, who "was of the opinion they managed the raiyats much better than the native thikadars did."[80] There is also some evidence that the raj found it advantageous to entrust them with the leases of distant villages in which there were no "substantial ryots" to coopt as intermediaries.[81]

---

74. O'Donnell estimates that a large indigo concern generally kept 2,000 to 5,000 acres in cultivation scattered over twenty to fifty villages.
75. Markham to Colltr., no. 240, April 26, 1899, Bengal Rev. Procs., Sept. 1899, no. 94 (encl.).
76. See, e.g., the correspondence over "Renewal of Mr. Fraser's Leases held from the Hutwa Estate," ibid., April 1873 to 1875, July 1873.
77. Mgr., H.R., to E. G. Chardon, Jaitpore Factory, no. 486, Jan. 4, 1886, and Chardon to Mgr., March 29, 1887; "Jogapore Factory: regarding renewal of lease, 1890," H.R. *Bastas*, 1880–1890.
78. Markham to Colltr., no. 549, May 18, 1900, ibid., 1900–1901, colltn. no. 37.
79. Ibid.
80. Markham to Colltr., no. 240, April 26, 1899, Bengal Rev. Procs., Sept. 1899, no. 94.
81. See Hodgkinson to Colltr., no. 230, July 2, 1873, ibid., April 1873 to 1875, July 1873.

The higher returns that indigo *thikadars* remitted are revealed by the smaller number of villages they held and the disproportionately larger amounts of rent they collected (table 8). Neither government nor estate records indicate that the villages leased to planters differed enough, either ecologically or sociologically, to account for the larger rentals. What can be documented, however, is that they recovered "high rents" for the raj, "as high as are to be found in any large tract in these provinces and that . . . [they took] all the risk of failure to collect and bear all the costs of rent suits."[82] Such an arrangement led to the inescapable conclusion, recognized by one official report, that "the Raj [Hathwa] became a partner with the planter in the profits of the indigo industry. This profit it got in addition to divesting itself of the duties of the proprietor; and it ran no risks either in collection of rents or in losses in the industry."[83] Additional sums also accrued to the estate from the security deposit of 50 to 100 percent of the annual farming rental it required of indigo planters (Indian *thikadars* deposited 25 percent). Hathwa invested this in promissory notes, a practice encouraged by the Court of Wards management. Furthermore, unlike their Indian counterparts, European *thikadars* received no commission for the collection of rent.[84]

As long as indigo remained a highly profitable enterprise, planters rarely complained about their lease terms. Although they attempted as early as 1888 to secure some of the advantages of native leases,[85] more concerted efforts followed only when German synthetic dye began to press hard on the indigo market at the turn of the twentieth century. The decline of the industry led Hathwa's planter *thikadars* to seek assistance "to make both ends meet" and to insist "that the ruin of the European thikadars could not but act prejudicially to the welfare of the raj."[86] Although their request for a 10 percent commission on rent collection was granted, security deposits remained, with the difference that the amount depended on the merit of each *thikadar*, Indian or European. Such caution was conditioned by "a recent case of a planter's taking a factory from a property under the Court of Wards in Saran [not from Hathwa] and of great loss of rents having been caused to the proprietor because sufficient security was not taken from the planter."[87]

82. "Note by Macpherson," June 18, 1900. See also Mishra (1966: 339–40), who asserts that indigo planters sometimes remitted more than they collected from the peasants.
83. "Note by Macpherson," June 18, 1900. For a similar point about north Bihar, see Fisher (1976: 169–222).
84. Markham to Colltr., no. 240, April 26, 1899, Bengal Rev. Procs., Sept. 1899, no. 94 (encl.); "Note by Macpherson," June 18, 1900.
85. See, e.g., their request for a 10 percent commission on rental collections (D. N. Reid, Mgr., Moniarah factory, to Bhubaneshwar Dutt, Mgr., H.R., Sept. 8, 1888, H.R. *Bastas*, 1880–1890, colltn. 12).
86. "Representation from—Messrs. D. Reid (Sadowa), M. Hutchins (Jogapur) and others, to the Manager, Raj Hathwa," March 1900, ibid., 1900–1901, colltn. 37.
87. "Note by Macpherson," June 18, 1900, and Hare to BOR, no. 450W, July 14, 1900, in ibid.

The Development of a *Khas* System

In the nineteenth century, at the initiative of the Court of Wards management, control began to extend from the Hathwa core to the other raj villages in the form of *khas* management. As the area subjected to this direct system expanded, so did the raj's concern with developing control down to the village level. As a result, intermediate agencies were designed to keep closer scrutiny of village society. Although the number of levels in the *khas* hierarchy and the number of personnel at each level varied, the basic structure was modeled after the idealized pattern of "a direct chain of Manager, Circle Officer, Sazawal [landholder's agent], Patwari and Barahil [peon] . . . [so that] money will pass through the Sazawal to the Treasury."[88]

Before the abolition of the raj's Sripur and Ambikapur indigo factories, few *khas* villages had *sazawals* in charge. In 110 of the 204 villages (see table 8) that were under indigo, patwaris collected the rents and made them over to the factory manager who then accounted to the estate manager every month.[89] In the remaining *khas* villages, *sazawals* were in charge of collection. This variation in the *khas* system apparently continued for a while after the closing of the factories. An 1898 report described the Sripur circle as comprising *khas* villages where patwaris collected and the other circles as under the charge of *sazawals*. However, this distinction was not a clear-cut one in practice. In the villages of the Hathwa circle, the large responsibilities of the *sazawals*—fifteen to twenty villages with rent rolls varying from Rs. 10,000 to 25,000—suggest that they functioned primarily in a supervisory capacity. Certainly, this increasingly became the trend, for by 1905 the *sazawal* of thirty or forty villages had to rely on patwaris to collect, while he became their insuring agency, "his security being held as a safeguard against misappropriation by the patwaris and an agency for controlling a group of villages."[90]

By 1905 the basic structure of the *khas* system had evolved. Below the assistant manager, the estate was broken up into several divisions (four in 1905), each headed by a circle officer whose major task was to supervise *sazawals* and patwaris. These four circles ranged in size from 45 to 389 villages, the *sazawal*'s area from 5 to 20 villages, the patwari's from 2 to 3.6 villages, and each village had a headman, a *gomastah* (agent or collector), and a peon (*barahil*).[91] (See table 11.)

Circle officers, generally paid from Rs. 150 to 400, numbered six in 1916: two were Europeans, two Bengalis, one a Bihari Hindu, and the sixth, a

---

88. Note by Commr. P. C. Lyon to Colltr., June 19, 1905, ibid., 1904–1905, colltn. 4. This pattern was also followed on other Bihar estates (Henningham 1983: 39).
89. "Management of Hutwa during 1873–74."
90. Offg. Mgr. S. Dutt to Colltr., July 25, 1905, H.R. *Bastas*, 1904–1905, colltn. 4; Buskin to Colltr., no. 1981, Feb. 21, 1898; Macpherson to Commr., no. 1 C.W., June 18, 1899, Bengal Rev. Procs., Sept. 1899, nos. 91 and 94 (encl.).
91. "Village Establishments under Hathwa Estate," Internal note to Mgr., March 12, 1905, H.R. *Bastas*, 1904–1905, colltn. 4.

Table 11.

Khas System in Hathwa Raj Circles, 1905

Circle	No. of villages	Total collect (Rs.)	No. of sazawals	No. of patwaris	Ave. no. of villages per patwari	Ave. collect. patwari (Rs.)
Bhorey	389	259,542	17	171	2.3	1,518
Hathwa	340	42,365	19	140	2.4	2,443
Gopalganj	189	200,936	12	89	2.0	2,257
Chapra	45	95,311	8	45	3.6	2,118
Total	963	598,154	56	445		

Source: "Village Establishments under Hathwa Estates," March 12, 1905, H.R. *Bastas*, 1904–1905, Colltn. 4.

Muslim. Each of them managed as many as fifteen *sazawals* who were stationed in particular villages. A list of *sazawals* in the Hathwa circle in 1903 identifies them as of high-caste background, primarily Bhumihar Brahmin, Brahmin, Rajput or Kayasth, or Muslim. Jagdishpur village, for example, was the headquarters of a *sazawal* whose charge covered an additional twenty-six villages nearby and a collection of Rs. 17,000 to 18,000; he appropriated 2 percent of the collection. His subordinate at the village level was the patwari who also worked in three other villages; in addition to his standard 1.5 percent commission, he collected another 1 percent because he also did the *gomastah*'s job. Five peons also represented the raj's interests in these twenty-seven villages for a monthly wage of Rs. 2 each.[92]

Among estate managers there was almost as much criticism of the *khas* system as there was praise of *thikadari* management, which colored the initial appraisal of the circle system in 1902–1903:

The appointment of the Circle Officers, which was a first step in the right direction has not been followed up by giving them an establishment capable of watching either the collection of rent, or the progress of civil suits or certificates, and thus the decentralisation sought for was not effected. The supervision of all main branches of management was still rigidly confined to the Head Office and the Circle Officers were little more than bailiffs. During the year under report an attempt has been made to impose upon the Circle Officers a much larger responsibility than was before vested in them and to make them supervise the work of litigation, of maintenance of records, and collection of all rents current and arrear whether from directly managed or farmed villages.[93]

Weaknesses in the direct system had repercussions at the village level, such as when *sazawals* appropriated the 1 percent commission intended for the peons:

92. Jagdishpur village and Belsara village, Mirganj *thana* nos. 13 and 1040, SVN; List appended to Dutt to Colltr., July 25, 1904, H.R. *Bastas*, 1904–1905.
93. "Hathwa Raj Estate Administration Report, 1902–03," P.C. *Basta* no. 166.

This led to many abuses, the peons were not paid for months together and were obliged to live on the rent payers, again disputes arose between these peons and the ryots and the peons not being enrolled Raj servants received no support from the Raj and the prestige of the Raj was impaired by the spectacle of these men being prosecuted by the tenants and having to admit that they were not regular Raj servants and received no pay from anyone except after delays which in themselves were tantamount to a license to extort.[94]

Peon inefficiency was also said to have caused *sazawal*s to leave large sums unrealized, thus compelling the raj to collect through lawsuits. Where such suits led to the purchase of holdings by the raj, the land was found to be of little value in many cases. An estimate in 1904–1905 put losses from such purchases at Rs. 11,956. *Sazawal*s often also dispensed with *gomastah*s and appropriated the 1 percent commission that the latter were entitled to as bankers for the former.[95]

Increasingly, however, the raj's *khas* mechanisms were developed to penetrate closer to the ground level. Although the raj's peons were not stationed in every village, as in the case of Jagdishpur village, the estate management was acutely aware of the gaps in its system of control. Especially in newly acquired villages, the absence of peons led to "purchased holdings . . . [being] stealthily sown down by their former occupants or by mere trespassers. Absconded and purchased trees, bamboos &c. are not effectually protected and generally the hold of the proprietor on the village is dangerously relaxed."[96] Local representation was considered vital, particularly in such holdings, to guard against the development of opposition.[97] New acquisitions were invariably placed under *khas* management.

Village-Level Controllers in Hathwa Raj

The relative ease with which the *thikadari* system was replaced by a direct system of management reflects the considerable control that the estate wielded over its intermediaries. Instead of *thikadar*s, Hathwa now linked up with the headman, the patwari, and other village notables, including former *thikadar*s. To tighten its grip further, it sought to have "some representative of the management, if not in every village, every small group of villages to assist the *patwari*s in collecting."[98] And when problems arose with the evolving *khas* system, organizational tinkering was sufficient to maintain it.

Officials and raiyats converged on Hathwa at *Dashara* to acknowledge the strategic position the Maharaja occupied as the major local controller and leading British connection in Saran. The rituals of this festival defined his vital hinge position, as well as his claim to monopoly over all sources of power in his "little kingdom."

94. "Note on Proposed Village Establishment," Markham, Mgr., June 2, 1904, H.R. *Basta*, 1904–1905, colltn. 4.   95. Ibid.   96. Ibid.
97. Dutt to Colltr., July 25, 1904, H.R. *Bastas*, 1904–1905.   98. Ibid.

This great estate's "sources of glory" were manifold. Symbolic of its authority in local society were the palace, *kachcheri*, market, and temple, which were clustered together in Hathwa and its contiguous villages, making this locality the hub of the great estate. These institutions embodied the elaborate control complex, which extended a variety of formal and informal, social, economic and religious networks outward, thus tying together the areas of the zamindari into one great estate.

A strong, central bureaucracy stood at the head of Hathwa's system of control. Unlike many other estates in North India, this powerful superstructure safeguarded the interests of the zamindari family against encroachments from other groups on the land. And, unlike many other estates, the bureaucracy was not only a professional organization, but also one staffed by "outsiders," Bengalis, and Europeans, who did not have an anchorage in local society and therefore did not develop their own vested interests at the expense of the zamindari.

Beneath this superstructure lay an administrative system that forged links to the farthest reaches of the estate, either through intermediaries called *thikadars*, or through a *khas* system of management. The *thikadari* system, the predominant form of management in the nineteenth century, functioned efficiently because *thikadars* were the substantial raiyats and moneylenders of their localities or were European indigo planters. In relation to the Hathwa raj, however, *thikadars* were in a weak position. They had little, if any, legal standing; and if they were issued leases, the terms of these documents spelled out in detail the raj's disciplinary rights over them. They were further restricted by Hathwa's elaborate administrative networks and its informal ties to them.

Hathwa's edge over its *thikadars* is also evident from the relative ease with which the *thikadari* system was replaced by a *khas* system at the turn of the twentieth century. Although the chain of command between the administrative center and the outlying villages was strengthened and developed under this direct system, the primary link remained the village-level controllers, now recruited as *sazawals*. As before, and in much the same fashion as the British Raj only defined its relations with its local controllers, the Hathwa raj was primarily concerned with the village-level controller as its connection. With the superior resources of the great estate supporting them, *thikadars*, *sazawals*, and other Hathwa coadjutors had a great deal of power over the rest of local society.

7

The Dynamics of Hathwa Control: Two Case Studies

Neither a carefully subordinated *thikadari* nor a highly economical management system fully explains the effectiveness of Hathwa's control system. This chapter completes the analysis of the system of control operating in Hathwa by showing how it actually functioned in two crisis situations at different points in time—1844 and 1879.

Between British Raj and Hathwa Raiyat

That the *thikadari* system worked efficaciously in the Hathwa raj was an article of faith among estate and government officials. Thirty-one years in the estate's service, M. Buskin spoke for several generations of managers and British administrators when he said he was "fully convinced of the superiority of the thika [indirect] over the *sir* or *khas* [direct] system of collection."[1] Such appreciation was prompted by several considerations. As one report on estate management noted, not only was it "greatly favoured by the late proprietor, who has been officially described as an admirable landlord . . . [but also] its abolition would involve serious injury to a very deserving body of men."[2] The late Maharaja Sir Krishna Pratap Sahi (1874–1896) favored the system because the institutionalized limitations imposed and enforced on *thikadars* were clearly in line with his intention to preserve all rights on his estate for himself. He also realized the worth of having *thikadars* whose standing as substantial raiyats and moneylenders in their leased villages enabled them to

---

1. Note by Commr. P. C. Lyon to Colltr., June 19, 1905, H.R. *Bastas*, 1904–1905, colltn. 4.
2. See "Management of the Hutwa Estate during 1873–74," Bengal Rev. Procs., Apr. 1873 to 1875, Aug. 1874, nos. 2–3.

monopolize power at the village level. For instance, in Maksudpur village it was the leaseholder who appointed the village headman, and, in villages where they did not already hold sway, *thikadars* usually replaced and transformed headmen into "mere social heads and elders."[3] In cases where *khas* villages were shifted to *thikadari* management, government insisted to the Court of Wards management that the new rent collectors be as far as possible "jyet ryots and persons living on the spot."[4] Other accounts consistently speak of the patwari as the creature of the rent collector or the landholder.[5]

A rental policy of "divide and rule" further consolidated Hathwa's interests at the village level. In the words of one estate report, there was "a very marked general difference between the rates paid by Brahmans, Babhuns, and high castes, and the rates at which lower castes hold.... [And] this difference has been increased by the mode of levying enhancements, *viz.*, a general increase of so much in each rupee of rent paid before."[6]

The late maharaja must have also found the *thikadari* system of management attractive because his main objective was reported to have been "to get as much money out of the estate as possible at as little expense as he could."[7] Estate officials knew that the *thikadari* management of the entire raj cost only 13.0 percent of the gross, while *khas* took up 15.7 to 17.2 percent. *Thikadars*, moreover, kept the estate's legal costs at a minimum because they paid for all such charges incurred in their jurisdictions out of their own pockets.[8]

Financial considerations also weighed heavily in favor of the continuing use of the *thikadari* system because the *khas* system involved

many unforeseen charges which cannot be estimated, e.g., criminal cases between the village agencies and the raiyats in connection with rent collection; cases with neighbouring proprietors in regard to boundaries; money is appropriated by the rent-collectors or stolen by thieves from the village cutcherries, or robbed on the way in transit to the head office; raiyats fall into arrears and abscond or die without leaving any heirs to pay up their dues.[9]

Thikadars, on the other hand, not only personally guaranteed the remittance of rent, but also acted as buffers against local dissonance. The European indigo planter *thikadar* played an especially important role in this respect. A better rentpayer and landlord than his Indian counterpart, he, in the estimation of one estate manager, also saved "the Raj and its officers a good deal of work

3. M. Buskin, Mgr., to Colltr., no. 1981, Feb. 21, 1898, Bengal Rev. Procs., Sept. to Oct. 1899, Sept., no. 91; Maksudpur village, Gopalganj thana no. 17, SVN, 1893–1901.
4. Offg. Junior Secy. J. Ware Edgar to Secy. GOB, no. 4882, Oct. 30, 1872, Bengal Rev. Procs., Oct.–Dec. 1872, Oct., 203.
5. Offg. Mgr. S. Dutt to Colltr., July 5, 1905, H.R. *Bastas*. 1904–1905, colltn. 4.
6. "Management of Hutwa during 1873–74."
7. "Annual Report of Hutwa Estate under Court of Wards for 1872–73," no. 71, April 30, 1873, P.C. *Basta* no. 103, Monthly Bundles, Gen. Dept., 1870–1875.
8. See Commr. J. A. Bourdillon to Secy. BOR, no. 363W, Aug. 4, 1899, Bengal Rev. Procs., Sept. to Oct. 1899, Sept., no. 94.
9. A. M. Markham, H.R., to Colltr., no. 240, April 26, 1899, ibid., (encl.), app. B.

by conducting all inquiries within his villages, and settling all composable disputes without resort to the law courts."[10] How much of a saving such *thikadari* efforts represented can be discerned from the enormous number of raiyats' petitions (e.g., 20,430 in fifteen months) that were directed at the central office "about rent matters, about alleged oppressive acts of thikadars, sazawals and patwaris, about alleged mistakes of entry of fields in the survey records, about grants for wells, about embankments, &c."[11]

Hathwa's European planters were also useful connettions for the raj, as they often interceded with government on behalf of the maharaja. Indigo *thikadars* acted in this capacity in 1876 when the subdeputy opium agent at Siwan clashed with the maharaja over the former's support of opium raiyats who refused to pay the increased rents demanded by Hathwa's rent collectors.[12] Zamindars generally considered planters as important allies because the latter had "the ear of the official."[13] In addition, Hathwa was also able to manipulate the legal system by virtue of its superior economic resources and close political ties and access to government. In the 1879 dispute, one of the case studies featured here, pitting the district magistrate against the maharaja of Hathwa, the former was cautioned by an indigo *thikadar* about the futility of acting on behalf of the estate's raiyats:

An argument put forward for my not interfering in the dealings between the Maharaja and his tenantry was that the action of the Magistrate on behalf of the latter would only lead to their utter ruin in the future. The instance brought to my notice was that of Arna village, where, upon some demand of the Maharaja being recently contested, the civil courts were utilized to procure decrees for three years' arrears of rents, and eviction of half the householders was the speedy result.[14]

The Consolidation of Hathwa Control, 1844

The "internal rising" of 1844 was the occasion of "survey riots" that challenged the legitimacy of the Hathwa raja. The opening salvo of this confrontation was fired by Bujahawan Misra, a Brahmin of Bhorey, who, with the support of the Bhumihar Brahmins and peasants of his locality, claimed an extensive tract of land, including the former zamindari headquarters of Huseypur, as his rentfree grant (*birt*). The ensuing riots involved several hundred people and constituted such a threat that, in the words of the local

10. Mgr. to Colltr., no. 549, May 18, 1900, H.R. *Bastas*, 1900–1901, colltn. 37. Indigo planters themselves also emphasized this aspect of their role. ("Representation from—Messrs. D. Reid (Suddowa), M. Hutchins (Jogapur) and others," April 1900, ibid.).
11. Colltr. W. C. Macpherson to Commr., no. 1 C.W., June 18, 1899, Bengal Rev. Procs., Sept. to Oct. 1899, Sept., no. 94 (encl.).
12. G. S. Park to Commr., no. 2007G, Aug. 31, 1876, and Commr. S. C. Bayley to Opium Agent, Patna, no. 93, Nov. 6, 1876, ibid., 1879, Dec., nos. 73–78.
13. D. N. Reid to H. H. Fowler, Her Majesty's Principal Secy. of State for India, Sept. 25, 1894, R 1530/94, GOI, Rev. Papers, 1894 L/E/7/357; Fisher 1976: 220–21.
14. Offg. Colltr. R. H. Pawsey to Commr., no. 345, July 29, 1879, Bengal Rev. Procs., Dec. 1879, nos. 73-78.

bards, the "Raja was reduced to diminutive, and his soldiers were reduced to the position of a cotton-dresser while Bajhawan Missir fought making the earth tremble under his feet."[15]

The first spark of an impending explosion came in 1842, when Maharaja Chatterdhari Sahi petitioned against government's plans to institute survey operations in Saran. Although his letter couched his objections on the grounds that the survey would run counter to the principles of the Permanent Settlement, be expensive, and result in conceding to government the right to transfer land, his real concern was the disputes it would foment between the estate and the vested interests who had secured their privileges from the Huseypur line. In dismissing his complaints about the proceedings, the provincial authorities noted that "opulent, powerful and encroaching landholders will naturally object to what puts a barrier to their encroachments.... It is the poor and the weak who be the great gainers."[16]

In early 1844, 151 petitions were submitted to the government by people calling themselves the *birtdars* (rentfree grantees) of villages that included one-third of pargana Kalyanpur Kuari. Their claim was that they had acquired these rights before and during the tenure of Raja Fateh Sahi. Some of these privileges, no doubt, were created by the rebel Raja to maintain his supporters in the protracted struggle against the Company Raj in the late eighteenth century. However, their petition was rejected with the statement that the only purpose of the survey was to plot the boundaries of the estates and villages and not to record the rights of any parties except those of the proprietors.[17]

When the petitioners assembled before the deputy collector to plead their case, on April 2, 1844, they were assaulted by the local police and arrested. However, their leader, Bujahawan Misra, and a number of others, escaped. The subsequent official inquiry report showed that this attack was instituted by the police in collusion with the Hathwa retainers to intimidate the petitioners. And when the petitioners engaged attorneys to defend themselves, Hathwa's agents persuaded the attorneys to resign from the case. Nevertheless, the petitioners were released by the local judge.[18]

On April 3 a fire ravaged the temporary shelter that had been built to house the deputy collector's records, including the documents collected from the *birtdar* petitioners. "Though no proof could be adduced," its occurrence on the heels of the police assault prompted government "to suppose that the same parties were instigators of both acts and that the object in the latter was to destroy all records by which the case of the Petitioners could be in any way supported."[19] In May the deputy collector rejected the 151 petitions that had

---

15. G. N. Dutt 1905: 19.
16. J. H. Young, Deputy. Secy. to GOB, to Secy. Currie, no. 410, April 13, 1842, Bengal Rev. Consltns., March 24 to April 13, 1842, no. 85.
17. "'Abstract translation of a petition from ... birtdars," Oct. 10, 1844, and Commr. E. C. Ravenshaw to BOR, no. 673, ibid., (hereafter cited as Ravenshaw Report), April 9 to May 7, 1845, nos. 91 & 93.   18. Ravenshaw Report.   19. Ibid.

accumulated by then, a decision upheld by the commissioner of the division. Although the *birtdars* then appealed to the Board of Revenue, they did not wait for its findings. On June 21 Bujahawan Misra assembled a band of 500 people; another one was led by Ishri Prasad, a *birtdar* petitioner who claimed fifty-two villages in Bhorey. Their forces ignited, according to an official report, a "flame [that] once lighted soon spread over the whole Pergana," at its height involving as many as 20 "ring leaders" supported by "5,950 men armed with swords, matchlocks and clubs." The ranks of the *birtdars* were swelled by the "hereditary enemies" of Hathwa: the family and supporters of the disinherited Huseypur line, now organized around the person of Fateh Sahi's grandson; the *birtdars* of Gorakhpur who sided with their Saran counterparts; and many tenants from villages held by the raja of Bettiah, "an inveterate enemy." These alliances produced ringleaders marching at the head of bands of three to four hundred people who stopped the payment of rent to Hathwa's rent collectors. Clashes quickly escalated into riots and affrays.[20]

When Hathwa retainers collected Rs. 300 from one *thikadar* in July, they were attacked by a crowd who demanded the return of the money, and, in the ensuing affray, there were a number of casualties. In August a sizable force of 4,000 men raided the Hathwa office at Bhorey and seized the sum of Rs. 5,365 that was deposited there; 4 men were killed and 4 wounded in this incident.[21] When local authorities dispatched 200 men armed with swords and spears to the house of Bujahawan Misra, they encountered, not as expected, a band of 500 men, but "upwards of 1500 men assembled, many armed with matchlocks."[22] In the face of such formidable opposition, the government force was compelled to withdraw. In September three troops of the Seventh Irregular Cavalry were sent to the area, their numbers designed to be "large enough to . . . overawe those be yet disposed to continue the disturbances."[23]

The crucial British role in suppressing the internal rising is only one indication of government's abiding interest in preserving and enhancing the primacy of the Hathwa estate. Much more revealing of the official stance in these disturbances is the clash that flared up between F. A. E. Dalrymple, the district magistrate, and W. Dampier, the superintendent of police. Their disagreement stemmed ostensibly from a difference in judgment about the cause of the riots: the former described the Hathwa raja as the "original aggressor."; the latter believed that the raja was merely exercising "his legal rights of collection for lands."[24] Dampier's contention was that the source of conflict was not "violence or oppression on the part of the Rajah . . . toward his tenantry" but stemmed from the seditious influence of Fateh Sahi's grandson

20. W. Dampier, Supt., Police, to Secy. F. J. Halliday, no. 2065, Sept. 7, 1844, Bengal Cr. Jdcl. Consltns., Aug. 22 to Sept. 16, 1844, Sept. 16, no. 84.   21. Ibid.
22. Dampier to Halliday, no. 2048, Sept. 3, 1844, ibid., no. 82.
23. Dampier to F. A. E. Dalrymple, Offg. Magte., Sept. 26, 1844, Bengal Rev Consltns., Oct. 2 to 30, 1844, Oct. 23, no. 71.
24. Dalrymple to Dampier, no. 356, Sept. 24, 1844, ibid., Oct. 16, no. 13.

(who still thought of himself as the rightful master of the great estate) and of the raja of Bettiah who was embroiled in a land dispute with Hathwa. Even Dampier acknowledged, however, that the underlying cause of the disturbances was a clash over rights in the land:

> I have heard it from tolerable authority, that some of the influential parties in these riotous acts had at the period of the permanent settlement some rights in under tenures given by Futteh Sahee, these were not then recorded as brought forward, and the [Hathwa] Rajah at the time of his assuming possession of his Estate, or shortly afterwards, took the opportunity of totally suppressing them, making their occupants mere assamees [cultivators], and this circumstance joined to some hope of success in case of a resettlement, helped to increase the feeling against him.
> The Rajah... is extremely averse to any holdings or tenures in his zamindari between himself and the cultivator.... He is not generally accused of acts of open violence, but through his influence, wealth and power... he has suppressed, not now but some time back, many subordinate rent free or other tenures in his property.[25]

Government's intervention, therefore, upheld Hathwa's rights to suppress any subordinate claims on its lands. Most of the ringleaders were rounded up. Bujahawan Misra eluded capture for many months but was finally arrested and sentenced to ten years' imprisonment. An official statement reported with satisfaction that the "presence of the Cavalry and the punishment of the ringleaders has had the effect of restoring tranquility, the survey of the Perganah has been completed and the Rajah is again enabled to collect his rents."[26]

Government's support of Dampier against Dalrymple must have served notice to Hathwa raiyats of the considerable backing that the maharaja enjoyed from the state. For not only did Dalrymple who described Hathwa as the "aggressor" find himself censured by his superiors, but his administration was also subjected to an official investigation.[27] This inquiry found him wanting and turned up the additional charge of having had "connexion with the wife of one of the parties concerned" in a criminal case over which he presided. Dampier, no doubt, did not hesitate to inform the Bengal government that the accusation made by the "wife" against Dalrymple aroused "considerable excitement in the place, and the people ask one another, whose wife is safe now, when the 'Hakim' [ruler, district head] does such acts?"[28] Although the charge was investigated, it could not be proven to have had undue influence in his decision on the case.

Dismissed from government service for the third time, in 1861, Dalrymple sought to reopen the 1844 case. In his defense he stated that many in the British community in the district and in Calcutta were prejudiced against him because they were scandalized by the action of the then Saran collector's wife,

---

25. Dampier to Halliday, no. 3511, Oct. 26, 1844, Bengal Cr. Jdcl. Consltns., Nov 6 to Dec. 27, 1844, Nov. 20, no. 36.   26. Ravenshaw Report.   27. Ibid.
28. Dampier to Halliday, Feb. 12, 1845, and A. Turnbull, Undersecy., GOB, to Dalrymple, no. 338, Feb. 27, 1845, Bengal Cr. Jdcl. Consltns., Feb. 5 to 27, 1845, Feb. 27, nos. 41 and 42.

Mrs. Farquharson, who had left her husband and sought his protection. In his 1861 plea, Dalrymple also claimed that many of the attacks against him, including the charges of having engaged in adultery with a native woman, were trumped up because of his involvement with Mrs. Farquharson. Furthermore, he accused Dampier of having conspired against him because the latter was in collusion with the maharaja and had wished to discredit him because he had refused to cooperate with them. He also attempted to turn the tables on Dampier by accusing him of having "a notorious and profligate and indecent life." It was the superintendent of police, "then a married man of nearly fifty years of age," he wrote, who "was a Keeper of Native Women who followed him in his tour about the country and was no great distance from Chupra when he attempted ... to degrade my character as low as his own."[29]

No doubt, Dalrymple and Dampier hurled accusations at one another because of personal animosities. But in the flurry of charges and countercharges, the official findings about the origins of the disturbances of 1844 were ignored. They did reveal that the clashes arose over a fundamental conflict between two parties claiming different degrees of rights in the land. According to the official report, which was really an inquiry into the petitions of the so-called *birtdars*, the maharaja of Hathwa, fearful of the possible deleterious consequences of the government survey, had for some time been engaged in securing decrees against the registration of any subordinate rights on his estate. Thus, he challenged not only the *birtdars* who were known to have enjoyed "long possession as Farmers," but also "Ticcadars of several villages."[30]

The British role in suppressing the disturbances of 1844 thus had the effect of establishing the maharaja of Hathwa's legal position as the "sole rais" of the great estate. Clearly, Hathwa's actions against the claims of the *birtdar* petitioners and its drive against the growth of rights in the land for *thikadars* represented its larger concern—to consolidate its power. And the survey operations triggered this effort to stake out the estate's supremacy, because, for Chatterdhari Sahi, as the first of the cadet line to assume the mantle of the former Huseypur zamindari, the awesome uprising of Fateh Sahi must have still been fresh in his mind. His fears were further heightened by the presence, in the wings, of his rebellious kinsman's grandson who had never renounced the Huseypur claims to the great estate. The grandson's involvement in the disturbances was well known, several hundred of his men having crossed over from his territory in neighboring Gorakhpur to join the rioters. The challenge

---

29. Francis A. Elphinstone-Dalrymple to Undersecy. of State for India, no. 261, July 5, 1861, India, Jdcl. Dept., Home Correspondence, 1861, L/P&J/2/201, no. 261. Government's curt reply was to refuse to reopen the case (H. Merivale to Dalrymple, no. 665, n.d., Jdcl. Dept., Misc. Letters, 1866–1872, L/P&J/2/198).   30. Ravenshaw Report.
31. Ibid. In the Mutiny/Rebellion of 1857, the maharaja of Hathwa's fear of the former Huseypur family led him to request government assistance against the possibility of an attack by his kinsmen (Magte. W. F. McDonnell to Commr. W. Tayler, demi-official, Aug. 13, 1857, P.C. *Basta* 105, Monthly Bundles, Gen. Dept., from 1854 on, from Magte. of Saran).

that the *birtdars* issued to Hathwa must have also loomed larger because it came from men who enjoyed the support of the Huseypur line and who were, in their own right, controllers over village-level society.[31] The 151 petitioners, for example, claimed to hold rights in 300 villages; the 20 ringleaders had at their command an army of 5,950 men; and Bujahawan Misra appeared with a following of 500 when the local authorities came to apprehend him. By beating back the challenge of these men and their "outside" patrons (the Huseypur family), the British Raj made the great estate safe for its "opulent, powerful and encroaching" maharaja.

The Desertions of 1879

By the late nineteenth century, the great estate of Hathwa wielded considerable power and influence over its *raiyats*. In 1879 its control was again buttressed by the authority of the British Raj. Five years before the "wholesale desertions," Hathwa had been released from a brief but beneficial tenure under the Court of Wards.

The bone of contention in the 1879 incident was whether "wholesale desertions" had occurred from several Hathwa villages in pargana Kalyanpur Kuari because of "oppression."[32] In April 1879 the head constable of the Katia outpost reported that large numbers of Hathwa peasants had fled to Gorakhpur and Champaran on account of "being pressed hard by the Ticcadars for rent and likewise in consequence of drought, the scantiness of the Rubi produce and the failure of the Aghani crop."[33] In May, at the behest of Charles James O'Donnell, the subdivisional officer of Siwan, J. F. Leadbeater, the inspector of police, investigated and ascertained that 366 families had left their homes. O'Donnell concluded, on the basis of census estimates for average homestead size, that at least 2,000 people had left. When additional police reports identified as many as 1,000 abandoned houses, he increased the estimate to 6,000 desertions.[34] Over two months after the initial report of forced migrations, in early July, O'Donnell personally inspected the locality of Katia and observed numerous abandoned houses. In a fifty-mile radius he encountered "at least 50 groups of villagers at different points, who alleged that ryots had absconded from their villages."[35]

32. C. J. O'Donnell, SDO, Siwan, to Magte. R. H. Pawsey, no. 164, June 21, 1879; and Maharaja Krishna Pratap Sahi of Hathwa to Colltr., no. 4A, June 21, 1879, Bengal Rev. Procs., 1879, Dec., nos. 73–78 (hereafter this correspondence is cited as "Desertions in Hathwa").
33. "Special Diary of Mr. Inspector J. F. Leadbeater, 18 June 1879"; O'Donnell to Magte., no. 164, June 21, 1879; Leadbeater to Dist. Supt. of Police, June 18, 1879; "Desertions in Hathwa."
34. O'Donnell to Magte., no. 172, July 8, 1879, ibid.
35. In the ensuing controversy, O'Donnell, sharply criticized for having delayed his visit to Katia, stated that he had deliberately stayed away so as not to alert Hathwa officials to the impending police investigation (O'Donnell to Magte., no. 172, July 8, 1879, ibid.). See also Pawsey to Commr., no. 345, July 29, 1879, ibid., which expresses concern about exciting tenants and setting "class against class."

The maharaja of Hathwa vehemently denied the charges of large-scale forced migrations from his estate. According to his reckoning only sixty-two persons had left forty-seven villages in the Katia outpost, and of these, only thirty-five had actually "exited," the other twenty-six had relocated in other parts of the estate. Nor did he accept the characterization of this flight as triggered by oppression. On the contrary, he attributed it to the "usual course of things . . . such as failure of crops, owing to drought, excessive rain, nature of soil, domestic afflictions, indebtedness, recovery of opium advances, &c." He also hinted at the possibility that personal animosities underlay "the mischief which Mr. O'Donnell and the police have been doing to the [Hathwa] Raj by putting up the ryots by threats against the *thikadars*."[36]

Although O'Donnell's immediate superior, R. H. Pawsey, the Saran magistrate, supported his case against Hathwa, their superior officer, Commissioner F. M. Halliday, sided with the maharaja. Not only did the commissioner consider the Hathwa rebuttals sufficient proof against any reports of "wholesale desertions," but he also mobilized what he said was additional evidence against the Saran officers' case. He noted, for example, that district returns of "emigration" for 1878–1879 showed that only eighty-four had departed, ignoring the fact that official statistics never included temporary or seasonal outmigration, let alone desertions.[37] Halliday also attacked the procedures followed in investigating the incident, particularly the deployment of police in a situation which he felt did not warrant a criminal investigation. Although this criticism simply echoed the maharaja's indignant complaint about police being "let loose in my estate," it subsequently became a major issue in the attack that the provincial authorities launched against the Saran administrators. In forwarding the correspondence of the case to the Bengal government, Halliday expressed dissatisfaction with Pawsey's role in the matter, but he saved his harshest words for O'Donnell, describing his actions as "injudicious and . . . open to censure."[38]

In concurring with Halliday, the acting lieutenant-governor of Bengal, Sir Steuart Bayley, ascribed the beginnings of this growing conflict to O'Donnell's "strong" personal views, which he called partial "to the depressed condition of the ryots in Behar generally, and specially in Sarun, and as [opposed] to the evils of the existing system of zamindari management." These biases, the lieutenant-governor believed, impeded a "full and impartial investigation" and produced instead a "report strongly against the Maharaja's management, on grounds which are to a great extent hypothetical."[39]

Despite the steady barrage of criticism from his superiors, O'Donnell held fast to his case. Although, along with Pawsey, he was transferred out of the

36. Maharaja to Colltr., nos. A, 2A, & 4A, June 24, June 25, and July 21, 1879, respectively, ibid.
37. Halliday to Secy., GOB, Rev., no. 85R, Aug. 4, 1879, ibid. See also Yang (1979a: 38–45) on the limited coverage of official records on migration and abscondings.
38. Halliday to Secy., Aug. 4, 1879, "Desertions in Hathwa." 39. Ibid.

district, he refused to withdraw his charges. On the contrary, he not only wrote repeatedly to the Bengal government, but also heightened his attack on Hathwa's estate management, broadening his indictment to include the entire zamindari system in Bihar and government's cooperation with it. In a letter written at the close of 1879, he announced his intention to carry his appeal to the highest level of Indian government, to the viceroy, and even further, to the Secretary of State for India. The Bengal government's reply to this long, detailed communication was a curt dismissal that referred him to a report submitted by the new magistrate of Saran, A. P. MacDonnell, which, it claimed, vindicated the official view. It also informed him that the proper course of appeal to the next level had to proceed through the local government.[40]

O'Donnell, nevertheless, wrote directly to the Secretary of State. His petition, published in England as a pamphlet, repeated his earlier attacks against Hathwa mismanagement and government's collaboration with the system of landholding in Bihar.[41] Reactions to this pamphlet in the Secretary of State's office ranged from indignation to deep concern about the validity of his charges. Most opinions, however, accepted the judgments that the new magistrate, A. P. MacDonnell, passed on the pamphlet at the invitation of the government. In declaring O'Donnell's criticisms no longer binding, MacDonnell pointed to the reforms that had been introduced after 1877, changing precisely those aspects of British administration and the estate management system that were under fire. "Though just be its strictures, and though merited its denunciation of a bad system, it conveys . . . a false impression of recent administration; it is unjust to individuals; it needlessly intrudes on private life . . . the only compensation . . . is the good it may do in attracting to this province a larger share of the public attention which is always wholesome."[42]

At the provincial level as well as the highest reaches of government, O'Donnell failed to gain a sympathetic hearing. His views were simply too controversial because his critical salvos were aimed at the entire system of colonial rule in Bihar, which, as elsewhere in India, rested on a policy of collaboration with local controllers.[43]

Although the continuing rounds of charges and countercharges generated additional information, government was never able to disprove convincingly

40. O'Donnell to Secy., Dec. 31, 1879, and Secy. to O'Donnell, no. 344-160 LR, Feb. 12, 1880, Bengal Rev. Procs., Feb. 1880, nos. 9-10.
41. O'Donnell 1880. See also L/E/6/13: 1880, Rev. Papers, 632-710, for the deliberations over this pamphlet in the office of the Secy. of State for India.
42. A. P. MacDonnell, Magte.-Colltr. of Saran to Secy., GOB, Jdcl., Sept. 7, 1880, L/E/6/13: 1880 Rev. Papers. See also Hill (1981: 56-83).
43. O'Donnell pursued every avenue of appeal: publishing his petition, writing to newspapers, and using the network of his fellow-Irish "Friends of India," Home Rulers who included his brother, Frank Hugh O'Donnell. For this group, O'Donnell's attacks fitted in well with their plans to take advantage of their representation in the House of Commons to mount "a grand inquest into both imperial and Indian affairs" (Brasted 1980: 37-63).

the occurrence of "wholesale desertions." Provincial authorities generally relied on the maharaja's version, which consisted of denials without actual evidence and reference to the fact that his *thikadars* were not legally allowed to raise rents without his consent. Saran administrators, on the other hand, ranging from the head constable of the Katia outpost to the district magistrate, were in complete agreement about the incident. Their sources of information included personal observations and data collected at the village level from chaukidars and patwaris as well as such local records as registers of village holdings. But the government remained steadfast in its support of the maharaja, a position it felt was vindicated by the MacDonnell investigation.

The MacDonnell report, however, was never printed in the official proceedings with the rest of the correspondence on the "wholesale desertions" and thus never became part of the public government records. Nevertheless, it was the Bengal government's trump card, and it was invariably produced every time O'Donnell attempted to deal a new hand. His long missive of December 31, 1879, for instance, was dismissed with the rejoinder that the MacDonnell report "fully confirms the opinions expressed by Sir Steuart Bayley."[44] But what the provincial authorities did not divulge was that this report had found "discontent" in the Hathwa estate, nor did they choose to cite MacDonnell's statement that this discontent was the result of the exactions of "native thikadars [who] abused their opportunities as native thikadars in Behar almost always do" or that while "the maharaja is confident of the legality of the demand the ryots are not; a widespread feeling of discontent with this enhancement prevails; and looking to the condition of this part of the district the fact is not surprising."[45]

Indeed, an inherent orientation of the raj's *thikadari* system was to press down heavily on its subordinates. Thus, the rent raises of 1878 or 1879 were felt keenly by Hathwa's raiyats because it followed on the heels of other increases made in the 1870s.[46] Earlier, in 1872, the estate manager had acknowledged this operating principle of the control system when he stated that "the lower classes . . . have had to bear most of the weight of the successive increased demand of rent made by the late Rajah on the villages. . . ."[47] The demands of the late 1870s were the filtering down of the new increased leases that Hathwa had issued to its *thikadars*. Information available on fifteen villages shows that the new rents that *thikadars* were made responsible for were, on an average, 19 percent more than they had been in 1871.[48]

44. H. J. Reynolds, Secy., to O'Donnell, no. 344–160LR, Feb. 12, 1880, Bengal Rev. Procs., Feb. 1880, no. 10.
45. MacDonnell to Commr., Jan. 1, 1880, P.C. Rev. *Basta* no. 331, 1879–1880. A copy of this report was eventually shown to O'Donnell.
46. O'Donnell to Magte., no. 172, July 8, 1879, "Desertions in Hathwa."
47. G. J. S. Hodgkinson, Mgr., Court of Wards, Hathwa, to Colltr. C. B. Garrett, no. A, Feb. 20, 1872, Bengal Rev. Procs., Jan. to April 1872, April, no. 149.
48. MacDonnell to Commr., Jan. 1, 1880, P.C. Rev. *Basta* no. 331. One way that higher rents were achieved "legally" was by "measurement jugglery" (the "discovery" of "surplus" lands).

The wholesale desertions were also induced by the coercive machinery of the Hathwa estate. In O'Donnell's words, the "oppressive enhancement" was accompanied by "unjust, oppressive, and often violent collection of these enhanced rents."[49] These methods were the immediate cause of the mass flight because they aimed at intimidating peasants or denying them their vital, everyday resources.

Physical violence by Hathwa retainers was common against peasants who resisted: Ujagir Rai was wounded with a sickle; Ramlal Tewari was imprisoned until he promised to pay; Lakshmi Narain Dubey and Mussamut Bhagmati were driven off their fields; and Ganga Rawniar was expelled from his home.[50]

The other tactic was to deny peasants access to their subsistence needs. Paddy and maize crops were confiscated. In other instances, crops were confiscated while they were on the threshing floor. Many tenants were unable to continue work because the estate's retainers prevented them from watering or plowing their fields. Enhanced rents were also enforced by stripping people of their cattle and bullocks. One tenant even returned home after an absence to find that the roof of his house had been removed by his *thikadar*![51]

In Karkataha, the "notorious *thikadar*," Nihal Khan, held sway and used similar tactics to disrupt the routine of everyday life. When Hirahman Koeri refused to pay an additional five rupees, Nihal Khan, accompanied by two retainers, seized him while he was enroute to his son's wedding. He was then dragged off, beaten, and kept confined until 9 o'clock that evening. His neck cloth containing Rs. 25 was confiscated.[52]

Resistance was also broken by tying a human "millstone" around the necks of some villagers. This was achieved by sending an estate retainer to the house of a recalcitrant tenant.

> He usually sits outside the tenant's door, seeking every opportunity of petty harassment, such as by preventing the ryot going to his daily work, by insulting his womenfolk, and by demanding his daily diet expenses—a demand which he does not hesitate to enforce by snatching his cloth from the ryot's shoulders, his turban from his head, or his brass plate from before him as he eats. When asked why he does not resist, the ryot simply answers that going to court would cost him as much as ten cloths or half a dozen brass plates; besides he would find himself opposed by the trained lawyers whom the Maharaja regularly employs, and, moreover, might have a sowar [horseman, retainer] from Hutwa, costing a rupee a day, appointed to further harass and beggar him. Such is the look-out of the poor ryot.[53]

See "the humble petition of . . . O'Donnell . . . to the Viceroy," April 11, 1881, P.C. Gen. *Basta* no. 284, 1881.
    49. O'Donnell to Magte., no. 169, July 4, 1879, "Desertions in Hathwa." Leadbeater to Supt., (June 18, 1879, ibid.) describes these methods as *zoolum* (oppression or tyranny).
    50. Compiled from "Abstract of cases . . . laid before Subdivisional officer . . . and other Magistrates," with O'Donnell to Magte., no. 172, July 8, 1879, ibid.   51. Ibid.
    52. Hirahman Koeri *vs.* Nehal Khan, case decided by Pawsey, July 1879, with Offg. Colltr. C. C. Quinn to Commr., June 25, 1881, P.C. Gen. *Basta* no. 284. It was MacDonnell who singled out Nihal Khan as the "notorious *thikadar*" (MacDonnell to Commr., Jan. 1, 1880, ibid., no. 331).
    53. O'Donnell to Magte, no. 172, July 8, 1879, "Desertions in Hathwa."

Hathwa also manipulated the state's legal system to secure an additional edge over its tenants. Both in the areas in which it had holdings as well as in the major administrative centers, it maintained law specialists. Although the Calcutta establishment was abolished by 1872 by the Court of Wards, the estate still had two pleaders and four legal agents (mukhtars) in Chapra, and additional legal representatives in Siwan, Shahabad, Champaran, Gorakhpur, Muzaffarpur, and Patna city.[54] With its superior legal establishment and resources, it successfully secured legal sanction for rent enhancements by instituting cases disguised as suits for arrears of rent. Often these and other cases were filed in the courts of Chapra sixty miles away. And if an enterprising tenant was bold enough to challenge the suit, he faced the additional danger of surviving litigation that could cost him immensely in time and money.[55]

Nor did the state's other institutions seek to contest the local power of Hathwa. Even as Saran administrators were investigating the desertions, the estate's functionaries—*sowars* (horsemen), *peadas* (peons), and high-ranking retainers on elephant-back—arrived to still the voices of discontent. And on another front, the maharaja succeeded in convincing the regional authorities that his version of the events of 1879 was the correct one—a triumph that led to the removal of O'Donnell and Pawsey from their posts in Saran.[56]

The Dynamics of Hathwa Control

The 1879 case highlights the dynamics of the Hathwa control system. As the reference to the "late" maharaja's views on accrual of rights suggests and as is also apparent in the analysis of the raj-*thikadari* connection, the estate monopolized all rights in its land. For the estate, *thikadars* were primarily rent collectors whom it could appoint and dismiss at will. Their intermediary role was further emphasized by the maharaja's exclusive rights to institute any and all legal action against raiyats.

The great estate of Hathwa was remarkable in that it had few villages in which it allowed long-term rights to accrue. A major exception was the fifty-seven villages in perpetual lease to supply the maintenance of the cadet line of Hathwa. This grant had been made to the cadet line in return for that family's withdrawal from the long and costly litigation over the existence of the custom of primogeniture in the Hathwa raj. However, in the absence of a male heir, these villages were to revert back to the estate.[57] Subordinate rights had also developed in three villages in perpetual lease to a distant relative of the

---

54. "Management of the Hutwa raj," no. A, Feb. 20, 1872, Bengal Rev. Procs., April 1872, no. 142.   55. Pawsey to Commr., no. 345, July 29, 1879, "Desertions in Hathwa."
56. O'Donnell to Magte., no. 164, June 21, 1879, ibid.
57. *Ekarnamah* (deed) executed by Maharaja Rajender Pertap Sahee, Feb. 24, 1862. A printed copy of this deed of agreement was given to me by Babu Bishwanath Pratap Sahi, descendant of the cadet line of Hathwa, June 22, 1974, Hathwa village, Saran. See also "Management of the Hutwa Raj," Bengal Rev. Procs., April 1872, no. 149.

Hathwa family; some rentfree villages were in the hands of family retainers, such as the descendants of the faithful Rajput lieutenant, Dujjoo Singh, who had been an important ally in the struggle against Fateh Sahi; still others were held as service grants by the estate's attorneys.[58]

The strong centralized power of Hathwa is especially apparent in contrast to the Bettiah and Ramnagar estates of Champaran where indigo planters secured permanent intermediate tenures (*mokarrari*).[59] Hathwa, on the other hand, consistently opposed even the development of rights at the lowest level of the peasantry. As one estate manager declared in the late 1870s, "the ryots of this estate are mere tenants-at-will and have therefore no occupancy rights."[60]

Clearly, the Hathwa raj claimed exclusive rights in the land, and, whenever possible, it preempted all other parties from acquiring any rights. But it was far less occupied with regulating relationships in which it was not directly involved. In other words, while designed to maintain a strong superstructure, its system of control allowed subordinate levels considerable latitude in obtaining advantageous exchanges with still lower ranks in the estate hierarchy. One institutionalized manifestation of this principle was the elaborate perquisites that raj officials received from *thikadars* and raiyats. For example, in the tahsildari of Bhorey in 1871–1872, the superintendent received Rs. 104; the tahsildar, Rs. 48; the assistant manager, Rs. 47; the *mohurrir* (writer), Rs. 37; and an additional Rs. 25 had to be given the patwari as a cess for acknowledging receipt of the rent payment. Although the Court of Wards was familiar with these practices, it made no attempt to stop them. And when a commissioner of Patna objected to them, the provincial authorities informed him that official action against illegal dues was futile because it would only lead to their being incorporated into the rent rolls.[61]

Thus, the dynamics of Hathwa's system of control generated a propensity among its intermediaries to maximize their resources at the expense of the raiyats. This principle was built into the estate structure because its strong, central management safeguarded the interests of the maharaja but had no mechanisms to restrain *thikadari* demands on village society. And as substantial peasants and moneylenders, *thikadars* were in an opportune position to abuse their power as village-level controllers. The estate's control over them was, therefore, designed only to check their interceptions of its share and not to regulate their dealings with village society. The subdivisional officer of Siwan ran up against this aspect of the system in 1879, when he found out that his

58. "Management of the Hutwa Raj"; "Note of D. N. Dutt" (on petition of Toti Singh and others, descendants of Dujjoo Singh), Nov. 29, 1899, H.R. *Bastas*, 1899–1900.
59. Mishra 1966: 399.
60. Cited in Pawsey to Commr., no. 345, July 29, 1879, Bengal Rev. Procs., Dec. 1879, nos. 73–78.
61. Commr. R. P. Jenkins to Colltr., no. 232, Mar. 1, 1872, Bengal Rev. Procs., April 1872, no. 149. The lieutenant-governor's opinions are in K.W. (Keep With) Procs. for April 1872, nos. 149–50.

complaints against the *thikadari* system were not only ignored, but the estate bureaucracy "*invariably* supported the ticcadars against the ryots."[62] And, whether by design or by default, as the *amla* and tahsildari perquisites reveal, Hathwa management generally condoned exactions from subordinates. The evidence strongly suggests that the description by a Court of Wards manager accurately characterized the manner in which Hathwa dealt with its connections in village society:

Formerly they used, no doubt to levy contributions in excess of the rents. A practice which was rendered the easier for the village papers being really in theirs [*sic*] without any check beyond that which a Patwaree whom they could and did turn out at will, could impose, and they thought little of depriving their ryots of any particularly good piece of land, to which they took a fancy. These practices were winked at, as long as the Raj received its rent regularly; and, indeed, were probably looked upon as more or less essential to the regularity in payment. At any rate they were practices which the principal *amlah*, themselves teekadars, could not be expected to expose.[63]

In times of agricultural distress, these *thikadari* impositions came down particularly heavily on the raiyats because the central management continued to demand its customary claim. The 1879 desertions illustrate this tendency on the part of the Hathwa system, as do the desertions that occurred in 1872 from several villages in Bhorey, when the area was stricken by three successive crop failures due to inundation. Because no allowances were made, many raiyats were compelled to sell their bullocks to pay their rents; others absconded. The estate manager's explanation of this situation identifies this inherent orientation of the *thikadari* system: "In the first place a ticcadar who has his own rents to pay to the landlord cannot be trusted to give the ryot any indulgence, and not to rigorously exact every pice [cent] that can be screwed out of him. In the second place, the ticcadars are often the village mahajan, which is another reason for fearing their exactions."[64] Thus, whether the management system of an estate was directly administered or indirectly managed through *thikadars*, the weight of the system—regardless of who or what superordinate group intercepted the largest share—fell squarely on the shoulders of the raiyats.

Hathwa even gained the upper hand during the survey and settlement proceedings of the late nineteenth century, which were ostensibly designed to produce a reliable record of rights on the land. In the "settlement of fair rents," 84 percent of the total increase was made in the Hathwa-dominated thanas of Mirganj and Gopalganj. In Hathwa 29 percent of raiyati holdings were affected, compared to 2 percent of raiyati holdings in other estates. Hathwa's rents were increased by 6 percent, whereas the increase in the rest of the district was 3 percent. Hathwa's greater success stemmed from the "accurate"

---

62. O'Donnell to Magte., no. 164, June 21, 1879, "Desertions in Hathwa."
63. "Annual Report of Hutwa for 1872–73."
64. Hodgkinson to Colltr., no. 436, Sept. 25, 1872, Bengal Rev. Procs., Oct.–Dec. 1872, Nov., 395.

records and maps compiled by the Court of Wards management in the 1870s. These the estate used "for all they were worth, and took advantage of every provision of the law in order to get the full benefit of the settlement operations." Or as the district settlement officer phrased it, "the Hathwa Raj has its pound of flesh."[65]

The rise of the Hathwa raj was the result of direct British intervention. British involvement was crucial in the elevation of the cadet line in the early nineteenth century and the dispossession of the family of the rebellious Fateh Sahi in the late eighteenth century, and it also figured in the development of a vital, strategic alliance. As the major prop of the Limited Raj, it was in the interests of government to preserve and enhance Hathwa's local power and control. Thus, when the estate's intermediate tenureholders—many with enduring loyalties to the family of Fateh Sahi—fomented an internal rising on the occasion of the survey operations of 1844, the British sent their cavalry to the rescue. In stamping out these riots, government ensured the continuing consolidation and development of the zamindari. In effect, the British facilitated the restructuring of networks of control at the village level, thereafter to be organized by and linked closely to Hathwa.

The success of this reorganization is evident from the wholesale desertions of 1879, when the great estate of Hathwa exercised its newly built capacity to intrude directly into the lives of its peasants. This ability was expressed through an elaborate network of control that subordinated the estate's villages to a highly centralized management system, with crucial links supplied by the *thikadar*s, who were generally substantial peasants or petty maliks of considerable social, economic, and political standing in their village communities. Confronted with this system of control, peasants were unable to resist the demands of their landholder, except by defensively engaging in mass exodus. The events of 1879 also clearly indicate government's continuing support of its major local connection. Because the extensions of the colonial state were limited, its ties to Hathwa formed a crucial connection to local society. In such a system of collaboration, as the events of 1844 and 1879 reveal, the result was that the maharaja of Hathwa enjoyed undisputed dominance as the lord of his great estate.

65. *SR*: 84.

8

Zamindars and Maliks: Structures and Strategies of Control

In contrast to the frequent official praise for the management of the great estate of Hathwa, the machinery of control in large zamindaris and the small estates of petty maliks received little official acclaim. In both cases, the views of "the man for Chupra" were shaped by specific concerns. In large part, they were based on political expediency because, for the Limited Raj to function optimally, its connections with the local society had to be strong and effective. The different roles envisaged for major and small landholders were frequently enunciated: "[P]etty maliks . . . are village tyrants and set authority at defiance, but owing to their numbers and comparative insignificance, have not the responsibility and influence of large zamindars, who can be and are of material assistance to a Collector in maintaining the authority of the Government."[1]

The systems of control in the smaller estates appeared arbitrary to the government because they seemed to lack central organization and cohesion. They were also said to be prone to excesses that threatened the stability of the rural order. Such descriptions of ineffective control in Saran's estates were not intended to highlight the proverbially recalcitrant raiyats, but to recognize the extent of pressure landholders exerted on their subordinates.

Several factors conditioned the systems of control in Saran estates. Although few large zamindars were able to maintain their holdings in the nineteenth and early twentieth centuries, let alone consolidate and expand, nevertheless their holdings remained fairly cohesive geographical units. Since the Permanent Settlement of the district had been made "with the old landed proprietors of

1. Note by W. Kemble, BOR, with no. 824T.R., Oct. 19, 1892, Bengal Rev. Procs., May to Aug. 1893, July, 286.

the country,"[2] many zamindars and maliks had, prior to the advent of the British, already secured compact territorial units, a process no doubt necessitated by the infrastructural limitations of transport and communications. Not surprisingly, then, the nineteenth-century holdings of large estates generally encompassed contiguous villages. Two notable examples of such geographical cohesiveness are the important Eksaria Bhumihar zamindaris of Bagoura and Parsa.[3]

Few estates, however, enjoyed the repeated British interventions that facilitated and enhanced cohesion and strong central management in the Hathwa raj. Nor did many estates have the opportunity to have the Court of Wards step in to build up their bureaucracies. However, the large estates generally had diffuse control networks that were more than adequate for their primary goal of rent collection. The absence of a Hathwa-like control superstructure did not mean a complete breakdown in superordinate control because their connections at the village level operated in much the same fashion.

The residential seats of large landholdings were usually marketing centers; a close correlation exists between the mid-nineteenth-century sites of zamindar forts and markets.[4] This coincidence of zamindari centers with markets was common in north India. As Richard Fox explains, "a local *raja, navab,* or big zamindar . . . endowed towns and began market places . . . [and] control of the market and the town . . . imposed a sense and structure of community upon what was an amorphous collection of primarily merchant castes, attracted by economic opportunity."[5]

Most petty maliks resided in the villages in which they had holdings. In eleven of the forty-four villages of Sonepur thana—the area with the smallest estates in the district—in which positive identifications of the landholders and their places of residence are possible, the maliks were local men; another twelve were from nearby villages. "Outside" proprietors were mostly from small market centers (*hats*). In addition, six villages belonged entirely and three partly to inhabitants of Patna city. The rest were held by combinations of resident and neighborhood landholders, or by proprietors from Chapra and the large zamindar of Goldenganj. And in the villages where proprietors cannot be identified, the village notes suggest that at least some rights belonged to villagers or nearby residents.[6]

The evidence from Sonepur also shows a bewildering range of rights in Saran's lands. Unlike the neat parcels of Hathwa's land package, most Sonepur maliks had highly fractional rights. In Baigalpur Keshor an estate paying

2. *SR*: 23.
3. See Parsa thana nos. 1–100, 101–200; and, for Bagoura, Basantpur thana nos. 1–100, 101–200, SVN. See also Cohn (1969: 53–151) for the argument that landholders remained in positions of power in villages even when they were legally dispossessed.
4. See Yang 1983.   5. 1969: 70.
6. See Sonepur thana nos. 1–100, 106–159, SVN. Manpur village, Sonepur thana no. 146, is an area where the maliks collected rents.

government revenue of Rs. 323 had forty-one separate accounts.[7] During the thana's survey and settlement, attestation officers noticed that the proprietors of one estate were often tenants on another, apparently as a result of fissiparous processes acting on an area in which the original settlement had been made with only a few large proprietors.[8] In effect, many of these estate holders were no better off than the average raiyat in the village.

Most landholders with substantial rights in at least one village tended to set themselves apart from their fellow villagers. Large landholders especially maintained a visibly different presence, one of the most conspicuous symbols of their distinction being their residences. Although none had palaces on the scale of Hathwa's, most had substantial houses (*kothis*).[9] In the late nineteenth century, others continued to live in forts such as the one the Salempur babus were routed from in the Mutiny/Rebellion of 1857.[10] Later in the century, the residential seat of many of the large estates also housed their *kachcheris*. These establishments, according to one descendant of a leading zamindari family, were modeled after the district collectorates.[11]

Although the number of employees in the large estates and their designations varied considerably, most had a staff of all or some of the following: manager, agent, diwan, and a host of retainers (commonly referred to as *amla*). In the prominent Manjhi estate in 1838, for example, the widow requested the Court of Wards to support the establishment she felt necessary to maintain as "a member of a respectable family." In addition to her household staff, which included a mahout for her elephant and eleven slave girls, she sought funds to have a mukhtar (presumably to act as her agent) and two peons.[12]

Relatives and fellow castemen of the proprietor formed a significant pool of recruitment for zamindari administrative positions. Even the peons in many important Bhumihar Brahmin estates were drawn from the ranks of fellow castemen. Each of the forty-one Bhumihar families in the village of Bedupur had at least one member working in the large estates of Chainpur, Parsa, Gabhirar, and Salemgarh.[13] Such practices suggest the assertion that "rural power in nineteenth-century India might be seen as being with the estate managers and their cronies."[14] In other words, a fixed pool of recruitment was conducive to the growth of alternate sources of power and influence within an estate. A striking example of such diversion of the landholder's resources is the

---

7. See Sonepur thana no. 65; also Dumri Buzurg village, Sonepur thana no. 22, SVN, which had two estates and 500 shares.   8. *SR*: 127.
9. Interview with P. T Mansfield, July 31, 1973.
10. Deputy Magte. J. F. Lynch to Magte. W. F. McDonnell, no. 61, Feb. 2, 1858, S.C., Letters received from 1854 to 1859 from Deputy Magte. of Siwan.
11. Interview with Hari Surendra Sahi, Manjha family.
12. Offg. Colltr. W. Luke to Offg. Commr. E. C. Ravenshaw, Oct. 4, 1838, Bengal BOR Conslns., Wards, 1838, Nov., no. 12.
13. These families added up to 265 individuals. See Bedupur village, Manjhi thana no. 173, SVN. For a similar configuration of zamindari staff in Patna estates, see Hagen (1981: 146).
14. Musgrave 1972: 270.

case of the Rampur babus, who rose from being the servants of the Chainpur estate "to the position of independent zamindars."[15]

In addition, many large estates retained mukhtars, who combined a working knowledge of "lawyer's law" with close ties to the landholder.[16] On most estates, as in the Hathwa raj, they were regarded as trusted officers. In many, including Hathwa, Goldenganj, Manjha, Parsa, and Rusi, they were also the "general agents."[17] In 1866, 30 mukhtars were licensed in the district with general powers of attorney, and 298 officially recognized as "revenue agents."[18] That the occupation of many was listed as both mukhtar and zamindar points to the customary dependent relationship between a landholder and his major servants, often expressed by an assignment of land in lieu of salary. Most legal agents were of the traditionally literate caste: Kayasths.[19]

The Structures of Control

Regardless of the diffuse nature of management structures at the top, from the perspective of the village, a complete breakdown of superordinate control in large zamindaris was rare. Weak intermediate links between the village and the estate, while cutting into the profits of the proprietor, also had the effect of enhancing the commanding power of the village-level connections. The zamindar's loss was invariably the *thikadar*'s or some other intermediary's gain. In such estates the intermediaries became, in effect, petty maliks.

Thikadars, generally men of wealth and power, were the crucial connections in most large estates. In Basantpur and Manjhi thanas, where the Chainpur and Manjhi babus held considerable territory, the largest areas in the district were in cultivation to "tenureholders," who were primarily Indian or European indigo planter *thikadars*, and rentfree holders under these babus.[20] This "ordinary" *thikadari* system exhibited a major difference from that of Hathwa: they lacked Hathwa's strong central supervision:

The farms are generally held by middle-men in consideration of loans or advances, and are as a rule leased by the maliks to the highest bidder. This inevitably leads to the worst form of rack-renting. The ticcadar does his best to squeeze as much as possible from the

15. See Nagdiha and Jahangirpur villages, Chapra thana nos. 50 and 51, SVN, 1893–1901.
16. "Lawyer's law" refers to "that set of norms sanctioned by the national and state courts and administrative systems and their personnel" (Cohn 1965: 82).
17. See "The humble memorial of the undersigned Native Inhabitants of Zillah Sarun," July 1870, India, Home Dept. Procs., Education, Jan. 1871, no. 2, which lists, in order of local importance, the names and occupations of some 1,500 individuals. The first five signatures were of rajas, followed by 11 "1st class zamindars," one "1st class zamindar and banker," 189 zamindars, 33 pleaders, 151 government servants and indigo planters, and 142 mukhtars. The remaining 778 consisted of "bankers, teachers, students, and inhabitants."
18. See "List of Mokhtars" with Colltr. Halliday to Commr. Dalrymple, no. 60, June 19, 1866, S.C., Letters sent to the Commr. of Patna commencing from Aug. 16, 1865.
19. Of the 298 "revenue agent" mukhtars, 246 were Kayasth; 41, Muslim; 5, Bhumihar; 2, Brahmin; 1, Rajput; 1, Koeri; and 1, Gurer (compiled from ibid.).
20. *Thikadars* were considered tenureholders (*SR*: 127; Basantpur thana nos. 301–401, SVN).

ryots, and the ryots in their turn are helpless. They are at once precluded from applying to their original landlord for protection, and they can obtain no redress from the courts of justice, because as a rule they hold no pottahs or written engagements. They are therefore entirely at the mercy of the ticcadars and putwaries. Any case which a ryot brings against the ticcadar must depend solely on the putwari's papers and these, as may be imagined are prepared for the occasion and filed to suit the objects of the ticcadars.[21]

Some estates employed the direct system of management. Although none were on the scale of Hathwa's circle system, they followed the same pattern of relying on tahsildars working in collaboration with village officials to represent the interests of the estate.[22] A *khas* system of rent collection also characterized most small estates, extending over several villages in full or in part, and almost always the estates of petty maliks, holding a village or two. In some Kayasth-held villages, even these connections were dispensed with and the maliks themselves made the collections.[23]

Although the absence of a strong central superstructure in many of the district's large estates meant a diffuse and often arbitrary system of control, it did not, at least for the raiyat, constitute a power vacuum in village society. A case in point is the zamindari of Amnour, where the "late proprietor, a kindly easy going landlord ... treated his tenants with the utmost leniency, and it was his boast that he had never brought a rent suit against any of them. His accounts were above suspicion, but showed that he had never realised a quarter of the rental entered in his jamabandis."[24] But under the existing structure of connections between estate and village, rarely was there a complete dissolution of *all* superordinate authority. Instead, as under the "lenient" hand of the late Amnour proprietor, it was not the raiyats who prospered but the estate servants "who collected far more than they made over to him."[25]

Recent debates about the structures of estate management, however, tend to ignore the important distinctions that need to be made between the central organization and the intermediate connections of the estate. As a result, findings about zamindars with less than complete control over their resources and the concomitant greater power of their underlings have prompted hasty conclusions about the "feet of clay" of the landlord raj. From the perspective of the raiyats, it made little difference if the village structures of control did ultimately link up with the larger estate network because the "man on the spot"—whether a *thikadar*, or a petty malik, or other estate functionary—still imposed his demands on them. Another facile generalization in recent writings has been to assume that indirect control, such as that wielded through the

21. Remarks of the Commr. of Patna cited in "Supplementary Report of Patna and Bhagalpur Divisions," Bengal Rev. Procs., Jan. to Apr. 1872, Feb., no. 107, app. B. For a similar assessment by the Saran Magte., see AGRPD, 1872–73.
22. See, e.g., Dohar village, Manjhi thana no 4. SVN.
23. As in Katuri Chak, Hayagaon, and Mahmud Chak villages, Sonepur thana nos. 21, 32, and 28, respectively, SVN.   24. *SR*: 71.   25. Ibid.

thikadars, automatically meant an enervation of the power of the landholder.[26] Neither the evidence on Hathwa nor the documentation on other Saran estates warrants this conclusion.

Many *thikadars* were also petty maliks, either of the village they had leased or of a nearby one.[27] And, as in the great estate of Hathwa, *thikadars* of other zamindaris were often also village headmen, and almost always the substantial raiyats and moneylenders of the village.

In localities where the *jeth*-raiyat (the "eldest" or the "principal" raiyat of a village) was not formally part of an estate organization, he was at least closely subordinated to the zamindar. Originally, however, he had been the intermediate agent between the landholder and other raiyats in all village affairs. But, by the late nineteenth century, instead of being linked to the village community, he was frequently noticed in every privately partitioned part of an estate, as was the case with the zamindar's other village-level connection, the patwari. One district magistrate described headmen as practically "the gomastah of the zamindar, owing to the frequency of their employment by landholders in that capacity."[28] By the early twentieth century, this village officer had become even more completely incorporated in the estate's network:

> He is usually found only in large estates. He is generally an important raiyat in the village, whose duties are sometimes to collect the rents and make them over to the patwari, and sometimes merely to induce the raiyats to go to the patwari to pay their rents. He is remunerated occasionally by a percentage in the rent collections, but usually by being given a remission on his own rent or by being allowed to hold his lands at a favourable rate.[29]

The selection of the headmen also highlights the control of the landholder, who appointed a replacement if the normally hereditary succession was interrupted because the headman's family was in reduced circumstances or lacked a member of sufficient standing. The villagers were often not consulted in this matter. At *Dashara* which, in the words of one Saran resident, "was looked upon as the festival of the zamindars,"[30] the subordination of the headmen was ritually enacted. In the ceremony held on this occasion, the landholder endowed him with a turban "in public, as a mark of distinction, on the day of his assuming office, and on every subsequent *Dashara* festival, but he has to pay in return salamee (douceur) to the zemindar."[31]

That many *thikadars* were also village moneylenders is not surprising because it reflects the importance of credit manipulation in agricultural societies.[32] Indeed, one veteran Bihar official noted that raiyats considered

---

26. See the conflicting viewpoints of Musgrave (1972: 257–75) and Henningham (1983: 35–37). The emphasis on opposing interests on an estate is also made by Robb (1979: 102–4).
27. See, e.g., Baraja village, Manjhi thana no. 173, SVN.
28. Report of Saran Magte. cited in *Papers regarding Village Agency*. 29. *SR*: 185.
30. Rajendra Prasad 1957: 12. 31. *Papers regarding Village Agency*: 49.
32. For a general statement, see Firth and Yamey (1963); also Musgrave (1978: 216–32).

villages without moneylenders to be "an abnormal state of things." Furthermore, the "impressions" he had accumulated from "mofussil wanderings over a period of some 17 years, are that the rajah, the ryot and the mahajan are so many parts of a machine; the one without the other would bring the whole to a standstill."[33] Combined with the *thikadar*'s other strengths, this role in the local economy fortified his position as village controller and connection.

The *thikadar* as headman and moneylender epitomizes the estate's connections with village-level society. In addition, there were other links, as is evident from the earlier observations made about the fit of the patwari and the chaukidar in the networks of state and estate control. One Bihar official even described the patwari as "a relation of the ticcadar, almost always his caste-fellow, and is himself an embryo ticcadar, whose best hope of success in life depends on doing the ticcadar's dirty work."[34]

By the mid-nineteenth century, the village peon (*gorait*), whose office was akin to that of the ehaukidar, was consistently characterized in the official records as an appointee of the landholder and also reported as "now afraid of the zamindar and of losing his Jaigeer."[35] Furthermore, while village officials increasingly articulated the interests of the landholder, other village institutions, such as panchayets (councils), declined in importance. Although caste panchayets were noted in Saran in the late nineteenth century, they, too, toiled under the shadow of estate controls.[36] In short, the primary networks of control in local society in the nineteenth and twentieth centuries derived ultimately from the estates of zamindars and petty maliks.

Strategies of Control

Because control depends on the maintenance and manipulation of unequal exchanges of resources, strategies of control refer to the ways in which superordinates attempted to ensure and enhance their commanding positions. In Saran, these strategies centered on maximizing rights and claims in the land and were worked out in an arena where many levels of interests intersected. Although the British regime constituted a Limited Raj at the district level, its supralocal power and authority made it imperative that local controllers either obviate the British presence altogether or rechannel resources to further their own objectives.

---

33. Note from C. T. Metcalfe, Nov. 4, 1875, London, Temple Papers, Condition of Peasantry, Bengal, 1875, Mss. Eur. F. 86/161.
34. C. J. O'Donnell, Joint Magte., Gaya, to Magte. of Gaya, in "Behar Rent Papers (1877–78)," I, (74) 1908/3, p. 22.
35. Lynch to McDonnell, no. 54, Sept. 15, 1856, S.C., Letters from 1854 to 1859 from Siwan; Gopalganj thana nos. 1–100, SVN.
36. *Papers regarding Village Agency*: 54.

LEGAL MANIPULATION

A case in point is the manipulation of the British legal machinery. On one hand, many disputes were kept out of court and settled by local controllers and their coadjutors. On the other hand, the "litigious native" was a stock British perception. Commonplace was the observation, enshrined in the Saran gazetteer, that the heavy volume of civil cases in the district "must be attributed to the litigiousness of a large population."[37] But the frequent recourse to the courts, as local officials acknowledged, stemmed from their ready manipulation as instruments of control.

In most estates, *thikadars* were expected not only to collect rents, but also to contain dissonance. Contemporary accounts describe an "informal courts" system, which played a leading role in the adjudication of local disputes. According to the commissioner of Tirhut division, this system was routinely handled "by planters, zamindars and zamindari managers and is regarded as an ordinary part of their business, raiyats naturally referring their disputes to them and agreeing to their decisions, although of course legally these decisions are not enforceable."[38]

The legal system was, therefore, used discriminately. When only six cases were instituted for the enhancement or abatement of rent in 1894–1895, the Saran collector explained that a "great many petty cases are . . . heard and decided by the landlords and the parties considered guilty punished by fine."[39] Or, as another Saran official put it in noticing only forty-three such suits, "resort to the courts for this purpose . . . [was] quite unnecessary in Behar."[40]

Suits for arrears of rent were much more commonplace because they proved to be effective leverages for superordinate control. Not unrepresentative was the year in which there were 43 cases for enhancement but 1,227 suits for arrears of rent. The difference lay in the tactical advantages that the latter provided for securing illegal enhancements:

The zamindar having ordered that all demands should be increased by one half, his agents framed their collection papers accordingly, and kept their accounts upon that basis for a series of years. Rent at the old rate, though tendered and apparently accepted as a discharge in full of all obligation, was credited only as a payment in part, no accounts were given to the tenants, and the receipts were so framed as to afford no indication as to the demand. After three years or more the agent brought over a few raiyats to swear that the desired rate had existed for a long period, hired half a dozen clubmen, and instituted suits, not for enhancement but for arrears. He probably obtained certain collusive decrees as foundation. The real suits were delayed as long as possible, and seldom came to a final determination, as the raiyats, after a skirmish or

37. *SDG, 1930*: 117.
38. B. Foley to GOB&O, March 10, 1914, B&O Jdcl. Procs., May to Aug. 1917, May, 50.
39. "Saran District Administration Report, 1894–95," Colltr. F. A. Slack to Commr., no. 398G, May 7, 1895, P.C. Rev. *Basta* no. 363, 1895–1896.
40. AGRPD, 1872–73.

two with the lathials [clubmen], followed by prosecution in the criminal courts, preferred to compromise for an increase of 25 per cent.[41]

Court decisions also testify to the manipulation of the legal system. Of the 3,131 suits in 1872–1873, only 21 were settled by arbitration; 2,037 were withdrawn, compromised, or decreed ex parte, or on confession. These figures convinced the district magistrate that "the civil courts are largely made use of for improper purposes by those who have means to do so."[42] Nor did the legal system become any less pliable once a record of rights was established in the region at the turn of the nineteenth century. In the quinquennium 1900–1901 to 1904–1905, 239,871 (78 percent) of the total 308,080 rent suits in Patna division were compromised or decreed ex parte, without reference to the record of rights.[43]

Recourse to the courts was a handy instrument of control because the British legal system ignored local power realities. Thus, the outcome of any legal contest between zamindar and raiyat was inevitable, as is suggested by the "typical" case of court abuse schematized by one Bihar administrator:

A, zamindar of Chapra, wishes to harass *B*, one of his tenants, or to make him pay an extortionate rent, or to part with some landed property. *A*, through an agent, causes a false civil suit to be brought against *B* in the Small Cause Court in Calcutta. He takes measures to prevent *B* from hearing of this suit and obtains a decree ex parte. The first thing that *B* hears of the suit is when execution proceedings are taken out and a civil court peon appears to attach his property.

Under the present procedures *B* is required to apply to the District Magistrate, who will investigate the case by the C.I.D. [Criminal Investigation Department]. The C.I.D. moves the Small Cause Court to declare the case false, after which *A* will be prosecuted . . . and may possibly be convicted, after about one year or 18 months. Meanwhile *B* will undergo constant harassment from police enquiries and from being required to give evidence in distant courts, and, since apparently there is no procedure to annul summarily and immediately the decree obtained in the false suit, he will not be saved from ruin. As a matter of fact in existing conditions *A* will probably escape conviction. He knows this and so does his tenants. As things are at present therefore *A*, though proceedings were pending against him, might well say to other tenants *C*, *D* and *E*, "Do as I want or I will treat you as I've treated *B*."[44]

In five fraudulent cases that the government pleader reported for Saran, the proceedings extended over at least one year and, in one instance, two years.[45] The secretary of the Saran Bar Association testified that the beneficiaries of "notoriously dilatory and expensive" civil court proceedings were "persons who . . . are usually men of wealth and leisure. They [courts] are also used to a

41. E. W. Collin, Secy. BOR to Secy. GOB, no. 210A, Feb. 24, 1902, Bengal Rev. Procs., May–July 1902, June, 1457.   42. Cited in AGRPD, 1872–73.
43. "Quinquennial Report of the Patna Division for the period from 1900–01 to 1904–05," Bengal Rev. Procs., June to Aug. 1906, Aug., 19.
44. Commr. B. Foley, Chota Nagpur, to GOB&O, Jdcl., April 5, 1918, B&O Jdcl. Procs., 1918, Oct., 12.   45. Note from B. C. Mukherjee, Govt. Pleader, Feb. 8, 1918, in ibid., 5.

regrettable extent . . . as a machinery for oppression and extortion."[46] The extent to which courts were arenas for "speculation" in control is also underscored by the experiences of a veteran Bihar administrator:

> Since I was subdivisional officer of Bettiah in 1895 I have been aware that certain Indian zamindars occasionally collected their rent and whatever else they wished from their tenants by means of false criminal cases. It was (not) till I was Collector of Saran in 1912 that I was aware that they used false civil cases brought in other districts for the same purpose. . . . Since then I had occasion to make enquiries and found the practice widely prevalent in Saran, Muzaffarpur, and Darbhanga. I remember discussing the question with an Indian gentleman at Chapra and venturing the opinion that 50 per cent of the cases brought in the Small Cause Court were false. This gentleman answered me I was quite incorrect; 90 per cent of such cases were false.[47]

But the legal levers that courts became for local controllers were never balanced by corrective legislation, despite widespread official awareness of the deleterious effects of the legal system.[48]

Perhaps nowhere was the failure of the legal system to neutralize the power of local controllers more apparent than in the legislative attempts to protect the rights of the tenantry. Beginning with regulations drafted in Bengal in 1826 to promulgate the so-called Rent Act of 1859, virtually no protective shields were created for raiyats against the superior resources of landholders.[49] The voluminous evidence compiled in the region in the late 1870s, leading to the Bengal Tenancy Act of 1885, clearly reflects the inadequacies of the earlier legislation. Although the provincial authorities believed that the deficiency in Bengal proper was the absence of any effective means of recovering rents (i.e., tenants were contentious), in Bihar the opposite situation was said to prevail:

> What is most wanted there is to provide some ready means of enabling the ryot to resist illegal distraint, illegal enhancement, and illegal cesses, and to enable him to prove and maintain his occupancy rights where the law gives them. Apart from the backwardness, weakness, and poverty of the ryots, the facts which tend most to support the present state of things are the tediousness and expense of rent suits in a civil court, the corruption of process-servers, the entire absence of pottahs [deeds of lease] and kaboolyuts [document of rental agreement], and the wretched system of keeping zemindaree accounts, by which loose papers, written up in the course of a night, are the only documentary evidence which, as a rule, is put before the court.[50]

Convened to draw up special measures, the Bihar Rent Committee found overwhelming proof of the shortcomings of the Rent Act of 1859. Although this

46. Cited in Commr. Foley to GOB&O, Jdcl., ibid., May to Aug. 1917, May, 50.
47. Foley to GOB&O, April 5, 1918, ibid., Oct. 1918, 11. See also Rothermund (1978: 89) on the landlord strategem of overwhelming a tenant in a court case in order to intimidate other potential tenant litigants.
48. For a good discussion of British attempts to regulate the effects of their law on local society, see Whitcombe (1971: 205–233).
49. Palit 1975: 156–92, 200–201; B. B. Chaudhuri 1976a: 51–62.
50. S. C. Bayley, Secy., GOB, Jdcl., to Commr. of Patna Division, demi-official, Aug. 7, 1877, Behar Rent Papers.

law granted tenants a prescriptive right of occupancy after possession for twelve years, it was largely unsuccessful. The committee's report revealed that less than 1 percent of the 60 percent who, according to estate rent rolls, had lived and worked in the same area for more than twelve years were in possession of the same plots. Landholders had thwarted the aim of the law by shifting their raiyats to other plots. Nor was this situation alleviated by the fact that less than ¼ percent of Bihar peasants held deeds of lease.[51]

The committee's recommendations for tenancy legislation emphasized the enactment of provisions to secure occupancy rights, fixity of tenure, certified annual rent rates, procedures to resist illegal distraint, and a reliable set of receipts of payments and demands.[52] The legislation eventually passed as the Bengal Tenancy Act of 1885 modified some of these proposals, although it ostensibly provided a wide range of protective devices, especially for occupancy raiyats.[53] However bold and innovative in the range of tenancy issues the act addressed, it remained merely a declaration of good intentions. Five years after its institution, an investigation found the beginnings of an appreciation of its provisions among "all classes," but widespread ignorance regarding its "novel" provisions.[54] The failure to implement the essential features of the act returned to haunt government in the early twentieth century when its provisions became the central issues of contention between peasants and landholders.[55]

THE RENT AND CESS SYSTEM

The rent and cess system exacerbated distinctions among various levels of the agrarian hierarchy. And, as in the case of *thikadari* management, such discriminations were instrumental to the effectiveness of the rent and cess structure because they created bulwarks that served as integrating links. Whereas the *thikadari* system only singled out the major raiyats in a village, the rent and cess system underlined much sharper distinctions among different social and economic categories. In effect, such divisions defined a series of superordinate-subordinate relationships in village society, fostering the growth of intra-raiyat cleavages and reducing the possibility of subordinate combinations for concerted action.

Rent represented the formal amount that the state recognized as a legitimate claim. It was also one of the major transactions of goods and services, in cash or kind, between landholders and raiyats. However, as is suggested by the

51. Tupper 1881: 150.
52. "Report of the Behar Rent Committee," in Behar Rent Papers.
53. Rothermund 1978: 101–9; Chaudhuri 1976a: 72–81.
54. C. W. Bolton, Secy. BOR, to Secy. GOB, no. 419A, April 30, 1892, Bengal Rev. Procs., Sept. to Dec. 1892, Sept., 252.
55. Most studies show that the act was "a document of declaration and was never uniformly implemented [in Bihar]" (Hauser 1963: 60). See also Jannuzi (1974: 8), who argues that "nowhere in contemporary India is the gulf between articulated ideals with respect to agrarian reforms and solid accomplishments more conspicuous than in Bihar."

paucity of rent enhancement suits, except those disguised as claims for arrears, a wide range of control strategems remained outside the pale of the state's framework. Legal procedures were followed only to secure official sanction or when all other measures failed. Thus, in addition to rent, the widespread practice of extracting *abwabs* (illegal dues or unauthorized cesses) also underscored the effectiveness of control in local society.

Rates of rent were more directly related to local power configurations than they were to ecological factors. In the Hathwa estate and throughout the district, different groups paid different rates of rent. W. W. Hunter estimated that high castes held the best lands in a village at rates varying from 50 to 75 percent below what low castes such as Koeris and Kurmis and Chamars paid for inferior lands.[56] The differential rent structure is also apparent in the rates for raiyats with varying degrees of rights in the land. Although the categories refer more precisely to legal statuses than to functional ones, the differences in rates are nevertheless illuminating. While "raiyats at fixed rates" paid an average of Rs. 3-4-9 per acre, less privileged raiyats, such as "settled or occupancy raiyats" and "non occupancy raiyats" paid more—Rs. 4-5-4 and 5-0-6, respectively. Under-raiyats described as "merely tenants at will" were levied the highest rent rates, Rs. 5-2-9 per acre.[57] This variable structure of rent was designed to acknowledge and reinforce village power realities. Rather than have the *thikadar* keep his own rents the lowest, this system institutionalized such practices: "The high castes pay irregularly, and sometimes not at all. They are rarely sued, as the amounts are not large, and the landlord or lessee finds it bad policy to quarrel with influential villagers; frequently they pay at lower rates than inferior castes are giving for the same quality of land."[58]

Similarly, the system of *abwabs* served as a buttress for the district's agrarian hierarchy. C. F. Worsley, an old Bihar hand, claimed that these illegal dues were as common in the late nineteenth century as they had been at the outset of British rule. Thus, the classic 1815 characterization of such zamindari demands remains an accurate description of existing practices: "Not a child can be borne, not a head religiously shaved, not a son married, not a daughter given in marriage, not even one of the tyrannical fraternity dies, without an immediate visitation of calamity upon the ryot. Whether the occasion be joyful, whether it be sad in its effects, to the cultivator it is alike mournful and calamitous."[59] Indeed, not only did illegal cesses and *abwabs* continue to persist, but they were tacked on to almost every facet of rural life. Following is a list, divided into three categories, of *abwabs* levied on raiyats in Saran District in 1872 (those only on 1903 list are noted).

---

56. Hunter 1877: 301; "Management of the Hutwa Estate during 1873–74," Bengal Rev. Procs., April 1873 to 1875, Aug. 1874, nos. 2–3. 57. *SR*: 37, 144.
58. Harrison 1890: 276.
59. Cited in Offg. Colltr. of Muzaffarpur to Commr., no. 115, June 28, 1875, P.C. Rev. *Basta* no. 323, 1875–76.

I. *Band Behari*: ¼ anna to 1 anna per rupee to recoup amount paid to government for embankment repairs; *Dak Behari*: ¼ anna per rupee of rent taken by zamindar to pay government zamindari charges; *Pul-bandi* (1903 list): For the ostensible object of repairing bridges, not usually paid; Chaukidari/*Kotwali*: A small fee to pay for the maintenance of rural police.

II. *Tahrir/Rasidana*: Levied by the patwari at rates varying from ¼ to 1 anna per rupee of rent, for writing receipts and keeping accounts (alternative names are *hisabana, furkaon,* and *neg*); *Badarat* (1903 list): ½ to 1 anna per rupee for favors shown by patwari to raiyats; *Dawat-Puja* (1903 list): A festival observed by all Kayasths in which the inkpot is worshipped, 1 or 2 annas per rupee to the patwari on this occasion.

III. *Batta* or *Batta* Company: ½ to 1 anna per rupee to compensate for the short weight of rupees introduced by the East India Company, also levied for short weight of any kind of rupees in currency; *Kharcha* or *Kharcha dehia*: 1 to 2 annas per rupee collection expenses of rent in a village; *Beshi* (1903 list): Excess enhancement payment, which rent-collector appropriates; *Salami*: Payment to malik or patwari when entries effected in rent roll; *Chauth* (1872 list): One-quarter value of houses and gardens whenever alienated by the owners; *Kist bojhai* (1872 list): 1 anna on every boat that loads or unloads at a *ganj* (market, port); *Burdana* (1872 list): 3 or 4 annas per annum on every bullock or pony that carries a load; *Kachcheri* (1872 list): A customary present to zamindars and others on the occasion of marriage or another auspicious event in their family, usually in grain; *Begari* and *Hurowai* (1872 list): Demand of free labor, plow, and cattle for cultivation of zamindar's private lands; *Khunti* (1903 list): 12 annas to Rs. 1-4 per bigha for cultivating tobacco; *Khapta* (1903 list): As above, levied for allowing raiyats to raise special crops, usually demanded of Koeris.[60]

Category I exemplifies the ways in which landholders recouped government impositions on them by exacting the same from their raiyats. These cesses and dues, however, are only some of the major exactions. For instance, the introduction of the income tax in the late nineteenth century—levied primarily on the high-income brackets in the district—led to the imposition on all raiyats of a cess known in the vernacular as "income tax." The same dynamic compelled raiyats to pay the chaukidari tax twice, once to fulfill the customary dues owed for the village watchman's maintenance and again toward the newly imposed government charge.[61]

Category II asserts the importance of written records and their monopoly

60. Compiled from "Statements of Illegal Cesses levied by Zemindars from their Ryots in the several districts of the Patna Division," Offg. Commr. S. C. Bayley to Secy., GOB, no. 251, July 2, 1872, Bengal Rev. Procs., 1873–1875, July 1874, 49–51; *SR*: 65.
61. Offg. Colltr. J. S. Drummond to Offg. Secy. GOB, Sept. 28, 1872, Bengal Rev. Procs., Oct. to Dec. 1872, Dec., 169.

by literate specialists, the patwaris. These dues were the most consistently reported ones in the village notes of both 1893–1901 and 1915–1921.[62] Their widespread prevalence reinforces the earlier characterization of patwaris as the leading men of village society. Moreover, the opportunities for record manipulation had increased as the British generated a vast, new array of paperwork—a "record-Raj"—which opened up additional possibilities for enhancing the wealth and power of village accountants.

Category III describes the considerable range of superordinate control in local society. As the 1815 observations suggest, landholders and their village connections exerted extensive leverage over every aspect of their raiyats' lives. Growing certain crops necessitated the payment of special charges, as did other kinds of routine activities, whether it was transporting goods or changing rent roll entries on account of transfer by inheritance or sale. In part, raiyats even subsidized the collection of rent from themselves!

Raiyats apparently largely acceded to such superordinate demands. There were "no records in this office [Saran collectorate] to shew that complaint or resistance was ever made," wrote one official, but quickly added, "it is not to be inferred on this account, that they [cesses] are any the less distasteful to the ryots, who from the nature of their position must find it safer to pay than to incur the displeasure of their zamindars."[63]

As with the system of rent, the illegal cesses system distinguished among various categories of raiyats. Hathwa raj's customary commands (*hukumat*) bound its tenants to varying degrees of obligations and dues, excepting only the higher castes. Otherwise each tenant had to lend his bullock and one plow for two days each year, once in Asarh (June–July) and again in Kartik (October–November) for use on raj land. In exchange, the estate provided the plowman with over two pounds (one seer) of coarse grain (*sattu*) each day. Tenants were also expected to give fodder for the landholder's cattle and different caste categories were obligated to offer their special services. *Chiragi* dictated that Telis had to give the estate's *amla* one ounce of oil daily when these retainers camped in their village. If there were no resident Teli, the oil presser who served the village had to act as a substitute. On the occasion of raj marriages and other ceremonies, Telis were bound to sell oil at rates of one seer over the market rate. Kandus and Gonds provided one man's menial services every day when estate officials stayed in the village. Similar practices obtained on other estates.[64]

Although the success with which any or all of these exactions were collected varied in Saran's estates, as also over time, their comprehensiveness clearly shows the extraordinary impositions of landholders, *thikadars* and patwaris on

---

62. See, e.g., Chapra thana nos. 1–136; Basantpur thana nos. 1–100, SVN. In 1911 only 4 percent of the district's population was literate (*SDG, Statistics, 1900–01 to 1910–11*: 25).

63. Drummond to Commr., no. 15, April 1872, uncatalogued P.C. *Basta*.

64. See, e.g., Belsara village, Mirganj thana no. 1040; Bhukuian village, Gopalganj thana no. 423, SVN.

the rest of village society. A sharply focused picture of the Limited Raj emerges here: one in which state authority and power faded at the levels of local society, except when it was manipulated by local controllers for their own benefit.

Credit Manipulation

Credit manipulation was another mechanism used to control raiyats. Its workings not only illustrate the dependency of raiyats, but also highlight the considerable standing of the *thikadar* in village society as an estate connection, a moneylender, and a substantial raiyat or petty malik.

Both the extent of indebtedness and the number of moneylenders in Saran reflect the considerable importance of credit manipulation in local society. Although few precise figures exist, most contemporary accounts included the majority of the district's inhabitants among the ranks of the indebted, and a frequently mentioned estimate was 75 percent.[65] A. Tytler, a subdeputy opium agent in Saran for thirty years, stated "that 95 percent of the ordinary raiyats live and die in debt."[66] Other government reports claimed lower figures based on statistics for mortgages and alienations of raiyats' holdings.[67]

Much of the survey and settlement data on Saran's villages, which judged the prosperity of a locality on the basis of its degrees of indebtedness, reported "not good" conditions for many areas. The observations of one village note writer, J. N. Mahapatra, are particularly insightful because he paid close attention to moneylenders and credit relations. In Bijauli village, he found thirty-two of its thirty-eight families under heavy obligations to creditors as a result of borrowing to clear off arrears of rent and to make "both ends meet in the trying parts of the year, i.e., from Asarh [June–July] to Aswin [September–October]."[68]

The identities of Saran's creditors further explains the manipulative possibilities of moneylending as well as of the considerable village-level control of moneylenders, many of whom were *thikadars* and petty maliks. Throughout the district and the region, small moneylenders predominated as the principal agricultural financiers. Jador Sinha, for example, was the moneylender of Bhataura village with a business of up to Rs. 5,000.[69] These small mahajans

---

65. Metcalfe note, Temple Papers. A similar estimation is made for other Bihar districts by Pouchepadass (1980a: 166–67); also Whitcombe (1971: 162).
66. Cited in AGRPD, 1897–98.
67. *SR*: 157. For a trenchant refutation of government methods of analysis, see B. B. Chaudhuri (1969b: 209–210), who also argues that indebtedness increased in Bengal and Bihar during this period.
68. Of the 38 families, 30 were Ahir, 7, Koeri and 1, Nuniya, a total population of 180. See Bijauli village, Mashrak thana no. 37, SVN. A raiyat in Bihar was said to take out loans for the following reasons: "1. to institute cases 2. to buy cattle 3. to pay his rent 4. to marry his daughter 5. to clothe himself and his family 6. to bribe the police 7. to feed the Brahmins when a death takes place in his family 8. in times of famine or scarcity 9. to buy seed and hire ploughmen" (Metcalfe note, Temple Papers).
69. Bhataura village, Mashrak thana no. 238, SVN.

were the major sources of rural credit because of their "local influence" and "easy accessibility." They provided credit for "all purposes" and were able to adapt "the nature of security and the period of each loan in accordance with the needs of each individual case."[70]

Most villages had moneylenders. A detailed inquiry of over 160 villages in Muzaffarpur District showed an average of three moneylenders per village and as many as ten in some. Over 50 percent of the creditors were agriculturists, 20 percent zamindars and *banias* and the remaining 10 percent "outsiders," such as Kabulis and Punjabis.[71] In Saran too most of the credit was extended by substantial raiyats and petty landholders, who were often *thikadars*. In the exceptional instances of villages without moneylenders, the credit facilities of neighboring areas were readily available.[72]

An extremely profitable venture, moneylending was an inviting investment for people with surplus cash or grain. No wonder agriculturist mahajans were described as "returned emigrants, ex-officers or large holders,"[73] that is, the individuals most likely to have such resources in village society. In the village notes, the substantial raiyat or the petty malik is consistently identified as the local moneylender. In Gaundri, twenty-five of the village's seventy-five families were Rajputs and in "affluent circumstances." Among them, Faujdar Sinha was specifically singled out. He cultivated 115 bighas of land, had eight bullocks, and two cows. Although his "family" consisted of twenty-eight to thirty members, he was not in debt; he saved about 4,350 lbs. of grain every year and was the village moneylender. Similarly, in other villages, surpluses made prosperous raiyats and landholders combine moneylending with cultivation. The main source of credit in Bangra villages was Sheobalak Singh, who owed his capital to his brother's "handsome income" in Calcutta. In Bahadurpur, the moneylender Deo Singh also dealt in elephants and horses and had landed property in the Bihar district of Purnea.[74]

Although these three examples were Rajputs, the district's mahajans were not uniformly of any particular caste or community. A large village of 3,769 inhabitants, Rasauli's nine moneylenders included two Brahmins, two Rajputs,

70. Evidence of V. M. Thakore, Secy. of the Bihar and Orissa Provincial Cooperative Bank, Patna, in *The Bihar and Orissa Provincial Banking Enquiry Committee, 1929-30*, 1930, 2: 76 (hereafter cited as *Bihar Banking Committee*).
71. Evidence of Sadashiva Prasad, Honorary Secy. of Patna College Chanakya (Economics) Society, and of Rai Bahadur Durga Prasad, Registrar of Cooperative Societies, ibid.: 5, 24, 402-4. *Kist-kothis* (moneylending institutions of big zamindars), which collected loans in regular installments, were not significant in Saran.
72. See, e.g., Bawandih village, Darauli thana no. 518; Pakari village, Mirganj thana no. 697. An interesting case of Saran men who operated as "outside" mahajans was Atiths, who advanced money in south Bihar (Dhubauli village, Mashrak thana no. 63; Phuchti Kalan village, Manjhi thana no. 129, SVN).
73. Evidence of Sadashiva Prasad, *Bihar Banking Committee*: 403. Also see Mukherjee (1979: 93) for a description of "the village mahajan, who generally rose from the ranks of the raiyats themselves."
74. Gaundri, Bangra, and Bahadurpur villages, Mashrak thana nos. 273, 19, and 17, respectively, SVN.

and two Muslims. Combinations of high and low castes also existed, as in Matihania Bind, where five Brahmin and one Sonar family advanced loans. And in some villages with many high-caste families, credit was advanced by the local Kalwars.[75]

Credit manipulation was clearly an important source of power and control in village society. The major raiyat in Arnwa village, Ajodhya Dubey, typified this equation. Considered a "very influential" man of the locality he had, by lending money in the neighboring villages, secured "possession of most of the lands of the raiyats by mortgages or sales."[76] He represented the fact that most mahajans were of the "higher class."[77]

Because a disproportionate number of high castes held rights in Saran's lands, their representation in the ranks of moneylenders was also considerable. In 55 villages of Mirganj thana where positive caste identifications are possible, 44 had mahajans of only one caste and 11 combinations of several. In the 44 villages, 19 had only Brahmin moneylenders, 8 Rajputs, 4 Raj Bhats, 3 Banias, 3 Bhumihar Brahmins, 2 Koeris, 2 Kalwars, and one each of Gadi, Rauniar, Kayasth, and Bairagi; in the other 11 villages, 8 had at least one Brahmin each.[78]

The identification of Mirganj's moneylenders reflects the "dominant caste" pattern of the locality.[79] Brahmins were the single largest high caste in this thana, and their superiority in overall numbers was reinforced by the settlement configurations of Mirganj's villages: Brahmin-dominated villages were clustered together in the western part of the thana. Of its 963 inhabited villages, 273 had only Brahmins in its high-caste populations. There were 39 with only Muslim "high castes" (Sheikh, Sayyad, or Pathan) and 26, 23, and 20 with Rajput, Bhumihar Brahmin, and Kayasth, respectively. Of the remaining 582, 412 had at least two high castes present, 145 had only low castes, and 25 had single-caste villages.[80]

As in the case of Brahmins in Mirganj, the predominance of Rajputs in Mashrak thana was enhanced by their settlement patterns. Although most of the thana's 260 villages consisted of mixes of high and low castes, as many as 93 of the total had only one high-caste category. Of these, 47 villages were Rajput, 14 Bhumihar Brahmin, 13 Brahmin, 7 Kayasth, and 2 Sheikh. Only 11 villages were entirely of low-caste residents.[81]

75. Rasauli village, Mashrak thana no. 71; Matihanai bind, Mirganj thana no. 3, SVN. The diverse backgrounds of village moneylenders is also noted in Musgrave (1978: 218–19).
76. Arnwa village, Mirganj thana no. 25, SVN.
77. Neehap and Tajhpur villages, Manjhi thana nos. 53 and 69, SVN.
78. Figures compiled from 11 volumes of village notes, Mirganj thana nos. 1–100, 101–200, 201–300, 301–400, 401–500, 501–600, 601–700, 701–800, 801–900, 901–1000, 1001–1064, SVN.
79. A standard definition of a "dominant caste" as a caste preponderating numerically and wielding superior economic and political power over other castes is in Srinivas (1959: 1–15; 1962: 89–90). See also Blair (1979: 139–76) for an application of this concept to Bihar politics.
80. Figures compiled from Mirganj thana, 11 vols., SVN.
81. Mashrak thana nos. 1–100, 101–200, and 201–285, SVN; 25 of the 285 villages were either uninhabited (18), not surveyed (6), or had no information (1).

Similarly, the village notes for the district's other thanas emphasize the estate's strong village connections. They also reveal that village-level controllers were of diverse social backgrounds, although primarily of high caste. In Mashrak thana, an area with a large Rajput population, most of the mahajans identified reflect this predominance. Where specific references to the leading families of a village exist, they are described as mostly Rajput and of wealth and influence: they enjoyed the largest holdings, often supplemented by a side business in moneylending or petty trading, and their commanding position in the village was confirmed by their *jeth*-raiyatship, which also meant their likely cooptation as supravillage connections.[82]

The local anchorage of Saran's moneylenders contrasts with the urban-based outsiders who dominated moneylending in other parts of India. In the north, such "intruders" were said to have dispossessed landholders and raiyats by purchasing their land rights under the new conditions (created by the British) of free sale and mortgage, and, in western India, *banias* increasingly were able to transfer land into their own hands. Their growing control of land in north India led to violence against them during the Mutiny/Rebellion, and, in western India, rural unrest erupted into the Deccan Riots of 1875.[83] Although interpretations casting "outside" moneylenders as villains have come under critical fire, they do show the growing infiltration of outsiders into the local agrarian structure through land transfers, mortgages, and usury.[84]

However, in other parts of India, rural credit remained in the hands of groups with well-entrenched interests in their localities. In the village economy of Bengal, *jotedar* (rich farmer) families played a key role as moneylenders and grain dealers. Although professional moneylenders and traders were predominant in some areas of the United Provinces, in the eastern districts adjoining Saran, "landlords and superior agriculturalists constituted the main source of agricultural credit.... No doubt rural credit and usury remained an important buttress for landlord elements to shore up their position in the east."[85]

Moneylending served as an important mechanism of control because of its sizable economic returns and its manipulative possibilities. A twentieth-century source described the rate of interest on grain transactions as 50 percent per year and 2 to 3 percent per month on cash loans.[86] At least three kinds of

---

82. Twelve of the 18 moneylenders whose castes are identified were Rajputs. Mashrak thana nos. 1–285, esp., thana nos. 19, 42, 61, 76, 77, 107, 177, 191, 192, 193, 194, 195, 231, 238, 249, 254, and 278, SVN.
83. See S. B. Chaudhuri (1957: 135–36); R. Kumar (1968: 153–88); and Catanach (1970: 11–23).
84. For a critique of S. B. Chaudhuri, see Stokes (1978: 159–84); for a reinterpretation of the Deccan riots, see Charlesworth (1972: 401–421).
85. Stokes 1978: 240. For Bengal, see Ratnalekha Ray (1979: 64–65).
86. Interest was only 25 percent in some areas if the loan was in seed and not grain for consumption (Evidence of Shambu Dayal, Income-Tax Officer, Darbhanga, *Bihar Banking Committee*: 295–96). See also Pouchepadass (1980a: 185–91).

interest rates prevailed in Saran: "ordinary" mahājani interest varied between 6 to 24 percent per year; *sawai* levied 25 percent per year on petty transactions of either cash or kind unless loans were repaid within three or four months; and *athrahaoni* charged the still higher rate of 50 percent a year on small advances repayable within three or four months.[87] The moneylender's profit on such advances was considerable:

As soon as the *makai* [corn] is harvested the debtor must pay up Re. 1-2-0 for every rupee taken by him during the preceding three months. The repayment is generally made in cash, but if it is made in grain, the mahajan makes an additional profit owing to the difference in the selling prices of grain before and after *bhadai* [autumn crop] is harvested. If a raiyat fails to pay up, the whole amount (Re. 1-2-0) becomes liable to sawai as though it were a cash loan of Re. 1-2-0 taken on the usual conditions.[88]

The rate of grain loans was usually 50 percent in six months with the advance made from Asarh to Bhadoi (June–July to August–September), which was the time of cultivation.[89] Cash loans also yielded high interest. One Hathwa estate manager reported a case in which "his assistance was invoked for the settlement of a debt, which on an original cash advance of Rs. 16, had amounted, with interest, to Rs. 56 at the end of three years, after payment by the debtor of the sum of Rs. 24!"[90] Often the rate was 12 to 25 percent, and loans were generally for one year, with interest compounded every six months. For instance, Jador Sinha, identified earlier as a fairly typical village mahajan, charged 25 percent on petty loans and 6 percent on loans of over Rs. 100.[91]

Such loans engendered strong dependency relationships between creditors and debtors. In Bijauli village, 1 *pauseri* (about 7 lbs.) of grain borrowed for consumption in June–July (Asarh) required a return of 1½ *pauseri* in November–December (Aghan), which was collected from the threshing floor.[92] This timing ensured the recurring indebtedness of the borrower, as he often had to meet rent and other contingency expenses soon thereafter. These terms also meant that the raiyat returned considerably larger amounts than he had originally secured, because he had borrowed when stocks were low and prices high, and repaid at harvest time when prices were low.[93] This process of unending indebtedness was vividly portrayed by one senior administrator:

Having reaped his rice and *rubbee* [spring] crops, and paid up part of his mahajun's demands, he [the raiyat] lives on till March doing little or nothing. He is then one day

---

87. *SRR*: 52.
88. Ibid. See also M. H. Siddiqi (1978: 76–77) on the practice of making loans of grains when prices were high and collecting them when prices were low.
89. Evidence of Shambu Dayal, *Bihar Banking Committee*: 295–96.
90. *Papers regarding Village Agency*: 398.
91. Bhataura village, Mashrak thana no. 238, SVN. Also, evidence of Khan Bahadur Saghirul Haque, Deputy Colltr., Central Co-operative Bank, Siwan, *Bihar Banking Committee*: 119.
92. Bijauli village, Mashrak thana no. 37. Apparently, this was a commonly used rate, e.g., Basatpur village, Mashrak thana no. 53, SVN.
93. A similar arrangement existed in the North-Western Provinces (Whitcombe 1971: 165). See also Amin (1983: 44–45).

summoned to the village cutcherry and pressed for his rent. A violent altercation then ensues between the putwaree, the debtor, and the village mahajun, who is generally present. It ends in the mahajun paying the rent in cash.... From time to time, as his stocks disappear and the ladies of the house get more abusive and demonstrative, as the grain runs short, he pays the mahajun a visit and gets advances.... Then the sowing time comes for the rain crop, and he has no seed, what is he to do? He goes to the putwaree, and there is another stormy interview, but the putwaree in the end gives in, for he well knows *no seed, no crop, no rent*. So the seed is advanced and the ryot lives on till the crop comes in. Again is the putwaree satisfied, and the mahajuns for the time being appeased, the crop gathered and expended, and the whole scene is re-enacted as it has been for generations before.[94]

Debts were, therefore, difficult to clear, often continuing from generation to generation. No doubt, as one expert witness testified at a hearing on banking in Bihar, it was to the mahajan's advantage to prolong this process in order to secure eventually the debtor's holdings.[95]

In short, moneylending was a powerful mechanism with which to exercise and maintain control. Particularly for the *thikadar* who combined his supravillage connections with his important village standing, the position of being a creditor further strengthened his grip over village society. Moreover, he enjoyed legal assurances for credit manipulation as he could seek redress in the courts against outstanding debts. Before the revised Civil Procedure Code of 1877, creditors could appropriate their overdue borrowers' belongings, such as "implements of husbandry" and "materials of an agriculturist's house or farm-building." But, following the passage of this act, moneylenders increasingly moved against the debtors' land, either by foreclosure, or mortgages, or sale.[96] This trend is reflected in the figures on the percentage of sales and mortgages of raiyats' rights between 1891–1901 and 1911–1921 (table 12). Between these two periods, there was an increase by 1,466 percent of the number of holdings transferred by sale.[97]

Table 12.
Transfer of Raiyati Rights, 1891–1901 and 1911–1921

	Area held by occupancy raiyats	Area transferred (%)	By mortgage (%)	By sale (%)	No. of holdings affected[a]	By mortgage (%)	By sale (%)
1891–1901	939,699.	5.8	5.6	0.2	15.6	15.3	0.3
1911–1921	1,185,829	12.9	10.8	2.1	24.4	23.1	3.3

Sources: Compiled from *SR*: 149; *SRR*: 47–48, app. 15 and 7.
[a] Number of transfers by hundred holdings.

94. Matcalfe Note, Temple Papers.
95. Evidence of Shambu Dayal, *Bihar Banking Committee*, 2: 296. For a similar observation, see Mukherjee (1975: 93). 96. B. B. Chaudhuri 1969b: 235. 97. *SRR*: 48.

On the assumption "that individual peasant families were the units of holding," B. B. Chaudhuri has convincingly argued that the 1891–1901 figures show that a considerable section of the peasant population was affected by such alienations, a pattern that continued in the decade between 1911 and 1921 (table 12). However, these findings do not warrant his conclusion that "continuing alienations at this rate would have resulted in the course of three decades in degrading half the owner-cultivator families of . . . Saran into landless labourers."[98] A useful corrective can be gained by examining the different categories of people who gained from these transfers. As official records indicate, the beneficiaries of sales and mortgages can be broadly divided into four classifications (table 13).

Table 13.
Categories of Transferees, 1891–1901 and 1911–1921

	Sales (%)		Mortgages (%)	
	1891–1901	*1911–1921*	*1891–1901*	*1911–1921*
Landlords	5.7	3.8	5.7	4.4
Lawyers	0.9	1.7	0.9	1.0
Moneylenders	9.4	22.9	9.3	29.9
Raiyats	84.0	71.5	83.9	64.5

Sources: *SR*: 150; *SRR*: 47.
Note: All figures represent percentage of total number of transfers.

Figures for the number of raiyati holdings with occupancy rights transferred in earlier years show approximately the same proportions, although they exclude mortgages. However, lawyers were not separately identified as a category of transferees. In the period 1881–1882 to 1884–1885, landlord purchasers numbered 15.2 percent, moneylenders 11.7, raiyats 60.8, and unspecified 12.1. In 1888–1889 to 1891–1892, these same categories accounted for, respectively, 21.2, 8.2, 66.1, and 4.1 percent of all the holdings alienated.[99]

These findings, however, fail to recognize the coincidence in identity between important raiyats and moneylenders. Many moneylenders were also landholders.[100] Small wonder, then, that raiyat purchasers, also identified as "small village mahajans—well-to-do cultivators," were said to "gradually absorb their poorer neighbours' occupancy rights, not so much with the

98. B. B. Chaudhuri 1969b: 235.
99. Compiled from "Statement B" with no. 1089R, Jan. 29, 1894, Bengal Jdcl. Procs., July to Sept. 1897, Sept., 145.
100. Ibid., 143. See also Commr. A. Forbes to BOR. no. 21C, March 5, 1896, ibid., 138–42.

intention of cultivating the acquired holdings themselves, as of subletting them at rack rent."[101]

Opposition from large landholders, especially to alienations by sale explains the higher incidence of mortgages, but only a few estates, such as the Hathwa raj, were able to prevent transfers. In the Hathwa-dominated thanas of Mirganj and Gopalganj, the number of transfers, particularly by sale, was the lowest. The raj's restrictions also influenced the low rate per acre advanced on mortgages in Mirganj (Rs. 47 per acre as compared to Rs. 138 and 109, respectively, in Manjhi and Sonepur thanas where petty maliks predominated). As frequent purchasers, petty maliks were naturally less likely to oppose land alienations.[102]

Credit manipulation was a powerful mechanism of control in Saran and, as in the neighboring region of the United Provinces, "far from bowling over the system of village control, it was filtered through and mediated by the system of village control."[103]

The "Ordinary" Control System

In the "ordinary" *thikadari* and *khas* system of management of large zamindars and petty maliks, the actual structures of control were often diffuse and arbitrary, but this made little difference in the basic pattern of control because most estates had accessible connections in the body of village controllers who combined their considerable village standing as officials, moneylenders, and men of wealth with this supravillage authority. Strains and stresses in this system, therefore, usually loosened the connections between the estate and the village but rarely touched village-level controllers who were firmly embedded in the grassroots of society.

In the Limited Raj, these indigenous control systems provided the effective government and rule in local society. Although estates increasingly grew smaller in size, there was no diminution in the degree of their power and influence. Rather, as the state's ground-level links became more attenuated, village notables became more securely bound to estate networks.

Furthermore, as the strategies of control reveal, state power and authority were often manipulated to articulate the interests of local controllers. On the one hand, a wide range of tactics remained outside the control of the government framework; on the other, the formal institutions of the British Raj, such as courts, were used to reinforce the grip of local systems of control. The primary focus of such strategems was to maximize the dues and claims from the land, as is evident from the mechanisms of rent, cesses, and credit manipulation.

Invariably, these systems of control bore down most heavily on the lowest levels of raiyats, who paid the most dues and had the least rights in the land.

---

101. Offg. Secy. BOR to GOB, no. 800A, June 20, 1894, Bengal Rev. Procs., May to Aug. 1894, Aug., 295.   102. *SR*: 152–53.   103. Musgrave 1978: 228.

And, as these systems created cleavages within village society, they militated against the development of unitary peasant movements. In the face of such local systems of control, both of the great estate of Hathwa and of other zamindars and petty maliks, the range of options available to raiyats was severely circumscribed.

PART IV

Peasant Options in a Colonial Society

9

Desertion and Migration as Peasant Options

Movement, either by desertion or by migration, was one of the mechanisms by which Saran raiyats sought to mitigate their hardships in the nineteenth and early twentieth centuries. Desertions were forced movement, often assuming the proportions of "avoidance protest."[1] Migration, though also motivated by necessity, was usually voluntary. In the former instance, the movement of raiyats was induced by "push" factors, generally a complex mix of superordinate, economic, and ecological pressures. In the latter, the impulse was generated by a variety of motivations—economic and noneconomic—some of which were "push" and others "pull" factors: in other words, local circumstances that repelled and external conditions that encouraged the movement of persons.[2]

Desertions

Despite Saran's high population density, deserted fields were not uncommon even in the late nineteenth and early twentieth centuries. They were particularly noticeable in the northwest, one of the least populated areas of the district and part of the great estate of Hathwa. To Sir A. P. MacDonnell, who had a long and active career in the Bihar administration, such scenes were reminiscent of Ireland. In a letter to the marquess of Lansdowne, he recalled a conversation he had had with an earlier viceroy: "I told him of whole villages depopulated

---

1. Recent studies of "avoidance protest" include Adas (1981: 217–47) and Asiwaju (1976: 577–94).
2. For general discussions of migration, see Jackson (1969) and Kosinski and Prothero (1975). See Pryor (1975: 33–35) for a discussion of the concept of "push and pull" that is widely used to explain the mechanism of migration.

by excessive rents and by indigo, the ryots going across to Nepal; in fact the same kind of scenes owing to analogous causes that I had been familiar with in the west of Ireland and in my childhood."[3]

Historically, Indian peasants have often abandoned their homes and fields under certain conditions. Irfan Habib's authoritative account of Mughal India considers the "capacity of mobility on the part of the peasant . . . as one of the most striking features of the social and economic life of the times. It was the peasant's first answer to famine or man's oppression."[4] Under the British Raj, when control of the land became the fundamental source of power, wealth, and status, flight became far less promising an alternative to the raiyats. Its continuance as an act of avoidance protest, therefore, highlights the intense pressures on peasants in Saran's agrarian system.

Desertions in Saran, as elsewhere in India, were a common phenomenon in the late eighteenth century.[5] They were especially frequent during the rebellion of Fateh Sahi when some villagers left to join him and others were uprooted by the constant hostilities. This trend continued throughout the protracted struggle of the Huseypur raja with the British, as evidenced by the large numbers of abscondings that took place in 1792.[6]

Natural catastrophes also precipitated flight. In 1795 several zamindars informed government that, as the result of the inundation of many of their villages, "ryots have been obliged to fly to other parts of the country."[7] Extreme conditions, such as those engendered by famines, also induced large numbers of peasants to flee. Desertions usually came from the ranks of people who lived close to the margin of subsistence in normal agricultural years. In the 1866 famine, the major casualties were among "the petty village artisans and day labourers, the dosads, mosaheers, domes, koormies, and others, who in a village community ordinarily receive a day's food, supplemented by some cash payment for a day's work [and who] could no longer obtain this employment when the day's food has assumed a value hitherto unknown."[8]

As the pressures exerted by the famine began to be widely felt in March 1866, people began "flocking about for food and dying in large numbers."[9] From another area, however, came the less gloomy news that, of the 3,159

---

3. MacDonnell, Offg. L.G. of Bengal to Marquess of Lansdowne, no. 149, Aug. 19, 1893, Marquess of Lansdowne, Correspondence with Persons in India, July to Dec. 1893, vol. 2, Mss. Eur. D. 558/25.   4. 1963: 117.

5. See Edward Golding, Supervisor, Saran, to Hon. John Cartier, Pres. and Governor, Rev. Committee, Calcutta, May 29, 1771, Calcutta Rev. Committee Consltns., April 1 to Dec. 31, 1771, June 24.

6. James Pearson, Lt. Commd., Barra Gawn, to Ewan Law, &c., Patna Council, Nov. 26, 1777; A. Montgomerie, Colltr., to Wm. Cowper, BOR, Jan. 24, 1792; Bengal Rev. Consltns., Jan. 2 to 27, 1778, Jan. 13, no. 48, encl.; May 4 to June 1, 1792, Jan. 24.

7. Outumnarian &c., zamindars of Sircar Saran, petition, Nov. 2, 1795, ibid., Nov. 13 to Dec. 19, 1795, Nov. 27, no. 9.

8. *Parliamentary Papers*, vol. 170, 1867, "Mr. F. R. Cockerell's Report," p. 34.

9. G. Macleod, in charge of the affairs of the Rajah of Hathwa, to F. M. Halliday, Colltr., Dec. 21, 1866, ibid., p. 85.

families on the rent rolls of one leaseholder's fifty-five villages, only five holdings had been vacated as a result of deaths or desertions.[10] In the famine of 1873-1874, one touring administrator found himself besieged "by people asking for grain." Another official reported encountering "many people in great distress . . . on the roads."[11]

Many incidents of desertions in the late nineteenth century were related to the extension of indigo cultivation in Saran, especially in the 1860s and 1870s.[12] By voting with their feet, indigo tenants expressed their disapproval of indigo. This phenomenon was not, however, as a recent study of northern Bihar indigo plantations avers, "a natural demographic adjustment, as people moved from the densely populated uplands to the less thickly settled rice lands of the border . . . and . . . independent of considerations of rent rates and *thikadari* oppression." This analysis is also inaccurate in contending that "it cannot be argued on the available evidence that indigo cultivation was a sufficient cause of desertion."[13] There are, on the contrary, many accounts of abscondings in the detailed estate records of Hathwa relating to indigo plantations, such as those of Akloo Nuniya and Parah Ahir in 1892, and those of Wallah Rai, Mohan Das, and Sobran Das in 1893. In 1894 twenty-seven raiyats were said to have deserted from seventeen villages in which the Maniara Indigo Factory had interests. And, in the most extensive list of abscondings from Hathwa's indigo areas, as many as eighty-three raiyats were reported to have fled between 1889 and 1892 from a number of villages that Hathwa had leased to the Maniara Factory.[14]

Most indigo deserters were small tenant holders. The average holding of the twenty-seven raiyats who fled in 1894 was 5.3 bighas, with individual holdings ranging in size from 0.3 to 15.4 bighas. The detailed list of deserters for 1889 to 1892 reinforces this characterization; thus, the concern when Bermal Kurmi of Sulkhpur Matcherra fled because he had one of the largest holdings in his village—over 27 bighas at a rental of Rs. 86-12.[15] According to Bermal Kurmi's indigo planter, D. N. Reid, the former left because he was deeply in debt to moneylenders. Although indebtedness was a common reason for leaving, as the records of the Hathwa estate show, most abandoned their villages because of "poverty," "inundation," "decree of Mr. Reid," "for failing to fulfill Mr. Reid's terms," "false charge of damage" instituted by Reid, and "dread of Mr. Reid."[16]

Underlying these grievances were the basic contradictions between indigo

10. Lewis Cosserat, Mgr., Burhoga Factory, to Halliday, Dec. 20, 1866, ibid., p. 93.
11. "Narrative of Scarcity . . . in Sarun . . . for the Fortnight ending with July 1874," *Famine Narrative*, nos. 21 and 22, June 26 to July 23, 1874, p. 6.
12. AGRPD, 1877–78. See also Fisher (1976: 43) on production of indigo in maunds between 1849 and 1897.   13. Fisher 1976: 117.
14. Mgr., H.R., to Mgr., Moniarah, no. 268, Nov. 15, 1892; Moniarah to H.R., June 9, 1893; H.R. to Moniarah, nos. 183 and 184, Oct. 25, 1894; "Moniara Factory 1891-92"; H.R. *Bastas*, 1880–1899.   15. Ibid.
16. "Moniara Factory, 1891-92," Reid to H.R., Feb. 22, 1892, ibid.

and the peasant system of agriculture: "The dislike of indigo derived from its anomalous position as a crop designed for plantation production being grown on small farms. The planters' need to apply compulsion to make the cultivators agree to indigo, and strict supervision over the processes of cultivation resulted from the peasants' decisions, as rational economic men, not to grow indigo as a free commercial speculation."[17]

Desertion was often the only viable option left because raiyats could not fulfill the planter's demands on their land and labor; nor could they easily resist the planter because he enjoyed "two forms of power: one deriving from the *zemindars*' traditional authority, and the other from his legal position."[18] Although abscondings satisfied the planters' urgent desire for land, they were also a source of concern because a mass exodus of raiyats could wreak havoc on the planters' equally pressing need for labor. Both estate and planters profited from desertions because the indigo factory assumed responsibility for the holdings of absconders at an enhanced rental of 20 percent.[19]

Desertions were not peculiar to indigo areas; they occurred regularly in estates throughout the district. Abscondings from zamindari estates were also induced by a complex of superordinate and ecological pressures. A standard instance is the forced migration of "hundreds of ryots" from several villages in the vicinity of Bhorey, in the great estate of Hathwa, in the late nineteenth century. Beginning in 1869 and continuing through 1872, Bhorey raiyats numbering in the hundreds abandoned their lands and sought refuge elsewhere in the district or in neighboring Gorakhpur. Their exodus was prompted by the estate's demands for high rent—even a rent increase in 1870—at a time of poor harvests. Moreover, the estate's rent collectors added to the burden of these levies because their position as moneylenders enabled them to compound their exactions into a more taxing rent-and-credit demand. Small wonder, then, that under these conditions new tenants were difficult to find to lease the abandoned lands. As a result, land was left lying waste "at an annual loss to the raj of not less than Rs. 20,000 or 25,000, very likely much more."[20]

In 1902–1903, in Bhorey in the Hathwa estate, the failure of four successive rice crops triggered another round of desertions. On this occasion too, the dismal harvests were exacerbated by the uncompromising demands of the rent collectors, thus precipitating a crisis "by the very injudicious way in which enhancements of rents on the ground of inadequate rate of rents were claimed and won in the settlement courts."[21] By the time the raj's Court of Wards management became aware of the severity of the situation, much damage had already been done:

17. Fisher 1976: 103.   18. Ibid.: 104.
19. Mgr., H.R., to G. R. Macdonald, no. 1025, March 11, 1893, H.R. *Bastas*, 1880–1899.
20. G. J. S. Hodgkinson, Mgr., Court of Wards, to Colltr. of Saran, no. 436, Sept. 25, 1872, Bengal Rev. Procs., Oct. to Dec. 1872, Nov., no. 121.
21. "Hathwa Raj Estate Administration Report, 1902–03," P.C. *Basta* no. 166, Court of Wards, Hathwa Estate.

With the failure of the crops, defaults in rent have been universal. Resort to process of law and the sale of the holdings has followed, and the Raj has had to purchase them for want of other bidders and on resettlement has had to write off all arrears. The Raj has therefore spent large sums of money on court fees and lawyers merely to evict unfortunate tenants whose only fault was poverty.... It is not to be wondered at that the tenantry in that locality have lost all and any respect for the Raj and there are constant petty disputes in the Criminal Courts in consequence.[22]

Why such conditions sparked forced migrations and not other kinds of actions can be gauged from the "wholesale desertions" of 1879.

The Wholesale Desertions of 1879

The wholesale desertions of 1879 were the largest reported case of forced migrations from either the Hathwa estate or Saran in the nineteenth and early twentieth centuries. The initial report of the investigating police subinspector noted "that 241 families have run away and the reason for their flight is, that during the last three years, the produce of the crops having been very limited owing to the drought and the Ticcadars having pressed the ryots for rent they have taken to flight."[23] A subsequent inquiry turned up as many as 1,000 abandoned houses, a number said to add up to 6,000 desertions. Of the thirty-five villages visited, a European police inspector found only four still inhabited. "All the villages I've been to," he noted in his diary, "I've personally seen the bare walls standing... and some houses all empty."[24]

So momentous were the events of 1879 that the memory of widespread discontent remained etched in the minds of Hathwa peasants long after the official controversy instigated by the subsequent investigation by local British administrators had subsided. A. P. MacDonnell, who had been sent to Saran to conduct a special tour of the locality after the removal of the subdivisional officer of Siwan and the Saran magistrate, encountered no difficulty in hearing the peasants' "storytellers." More than a quarter of a century later, in 1905, a touring manager of the Hathwa estate inadvertently recorded its continuing currency in the oral traditions of the locality when he inspected Karkataha village, one of the communities from which many peasants had fled. His diary of February 10 states:

Rode to Karkattaha and inspected the earthworks.... The large area which is being now improved by these earthworks is of very poor quality and is largely waste owing to the abandonment and poverty of the tenants. The rental of the village is said to be nearly five rupees a bigha against three in the surrounding villages. I questioned some of the tenants as to their holdings and found them all between five and six rupees a bigha

22. Ibid.
23. Md. Ayud Khan, Sub-Inspector of Burragaon, June 5, 1879, with Commr. F. M. Halliday to GOB, no. 386, Aug. 8, 1881 (draft), P.C. Gen. *Basta* no. 284, 1881.
24. "Special Diary of Mr. Inspector J. F. Leadbeater," no. 164, June 18, 1879, with C. J. O'Donnell, SDO, to Magte., June 21, 1879, in "Desertions in Hathwa."

which the quality of the land certainly does not justify. I rode all round the villages so as to see exactly what the capabilities were and I consider the lands to be not one whit superior to those of the surrounding villages. The villagers stated that the rates were largely increased during the thikadari of one Nehal Khan in whose time the rent was doubled from 1200 to 2400.[25]

Thus, this Hathwa manager unwittingly served as the storyteller of experiences that had passed into oral traditions. Their preservation in the form of remembrances had survived the attempts by Hathwa retainers to restrain peasants from testifying to local administrators in 1879 as well as efforts by government to relegate them to obscure files. Their persistence also reveals the awareness that Hathwa peasants had of the importance of speaking out about their conditions. For silence, as the forty peasants from six villages who assembled before O'Donnell, knew, was a powerful weapon against them. Therefore, they, "without exception begged me to take their statements and the evidence in support of them at once, as they believed if they went home they would never be allowed to appear in court again."[26] In 1879, as later in 1905, peasants appreciated the significance of memory as "a mode of resistance to the *longue durée* [long duration] of rule which others have exercised over peasants. That is, where there is domination exercised so effectively as to prohibit active resistance for (long) periods of time, memory . . . serves as the record of injustice, loss, etc., and also of successful resistance, rebellion, etc. . . . Memory, as history, waited to be acted upon."[27]

THE DESERTERS: FACES IN THE CROWD

The wholesale desertions were the result of widespread discontent across a large area of the great estate of Hathwa. A. P. MacDonnell identified the locus and origins of the discontent when he observed the difference between "the richly cultivated and fertile country towards the centre of the district, [and] the Koari perganah [which] seemed by comparison poor and unproductive. The character of the soil, the degree of comfort observeable in the village, the physique of the people all appeared inferior to what I had seen in my earlier marches. I saw neither good rice nor good rubee in the Kateya police jurisdiction yet the rents of the land seemed high."[28]

The arithmetic of the events of 1879 highlights their scale and intensity. In a tour of the Hathwa-controlled locality of Katia in which he covered "fifty miles in various directions," O'Donnell encountered "at least fifty groups of villagers

---

25. "Manager's Tour Diary," Feb. 4 to Feb. 15, 1905, H.R. *Bastas*, 1904–1905. Nihal Khan had been singled out by numerous reports, including MacDonnell's, as one of the most oppressive of Hathwa thikadars.
26. O'Donnell to Magte:, no. 164, June 21, 1879, "Desertions in Hathwa."
27. Kaye 1982: 90.
28. MacDonnell to Commr., Jan. 1, 1880, P.C. Rev. *Basta* no. 331, 1879–1880.

at different points who alleged that ryots had absconded from their villages."[29] And the estimate that 6,000 individuals had fled from 168 villages in the Katia outpost did not include people who were disaffected but did not leave. About 3,000 of these formed "a sufficiently menacing army of discontent," marched sixty miles to Chapra and surrounded the house of Magistrate Pawsey, dispersing only after he agreed to inquire into their grievances.[30]

The majority of the forced migrations were from twenty-one villages in the Katia outpost. Inspector Leadbeater's tour of the area identified the absence, added to the abscondings from Nehruwa, Kapuri, Karkataha, and Misrauli, of a total of 366 families.[31] Most of the deserters fled to Gorakhpur or Champaran, choices no doubt dictated by the fact that these districts lay within easy access, across administrative frontiers, and represented a convenient alternative to remaining in Saran which, at least in the north, was largely controlled by Hathwa. Some absconders merely moved to another part of the great estate, because of the immense size of Hathwa and the costs of entering another territorial system. At best this move offered them the dismal prospect of sinking "from the grade of farmer, cultivating their own lands, to the position ... of starving labourers on the farms of unknown masters."[32]

The wholesale character of the exodus is also embodied in the identities of the deserters. Clearly, not all of them were, as the maharaja attempted to convince the authorities, of the "floating population" of landless laborers, "people belonging to the 'Gomta Koeri' and 'Oudhia Koeri' [sic] classes, who as it is notorious, never settle in any village permanently."[33] This statement was inaccurate because the standard ethnographies—"Sherring's Hindu Castes, Magrath's Castes of Behar, and Dr. Hunter's Statistical Accounts of the Behar Districts—proved that Koiris and ['Oudhia'] Kurmis are, without rival, the most respectable of all the cultivating castes."[34] Indeed, many of the deserters were of the prominent agricultural castes; others were of castes that typically round out the tenant population of the locality. Of the thirty-one families who abandoned Kapuri, for instance, twenty-two were Koeris, three Shepherds (Bherihars), three Gores (Goria Ahirs—cattle herders), one Teli (oil-presser), one Kurmi, and one household headed by a woman whose caste could not be identified.[35] From other villages, "fairly substantial men" swelled the ranks of

29. O'Donnell to Magte., no. 172, July 8, 1879, "Desertions in Hathwa."
30. O'Donnell to Secy., GOB, Dec. 31, 1879, Bengal Rev. Procs., Feb. 1880, no. 9.
31. "Special Diary of Leadbeater," June 18, 1879; Leadbeater to Dist. Supt. of Police, June 18, 1879; Maharaja Krishna Protab Sahai, Bahadur, to Colltr., no. 4A, July 21, 1879; "Desertions in Hathwa." Location of these villages has been cross-checked with village notes and thana maps.
32. O'Donnell to Magte., no. 172, July 8, 1879. See also Report of Head Constable of Katia, April 17, 1879; Maharaja to Colltr., no. 4A, July 21, 1879; ibid.
33. Maharaja to Colltr., no. 4A, July 21, 1879, ibid.
34. O'Donnell to GOB, Dec. 31, 1879, Bengal Rev. Procs., Feb., 1880, no. 9. See also, *SDG, 1930*: 45, which describes Koeris as "industrious, peaceful and contented cultivators," and Kurmis as "an agricultural class, mainly in cultivation."
35. "Diary of Leadbeater." Koeris comprised 12 percent of the population of Mirganj thana.

the deserters. The affected parties in Bathnarup included nine families of Tewari Brahmins; among them the smallest tenant holder was Gya Tewari with 7 bighas, the largest, Liladhur Tewari with over 12 bighas.[36]

Most of the faces in the crowd of deserters, however, were of people of low caste and economic position. From Line Bazaar, the people who left included Bodhi Boldar who "had only 1 cottah [one-twentieth of a *bigha*] of land . . . [and] used to live by working for other people," Hoosani Koonjra who "held beegha 1-8-9 of land . . . [and] lived by selling vegetables from bazar to bazar [*sic*]" and Chandu Khan who "held beegha 0-11-9 of land . . . [and] used to live by working for other people."[37] That so many poor peasants joined the streams of deserters is not surprising because they were the easiest to oust from their homes. They were also probably more inclined to leave in the face of threats because they had the smallest stakes in their villages.

Whereas some of the poor peasants, especially, belonged to the category of "floating population" that the maharaja attempted to apply to all the deserters, the mass exodus was not, as he claimed, synchronized to "flitting time"[38]—the slack period in the agricultural year during which many Saran peasants temporarily moved to the "East" to supplement their incomes. Obviously, the maharaja wanted to downplay the wholesale desertions by passing them off as part of a seasonal migration, but the diverse economic and social backgrounds of the deserters and the involvement of their entire families did not conform to the characteristics of seasonal migrants.

Desertion as a Peasant Option

The desertions by Hathwa peasants in 1879 were an alternative to collective action and violence or staying on in the estate. Although "hundreds of ryots" had fled the estate between 1869 and 1872, the scale of that movement was quite different from that of the mass exodus in 1879, as was also the intensity of the discontent, which was so visible in 1879. In part, the difference in peasant response in these two instances lay in the greater pressures that were exerted by the estate in 1879, especially in its demands for higher rents. Although the enhanced rent of 1878 and 1879 may not in itself have been sufficient to trigger a mass exodus, it was exacerbated by other enhancements made in the 1870s, which, in turn, had been tacked on to a whopping 25 percent increase in 1854 and an additional augmentation of 12.5 percent a few years later. Rent receipts in one area of the estate revealed that enhancements of 9 to 25 percent had been demanded in 1878 and 1879 on rents that had been raised by 15 to 20

---

36. O'Donnell to Magte., no. 164, June 21, 1879, "Desertions in Hathwa." The average size of holdings in Mirganj thana was 4 bighas for "occupancy raiyats" who constituted 86 percent of all cultivators; this holding was considered sufficient to generate a subsistence income for a family of five persons (*SR*: 133, 156).
37. M. Buskin to Maharaja, no. 4A, July 21, 1879, "Desertions in Hathwa."
38. Maharaja to Colltr., no. 4A, July 21, 1879, ibid.

percent in 1874. In the locality of Katia, there had been three increases in the 1870s: 12.5 percent in 1871, another 15 percent between 1875 and 1879, and yet another of 10 to 15 percent in 1879. These demands came in the wake of the new enhanced leases that Hathwa had issued to its *thikadars*.[39]

According to MacDonnell, the widespread enhancement in rent—in his estimation an increase of 25 percent in the decade of the 1870s—was legal because the new rates were levied after the estate had discovered the presence of "surplus land" in the holdings of most of its tenants.[40] But noticeably absent from his findings was any reference to the possibility that the estate may have resorted to the familiar tactic of manipulating its control of village records and recordkeepers to secure legal recourse for its new claims. Certainly, the survey and settlement operations conducted between 1893 and 1901 found ample evidence that Hathwa had exploited its "accurate" records and maps "to get the full benefit of the settlement operations." These operations also ascertained that a 12.5 percent rent enhancement had been introduced throughout the estate in 1870 (implemented in some areas, as in Katia, in 1871), followed by other increments added on between 1874 and 1880. Thus, the exactions of 1879, representing the culmination of a spiraling rise in rent from 1854 on, added up to an enhancement that exceeded the bounds of demands considered legitimate in the "moral economy" of peasant society.[41]

As in the early 1870s, even though agricultural conditions were poor, the 1879 increases occurred "after a period of at least two years of the most grave agricultural depression and high prices of food."[42] The entire decade of the 1870s, moreover, were not "years of plenty . . . [but] when the people were suffering from the effects of the Famine of 1874 and . . . years of short harvests. . . . [Thus] a series of bad years had diminished . . . the ability of the ryot not [only] to pay an enhanced, but to meet even the old, demand."[43] In the face of these conditions, many Hathwa peasants could no longer remain on the estate.

In 1879, unlike 1872, the "moral economy" of the Hathwa peasants was further violated because the estate took no conciliatory steps and made no efforts "to achieve mutually acceptable outcomes." In 1872 the Court of Wards took immediate action to encourage absconded tenants to return, allowed partial remissions of rent (an average of 25 to 30 percent), advanced loans for the purchase of seed and bullocks, and even stripped rent collectors of their leases of affected villages for fear that they would continue to exact their customary dues.[44]

39. O'Donnell to Magte., no. 172, July 8, 1879, ibid.; *SR*: 141.
40. MacDonnell to Commr., Jan. 1, 1880, P.C. Rev. *Basta* no. 331. MacDonnell added that the Maharaja was "confident of the legality of the demand [but] the ryots are not."
41. See Scott (1976: 6–8) on "moral economy" as a standard rooted in a subsistence ethic that seeks a "minimal guaranteed return" for peasants.
42. O'Donnell to Magte., no. 172, July 8, 1879, "Desertions in Hathwa"; Hodgkinson to Colltr., no. 436, Sept. 25, 1872, Beng. Rev. Procs., Nov. 1872, no. 121.
43. MacDonnell to Commr., Jan. 1, 1880, P.C. Rev. *Basta* no. 331.
44. Hodgkinson to Colltr., no. 436, Sept. 25, 1872, Bengal Rev. Procs., Nov. 1872, no. 121.

In addition, the enhanced rents of the early 1870s had been more acceptable: "the ryots paid the increased rent more resignedly to the Courts of Wards (as being identified with the Government) than they pay to their landlord."[45] The involvement of local administrators in 1879 had the reverse effect. Instead of legitimizing Hathwa's enlarged demands, the active and sympathetic investigations carried out by O'Donnell and other Saran officials were probably perceived by peasants as championing their cause; crowds of peasants flocked to them to articulate their grievances. Indeed, the maharaja was not entirely inaccurate in charging that his peasants had lodged no complaints until the police were "let loose on my estate" and that they had been "instigated" and "goaded" into seeking redress from the authorities.[46]

The wholesale desertions were also induced by the coercive machinery of the Hathwa estate, which bore down heavily on an already hard-pressed peasantry. The methods of suppression—described as oppression or tyranny (*zoolum*)—while successful in containing dissidence, left Hathwa peasants with no choice but to resort to "avoidance protest" as they aimed at subduing peasants physically or denying them their everyday subsistence.[47]

Abscondings were not, however, confined to the great estates. As the maharaja of Hathwa admitted, albeit to minimize the gravity of the events of 1879, "such desertions afford no matter for surprise or comment; as they must and do occur more or less in every zamindari."[48]

Migration

The 1891 census described Saran as "one of the greatest emigrating districts in Bengal."[49] That year 364,315 of its inhabitants (212,790 men and 151,525 women) were enumerated in other districts of India. Nonmigrants (those born and remaining in the district) totaled 2,427,851. The total outmigrants represented 15.2 percent of the population. Only 32,023 women and 7,603 men from other districts migrated into Saran, which meant a net outmigration of 324,689 people. Although this outmigration was unusually large because of heavy floods in the district,[50] Saran was a major district of outmigration throughout the late nineteenth and early twentieth centuries (table 14).

In years not covered by these censuses, similar volumes of outmigration can be traced through the district's annual administration reports. Except when circumstances in the district or in potential destinations inhibited movement,

---

45. MacDonnell to Commr., Jan. 1, 1880, P.C. Rev. *Basta* no. 331.
46. Maharaja to Colltr., no. 4A, July 21, 1879, "Desertions in Hathwa."
47. Leadbeater to Police, June 18, 1879, ibid.
48. Maharaja to Offg. Colltr., no. 2A, June 24, 1879, ibid. See also Fisher (1976: 116–17); Rothermund (1977: 230–42).   49. Bourdillon 1898: 66.
50. Floods inundated 600 square miles in the south of the district and almost entirely destroyed the autumn and winter crops of 1890–1891 (AGRPD, 1890–91). See also Bourdillon (1898, 3: 102–3). Only Hooghly with a proportion of 15.9 percent of outmigrants ranked above Saran.

Table 14.
Outmigration from Saran, 1881–1921

	Male	Female	Total	Net Outmigration
1881	124,211	66,941	191,152[a]	—
1891	212,790	151,525	364,315	324,689
1901	174,168	68,320	242,488	186,064
1911	203,000	80,000	283,000	235,540
1921	147,854	62,036	209,890	165,154

Sources: Compiled from Bourdillon 1898, 3: 102–3; Gait 1913, 6, pt. 1: 145–46; O'Malley 1913, 5, pt. 1: 187, 189; Tallents 1923, 7, pt. 1: 115–16.
[a] Does not include outmigration outside of Bengal.

these reports note with unfailing regularity the "usual exodus," as was the case in 1879–1880 and throughout the quinquennial period between 1905–1906 to 1910–1911.[51] In some years sizable increases were noticed, as in 1897, when the collector on tour reported that "it was a matter of common observation, that the number of emigrants was much larger than usual. The villages I visited seemed deserted of their able-bodied male population, and the roads were levied with travellers of the East."[52] Precisely when these patterns of migration developed cannot be determined, but there have always been people from the Indian countryside who have moved elsewhere in response to better opportunities.[53] For example, when Robert Clive organized the first sepoy battalion in Bengal in the 1770s, a number of recruits were drawn from Bihar, probably including some from Saran. By the mid-nineteenth century, the district had provided 10,000 sepoys.[54]

The mobility of Saran's population in the early nineteenth century is also evident from retracing the steps of its many inhabitants who joined the initial streams of emigrants to the sugar plantations of Mauritius, British Guiana (now Guyana), Trinidad, and Jamaica. Because little or no organized recruiting was conducted in the interior, many of Saran's emigrants were enlisted in Calcutta.[55] By the late nineteenth century, the streams of migration toward Bengal were well-established flows. Outside of the adjoining districts of

---

51. AGRPD, 1879–80; "Report on the General Administration of the Tirhut Division for the Quinquennial Period from 1905–06 to 1909–10," Bengal Gen. Procs., April 1911, 226.
52. AGRPD, 1897–98.
53. For a similar point, see Morris (1965: 42), where he argues against the proposition that such aspects of Indian rural social structure as "joint family, caste, and village organization... [have] acted as barriers to population mobility." See also Omvedt (1980).
54. Rankine: 34. See also Barat (1962: 48, 119); Hunter (1877: 240).
55. GOB, *Report of Committee on Coolies and Mr. Doomsun's Minute*, 1840, no. 3. The demand for labor in these areas developed following the abolition of slavery in 1834. The initial Indian immigrants were the hill coolies from Chotanagpur, but recruits in the 1840s and 1850s were drawn increasingly from eastern U.P. and Bihar (Saha 1970: 28–30; Tinker 1974).

Table 15.
Principal Destinations of Saran's Outmigrants, 1881–1921

	1881	1891	1901	1911	1921
Bengal					
Hooghly	1,057	1,041	7,468	8,751	n.a.
Howrah	2,627	4,160	8,561	7,629	6,562
24-Parganas	8,849	5,913	15,048	28,026	24,768
Calcutta	11,132[a]	14,024	17,756	14,719	10,331
Khulna	1,117	415	1,272	n.a.	n.a.
Murshidabad	1,438	2,569	716	n.a.	n.a.
Dinajpur	2,274	4,266	5,455	n.a.	n.a.
Rangpur	7,935	16,371	22,161	n.a.	n.a.
Pabna	415	1,801	2,125	n.a.	n.a.
Darjeeling	771	3,463	2,851	n.a.	n.a.
Jalpaiguri	2,023	3,588	4,481	n.a.	n.a.
Dacca	748	3,508	2,937	n.a.	n.a.
Faridpur	481	1,469	2,160	n.a.	n.a.
Mymensingh	5,247	13,618	13,746	n.a.	n.a.
Tipperah	1,705	1,968	1,961	n.a.	n.a.
Bihar					
Patna	14,826	24,578	8,872	8,314	9,169
Gaya	1,754	1,197	1,103	890	744
Shahabad	5,936	33,682	7,190	5,028	4,359
Muzaffarpur	22,070	13,978	12,637	9,114	5,429
Darbhanga	5,211	4,570	4,054	4,132	3,062
Champaran	76,670	83,241	25,452	21,694	12,494
Monghyr	2,810	1,825	1,568	1,653	1,676
Bhagalpur	4,578	3,486	2,946	3,347	2,418
Purnea	3,592	5,164	4,595	4,817	3,369
Santhal Parganas	1,405	15,145	1,370	1,087	1,247

Sources: Compiled from Bourdillon 1883, 2: 340–65; Bourdillon 1898, 4: 347–89; Gait 1913, 6B, pt. 2: 140–74; O'Malley 1913, 5, pt. 1: 182, pt. 3: 70–76; Tallents 1923, 7, pt. 1: 110, pt. 2: 70–84.
Note: Only localities receiving more than 1,000 outmigrants are identified. N.a. = not available.
[a] Includes 3,930 enumerated in the "suburbs."

Shahabad, Muzaffarpur, Patna, and Champaran in Bihar, and Gorakhpur, Azimgarh, and Ballia in U.P., the majority of the district's outmigrants went to the area they referred to as the East.[56] (See table 15.)

Two major trends of migration can be seen. The farther removed the destination from the district and its region, the lower the proportion of women to men. In Bengal proper, women migrants were generally outnumbered ten to one. Juxtaposed with other kinds of data, the ratio of female to male outmigrants over distance reveals the difference in volume between permanent (and especially marriage) migration, and the well-documented seasonal exodus of primarily males from Saran during the cold weather. According to one source, by subtracting all the women and an equal body of men from the total number of outmigrants as permanent migrants, the number remaining would constitute the seasonal outmigrants. By this method, 80,000 seasonal outmigrants were estimated for 1891.[57] Such a procedure is biased toward underestimation, however, even though it does not include the volume of predominantly female outmigration to U.P. Not all the women who moved left the district permanently because many accompanied the men on seasonal migrations. In 1891, for instance, a large number of women joined the annual movement, including that to the neighboring districts.[58]

Furthermore, although village exogamy explains the high proportion of women enumerated as outmigrants, marriage migration cannot be assumed for the distinctly different cultural region of Bengal. For Bihar's ties lie to the "West," to U.P., an area with which it historically enjoyed close social and cultural affinities. Within this region, the field of marriage migration for Saran is confined to a fairly restricted area. A recent study estimates median marriage distance for Saran women as only 4.5 to 9.4 miles.[59] This relatively delimited area reflects the confining configuration of the districts' great rivers, particularly the Gandak which has long inhibited intermarriages between Champaran and Saran, and the Ganges between the districts of north and south Bihar. Moreover, it is generally the socially and economically higher castes who seek alliances from a wider radius than those of lower groups.[60] Migrants, however, were drawn primarily from the latter category.

The extent to which the figure of 80,000 seasonal migrants in 1891 is an underestimation is also suggested by the fact that Bengal alone received more than that number of male migrants. Nor does it include the many seasonal

---

56. Place of birth data are especially useful for the study of seasonal migration because censuses were taken in the early months of the year, generally Feb. or March, also the height of the migration season; most absentees were therefore considered migrants. J. A. Bourdillon, Magte., to Commr., no. 1401, July 8-10, 1890, Bengal Gen. (Misc.) Procs., Sept. to Dec. 1890, Dec., nos 3-4 (hereafter cited as Bourdillon Report). See also Zachariah (1964: 42-43).

57. O'Donnell 1893: 106.   58. Ibid.: 102-3; AGRPD, 1890-91.

59. Libbee and Sopher 1975: 352-53. See also Bourdillon (1898: xii), who asserts that, because over 95 percent of female "migrants" were enumerated within the district, "marriage migration ... is ... largely confined to places within the district."

60. Bourdillon 1883, 1: 157; Libee and Sopher 1975: 353.

migrants who were in the nearby districts of Bihar. Thus, Bourdillon's calculation that only one-tenth of all males enumerated outside the district were quasi-permanent migrants, with the remaining nine-tenths only temporarily away appears much closer to the mark. By his estimate, the number of seasonal migrants for 1891 was closer to 200,000 and not 80,000. Additional evidence also supports this finding that the outmigration from Saran was of an overwhelmingly seasonal character.[61]

Compared to this massive seasonal movement, only a handful emigrated to the "colonies" outside India, despite considerable government effort. Between 1868 and 1909, the highest number of emigrants overseas in a year (799) was in 1890–1891; the lowest in 1909 (47). Attempts to relocate inhabitants to other provinces in India also yielded few results; the plan to send Biharis to the Central Provinces, for example, was an acknowledged failure. Assam and Burma were then regarded as good possibilities. Following a conference of indigo planters and administrators, efforts to encourage movement to Burma were intensified. Recruiters were dispatched to the districts, and leaflets were circulated. Each emigrant was offered an advance to cover expenses to Calcutta and Burma, which was to be deducted later from his wages. Of the 83 Saran men who secured advances, many absconded.[62]

PEASANTS ON THE MOVE

Most outmigrants came from the southern thanas, which lay along the main communication arteries connecting Saran by road and waterways to points east and south. Initially, the thanas of Mashrak and Parsa were heavily represented. Sonepur subsequently became "a great emigrating *thana* and also the *thana* most largely inhabited by the class who most enlist as soldiers."[63] In 1891 the inhabitants of Manjhi and Basantpur thanas were also said to have joined the seasonal travelers; in the former case, the "vogue" had caught on following the severe floods of 1890–1891.[64]

These observations are confirmed by the relative proportion of the sexes in these thanas. Because censuses were compiled in the cold weather, and most seasonal migrants were males, many more women than men were consistently counted in the areas of outmigration. The highest proportion of women to men was in Sonepur with 133 females for every 100 males, Manjhi (128), Parsa (126), Mashrak (124) and Basantpur (122)—the very thanas from which large numbers flocked east.[65]

Further identification of the seasonal outmigrants from Saran confirms the

---

61. See *District Census Report, 1891, Champaran* 1898: 94; Bourdillon Report; *SR*: 159.
62. "Memorandum on the Material Condition of the Lower Orders in Bengal," 1888, in Parliamentary Branch Papers, L/Parl/1/220; AGRPD, 1891–92. See also AGRPD, 1872–73, 1882–83, 1890–91; "Report . . . of Tirhut Division for . . . 1905–06 to 1909–10," Bengal Gen. Procs., April 1911, 227.
63. Bourdillon 1898: 68; Hunter 1877: 26.
64. Bourdillon 1898: 68.
65. Ibid.: 66.

"cliche that migrants will be disproportionately drawn from among the segments of the rural population which occupy the least favored structural position."[66] A 1901 report indicates that few high-caste persons went to Bengal from Bihar. Those who did were generally Brahmin or Rajput; few upcountry Kayasths or Bhumihar Brahmins were noticed. The migrants were usually of the lower castes: Tanti, Ahir, Kurmi, Kahar, Kalwar, Bhar, Dusadh, Nuniya, Bind, and Chamar.[67]

The 1915–1921 village-by-village information for the four thanas of Manjhi, Mashrak, Parsa, and Sonepur, which provided the bulk of the people who moved from the district, reveals similar faces in the crowds of outmigrants. In Nawada, a village of 148 families of eighteen different castes, ranging from 4 families of Brahmins to 1 of the sweeper caste, it was the Ahirs, Nuniyas, Chamars, and Dhuniyas who moved out annually. Together these castes constituted 19 percent of the village's total inhabitants. From Bal village, whose 107 families included only 5 upper-caste families of Brahmins, two or three men from each family were said to migrate every year. From Gangoi many went to Bengal except for the local Rajputs and Brahmins; from Rasidpur all petty cultivators and Muslims moved east. In some villages of Parsa thana, only the Chamars were known to be outmigrants, working in hide godowns in Bengal. And for Sonepur, the notes report that many who did not earn sufficient income from agriculture resorted to temporary labor and service in Calcutta and elsewhere.[68] Similar identifications are also provided by accounts of the localities that received these streams of migration.[69]

Such generalizations gain additional focus in the case of Hira, a 42-year-old Teli who lived in the village of Usri with his wife and two children. By serving as a porter or laborer in Calcutta four months a year, he returned home with a savings of Rs. 36 to supplement an income of Rs. 208 derived primarily from his holdings and his work as an oil-presser. As a tenant-at-will, he held 1 bigha 4 *cottahs* on a cash rent basis and 12 *cottahs* on a produce rent system. Nevertheless, his total income of Rs. 256-12 annas was only barely sufficient for the year because he had gained Rs. 28 from the sale of a bullock.[70]

A high incidence of people with low economic and social status inhabiting heavily populated localities was considered the distinctive feature of areas of potential labor supply for the growing industrial centers of the early twentieth century.[71] Saran not only had a high population density, but its southern thanas, from which outmigration was the heaviest, were the most crowded and

---

66. Graves and Graves 1974: 117.   67. Gait 1902: 143.
68. Nawada and Bal villages, Manjhi thana nos. 104 and 105; Gangoi and Rasidpur villages, Mashrak thana nos. 226 and 280; Sirampur and Bedowlia villages, Parsa thana nos. 399 and 400, Mohamatpur, Sonepur thana no. 118, SVN.
69. See Vas (1911: 82); Tea District Labour Association, Calcutta (1924: 248–326).
70. See "Family Budget of Hira, Teli by caste, of the Village Usri," *Chanakya Society, 6th Annual Report, 1915–16*, pp. 92–96.
71. Fremantle 1906: 43–44; Foley 1906: 38–58. For a similar identification of the low economic and social status of factory labor, see Gupta (1976) and Baniprasana Misra (1975).

demanded higher rent rates than the relatively nonmigrating northern areas. Furthermore, according to a 1903 estimate, only 64 percent of the district's population held above the minimum subsistence level of 2.5 acres for a family of five. Far below this standard were the "cultivating and landless laborers" consisting in equal proportions of people whose holdings did not amount to 2.5 acres and those with no land at all. The propensity to migrate appears almost a part of their official definition as "persons whose holdings are insufficient for the support of themselves and their families and who are consequently obliged to supplement their income."[72] Over 600,000 people, primarily of the following castes, were included in this category: Ahirs, Baris, Binds, Chamars, Dhanuks, Dhobis, Dusadhs, Gonds, Hajams, Jolahas, Kandus, Koeris, Kumhars, Kurmis, Mallahs, Nuniyas, Sheikhs, Tatwas, and Turhas.[73]

These conditions explain why Saran was a major district of outmigrants in the late nineteenth and early twentieth centuries. The push was felt particularly by persons of low economic and social status because "this class of population had little inducement to stay at home for agricultural wages are notoriously low, and (they) will be ready to go abroad in order to earn a fair wage."[74] And such opportunities existed in the east "in the mills, factories, docks, and coal mines, or on the roads and railways, or in harvesting the crops of other districts."[75] Their pull for the outmigrants is clearly discernible from the comparison of wages (table 16).

Table 16.

Average Daily Wages in Saran, Dacca, and 24-Parganas
(All figures in rupees-annas-pice)

	Saran (April 1911)	Dacca[a] (March 1911)	24 Parganas[a] (March 1912)
Coolie or unskilled labor	-2- to -3-3	-8-	-5-1
Blacksmith	-4- to -5-6	-12- to 1-4	-12- to 1-0
Carpenter	-4- to -5-6	-10- to 1-6	-12- to 1-0
Thatcher	-4- to -5-6	-8-	n.a.

Sources: SDG, B Vol., *Statistics, 1900–1901 to 1910–11*, p. 10; *Bengal District Gazetteers*, B Vol., Dacca District, *Statistics, 1900–1902 to 1910–11*, 1914: 10; *Bengal District Gazetteers, 24-Parganas* 1910: 141.

[a] For Dacca and 24 Parganas, wages indicated are for common to superior blacksmiths and carpenters.

72. Three acres provided "fair" comfort; 64 percent were "pure cultivators"; 20 percent, "cultivating and landless laborers"; and "others," 14 percent (*SR*: 160, 18, 156). These figures are for the agricultural population only; otherwise the estimate for cultivating and landless laborers is 27 percent. See also Hunter (1873: 29) for an estimate of 20 percent for "labouring classes"; and AGRPD 1878–79, for a higher figure of 25 percent.

73. *SR*: 17. Although comprising 26 percent of the district's population, agricultural and low castes held only 3.3 percent of the land.   74. Fremantle 1906: 44.

75. O'Malley 1912: 4.

Compared to Bihar, the wages in Bengal were considerably higher both in agriculture and industry. For Bihar migrants, the attraction to Rangpur district during the cultivating and harvesting season was the possibility of earning as much as 10 annas a day in jute harvesting and retting operations. The gains from factory work, for skilled or unskilled laborers, were also much more than could be attained in Bihar. In jute mills, which had large numbers of Saran hands, ordinary unskilled labor by men earned a weekly sum of Rs. 2-4 or over 5 annas per day.[76]

One indication of the benefits that were reaped by moving east is the estimate by a 1903 report of the "remittances made by Saran emigrants.... The average value of the money orders cashed annually in Saran is 15 lakhs and much of this doubtless represents the earnings of Saran cultivators in other districts. In the famine year the amount rose to over 34 lakhs."[77]

Most migrants made modest gains. R. H. Pawsey, who was previously collector in Mymensingh, recalled seeing Saran laborers in his former district, "each individual one of which readily admitted having saved Rs. 40 to Rs. 80 in cash, and sometimes even more, in his six months' labour."[78] Bourdillon estimated an average of Rs. 50 to 60 profit. Part of this sum was remitted home by money order midway during the temporary stay, and the rest brought back in May, but the net profit that "an ordinarily fortunate man makes over the trip," was only Rs. 30 or 40 because the moneylender had to be repaid for advances on travel expenses and "the immediate wants of the family at home till remittances arrived from the eastward."[79]

An approximate estimate of the total earnings of Saran migrants from their employment abroad can be tabulated from money order figures. Of Rs. 1,122,350 paid on money orders in Saran between January 1 and December 31, 1889, Rs. 1,040,294 were sent from the following sixteen districts: Calcutta, Rs. 144,935; Darjeeling, 65,548; Champaran, 51,671; Mymensingh, 47,884; 24-Parganas, 45,649; Julpigoree, 40,507; Howrah, 40,461; Hooghly, 35,756; Purnea, 31,086; Rangpur, 29,595; Muzaffarpur, 25,274; Dacca, 23,182; Darbhanga, 22,782; Patna, 22,325; Bhagalpur, 20,311; and Monghyr, 18,727.[80] These were precisely the districts that were important receiving localities for the district's migrants.

Large remittances through the post office also characterized other years. Between April 1893–March 1894 and April 1894–March 1895, Rs. 1,333,450 and 1,642,900, respectively, were paid out to discharge money orders. In 1910

---

76. According to the chairman of the Jute Mills Association, Saran provided the largest number of workers in the major mills of Victoria, Titaghur, and Shamnagar—1,280, 741, and 1,436, respectively (Foley 1906: 9, 14–15).   77. *SR*: 159.
78. Cited in AGRPD, 1878–79. See also Rajendra Prasad (1957: 521), who writes that his village received Rs. 4,000 to 5,000 weekly.   79. Bourdillon Report.
80. That these sums do not represent commercial transactions is evident from their general average value—Rs. 20—and the fact that *hundis* (bankers' drafts) and checks remained the means of commercial transactions (ibid.).

Rs. 38,600,000 was paid out for sums remitted by the district's migrants.[81] The contributions that such large sums made to the local economy were significant:

> [They] are not payments for exports, but they represent a vast number of small remittances to the homes by persons in service in the army, as durwans [doorkeepers] in Calcutta, and in other more or less menial appointments in Lower Bengal and elsewhere. It is to the money brought into the district in this way, as well as the large payments by Government to the opium cultivators and the very considerable local outlay by the numerous indigo factories, that the lower classes in Saran owe their safety from being in a chronic state of want.[82]

According to one district collector, who estimated that an average of Rs. 400,000 was sent home monthly, "credit is due to these men for their energy and the enormous sum which they remit for the support of their families."[83] In other words, these gains from employment "abroad" represented the efforts of the district's poorer peasants to survive the growing agricultural crisis of the late nineteenth and early twentieth centuries.

Within village society, the benefits of seasonal migration were often noticeable. In village Deuria, for instance, those who went to Bengal were said to live in "better style." In Chan Chaura village, anyone who migrated was "looked upon with respect by his family, no matter however junior he may be simply because he is an earning member of the family. These migrants considered themselves above the category of their brethren."[84]

Seasonal migration, however, also had some deleterious effects on the migrants' communities of origin. Because most women remained behind, the separation brought on by the annual exodus caused considerable anguish at home. The "psychic costs" of such separation have been vividly portrayed in the folklore of the region. A popular folksong sung by women in Gorakhpur recounts this grief through the device of a parrot given by a woman's beloved as a parting gift before he leaves for the east. The parrot becomes the object of her attention as she sings to it: "By day I will feed you, parrot, with milk and rice in a dish. And at night I will take you to sleep between my breasts." Finally, she sends it off to her husband in Calcutta, and there, perched on her beloved's turban, the parrot responds to the husband's question about the well-being of his family at home: "Thy wife weeps daily and hourly (Ah Ram!) thy mother weeps; yes, thy mother weeps the whole year through."[85]

The pangs of separation are also poignantly evoked in the Bhojpuri writings of Bhikhari Thakur whose "Bidesia" plays gained an appreciative audience in the Bhojpur region; according to one source, becoming as popular as the much-loved epic of the *Ramayana*.[86] An illiterate barber from Chapra, Thakur

---

81. AGRPD, 1894–95. For 1910 figure, see O'Malley (1912: 5); for 1915–1920, see Tallents (1923: 108). 82. AGRPD, 1894–95.
83. Cited in "Report on Tirhut from 1905–06 to 1909–10," Bengal Gen. Procs., April 1911, 2.
84. Deuria village, Mashrak thana no. 79; Chan Chaura village, Manjhi thana no. 117, SVN.
85. Fraser 1883: 7–8. See also 'Vinod,' (1958) and Upadhyya (1960).
86. Tiwari 1960: xxvi. See also Thakur (1931).

left home as a boy, wandered east and formed a traveling team of performers. His plays were called "Bidesia" because many of them depict the plight of the wife who has to remain behind while her husband seeks employment in what seems to her *bidesh* (a foreign country). "The pathos of the play finds reponse in countless hearts," J. C. Mathur's study of rural drama explains, "because many villagers from West Bihar go to Calcutta and some of them form attachment with city-women, neglecting young wives in their homes."[87]

In their receiving communities, especially if they were employed by the jute mills, Saran's migrants, along with other Biharis, lived in makeshift huts in the proximity of the factories. The squalor of their living condition was documented by government medical officers, who explained that the millhands from up-country lived "in the meanest huts, and eat the worst food, because these are the cheapest."[88] But the experience of working and living together in a "foreign" land fostered community consciousness, and its development was also aided by the networks of support that grew naturally among the large numbers of Bhojpuri-speaking migrants thrown together. In Calcutta, this spirit was particularly conspicuous: "[At] the foot of the Ochterlony Monument in the 'Maidan' there is a large informal gathering of Bhojpuri people, particularly on Sunday evenings, where the shadow of the 'Mauni-Math' (as the Bhojpuri speakers have transformed the English word monument), we have the regular sight of Bhojpuri people amusing themselves with folk-songs, folk-tales and informal talks and speeches."[89]

Internal Migration as an Option

The persistence of seasonal migration as the predominant form of internal migration in the late nineteenth and early twentieth centuries highlights its importance as an option for Saran peasants. Given the risks of permanently moving away from a familiar setting on the one hand and the uncertainty of relocating in a new environment on the other, the development of temporary movement as a mechanism for "maximization" reflects the "rationality" of peasant decision making and action.[90]

The basis for seasonal migration from Saran as well as other Bihar districts was the local agricultural calendar. Intensive labor was necessary primarily at the times of harvest. In Saran the peak demand was during the months of August to September for the autumn harvest, November to December for the winter harvest, and March to April for the spring harvest. In addition, the

---

87. 1964: 82. 88. GOI 1899: 3.
89. Tiwari 1960: xxvi. This community consciousness could also assume a virulent form (Chakrabarty 1981). Also see Weiner (1978) for a macro-picture of the problems engendered by intercultural and interstate migration.
90. See Beals and Menezes (1970: 111), who argue that seasonal migration enabled an efficient allocation of resources "because the combined income . . . exceeds income from the alternatives: namely, 'full time' employment . . . or permanent migration."

transplantation of the winter rice in June and July required intensive work. Whereas the months from June to November required continuous agricultural work, December to May was a slack period. It was during these months, the dry season, that the annual exodus of primarily males took place. Except for poppy cultivators, there was usually little to do in the fields during this period. The spring crops were sown by mid-November, and its harvest in March or April was light enough to be gathered by women and children. Intensive work only began with the outbreak of the monsoon, usually June or July when the lands had to be prepared for sowing *bhadoi* and rice.

This agricultural calendar also explains why streams of outmigration from Saran flowed not only toward Bengal, but also to the nearby districts of Bihar. In Saran, unlike Champaran, for instance, although rice was the major food crop, it occupied a relatively small area. Thus, labor from Saran, where the winter rice was the smallest of the three harvests, migrated to the considerably less populated district of Champaran where the winter rice crop was much more productive. The seasonality of labor demands in Saran also enabled its inhabitants to move to eastern Bengal to cut its crops.[91]

The sole alternative to outmigration was to remain in the locality to work in the region's indigo plantations, but this never developed as an option for several reasons. Substantial manpower for this labor intensive industry was required between June and September when the indigo was cut and manufactured and also between October and February.[92] In spite of the overlap of this later period with part of the slack season in agriculture, indigo planters consistently encountered difficulties in recruiting labor, because of the reaction that developed in local society to indigo and the predominantly European indigo planters and because of the low wages offered, often less than the prevailing rates in the locality.[93]

Seasonal migration also persisted as the major type of movement because of developments in communications, which added greater flexibility to the agricultural calendar. Better transportation facilities opened up a wider range of areas to migration. Initially, migrants from Saran went to their destination on foot. To travel to Bengal, they generally crossed the Gandak River at Lalganj, and then proceeded across Muzaffarpur and Darbhanga to Purnea and other localities farther east, a journey lasting between one to two months. As late as the 1880s, the district magistrate's informants told him that "a vast majority of

---

91. Foley 1906: 39; BOR's letter no. 904A, Aug. 13, 1891, by D. R. Lyall, Commr. of Patna, P.C. Rev. *Basta* no. 355, 1891–1892; *Champaran Census, 1891*, p. 94.

92. In 1883 indigo manufacturing employed as many as 18,680 laborers per day, according to the Secretary of the Saran Committee of the Bihar Indigo Planters' Association (AGRPD, 1882–83).

93. Fisher 1976: 223–71. Plantation efforts to recruit labor were also hampered by the controls exerted by local landholders over the existing supply of labor and the ritual objections of many high caste and Muslim cultivators to working with indigo. See also, C. F. Worsley, Offg. Colltr. of Muzaffarpur to Commr., Patna, Dec. 29, 1875 and Commr. C. T. Metcalfe to Secy., GOB, April 25, 1876, Bengal Gen. (Misc.) Procs., April 1876, 7–8.

the Saran emigrants tramp every foot of the way out and home."[94] Increasingly, however, the railways became the major mode of transport for migrants. By the mid-1880s, with north Bihar linked to the Bengal and North-Western railways, which in turn was connected to the Eastern Bengal State Railways, all of Bengal became easily accessible. As a result, the streams of movement to Bengal grew in size with the development of "familiarity with the railways and railway extensions."[95]

Better transportation facilities not only increased the volume of migration to many more areas but also facilitated adaptations that further increased the size of the movement. More members of a family moved out as the duration of the trip itself was reduced from one to two months to a matter of a few days. In the early twentieth century, family parties were noticed who stayed out for only three to four months.[96] From Manjhi thana, many went for only two months and returned in time to harvest the spring crops—a striking contrast to the extended December to May migration periods of the nineteenth century.[97] Shorter-term migrations were also possible because labor demands in many receiving communities was seasonal. In Hooghly, for instance, during the winter months of October to March, there was a constant demand in towns for factory hands and in the rural tracts for the winter rice and spring crops.[98]

Closely related to the fluctuations in the migrant streams were also the vagaries of the season and the changing job opportunities at home and abroad. "If bumper crops are reaped, it [outmigration] diminishes, if they are short, the exodus is largely increased and lasts longer."[99] Thus, when heavy rains inundated one area of the district and almost destroyed its autumn and winter harvests in 1890–1891, many more people than usual migrated from the flooded tracts. And when employment prospects at home were good, as in the 1880s, with the numerous railway construction projects in and around the district, the number who moved out fell sharply.[100]

Conditions in the prospective place of employment had similar effects. When crops failed in the northern districts of Bengal in 1891–1892, the number of travelers decreased noticeably. In 1919–1920, only four villagers went to Calcutta from Sonebersa, whereas previously large numbers took the trip. According to the villagers, they were aware of Calcutta's dull business year and its lack of "ready employment."[101]

94. Bourdillon Report; Hunter 1877: 269.
95. "Report on Tirhut from 1905–06 to 1909–10," Bengal Gen. Procs., April 1911, 285; Skrine, "Material Condition of the Lower Orders in Bengal," p. 48.
96. Tallents 1923: 110.
97. Tole Madhopur village, Manjhi thana no. 107, SVN; also, "Budget of Mawal, Teli by Caste, of Village Pachlakhi," in *Chanakya Society, 9th Annual Report, 1918–19*, p. 93, which notes that one of his two sons would go "once or twice a year to Eastern Bengal or Assam to earn money."
98. Factory labor was in demand particularly between November and February when epidemics of malaria reduced the number of workers (O'Malley and Chakravarti 1912: 169–70).
99. O'Malley 1912: 4.   100. AGRPD, 1890–91, 1883–84.
101. Sonebersa village, Darauli thana no. 327, SVN; Skrine, "Material Condition of the Lower Order in Bengal," p. 55.

Although push-and-pull factors were the major determinants of the patterns of movement, the migration decision was ultimately rooted in personal considerations. The district's inhabitants "having once acquired the habit of emigrating for wages, and having found that it is easy to save money in this way," a contemporary observer noted, "now emigrate yearly as a matter of habit to supplement their incomes, whether agricultural conditions are prosperous or the reverse."[102] Much the same pattern was noticed by George Grierson who considered the "native community" generally averse to emigration but acknowledged that "every coolie who emigrates, on his return becomes an apostle of it."[103] A slightly different formulation of this relationship between feedback and migration behavior is the assertion that those who went to the distant districts from Saran followed "some friend or relation."[104]

Because migration was an "old habit" from Saran, its advantages were widely recognized. An investigation in the early twentieth century confirms how commonplace such knowledge was:

I believe the rates and conditions of work in the Calcutta industries are well known in the district. There is a constant flow to and from the mills, and one man will inform a whole village as to what his earnings and his work have been. To test this I attended a *chaukidari* parade. Several chaukidars told me, as I thought correctly, what some weavers from their village had made in a Jute Mill, another what another kind of worker had made in a Jute Mill, and a third seemed to know a good deal about Jute Presses.... The people of Saran . . . are well aware of the benefits to be derived from employment in the industrial centres, and a larger number than from any other district seek employment in those centres spontaneously.[105]

Familiarity with an area also enabled migrants to return to that locality, even after their original project was finished. When the Mymensingh-Dacca branch of the Eastern Bengal Railway was completed, in part due to the efforts of Saran migrants, many went back annually to the area to cut and load jute in Mymensingh, Dacca, and Naraingunge.[106]

Indeed, the steady flow of remittances, and money and articles brought back home from successful "foraging" abroad, must have acted as powerful incentives for those who had not as yet moved out. Information passed on through existing social and kinship networks may explain, in part, why only selected villages in a locality consistently sent people.[107] Clearly, the habit of migration developed not only because of a number of push-and-pull factors but also because, as was noticed for village Deuria, those who moved to Bengal lived in "better style."

In addition, organized efforts were also made to facilitate and encourage migration. At one time, a district resident started an emigration agency, which

102. Cited in O'Malley (1912: 5). See also Lee (1969: 287). 103. Grierson 1883: 18.
104. Bourdillon Report. 105. Foley 1906: 39. 106. Bourdillon Report.
107. See Parsotimpur and Nilki villages from where nobody migrated, and the neighboring villages of Ahimanpatti, Kesarpur, Isamailee, and Sobhapur, which sent out many of its inhabitants (Sonepur thana nos. 6 and 24, 7, 8, 13, and 21, respectively, SVN).

offered information on routes, coordinated travel groups and loaned money for a fee of 1 rupee for services and 25 percent interest on advances. Factories from the east also took the initiative by sending out representatives to recruit gangs, varying in size from two to six men, who were generally all drawn from one village. In some cases, entire families, including women and children, were recruited.[108]

In their jobs Saran migrants also showed adaptability: they took up all kinds of field labor, "digging and cleaning tanks, repairing roads, making railway embankment and harvesting the winter rice crop. When women go they either work with their husbands, or else earn an income by grinding corn for the Banias."[109] Much of the earthwork of the Assam-Bihar Railway through Purnea and the Northern Bengal Railway in Rangpur, Bogra, and Dinajpur was accomplished by migrant labor. In the vicinity of Calcutta and Howrah, employment was mainly as coolies or millhands.[110]

Many migrants also adopted new occupations in a number of ingenious ways. Brahmins usually became pilgrim conductors, priests, clerks, peons, cooks, and, occasionally, coolies and day laborers. Rajputs were primarily constables, doorkeepers, jail wardens, peons, and railway porters. Ahirs were laborers, domestic servants, or shopkeepers. Kahars, Kurmis, and Dusadhs were laborers or millhands; many Kahars also became domestic servants; and Dusadhs often syces.[111]

The largely menial nature of employment reinforces the earlier identification of seasonal migrants as of low economic and social status.[112] Such a profile explains the relatively modest gains made by most peasants who moved. Although such movement enabled many in the district to maximize their living conditions, by its very nature it draws attention not to the receiving communities, but to the migrants' own place of origin. Thus, seasonal employment was economically beneficial ultimately not only to the travelers but also to their landholders and moneylenders.

Not surprisingly, the more distant and permanent kinds of outmigration were not encouraged by local controllers. As George A. Grierson reported, landholders were opposed to colonial emigration because "every coolie who emigrates is looked upon as so much property lost."[113] That such attitudes prevailed among all levels of land controllers is apparent from the testimony of Arikishan Sinha, a self-professed "cultivator" employing ten to twenty persons in his fields, to the Royal Commission on Labour in India:

D-568. *If they go to Assam or Burma they are not able to work for you?* No, they are not.
D-569. *And you yourself would like to see no recruiting for Assam or Burma?* As a cultivator and

108. Foley 1906: 25; Fremantle 1906: 37; Bourdillon Report.
109. Bourdillon Report. See also Rajendra Prasad (1957: 521) on migrant occupations.
110. Bourdillon Report. 111. Gait 1913: 143.
112. Note the contrast with the profile of internal migrants. (Pryor 1977: 66); Connell 1976: 156–96). 113. 1883: 16–17.

one who is desirous of improving the condition of agriculture in Bihar, I would not like that labourers from this place should go to other places.

D-570. *If the labourer has any choice of employment and is not confined to work on the land in Bihar, to that extent it sends up his rate of wages?* Yes. I will have no objection if he were to go seasonably, say, for six to nine months in a year.[114]

Thus, despite government encouragement, overseas migration was not a route many Saran peasants chose in the late nineteenth and early twentieth centuries. In part, it did not develop as an option because of the risks it entailed; in part, it remained a trickle because landholders were opposed to a permanent transfer of their supply of labor. Seasonal migration, on the other hand, was a viable option, because it reaped benefits for the peasants as well as their superordinates. In the sense that it allowed them to enhance their resources (although primarily to pay off their dues to their landholders and moneylenders), seasonal migration describes the kind of limited option that peasants have in many agrarian societies.

Stopgap Measures

Saran peasants historically moved under certain conditions. A common response to adversity was flight, which often assumed the proportions of avoidance protest. Indigo plantations often produced these conditions because their demands on land and labor clashed with the peasant system of agriculture. Desertions, a regular occurrence from zamindari estates, were desperate acts of evasion from situations, often triggered by disastrous ecological and manmade conditions, in which raiyats were unable to meet the persistent demands imposed on them by superordinates. A combination of such pressures compelled many peasants to flee Hathwa in 1872, 1902–1903, and in 1879 in the so-called "wholesale desertions," the largest reported case of forced migration from the district in the nineteenth and early twentieth centuries.

Deserters were disproportionately drawn from the poorer peasantry—people of low economic and social position. And as the detailed information on the desertions of 1879 reveals, most deserters had no choice but to respond defensively, because they were confronted with Hathwa's effective system of control. Flight was the only way to avoid complete ruin.

Notwithstanding the maharaja of Hathwa's attempt to explain away the wholesale desertions by characterizing them as the well-known annual exodus from Saran at "flitting time," seasonal migration was a different kind of movement. Over 10 percent of the population of the district, especially from its overcrowded southern thanas, was consistently reported outside the district in the late nineteenth and early twentieth centuries. The predominant form of movement was seasonal migration, increasingly directed at the districts of

---

114. He was also Gen. Secy. of the Bihar Provincial *Kisan Sabha (Royal Commission on Labour in India* 4, pt. 2: 67). See also Omvedt (1980: 185–90) and Standing (1981: 173–211).

Bengal, where opportunities existed for employment in menial jobs, such as harvesting, manual labor, or unskilled jobs in factories. On an average, a seasonal migrant netted earnings ranging from Rs. 30 to 80.

Seasonal migration persisted in Saran because it was a relatively safe proposition for peasants. It offered prospects for gains, while minimizing the uncertainties beyond the ordinary. Its basis was the local agricultural calendar in which, for up to six months in a year, in the period of relative slack, peasants left their homes to seek higher wages elsewhere. The introduction of railways in the mid-1800s provided additional "elasticity" to seasonal migration as a source of additional income. More members of a family now migrated, and the duration of their stays in the east became more closely tied to the levels of risk and uncertainty at home and abroad. And as such movement became a habit for many, a reliable resource pool of information developed that assisted potential migrants in their evaluation of prevailing push-and-pull factors. The continuing use of the option of seasonal migration therefore reflects on the rationality of peasant decision making and action.

By its very nature, seasonal migration also highlights the migrants' local society, because temporary movement was intended to benefit migrants and their families in their homes, and not in the receiving community. But it was not solely a mechanism for peasants to enhance their resources. As is evident from the social and economic identities of the annual migrants east, such movement represented the efforts of low caste peasants with minimal economic resources to earn supplementary incomes to meet the demands of landholders and moneylenders. Unlike overseas emigration, it was an option that peasants were not discouraged from using. Permanent movement on the other hand was not only less promising in pecuniary returns for superordinates, but also meant a reduction in the district's labor force, which it was in the landholder's interest to maintain.

The monetary gains of seasonal migration were eked out, however, at the expense of "psychic costs," which the communities at origin had to bear. A predominantly male phenomenon, this annual movement compelled many families to live apart during the slack season. So widespread was the habit of outmigration that the theme of the pangs of separation became enshrined in the popular literature of the Bhojpur region.

Desertion represented a desperate act of evasion and an attempt to flee utter ruin, but seasonal migration was much more of a positive step toward enhancing one's resources. And in developing it as an option the Saran peasant displayed both considerable skill and sophistication in tailoring it to his needs and abilities. Who moved, where he went, and what he did—all testify to this capacity to operate under some degree of risk and uncertainty to create an opportunity for financial gain. But, as with avoidance protest, the seasonal exodus ultimately reflected the Saran raiyats' inability to break out of the prevailing systems of local control. At best, desertions and migration were stopgap measures that kept zamindars and maliks at bay.

10

Resistance, Violence, and Collective Action as Peasant Options

Two images recurred in the British characterizations of the inhabitants of Saran. On the one hand was the description of the "people of this district... [as] all armed. Almost every man you meet on the road has a long 'lathee' [club], and very many carry swords."[1] Equally current was the perception, applied generally to the entire peasant population of Bihar, that they were "ignorant of their rights, and so imbued with the tika [stamp] of the feudal subjection that combined open conflict with the zamindars is but a rare occurrence."[2] Although seemingly contradictory, both images accurately depict facets of the complex relations between landholders and peasants in Saran.

Resistance and Recalcitrance

Acts and behaviors designed to uphold threatened rights occurred routinely in Saran. These everyday forms of resistance were usually aimed at alleviating subsistence crises, removing specific grievances, or seeking assistance against superordinates who had exceeded the norms prescribed by the prevailing moral economy.

A common mode of protest was the appeal peasants made to their landholders or to government by assembling en masse to state their concerns.

---

1. "Prevalence of Heinous Crime in District," Magte. F. Macnaghten to Commr., no. 95, July 31, 1862, P.C. *Basta* no. 105, Monthly Bundles, Gen. Dept. from 1854 on, from Magte. of Saran. See also Charles Boddam, Judge and Magte., Saran, Dec. 16, 1801, "Answers to Interrogatories of the Governor General (1801)," *Parliamentary Papers, 1812–1813* 9: 238.

2. Cited in AGRPD, 1878–79. See also Edward Golding, Supervisor, Saran, to Calcutta Council, May 29, 1771, Calcutta Rev. Committee's Consltns., April 1 to Dec. 31, 1771, June.

Official records reveal numerous cases of administrators being surrounded by pleading peasants. Before the survey riots of 1844, raiyats had sought to win the backing of government for their rentfree rights by personally presenting their case to the touring deputy collector.[3] Hathwa's tenants again employed this method in 1879 to protest the repeated rent raises imposed on them. In a fifty-mile radius, O'Donnell encountered "at least 50 groups of villagers at different points"; in another instance, he was visited by "40 ryots coming from 6 villages . . . [who] declared that they would immediately abscond if Government did not interpose in their behalf."[4]

Appeals to the government were both against its measures and for its support against the designs of other parties. When the British reorganized the district's chaukidari force and levied its costs on the inhabitants of certain localities, the Saran judge found his bungalow surrounded by 200 to 300 women of the "lower orders praying for remission of their share of the . . . assessment."[5] On another occasion, when a special investigator was dispatched to inquire into the origins of the famine of 1866, he ascertained that "on the part of the ryots [there was] a preconceived notion that the object of my deputation was to enquire into the system of indigo cultivation prevailing there. The only possible ground that I can suggest for the existence of such an impression . . . is, that with some of them at least there may be an objection to this cultivation."[6] During the famine of 1873-1874, the fortnightly accounts typically reported famine officers "besieged daily by crowds of people for advances of grain."[7]

Entreaties for immediate redress are also preserved in the innumerable petitions that were submitted to district officials and zamindars. In 1824, for instance, petitions addressed to the district administrators focused on a variety of grievances. One set complained about the abuses of the court inspector's office whose peons apparently repeatedly harassed people. Another set of 180 petitions included one that related that a Sheikh Zuman wanted reparation from an indigo planter who had inflicted injuries on him—his persistence in the matter was reflected in the fact that he had gone first to Calcutta to present his case to the governor-general and later to Chapra to submit it to the magistrate. A missive sent in by a Parmeshwar Tiwari complained of the "oppressive conduct" of "a great zameendar named Baboo Chutterdharee Sahee [Maharaja of Hathwa]."[8]

3. Commr. E. C. Ravenshaw, to Sadr BOR, no. 673, March 8, 1845, Bengal Rev. Consltns., April 9 to May 7, 1845, April 23, no. 93.
4. O'Donnell to Magte., July 8, 1879; O'Donnell to Magte., no. 164, June 21, 1879; "Desertions in Hathwa."
5. J. B. Elliot, 4th Judge, to W. H. Macnaghten, Registrar to the Nizt. Adlt., Dec. 10, 1824, Bengal Cr. Jdcl. Consltns., Feb. 17, 1825, no. 15.
6. F. R. Cockerell, on special deputation . . . to Secy., GOB, Feb. 15, 1867, Bengal Jdcl. Procs., Jan. to March 1867, March, 40.
7. See, e.g., "Narrative of Scarcity . . . in Sarun . . . for the Fortnight ending 11th July 1874," *Famine Narrative*, nos. 21 & 22, June 26 to July 23, 1874.
8. Elliot to Macnaghten, Dec. 10, 1824, Bengal Cr. Jdcl. Consltns., Feb. 17, 1825, no. 15.

A sampling of petitions directed at the government in 1867 indicates a similar range of concerns. Saliknand wrote in, praying for return of his interests in Punscona village, which had been purchased by a "public woman." Dharam Deo Narain and others complained about the "arbitrary and oppressive conduct" of the deputy magistrate of Siwan and requested "enquiry and justice."[9] In 1854 the residents of Mohummedpore boldly submitted their communication directly to the governor-general; their request was for deliverance from the hands of their zamindars who were "addicted to compel them by force and oppression to servitude."[10]

Peasants also submitted complaints directly to their landholders. In one fifteen-month period, the central office of Hathwa received 20,403 petitions "about rent matters, about alleged oppressive acts of thikadars, sazawals and patwaris, about alleged mistakes of entry of fields in the survey records, about grants for wells, about embankments, &c."[11] Many that year were also aimed at the Kehunia Indigo Factory against which raiyats had numerous grievances. Petitions from 1899/1900, while touching on a variety of complaints, included appeals to Hathwa regarding its indigo planter *thikadars*. One plea issued over the names of a number of raiyats declared:

Hail cherisher of the poor! We beg to state that from the time the villages Bangra, Majharia, Mathia, Rampore, Chitawni and Karanpur, Parganah Kuadi, have been leased to Kehuniah Factory, we the ryots of these villages have been reduced to poverty. We have no respect in the eyes of the factory nor our requests are ever listened to and considered by it. The manager of the factory only hears and believes what his amlas say. We know not where to go, and we are in a very wretched condition. A number of ryots having been too much oppressed by the factory absconded and their holdings instead of being settled with other ryots are taken in zeerat possession of the factory. Any ryot if he grows poor or becomes widow, his holdings are as well taken away forcibly.[12]

A career of "crime" was another alternative peasants fashioned for themselves when faced with natural or manmade hardships. One kind of criminal activity closely followed the pattern of seasonal migration, suggesting perhaps the latter's relation to desertions and avoidance protest. Among the annual travelers east, some took to the road to seek "other" sources of income. With a few minor changes, the following description could well be applied to seasonal migration: "In the month of November, after the Rubbee is sown crowds of Gowallahs [Ahirs], Dosadhs and even Rajputs leave their homes ostensibly on

---

9. "Petition of Saliknand" and ". . . of Dhurrum Deo Narain," Bengal Rev. Procs., April 1867, B, no. 53, and May to July 1867, May, B, no. 174.
10. "Humble petition of Pursun Sah . . . and others," Bengal Cr. Jdcl. Procs., Oct. 18 to Nov. 1, 1855, Oct. 18, no. 33.
11. Colltr. W. C. Macpherson to Commr., no. 1C.W., June 18, 1899, Bengal Rev. Procs., Sept. to Oct. 1899, Sept., no. 94 (encl.).
12. "Petitions," Jan. 18, 1899, H.R. *Bastas*, 1899–1900, colltn. no. 38; "Complaints against Kehunia Factory by ryots," ibid., 1898–99, colltn. no. 39, file no. 40. Such appeals remained a major mode of "resisting" superordinate pressures, as is evident from the many appeals made to the Bihar Provincial *Kisan Sabha* in the 1930s and 1940s (Hauser 1983).

a pilgrimage, but in reality on thieving expeditions: the weeding &c of their field is carried on by their wives and younger offspring[s], and when the rubbee is ready to be cut, the campaign is over and back they all come with their spoil."[13]

An appreciable increase in certain kinds of crime, such as offenses against property and riots, invariably occurred in famine years. In the aftermath of the 1866 famine, government discovered that many of the "dacoits" incarcerated for offenses against property were not habitual thieves or known bad characters, but people who had committed grain robberies on account of starvation and "under the pressure of want."[14] Grain robberies were also regularly reported in the famine reports of 1873–1874.[15]

Peasants also sought to minimize their losses by being the proverbial refractory rent-payer. Dismissing the prevailing view in administrative circles that settlement work turned civilians against landlords, P. T. Mansfield, a settlement officer in Saran in the early twentieth century, argued that the opposite had happened in his case. Not only did he find himself prejudiced against raiyats, but also against "the race as a whole." In his diary he explained his views: "You see so much of the ryots, their awful lying, their absolute unscrupulousness . . . that by the end of the day you feel utterly disgusted with the whole crowd."[16] Other officials, however, were aware that this behavior evolved out of a particular setting. In discussing the "popular belief" in north Bihar "that the Tirhoot ryot will never be a willing rent-payer," A. P. MacDonnell wrote that the "difficulties experienced in realizing rents by zemindars and others in Behar are the direct consequences of the numerous oppressions from which the ryots have suffered."[17]

As the survey and settlement operations of 1893 to 1901 discovered, rent disputes between zamindar and raiyat were "the rule rather than the exception" in Saran. Only in the great estate of Hathwa were they unusual, and there, the maharaja with his superior records and familiarity with the system was able to win, or to avert, most contests.[18] An indication of the volume as well as the nature of disputes that arose during the operations of the survey and settlement can be gauged from the "objections" that landholders and tenants registered against the draft record of rights showing "the extent and legal conditions of their interests."[19] In the settlement of 1893 to 1901, a total of 66,105 objections

13. "Yearly Statement for 1854," Robert R. Richard, Magte., no. 68, Feb. 13, 1854, P.C. *Basta* no. 105.
14. A. Hope, Sessions Judge, Saran, to GOB, Bengal Jdcl. Procs., Jan. to Mar. 1867, Feb., 132; Commr. J. W. Dalrymple to Secy., GOB, March 27, 1867, Bengal Jdcl. Procs., Apr. 1867, no. 63.
15. See, e.g., "Narrative of Scarcity . . . Fortnight ending the 30th May 1874," *Famine Narratives*, nos. 19 and 20, May 29 to June 25, 1874, p. 4. See also Arnold (1979: 140–67) for a study which relates rural crime to elements of protest.
16. Mansfield Papers, vol. 1, Nov. 14, 1915 to March 18, 1918, Nov. 19, 1916.
17. Offg. Colltr. of Darbhanga, MacDonnell, to Commr., no. 1174, Oct. 10, 1877, "Behar Rent Papers," I, p. 34. 18. *SR*: 64.
19. GOB, *Guide and Glossary to Settlement Operations in Patna* 1907: 1.

were filed; 29,598 of them were allowed, and 36,507, disallowed. Of these, 1,479 pitted raiyats against landholders on the issue of possession; 2,028, on money rent; 581, on produce rent; and 655, on "status." Almost an equal number of objections in each of these categories were disallowed. Landholders, on the other hand, were granted objections against raiyats for 2,629 cases involving "possession"; 6,207 and 2,411, on money rent and produce rent disputes, respectively, and 2,515 cases, on questions of "status."[20] In the revision settlement of 1915 to 1921, the number of objections were far fewer: 111 allowed cases of tenants versus landholder on matters of possession; 61, on money rent; 19, on produce rent; and 11, on status.[21]

These "objections" constituted only a tiny fraction of the total number of disputes that surfaced in the course of the settlement proceedings. Although the overall figures are aggregate numbers, which include intralandholder and peasant squabbles as well as intergroup conflict, the magnitude of the agrarian tension is better suggested by the enormous volume of disputes that characterized the preliminary stage of record writing of the operations. One estimate placed the number at 20,000 to 30,000 disputes filed each year, with the area covered in a typical year extending to about 600 square miles. At the end of 1895, in the three years since the commencement of the operations in 1893, Saran's officers had settled over 1,787 cases relating to rent, which involved over 20,000 tenants.[22]

The strained nature of agrarian relations in Saran is also reflected in the extensive lists compiled of disputes on a village-by-village basis (*fard tanaza* records). Consisting of forty-eight volumes for the revision settlement of 1915 to 1921, these records illustrate in great detail the extent to which conflict erupted over issues of possession, rent, status, and other matters. In Neori village, the disputes stemmed from both the actual party in possession of a plot of land as well as the rights under which such claims were made. In village Malikana, held by the Hathwa estate but given as a rentfree grant to Udai Singh, the land was divided up into sixteen cash rent-paying holdings, in each of which the raiyats successfully challenged the rate of rent that was claimed as a customary right. Disputes over status also existed in this village as tenants claimed, in opposition to Udai Singh, that their plots were in their cultivating possession (*bakasht*).[23]

Conflict over trees was also commonplace. Throughout the Hathwa raj and on the estates of most landholders in north Bihar, settlement officers had to deal with the vexing question of the rights of landholders and tenants in trees and the fruits of trees. Hathwa typified the landholder claim by asserting its share in the fruit and timber of every tree on its zamindari. However, with

20. *SR*: 76.   21. *SRR*: 28–29.
22. "Memo. by Finucane," no. 16A, Jan. 7, 1896, Bengal Rev. Procs., Jan. to Feb. 1896, Jan., 501; *SR*: 43.
23. Mirganj thana no. 457, Gopalganj thana no. 214, Saran *Fard Tanaza*, 1915–1921.

tenants vigorously refusing to relinquish their own rights, government had to recognize the claims of both parties. As a result, some trees were declared to belong entirely to the estate; the fruit and timber of others were to be shared between the two claimants; and still others were the absolute right of only the tenant.[24]

In both the original and subsequent revision settlement, lands formerly held by indigo factories in Chapra and Mashrak thanas generated many disputes. With the indigo industry on the wane in the late nineteenth and early twentieth centuries, the factories had little use for the lands they had acquired and, therefore, increasingly gave up the lease of large areas. Instead of reverting to the raiyats from whom the leases had been originally secured, the lands fell into the hands of landholders who stepped in to recover them for their own direct possession or to offer them to tenants at greatly increased rates. In villages such as Usuri Kalan, disputes over rent alone tallied seventy-six. Additional complications arose when the factory sided with the landholders in the latter's attempts to dispossess tenants of their rights and to raise rents.[25]

No doubt, raiyat acts of recalcitrance and resistance periodically produced victories. On the whole, though, such occasions represented only momentary breaches in the systematic structures of control that zamindars and maliks had erected in Saran. Acts of resistance were only minor deviations from a pattern of relations in which local controllers set the rules of the game. Thus, even as the report of the first survey and settlement of the district acknowledged the presence of extensive conflict, it recognized that the balance existing between landholders who sought to extract as much as possible and peasants who sought to elude their grasp by withholding as much as possible was tilting in favor of the former because of their ability to manipulate the legal system. In the courts, "[t]he end is always the same, the eventual sale of the holding and the ruin of the raiyat."[26]

Over a decade later, in the revision settlement between 1915 and 1921, the official report concluded that raiyats had become more contentious. Its explanation was that "the cult of non-co-operation [the nationalist campaign organized by the Gandhi-led Indian National Congress] ... [had] diminished the raiyats' respect for authority, and in some parts they have combined in opposing the payment of even lawful duties."[27] However, from the vantage point of one settlement officer working in the field, it was also clear that peasants continued to be on a weak footing in relation to their superordinates:

In some villages you hear terrific stories of the 'Zabbardasti' of the landlords (i.e. literally high handedness). The tenants come and say they are afraid to go near the amin [land measurer] to claim their field because the landlords will beat them, and generally give them a bad time, by not granting rent receipts, turning them out and so on. You

---

24. *SR*: 57–58.
25. Mashrak thana no. 220, Saran *Fard Tanaza*; *SR*: 68.   26   *SR*: 64.
27. *SRR*: 12.

really find yourself here in feudal surroundings. The law is almost unfairly on the side of raiyat, but owing to their ignorance, the hold of the landlords, the remoteness of the village, and the impossibility of getting reliable evidence, this favouritism is entirely counteracted.[28]

Collective Violence and Action: Agrarian Riots

Violent agrarian disputes, recorded in government reports as "criminal" affrays and riots, or lumped together under the category of "unlawful assembly," were an endemic feature of the district's history of collective action. A special investigation concluded in 1812 that the "worst feature in the police of the district of Chuprah, as generally in that of the province of Behar, appears to be the frequent recurrence of violent affrays denominated Ghooraree."[29] This complaint was again registered in 1832 when government took the stern step of executing "a wealthy zamindar" for killing a man in an affray. But after a brief lull, such clashes erupted again. In an account tinged with concern, the Saran magistrate noted that "[t]he sources of affrays being . . . so many and the difficulty of anticipating them being undeniably great—the frequency of their occurrence can scarcely be a matter of wonder." He also observed that the district's police force, "considering its numerical strength, and the space over which it is spread" was no match; they could not "be safely or reasonably relied on, to obviate the evil by prevention."[30] A similar charge was echoed in the "crime report" of 1882 which declared that "the most important offence with which police have to deal . . . is rioting."[31]

Figures on riots, as with all crime statistics in British India, were generally underestimations. Many cases went unreported; others remained concealed because of their categorization as murders, or "offences against public tranquility," a classification that included "affrays" and "unlawful assemblies." The inspector-general of the police admitted in 1887 that there was no offense

which is subject as rioting [is] to the caprices of classification, and in many districts there is a great and perfectly intelligible objection to call it by its right name. A petty squabble in the hat [periodic market] and a pitched fight with spears and firearms attended by bloodshed, may be equally riots. . . . The figures submitted do not in my opinion at all accurately represent the real state of things.[32]

Although grossly underreported, the arithmetic of riots indicates that they were an endemic part of Saran's agrarian life. The data for the years prior to

28. Mansfield Papers, vol. 1, Dec. 3, 1916.
29. W. Blunt, Supt. of Police, Muzaffarpur, to George Dowdeswell, Secy., Jdcl., Jan. 21, 1812, Bengal Cr. Jdcl. Consltns., Feb. 25 to Mar. 16, 1812, Feb. 25, no. 24.
30. "Extract from Magte . . . June 1, 1833," with Commr. W. Ewer, to Registrar, Nizamat Adawlat, J. F. M. Reid, May 4, 1833, ibid., Jan. 5–26, 1836, Jan. 26, no. 1.
31. "Annual Crime Report for 1882," no. 346, Feb. 14, 1883, S.C. *Faujdari Basta*, 1883.
32. "Quarterly Return of Serious Crime (1st Quarter of 1887)," April 22, 1887, Bengal Jdcl. Procs., Police, April to June 1887, June, 160. Rioting persisted as one of the major types of crime in the early twentieth century (*SDG*, 1930: 117).

the mid-nineteenth century, though incomplete, show repeated fluctuations. Between 1819 and 1821, as many as 56 cases of affrays reached court, constituting an average of 18.6 per year. In the period between 1822 and 1824, the number rose to 101, making an annual average of 33.6.[33] Between 1831 and 1833, they ranged from a total of 8 in 1831 to 11 in 1832 to 20 in 1833. Comparable statistics for the years between 1849 and 1853 added up to a median of 6.6 per year. In 1854 the total stood at 8.[34] For the period between 1862 and 1920, systematic figures exist, which reveal that the smallest number of riots reported in these years was 5 in 1862, the highest 122 in 1871, and they averaged almost 50 per year (table 17).

Police reports consistently observed that "crime" followed "the chances of the crop[s]."[35] Famine years, therefore, invariably registered appreciable increases in certain kinds of crime, such as offenses against property and riots.[36] The incidence of riots also varied with each agricultural season. Although the fragmentary nature of the data defies statistical equations, local observers regularly advanced economic analyses. Fluctuations were attributed to both prosperity and poverty-related causes. When sixteen cases of rioting were reported for the last quarter of 1880, as opposed to six in the preceding quarter, the explanation offered was that the abundant harvest had led to an increase in disputes among various claimants. Similarly, floods and the consequent rise in prices of food in 1890 were also said to account for the rise in rioting.[37] And, within an agricultural season, riots occurred particularly at the time of harvest.[38]

That the ebb and flow in the incidence of rioting was closely related to the "chances of the crop[s]" reflect the fact that they stemmed from petty agrarian disputes. Except for a few notable exceptions, most riots in the nineteenth and early twentieth centuries were, as an 1812 report stated, "disputes respecting lands or crops."[39] A few, however, every year involved issues other than rights or claims in the land and its produce. In 1824, for example, a special report

33. W. Lowther, Magte., to W. H. Macnaghten, Regtr. Nt. Adlt., March 21, 1825, Bengal Cr. Jdcl. Consltns., July 21 to Aug. 4, 1825, Aug. 4, no. 44.
34. "Comparative Statement of Crimes Committed in . . . Patna," Jan. 2, 1855, ibid., Jan. 3 to 17, 1856, Jan. 10, no. 114; Ewer to Registrar, May 4, 1833, and Commr. G. Mainwaring to Secy. C. Macsween, Feb. 19, 1834, ibid., Jan. 5–26, 1836, Jan. 26, nos. 1 and 6, respectively.
35. "Annual Police Report of Saran District for 1874," S.C. *Faujdari Basta*, 1875.
36. See Statement of A. Hope, Sessions Judge, Saran, Dec. 22, 1866, Bengal Jdcl. Procs., Jan. to Mar. 1867, Feb., 132; Commr. Dalrymple to GOB, March 27, 1867, ibid., April 1867, no. 63.
37. Burglaries also increased ("Criminal Administration Report of Saran District, 1890," no. 660, Feb. 12, 1891, S.C. *Faujdari Basta*, 1892; "Crime Report for the Fourth Quarter of 1880," Bengal Police Procs., Feb. 1881, 69–75). The changing character of police control, such as better vigilance in suppressing crime and in reporting cases, also influenced crime rates (e.g., "Police Administration Report for 1892," no. 124G, March 14, 1893, in P.C. Gen. *Basta* no. 307, 1893).
38. "Police Administration of Saran for 1869," May 23, 1870, S.C. *Faujdari Basta*, 1870; "Quarterly Return of Serious Crime," Lower Provinces, Sept. 2, 1910, Bengal Police Procs., Feb. 1911, 47.
39. Blunt, Supt., to Secy., Jdcl., Jan. 21, 1812, Bengal Cr. Jdcl. Consltns., Feb. 25 to March 16, 1812, Feb. 25, no. 24.

Table 17.

Number of Riots in Saran, 1862–1920

Year	No. of incidents	Year	No. of incidents	Year	No. of incidents
1862	5	1882	22	1902	36
1863	14	1883	36	1903	36
1864	18	1884	22	1904	41
1865	34	1885	n.a.	1905	44
1866	72	1886	40	1906	31
1867	73	1887	62	1907	23
1868	35	1888	43	1908	43
1869	55	1889	68	1909	29
1870	111	1890	93	1910	n.a.
1871	122	1891	70	1911	n.a.
1872	79	1892	62	1912	n.a.
1873	42	1893	79	1913	n.a.
1874	61	1894	63	1914	n.a.
1875	74	1895	44	1915	30
1876	52	1896	57	1916	32
1877	27	1897	36	1917	38
1878	45	1898	54	1918	47
1879	26	1899	40	1919	19
1880	41	1900	60	1920	42
1881	23	1901	57		

Sources: For 1862–1868: *Report on the Police of the Patna Division*. For 1869–1871: *Annual Crime Report of the Patna Division* (retitled) 1863–1872. For 1872–1887: annual police and crime reports in *Faujdari Bastas*, 1873–1888. For 1878–1887 and 1887–1895: annual police and crime reports from P.C. Gen. *Basta* nos. 291–303, 1879–1896. For 1895–1899, 1900–1904: "Quinquennial Report of the Patna Division for the period from 1900–1901 to 1904–1905," Bengal Rev. Procs., June to Aug. 1906, Aug., 23. For 1900–1909: "Report on the General Administration of the Tirhut Division for the Quinquennial Period from 1905–1906 to 1909–1910," Bengal Gen. Procs., 1911, April, 236; *Bengal Police Reports, 1866–1912* and *Bihar and Orissa Police Reports, 1912–1920*.

Note: Wherever possible, figures have been checked with at least two different sources; N.a. = not available.

regarding police noted the difficulty of suppressing affrays relating to disputes over women. In 1871 a highly publicized clash occurred in the streets of Chapra city over a wealthy courtesan.[40] But most disturbances fit the following description of a hypothetical riot by one Saran magistrate: "Two men quarrel about a piece of land, on that spot of land; there is an interval of abuse, and then the fight commences between the two principals aided and abetted by any

40. "Annual Police Report for 1871," Jan. 29, 1872, S.C. *Faujdari Basta*, 1872; Elliot to Macnaghten, Dec. 10, 1824, Bengal Cr. Jdcl. Consltns., Feb. 17, 1825, no. 15.

villagers who may have run up."⁴¹ This "petty nature" can also be seen in the number of disputes that flared up over cattle-trespass and issues relating to irrigation. Another source of conflict was "[i]ll defined boundaries and disputed titles."⁴² Still others, as an identification of thirteen affrays that occurred in the first six months of 1833 reveals, erupted over a variety of land-related conflicts: disputes over rights of grazing, right of establishing a bazaar, over building a wall, for possession of a field, and over property rights in a village.⁴³

The limited scale of Saran's riots can also be computed by counting the number of participants in the disturbances. One figure commonly cited was that the "disputes were . . . quarrels . . . in which more than five persons were occasionally engaged on one or both sides."⁴⁴ Figures for the number of persons implicated in the disturbances in the 1860s and 1870s show an average of 6 to 7 rioters. Similarly, the number held directly responsible or "bound over" for the riots in the 1880s averaged 3 to 4.⁴⁵ Occasionally larger numbers were involved, as in 1824 when 400 to 500 people were embroiled in an affray.⁴⁶

Typically, these perennial disturbances did not result in killings or grievous woundings. As the report for 1874 summed up, "no serious case, but quarrels regarding rights of certain kinds," or, as in 1877, "no cases of rioting with loss of life, or serious rioting with hurt."⁴⁷ Less characteristic, but not rare, were conflicts that ended in homicide or severe injuries. In 1824, in the year of the "heavy affray," clashes involved several hundred people and produced deaths in eight cases and woundings in eighteen instances.⁴⁸

Such details suggest that the average riot was a momentary affair. Perhaps by the time the local authorities appeared on the scene only a few clubs and battle-axes, and a few smoldering tempers and bruised heads remained to mark the event.⁴⁹

Regardless of the size, intensity, and duration of the disturbance, the faces in the crowd were generally of people with some degree of resources. Any unlawful assembly involving force required at least two antagonists with sufficient economic and social standing to mobilize a few *lathials* (clubmen) and other supporters. Furthermore, because the issues at stake in these conflicts centered on land and its produce, or as one official report put it,

41. "Yearly Statement for 1854," P.C. *Basta* no. 105.
42. "Extract from Magistrate . . . June 1, 1833"; "Quinquennial Report of the Patna Division for the period from 1900-01 to 1904-05," Bengal Rev. Procs., June to Aug. 1906, Aug., 23.
43. Mainwaring to Macsween, Sept. 2, 1833, Bengal Cr. Jdcl. Consltns., Jan. 26, 1836, no. 3.
44. "Annual Crime Report for 1884," S.C. *Faujdari Basta*, 1885.
45. See, e.g., "Annual Crime Report" for 1882, 1886, and 1887, ibid., 1883, 1887, and 1888; *Report on the Police of the Patna Division for the Year 1866, 1867, 1868*, 1867-1869; *Annual Crime Report of the Patna Division for the Year 1869, 1870, 1871*, 1871-1872.
46. Elliot to Macnaghten, Dec. 10, 1824, Bengal Cr. Jdcl. Procs., Feb. 17, 1825, no. 15.
47. "Annual Crime Report for 1877," S.C. *Faujdari Basta*, 1878; "Annual Police Report for 1874."
48. Elliot to Macnaghten, Dec. 10, 1824, Bengal Cr. Jdcl. Consltns., Feb. 17, 1825, no. 15.
49. "Resolution . . . on Reports by Divisional Commissioners," Oct. 21, 1887, Bengal Jdcl. Procs., Police, 1887, Nov., 123.

"disputes for proprietary right," the leading rioters were frequently local or village-level controllers. To cite another finding: "The influential Zemindars and Thiccadars . . . are in 19 cases out of 20 cases, the very persons who foment them, and array the ignorant and misguided ryots against each other for the purpose of determining by force some question affecting their own particular interests."[50] A similar identification was made by a police report which stated that riots "occur between people pretty well off."[51]

The active role of people "pretty well off" in the ranks of rioters was a well-known feature of agrarian disturbances in the nineteenth and twentieth centuries. This police label described a range of categories, from the landholder down to the ranks of the powerful and privileged in village society, the petty maliks, and the substantial raiyats. Additional details can be gleaned from the identifications made in police reports. One major clash in 1844 pitted the supporters of the maharaja of Bettiah with the rent collectors of the maharaja of Hathwa. A riot in 1861 stemmed from a boundary dispute between the maliks of two estates. Of the two notable cases in 1872, one involved a dispute over rights in trees between the shareholders of a small estate, and the other, petty maliks who clashed over "a feet of ground and a feeding trough for cattle."[52]

Thus, to highlight the faces in the crowds of Saran's rioters is to identify once again the village-level controllers and their pivotal roles in all spheres of action at the village level. As the vital links who integrated the village community into the networks of the estate and as the principal "men on the spot" in agrarian disturbances, they were the prime movers in the local agrarian arena. From the perspective of both control and conflict, they were the keys to stability and dissidence in local society. And, because the systems of local control were invariably based on the cooptation of these "men on the spot" as the connections for the estate, sustained conflict between landholders and peasants was rare.

This emphasis on the predominance of the village-level controllers in the ranks of the district's rioters does not mean that there were no violent dissensions between superordinates and subordinates, but that such competition was either minimal or did not take the form of open, organized conflict. Certainly, the data on the nature and structure of agrarian disturbances suggest that there was little systematic resistance on the part of peasants and that their protests rarely went beyond individual acts of violence.

In the instances when peasants acted collectively and beyond momentary outbursts of violence, exceptional circumstances usually provided the solidarity.

---

50. "Extract from Magistrate . . . 1 June 1833."
51. "Crime Report for 1870," S.C. *Faujdari Basta*, 1871.
52. "Annual Police Report for 1871." See also "Report of the State of the Police in the Lower Provinces for the Year 1844," June 25, 1845, Bengal Cr. Jdcl. Consltns., July 9 to 23, 1845, July 23, nos. 1 to 3; *Report on the Police of the Patna Division for the year 1861*, 1862: 40.

A case reported in 1884 as illustrative of the widespread hostility of raiyats toward petty maliks reveals one such important ingredient:

> An unusually powerful member of this class [petty maliks] . . . who living in Patna, chances to have inherited an 8 as. share in the village of Mohamedpore . . . [and] pushed his exactions to such an extent, and so harassed his ryots by vexatious litigation, that one dark night, they . . . surrounded his local agent, the putwari, as he lay sleeping in his yard, and then and there beat him to death with their *lathis* [clubs].[53]

As in the case of the Deccan riots of 1875, an outside target provided a common cause. Similarly, the intrusions of the local representatives of the state, especially the constabulary, on occasion provided the impulse for unified action. Three such incidents were reported in 1824 alone. In the first, a "large party of villagers" attacked and beat the peons of the local judge and police officer, releasing the cattle that they had seized. In another part of the district, a zamindar assisted by 200 followers shot a chaukidar and forced the police officer of Darauli thana to flee. In the third instance, when a police party, including cattle thieves and cattle they had apprehended, stopped at a village for the night, the local inhabitants attacked the police officer and his constables. Not only was the officer wounded, but the villagers "left him almost in a state of nudity having plundered him of his clothes, saddle cloth, shoes and arms."[54] In a serious case of rioting in 1878, 300 inhabitants from a number of villages confronted several constables when the latter attempted to stop them from cutting a government embankment to drain excessive water from their fields.[55]

The disturbances resulting from the attacks on police by the inhabitants of Degra, Murhur, and Chack-Shobaz villages also reveal the necessary components for a serious riot. In 1863 as a police force was leaving Degra with several arrests for burglary, a group estimated as 100 to 150 men attacked and rescued the prisoners. Later, when a posse of 40 men returned to the village, an even larger force of 500 people armed with clubs, battle-axes, and swords challenged the authorities. A similar occurrence ten years later prompted government to post a special police force in the locality at the expense of the three villages. Such stringent measures were considered necessary because "the Aheers [Ahirs] of Degra seem a very homogeneous body and the riot to have been the act of the whole community." Strong bonds were clearly forged out of caste ties and hostility for a common enemy. Furthermore, these links were reinforced by the leadership of Alim Singh, identified in the official report as the ringleader and a rent collector for the part-owner of Degra village.[56]

The decisive role that village-level controllers, such as Alim Singh played in defining the form and intensity of agrarian disturbances is also evident from

---

53. AGRPD, 1883–84.
54. Elliot to Macnaghten, Dec. 10, 1824, Bengal Cr. Jdcl. Procs., Feb. 17, 1825, no. 15.
55. "Criminal Administration Report for 1878," P.C. Gen. *Basta* no. 284, 1879.
56. Offg. Commr. S. C. Bayley to Insp.-Gen. of Police, no. 267J, June 30, 1873, Bengal Police Procs., 1873–1874, June 1874, 130–33.

the indigo riots, which occurred almost every agricultural season in the late nineteenth and early twentieth centuries. These were generally serious riots, involving large crowds and a high incidence of violence. When the servants of an indigo planter attempted to plow some contested land in 1860, the villagers, who also claimed a right to its cultivation, attacked and injured the servants.[57] Both of the major riots reported for 1882 resulted from indigo disputes. In one incident, a planter was seized and beaten by a number of raiyats, and in the other, another planter was attacked by the inhabitants of a village in which he had recently acquired a share. According to Sir Alexander Muddiman, when he was magistrate of Saran in 1900, indigo disputes often took the form of criminal assaults and riots.[58]

At the heart of most indigo disputes was a fundamental conflict over land. "The raiyat wanted to grow grain or poppy (opium) which are more paying crops than indigo, while the factory claimed the right to make him sow a portion of his land, generally the best land, with indigo."[59] Planters usually grew indigo on lands in which they had secured intermediary rights, such as by obtaining leases from zamindars. These rights did not necessarily mean, however, that they could enforce the cultivation of indigo in their leased villages. On the contrary, unless the zamindar lent his authority and influence, a clash between the planter and the peasants was inevitable. Minden Wilson, a planter in Muzaffarpur, testified that the support of zamindars was crucial in determining the willingness of raiyats to plant indigo. He also deposed before a civil court in 1876 that planters were generally prepared to use force to attain "factory influence," which he defined as "generally represented by a *peon* with a stick. . . . I do not think the factory influence extends beyond that. It is all due to coercion."[60]

Few indigo disputes in Saran were outright confrontations between planters and peasants. Instead, most conflicts grew out of tensions produced among local or village-level controllers by the introduction of indigo and followed a standard pattern:

The village in which the introduction of indigo is followed by disputes are, as a rule, villages in which a previous quarrel existed between the malik who gives his share to the factory and his co-sharers; and although in the complaints against the planter which follow, the role of complainant is played by ryots, yet they are in 9 cases out of 10 merely the representatives of their masters.[61]

Government was clearly aware of this structure of riots when it sought to contain a major indigo disturbance in 1913 by enlisting the usual ringleaders

---

57. *Report on the Police of the Patna Division for the year 1860*, 1861: 42. See also Fisher (1976: 122, 161–67) and Mishra (1978: 231–95) on the rise of indigo agitation in the late nineteenth and early twentieth centuries.   58. 1930: 40; "Annual Crime Report for 1882."
59. Muddiman 1930: 40.
60. Cited in GOB, *Selections from Papers, Bengal Tenancy Act* 1920: 9.
61. A. Forbes to Colltr. of Tirhut, no. 163–64, Jan. 28, 1872, demi-official, Bengal Gen. Procs., Aug. 1873, 165. For a detailed example of this type of dispute, see "Dispute between the raiyats of Dhamour [village] and the Manager of Arroah [Concern]," P.C. Gen. *Basta*, no. 289, 1884.

to act as a special police force. Between 1910 and early 1913, a series of incendiary acts, assaults, and riots were directed at the Rajapatti Indigo Concern leading to "lawlessness" between the factory and a cluster of villages, especially four of them, within a five-mile radius.[62] Lacking a sufficient police force to check the hostilities, the district authorities appointed several local residents, drawn from both the ranks of enemies and friends of the factory to be special constables responsible for law and order. Of the fourteen selected, four were the ringleaders of the opposition and described as the influential landholders and peasants of the four antagonistic villages.[63]

As in other cases of riots, especially serious disturbances, indigo disputes were not clear-cut acts of peasant solidarity and violence directed at the superordinate, but action usually generated by the local zamindar or substantial raiyat. In Saran the mutually beneficial pattern of exchanges between planters and zamindars in many estates, including Hathwa, diminished the possibility of indigo disputes with raiyats. Under the prevailing system of local control in Saran, the support of the landholder or the village-level controller ensured the relative absence of resistance to the cultivation of indigo. But, without such assistance, as the Maniara factory discovered, when it attempted to deal directly with peasants rather than through their landholder, the maharaja of Hathwa, raiyats were uncooperative.[64]

The significant role of local controllers in directing and determining the course and intensity of agrarian violence is also evident in the "internal rising" of 1844 when former Huseypur *birtdars* mobilized thousands of peasants against their "new" zamindar, the maharaja of Hathwa. The ringleaders—men such as Bujahawan Misra and Ishri Prasad—were *birtdars* who clashed with Hathwa over their claims to large numbers of villages. Additional supporters came from "abroad."

The basic structure of collective action and violence in Saran can also be delineated by an examination of the Cow Riots of 1893.[65] So threatening were these disturbances to the authority of the British Raj that their organization and scale prompted many comparisons to the rebellion of 1857.[66] These very aspects, as the prosecutor of the major cow riot case in Saran recognized, set the events of 1893 apart from the usual cases of rioting, which were

committed in connection with land or something belonging to land . . . [and] resorted to for taking forcible possession or forcibly dispossessing. It is also committed with respect

62. Commr. to Chief Secy., Jan./Feb. 1913, B&O Jdcl. Procs., April to June 1913, May, 59–62. See also Freitag (1978: 27–41), for a study showing similar government use of local controllers in regulating and curbing conflict.
63. Magte. B. Foley to Commr., no. 5168, Jan. 11, 1913, B&O Jdcl. Procs., May 1913, 59–62.
64. AGRPD, 1889–90.
65. The ostensible issue in these riots was the difference between Hindus and Muslims regarding the religious significance of the cow (Yang: 1980; Freitag 1980; McLane 1977: 271–331).
66. See GOI, Public and Judicial, L/P&J/6/365 and L/P&J/6/367, 1894, for a sampling of the different official interpretations of this agitation.

to the various methods of irrigation. There is another class of rioting for rescuing cattle taken to be impounded under the Cattle Trespass Act. Now in this particular case, none of the subjects are put forward to which form the large majority of cases for rioting. You will find here, from the charges drawn up against the accused with respect to rioting, that their common object was to take forcible possession of 129 head of cattle, more or less, which were then in the custody of the Police.[67]

Between August 31 and September 7, 1893, a series of cow riots broke out in Basantpur thana as a herd of cattle were being driven across the district for slaughter in Patna. The initial confrontation was in Bala village, on August 31, when a "mob" of over 150 persons assembled but dispersed when the local indigo planter appeared on the scene. The attacks were renewed, however, as the cattle were being moved toward Basantpur, six miles away. On the night of September 6, several hundred persons charged the police station in Basantpur where the cows had been quartered, ceasing only when the police counterattacked and fired into the crowd, killing one and injuring four.[68]

The existing data clearly show that these riots were well-planned and coordinated. As early as 1887, a Cow Protection Society (*Gaurakshini Sabha*) was founded in the district, and various prominent men, including the Maharaja of Hathwa, pleaders, and religious figures (sadhus), enlisted as members.[69] Through anonymous letters passed from village to village, anti-cow slaughter propaganda was circulated throughout the district. In addition, prominent speakers from within the district and outside preached regularly on the sacred aspects of the cow. Five days prior to the first riot at Bala, a *Gaurakshini Sabha* meeting was held at Basantpur, and, according to the police report, "several seditious speeches were made by a propagandist Pandit [a learned man] and others."[70]

These networks of communication and coordination explain the large-scale participation and duration of the cow riots of 1893. In the first major incident, the riot at Bala, the name of a prominent local landholder was repeatedly invoked by the crowd. According to the rioters, this zamindar of a village near Bala, Parmeshwar Singh, had issued the orders to attack. During the riot, he was seen on horseback at the head of the crowd.[71] Next he reappeared in the raid on the Basantpur police station, again as one of the ringleaders. The crowd, larger on this occasion, was estimated at 2,000 to 3,000 people. Nine hours before the actual disturbance, *lathial*s were noticed converging on Basantpur from nearby villages, and, just prior to the attack, the crowd

67. *Trial of the Basantpur Riot Case in the Court of the Sessions Judge of Saran, 1893*, 1894: 6. Communal riots also erupted in other parts of India in 1893 (Krishnaswamy 1966; Lambert 1952; Freitag 1979).
68. Commr. A. Forbes to Chief Secy., GOB, L/P&J/6/365, 1894, encl. 7.
69. Magte. G. E. Manisty to Commr., no. 2303, Sept. 11–12, 1893, Bengal Jdcl. Procs., Police, Oct. to Dec. 1894, Nov., nos. 30–31.
70. Commr. Forbes to Insp.-Gen. of Police, no. 585G, Oct. 14, 1893, ibid. Two samples of *gaurakshini* literature are Narayan (1896); Suhai (1886).
71. Manisty to Commr., no. 2303, Sept. 11–12, 1893, Bengal Jdcl. Procs., Nov. 1894, nos. 30–31.

assembled at a bridge one-quarter of a mile away.[72] The rioters were later traced by the district authorities to villages as far as eighteen miles away. And following the riots, punitive police were posted in the "disturbed area" of twenty-three villages with a total population of over 30,000 inhabitants.[73]

A number of characteristics clearly distinguish the "internal rising" of 1844 and the cow riots of 1893 from the other riots in Saran in the nineteenth and early twentieth centuries. In size, duration, the kinds of issues at stake, and their intensity, the two disturbances represented the rumblings of an organized movement. Nevertheless, as in all other notable acts of collective violence, men with considerable social and economic resources were the leaders. The prosecutor of the Basantpur case made precisely this kind of positive identification when he termed the rioters not habitual criminal offenders, but "well-to-do zamindars, who in the village in which they live and in the other villages in which they own property are men who exercise a great deal of influence."[74] Similarly, the ringleaders from the twenty-three villages said to be actively involved in the 1893 Cow Riots were identified as "maliks or their agents."[75]

The cow riots of 1893 also reveal new forces that were beginning to impinge on local society in the late nineteenth century. According to the official explanation of the rash of "religious" riots in 1893, one important cause was the "greater frequency of communication and the interchange of news by post and telegraph between different parts of the country. A riot which occurs in any place, even the most remote is speedily heard of all over India."[76] Furthermore, the development of first, regional, and later, national, political associations and organizations was also beginning to link different levels of society, for example, many of the reports on the cow protection movement claimed that the Indian National Congress was instrumental in stirring up the agitation.[77]

The Emerging Pattern: Raiyats and Riots

Although there were no significant changes in the character of agrarian disturbances in Saran between 1793 and 1920, the sources of contention between peasant and landholder were ever present and immanent. That these tensions did not erupt into sustained and open conflict was a testimony to the effectiveness of the zamindari networks of control and the Limited Raj, and not

72. Manisty to Commr., no. 2622, Oct. 10, 1893, ibid., Police, Nov. 1894, no. 33. The day of the attack being market day in Basantpur, the presence of such a large number of people went unnoticed.
73. Forbes to Insp.-Gen., no. 585G, Oct. 14, 1893, ibid., Nov. 1894, no. 32.
74. *Trial of the Basantpur Riot Case* 1894: 5.
75. Forbes to Insp.-Gen., no. 585G, Oct. 14, 1893, Bengal Jdcl. Procs., Nov. 1894, no. 32.
76. Lord Lansdowne to Secy. of State for India, Dec. 27, 1893, L/P&J/6/365, 1894. See also the confidential files on the important propagandists of the Cow Protection Movement, e.g., GOI to Secy. of State, Jan. 7, 1890, L/P&J/6/269, 1890.
77. "Note on the Agitation against Cow-killing" (strictly confidential) by D. G. McCracken, Offg. Gen. Supt., Thagi and Dacoity Dept., Aug. 9, 1893, L/P&J/6/367, 1894. An excellent general statement of political developments in the late nineteenth century is McLane (1977).

a reflection on the inherent lack of historical initiative on the part of the peasantry. On the contrary, Saran's raiyats sought to fashion options for themselves wherever and whenever possible, whether these took the form of occasional assaults on the local system of control, resistance by raising their voices directly or by petitions, or evading the system entirely by flight. Under the right circumstances, these steadily burning fires of protest could be ignited into a conflagration, as the study of disturbances in a cluster of villages around Bhorey, in the Katia area of the estate of Hathwa, reveals.

In over a twelve-month period in 1921 and 1922, numerous acts of violence broke out in an area of over thirty-eight villages. The district authorities attributed the "spirit of lawlessness" to the forces of Noncooperation, a movement Gandhi had launched in 1920. In February 1921, according to a government report, the "exponents of non-violence painted a woman black and took her naked round village Deoria."[78] When the police subinspector of Katia went there to investigate, he and his party of constables and chaukidars were beaten back by a force of 2,000 men. This armed crowd, drawn from nineteen villages and diverse socioeconomic backgrounds, confronted them with the cry of "Gandhi *ki jai*" [Long live Gandhi] and demanded that they kneel and repeat the chant.[79]

Attacks and threats of intimidation were also directed at chaukidars who, along with the police, were regarded by noncooperators as "the limb of a Satanic Government."[80] In the aftermath of the February 1922 rioting at Chauri Chaura (a village in Gorakhpur some thirty miles from Bhorey), "crimes" increased. Local inhabitants set fire to the property of some chaukidars, looted "English cloth" from a trader, and threatened five rural police stations. Resistance to the payment of the chaukidari tax also heightened.[81]

The targets of violence were not only the local police, but also the representatives of the local zamindar, the Hathwa raja. As Hathwa's rent collectors discovered, such acts of noncooperation as boycotts and strikes against government represented only one course of action; raiyats of this locality were also reluctant to pay their dues. In four instances, Hathwa's patwaris were threatened with assault and arson, and in other cases, various other officials of the estate were attacked.[82] Although the provincial authorities were concerned primarily with the political aspects of the disturbance, at least the Saran magistrate was well aware of its agrarian origins. In questioning the levying of costs on this entire locality for the quartering of punitive police, he pointed out

78. E. A. O. Perkin, Supt. of Police, Saran, to Personal Asst. to Insp.-Gen. of Police, no. 3168, May 8, 1922, B&O Polit. Procs., 1922, no. 50.
79. Ibid.; Henningham 1982: 100–1.
80. *Report on the Administration of the Police in the Province of Bihar and Orissa for the year 1921*, 1922: 26. See also *Report for 1920* and *1922*, 1921: 24; 1923: 3.
81. Perkin to Insp.-Gen., no. 3168, May 8, 1922, B&O Polit. Procs., June 1922, no. 50. On Chauri Chaura, see M. H. Siddiqi (1978: 205).
82. Perkin to Insp.-Gen., no. 3168, May 8, 1922, B&O Polit. Procs., June 1922, no. 50.

that, throughout much of this area, "the Hathwa raj is on bad terms with its tenants ... and that though the Raj as Zamindar would have to bear its share of the cost, the assessment of the entire area would tend to create the idea it is specially directed against recalcitrant tenants of the Raj."[83]

In other words, in their origins in land disputes, these "political" disturbances followed the basic historical pattern of collective violence and action in Saran. That they erupted in the Bhorey area of Katia, in the great estate of Hathwa, also draws attention to the ways in which local and supralocal movements were generated by the same impulses, because it was precisely this locality in which the Hathwa raj had recurring problems, beginning with the "internal rising" of the Brahmins of Bhorey in 1844 and followed by the large-scale desertions of the late nineteenth and early twentieth centuries.[84] Small wonder, then, that these antecedents engendered the organized disturbances associated with Gandhian Noncooperation in the 1920s, which in turn served as the foundation on which the Bihar Provincial *Kisan Sabha* attempted to launch a full-fledged peasant movement in the late 1930s and early 1940s.[85] Nor has this dynamic, born of protest and resistance at the grassroots level by peasants who wish to shape their own options in a world of their own making, been played out as yet. The peasant quest for an universe ordered by principles of moral economy remains a central concern in the 1980s, informing their acts and behavior in everyday life as well as in their expressions of discontent in the forms of routine outbursts of recalcitrance or intense episodes of violence and collective action.[86]

Peasant resistance, violence, and collective action in the nineteenth and early twentieth centuries rarely assumed the form of a sustained agitation or movement in Saran. Raiyat options for protest were limited by the nature of the local systems of control, which had coopted the immediate superordinates in village society as connections for the networks of the landholders' estates. As a result, protest was often registered in ways that sought to avoid open, direct, physical confrontation while, at the same time, articulating the grievances of peasants. Acts of recalcitrance conveyed such concerns clearly, as did raiyat appeals to government and their landholders in person and by petitions. A career of crime was another option that some peasants resorted to in order to overcome hardships.

Collective violence and action were not uncommon in the district, as the study of "criminal" riots show, but they followed a systemic pattern of agrarian conflict. An overwhelming majority of the average of fifty riots per year were highly localized and momentary affairs, involving as few as five

83. Comments of Dist. Magte. A. P. Middleton, cited in H. W. P. Scroope, Commr., Tirhut, to Insp.-Gen., no. J-1987, May 22, 1922, ibid., June 1922, no. 50.
84. On the links between local agitations and supralocal movements, especially the Noncooperation movement of 1920–1922, see Henningham (1982: 36–108); M. H. Siddiqi (1978: 174–88); Brown (1972: 250–349).   85. See Hauser (1961, 1983).
86. On the current scene, see Das (1982).

people in dispute over rights and claims in relation to land and its produce. Occasionally, peasants attacked their superordinates, but more usually clashes occurred between men of important village standing—the substantial peasants or the petty landholders.

Village-level controllers were also the organizing force in the instances when peasants acted collectively in local agitations that embraced stakes beyond their plots and fields and endured beyond brief lapses into violence. Solidarity in such cases was often generated by the presence of outside targets in the form of the police, other communities, and foreign indigo planters. Similarly, the ideology and organization of the Cow Protection Society of the late nineteenth century and the Noncooperation movement of the early twentieth century activated these dynamics of the local society and thus channelled localized actions into large-scale movements. At the fundamental level of Saran's agrarian society, the immediate arena of action for any peasant, the village-level controller was the key to both control and conflict.

Conclusions

Between 1793 and 1920, the Limited Raj of the British in Saran District turned over actual control of the land and its people to local zamindars and petty maliks. Viewed metaphorically from the perspective of the Sonepur Mela and Meet, a vivid portrait emerges of the power and influence wielded by the colonial state, on the one hand, and by the local and village-level controllers, on the other. At this site of pilgrimage and worship, enshrined in the religious tradition of the region, the British penetration into local society was reflected in the superimposition of their own event to coincide with the imperatives of this sacred place and sacred time. By foisting their own "sacred" meet on the special occasion celebrated by indigenous inhabitants in rituals and in a festive mela, the new rulers expressed their superior authority as well as their links to indigenous systems of rule.

At Sonepur, the British staked out a distinct mental and physical terrain, which expanded at the expense of the Indian event without completely disrupting it. On the contrary, the colonial presence there remained separate from the ritual and economic activities of worship and fair involving several hundred thousand people. But some points of contact existed. An administrative supervision was maintained over those activities, and major regional and local Indian notables were incorporated into the British gathering, thus enabling the colonial state to exert its superior authority and to be endowed with, and reciprocate, the support and recognition of powerful local controllers. As long as "Hathwa's cheer" provided resounding support for the meet and commanded attention in rural society as well, the meet-goers virtually ignored the throngs of raiyats whose presence signified the centrality of Sonepur in the region. As yet, the rising tides of nationalism, which later made the place unsafe for the "man for Chupra," were but ripples scarcely ruffling the annual routine of "Christmas pleasures" and "native" fair.

From the outset of British rule in the region in the late eighteenth century, when the instrument of authority was the British East India Company, the new regime's presence can be described as a Limited Raj. Although the initial takeover required the threat and the actual deployment of force to beat back the challenges of recalcitrant local controllers, in the case of Saran it also involved the suppression of a protracted rebellion by the major landholder—the raja of Huseypur. Once the Raj established its dominion, its attention turned to fashioning a collaborative colonial system. This pattern of conquest and consolidation of colonial rule fits in well with the emerging scholarly picture of European expansion into Asia and Africa in the late eighteenth and nineteenth centuries. No longer is it sufficient to highlight only the better technology or the superior military and social organization of alien intruders to explain their decisive edge over indigenous rulers. Instead, attention has turned to the "non-European foundations of European imperialism."[1] In other words, the collaborative arrangements worked out between Europeans and important elements in the local population formed a major prop of colonial rule.

In eastern India the foundations of this system were erected on the Permanent Settlement of 1793. By this settlement, 353 zamindars were sanctioned as the major controllers of the land in Saran. Most—such as the raja of Huseypur, and the zamindars of Chainpur, Manjhi, Chirand, Siwan, Barharia, Bagoura, and Manjha—were upper-caste landholders whose claims to superior rights in the land antedated the advent of Company Raj. Thus, the initial penetration of British rule induced virtually no changes in the existing indigenous controlling structure of the district, especially at the highest level of rights. Nor was there a caesura in the nineteenth and early twentieth centuries in this pattern of relations between the colonial state and the local controllers who became the "permanent" connections linking the former to the local society. What changes in landholding patterns occurred were primarily shifts in proprietary rights between members of families, lineages, and kinship groups belonging to the same "twice-born" castes. Similarly, the grip of upper castes over tenant rights remained largely intact. Relative stability in the agrarian social structure thus characterized the district between 1793 and 1920.

In this respect, the Saran pattern conforms more closely to the current view of the effects of the Permanent Settlement on the region than the earlier interpretation of such scholars as Rajani Palme Dutt, B. B. Misra, and N. K. Sinha. In their characterization, this settlement brought down the traditional structure of Bengali rural society and ushered in an opportunistic commercial and urban-based class who eagerly purchased rights on the land as a means of capital investment.[2] Local-level studies, however, reveal a much

1. Louis 1976.   2. Ratnalekha Ray 1984: 238–39.

more complex picture of the agrarian landscape. One feature that has consistently cropped up in such intensive investigations is the fact that the existing local structures of dominance and control were far more resilient in the face of the initial changes wrought by British rule than was formerly believed. The portrait of neighboring Champaran, for instance, bears a strong resemblance to that of Saran. Other than one revenue official who secured interests amounting to less than 2 percent of that district's total revenue, all the local controllers in 1793 were "local chiefs" or "revenue collectors" with roots in the locality dating back into the pre-British period.[3] With minor variations, detailed accounts of localities in Bengal offer a now-familiar outline. Ratnalekha Ray's fine study of several Bengal districts delineates the contours of this emerging picture:

> The Permanent Settlement brought about a great circulation in titles, but not of lands; and circulation of titles had been going on before at such a rate that the zamindars whom the British recognized as landlords were mostly a mushroom class of adventurers raised to their position of pre-eminence in the first half of the eighteenth century by the reduction of the old proprietors. Many of the reduced older proprietors no doubt survived as small taluqdars. And it was this smaller class of taluqdars and zamindars who succeeded in buying up the greatest number of the titles brought into circulation by the sale of zamindaris.[4]

The pattern for eastern India is clear enough for the authoritative *Cambridge History* to declare unequivocally: "The social foundation of the new set-up of 1793 was the old landed aristocracy, with only a sprinkling of the new men here and there."[5]

Findings from other parts of South Asia also reinforce the need to resuscitate the local controllers from the premature deaths assigned them by earlier historiography, which attached great significance to the legal innovations accompanying the array of British revenue settlements. Even for U.P., where the rush to judgment based on the enormous volume of transfers of proprietary titles in the first half of the nineteenth century formerly appeared warranted, a much more cautious interpretation now seems justified. Stokes's careful investigations furnish helpful clues in this regard in showing that these transfers "represented for the most part circulation within existing dominant landholding castes" and thus, in the first century of British rule, "there was no complete structural change."[6] What appeared disruptive on the surface in U.P., as superior rights on the land fell into the hands of different sets of people, reveals a different face under closer historical scrutiny. Even the taluqdars of the North-Western Provinces, whose experiences were formerly cited to illustrate the transforming effects of the British system, now represent a different archetype. That they were shorn of some of their sources of wealth and power in the early nineteenth century endures as an accurate report of

3. Mishra 1978: 10.
5. B. B. Chaudhuri 1984: 91.
4. 1979: 252.
6. 1978: 35.

their initial condition, but their subsequent fate has been revised to disclose that they recouped their losses in the later half of that century. To track the careers of the "dispossessed" of Banaras is to see "that the majority of individuals, families and lineages who 'lost' land between 1795 and 1885 retained their positions, economically, politically, and socially *within* the local areas in which they had held rights as zamindars."[7]

To what extent pre-British local controllers persisted in power well into the nineteenth and twentieth centuries throughout the subcontinent remains to be uncovered by additional micro-level investigations. But the first reassessments of this situation suggest more continuities than changes in the agrarian structures of control. Whether the initial penetration of the colonial state into the local society took the form of a Permanent Settlement, as in the East, or the *Raiyatwari* Settlement in the south, or a combination or permutation of the two, as carried out elsewhere, the result was the eventual reinvigoration of the controlling groups on the land: landholders in some instances, village-level controllers on the scale of Saran's petty maliks and small landholders in other cases. Local peculiarities notwithstanding, this process was replicated over and over again in many areas, as is exemplified by the experience of the southeastern Indian district of Thanjavur. Although the initial imposition of British revenue demands in Thanjavur led to sharp reductions in the accumulated resources of big landlords, they also pressed heavily on small landlords and peasants, compelling these two groups to become indebted to the still wealthy big landlords. In the late nineteenth century, the major landlords of the district became the bulwarks of British rule, as well as the prime beneficiaries of its new system. Although small landlords did not reap similar advantages, they too accepted the new conditions because "their positions as employers and village managers set them in opposition to their tenants and laborers."[8]

Whether government formed "permanent" connections to the local society from the outset or subsequently developed them by choice or necessity, the circumstances of such arrangements were conditioned by the character of the colonial state. The acceptance of powerful Indians as collaborators fitted in well with the financial imperatives of the Raj, which centered on maximizing revenues and minimizing costs of administration. By defining this relationship as the fulcrum for its rule in local society, the state entered into a bargain of sorts: collaboration vitiated the need for a strong official presence in the interior, but the price in return was that local power devolved on its Indian allies. Anil Seal has described the terms of this agreement:

Local bargains of this sort were of great advantage to the British because they reduced Indian politics to the level of haggles between the Raj and small pockets of its subjects, a system which kept them satisfactorily divided. . . . In return, the British had to acquiesce in an arrangement where strong local intermediaries could block them from

---

7. Cohn 1969: 89; Metcalf 1978: chaps. 7–8.   8. Gough 1978: 36.

meddling in the affairs of those who owned land, or controlling the others who tilled it. . . . At these levels it might be the British who governed, but it was Indians who ruled.[9]

Anchorage of the colonial regime at the local level was, therefore, attained by setting up a system that tacitly, if not explicitly, was geared toward the maintenance and enhancement of the prevailing indigenous system of superordination and subordination.

The advantages accruing to local controllers in this collaborative system of rule are distinctly indicated by the history of the Hathwa family. In the wake of the rebellion of the Huseypur raja, the British subsidized and developed his cadet line into the Hathwa maharaja. This process included the quelling of an "internal rising" by village-level controllers and the legal establishment of primogenitural succession and proprietary impartibility of the Hathwa estate. Saran's lesser zamindars, whose ties to the British also extended back to the late eighteenth century, also received patronage and honors for their loyalty.

A major institutional embodiment of the Limited Raj system was the Court of Wards, which acted as an extraordinary shelter for government's permanent connections. Although this mechanism provided the state with an opportunity to enhance its control over local landholders, it was used primarily to bolster and augment the power and resources of the "captive" estates.[10] Hathwa again serves as an apt illustration because its three tenures under the Court of Wards transformed it significantly. As a stabilizing sanctuary against the endemic processes of subdivisions and fragmentation that characterized the "majority story" of Saran's estates, government management was also beneficial to other zamindars.

Bihar landholders were not alone in enjoying the cosseting hand of the Raj. One element of the success story of Oudh taluqdars in the aftermath of 1857 was the protection afforded them by the law of primogeniture and the Court of Wards—which enabled them to hold their ground as well as add to their holdings through purchases.[11] Where such "shields" were not sufficient to turn back the tide of land sales, they at least sought to safeguard the properties of families officially designated as " 'ancient and prestigious' "—in colonial shorthand, local allies.[12]

With the British leaning heavily on local allies and imperial considerations weighing decisively in favor of minimizing the economic costs of rule, a strong administrative machinery became less of a requisite for colonial government. Although an important prop of colonial rule, at the local level, the bureaucratic apparatus was necessarily minimal, even fragile, especially in its extensions into the countryside. An attenuated institutional presence, moreover, posed no threat to the authority of the Raj because it was ultimately backed up by a monopoly of armed power. Not only did the British possess overwhelming

9. 1973: 328–29.
10. Yang 1979a.
11. F. C. R. Robinson 1973: 402.
12. Washbrook 1981: 675

military superiority, but their paramilitary forces, such as the police, occupied strategic centers throughout the subcontinent. Thus, the nexus shaped by the collaborative system of rule had far-reaching repercussions for the rest of society. Because the main concern of the colonial regime was to maintain and exercise its superior authority—to provide a semblance of law and order—to facilitate its economic interests, it allowed vast arenas of power and control to devolve on its local allies. A Limited Raj, in short, was not only sufficient to guarantee the interests of the colonial state, but also crucial in accommodating its collaborative arrangements.

No wonder official attempts to secure links to the subdistrict levels of society consistently failed. Especially in the late nineteenth century, when the British made their most strenuous efforts to extend their reach into the interior, their endeavors ran counter to the tendency of local control institutions to be organized by estate and village systems of control. Thus the campaign to revitalize the *qanungo*-patwari connection was thwarted by an already existing system of zamindari control revolving around estates, while the experiments with chaukidars faced not only the networks emanating from estates, but also that of village society. British inability to incorporate these officials into their own administrative machinery was proof that the framework for their organization of local control systems lay beyond their circle of power. Whether viewed from the perspective of government's relations with its allies or from the angle of its control institutions, the colonial system of rule in local society was a Limited Raj.

Throughout much of the countryside in eastern India, the extensions of British administration into the countryside remained fragile over the long haul of colonial rule. For Bengal, assessments of the weaknesses of the official system and the strengths of the local controllers have produced judgments ranging from characterizations of the situation as indicative of a "parallel government"—a "landlord raj"—to being "notoriously undergoverned."[13] Although this appraisal has hitherto distinguished the permanently settled areas of eastern India from the rest of the subcontinent, where different revenue settlements were enacted, the new historiography, grounded in microlevel studies, has tended to accent the similarities more than the differences. Certainly, reconsiderations regarding the disruptiveness of British revenue and legal innovations in the north evoke a less dissimilar portrait of taluqdar and zamindar power in the countryside than has been the impression conveyed by earlier scholars. Much the same conclusion regarding the limits of colonial control can be drawn for rural south India because the administrative apparatus there too failed to penetrate deeply into local society.[14]

Such measurements of the distance of the colonial system from their subjects do not, however, warrant painting the "classic" Guntur scenario onto every

13. Palit 1975: 206; Gallagher 1973: 590–91; Chattopadhyay 1985: 151–52.
14. Washbrook 1976: chap. 3; Metcalf 1979: 200–36; Ludden 1985: 59–74.

setting where the British governed but did not rule. While the Guntur account of local influence undermining central authority rightly challenges the idea of "all-wise, all-knowing" district officer—the man for Chupra, the magistrate of yore—it endows his coadjutor with those attributes. Thus, in this interpretation, the chief secretary "became the all-wise, all-knowing, ever-efficient prime-minister of the district."[15] But the Guntur perspective, while perceptive in identifying the weaknesses of the colonial system at the hub of its power, the district headquarters, ignores the fact that India lives in its villages, also the level of society where gaps in the official system were more likely to be adeptly occupied by local controllers.

To move away from the intrigues of the district collectorate offices to the countryside is to observe a different reality. The Raj was never "merely a nightwatchman and receiver of tribute; or that its system of collaboration simply meant confirming things as they were ... government ratified, or upset, social and economic arrangements which extended far beyond the localities."[16] The fall of the Huseypur raja and the rise of the Hathwa maharaja is a striking illustration of the active role the state played in Saran. So is the British involvement in the life of the taluqdars of Awadh. The limits of the colonial system, in other words, were not entirely the function of failures in attaining an effective system of government-cum-rule, but also the result of self-imposed structural constraints. The system put in place in local society was not shaped only by the manipulations of adroit coadjutors but also by a pattern of colonial rule determined by the policies of political and economic expediency formulated in London and Calcutta.

The structural constraints of the Raj meant that the real locus of power and control in local society resided with the key groups on the land. Again, a telling example of this configuration of control, shaped by state-local relations, is the historic role of the great estate of Hathwa. A well-developed system of control was not unique to Hathwa. Another great estate in Bihar, which possessed the management system to exert considerable power and influence over its enormous territory, was the Darbhanga raj.

The experiences of both these estates, as well as of those of others, such as the zamindari of Jaykrishna Mukherjee of Uttarpara,[17] contrast sharply with the well-known characterization of control systems in U.P. estates between 1860 and 1920. Although rightly taking issue with the classic "Oudh school" notion of landlords in north India enjoying undisputed dominance in their zamindaris, this interpretation shifts the balance completely to the other extreme: "The landlord, rather like the Collector, was hardly the 'Lord of the Land,' but rather the head of a complex and arcane system of government, which seems to have been adept at all levels in concealing information. In

15. Frykenberg 1965: 241. 16. Seal 1973: 329.
17. Henningham 1983: 35–57; Mukherjee 1975; 106–9; M. H. Siddiqi 1975: chap. 2.

some ways, then, rural power might be seen as being with the estate managers and cronies."[18]

Such an interpretation also fails to locate its assessment of estate management in the setting of the nineteenth and early twentieth centuries in which the growing pressure of numbers on the land was heightened by scanty development of alternative sources of employment.[19] To what extent this conjunction of processes provided a favorable backdrop for a drama of control to be enacted successfully is demonstrated by the agrarian system of Saran, which was increasingly beset by agricultural crisis. The impact of this crisis, however, was felt unevenly because the local agrarian society was sharply divided not only between the zamindars and the raiyats, but also among the different categories of landholders and peasants. And, by far the worst affected were the agricultural laborers who had no land at all.

Notwithstanding arguments to the contrary, estate systems of control, whether organized bureaucratically (the *khas* system) or managed indirectly through *thikadars*, were equally capable of asserting the primacy of their landholders. Although bureaucratic management usually endowed zamindars with a greater measure of centralized authority, the structures themselves were no guarantee of effective administration. Hathwa underscores the possibility of an estate operating equally efficiently under both an indirect and direct system of management. The key to Hathwa control, prior to its switch to a direct system of management, lay in its well-regulated ties to the *thikadar* who was the crucial figure for the estate at the ground level and the mainstay of the system of control in the nineteenth century. Because *thikadars* were village-level controllers who were substantial raiyats, petty maliks, or moneylenders, and, in some cases, European indigo planters, their power and influence enabled the successful and prompt collection of the estate's demands. They also served the interests of the great estate by assuming the burden of curbing local dissidence.

Hathwa's relations with its intermediaries constituted a different kind of collaborative bargain than the one that the colonial state entered into with Hathwa and other local allies. Whereas the British largely abandoned the countryside to its connections, Hathwa retained control over its villages through an array of devices. *Thikadars* were kept in a weak position in relation to the estate. They had virtually no legal rights, and, if they were issued leases, the terms of the agreement spelled out in detail the raj's disciplinary rights over them. Furthermore, Hathwa's powerful centralized administrative structure and efficient professional bureaucracy restricted the *thikadars*' command over village society. But there was one parallel between the colonial and Hathwa systems: each was primarily concerned with defining only its own

---

18. Musgrave 1972: 270.
19. See also Henningham (1983: 50–51) for a similar point; for a rebuttal to Henningham, see Musgrave (1983: 56–57).

rights in relation to its intermediaries, leaving to the Hathwa estate considerable latitude in operating in its own society as long as the superior authority's interests were maintained and enhanced.

Under this dynamic, the landholder's supremacy over his tenants continued to be exerted. Regardless of the extent to which other interests on his estate cut into his customary dues and obligations, this prevailed because his losses were generally translated into gains by estate functionaries or ground-level controllers, such as the *thikadar*s, who made the most of their enlarged control over their subordinates. With varying degrees of intensity, this principle of estate management was built into all zamindaris. Strong central management circumscribed the scope of this dynamic, leaving room for its application only to the lowest rungs of rural society; weak estate administrations, inherently unable to curtail its reach, sought a measure of security in deflecting its attention away from the core of the zamindari to the more vulnerable periphery. The law that governed this principle was that each and every level of interests on the estate was directed to seek its profits at the expense of the next lower rung—a system that ultimately rested on the shoulders of the weaker raiyats. Breakdowns in management, therefore, usually led to shifts in the center of gravity.

The history of the sizable Bettiah raj indicates that, even where central administration was virtually in a state of collapse for several decades, no easy conclusions can be drawn about the simultaneous downfall of the "Lords of the Land." Instead, the 14 percent increase in its income (an increment of Rs. 200,000) between the 1860s and the 1890s suggests a different picture of estate management. The cracks at the center merely promoted the emergence of many petty lords of the land—*thikadar*s, in the Bettiah case, who usurped some of their superiors' powers and subsequently buckled down on the rest of estate society with their newly acquired strength.[20] Similarly, the minimal bureaucracies of Tamilnad estates in the twentieth century do not warrant snap judgments regarding the weaknesses of superordinate control. Instead, when zamindars ignored such tasks as "assessing and collecting revenue, keeping records, and policing the villages," they were taken up by village officers: "The village headman, who made collections, kept order and often arbitrated in petty disputes, was often the rich ryot in the village . . . the karnam [patwari] was often a major landholder as well. Even where they were lesser men, they resided in the village and were tied closely to its economically and socially powerful members."[21]

"Subinfeudation" in Bengal, a phenomenon that invariably invites questions about the power of that region's zamindars, also repays closer scrutiny. Even the condition of the Burdwan raj—where the declining fortunes of the maharaja led to his selling parcels of his estate as perpetual leases and these leaseholders (*patnidar*s), in turn, sold their rights to other purchasers, thus creating additional "subdegrees" of lease rights—ultimately reflects the deeply entrenched

20. Mishra 1978: 36–37, 68–69. 21. Baker 1976: 18.

strengths of zamindars. Certainly, the sale of perpetual leases was a sign of the internal weaknesses of the zamindari system, but the growth of such intermediary rights did not necessarily dissolve superordinate control over the peasantry. On the contrary, "few upper and wealthier peasants" became the holders of these rights, and, with each new degree of tenure rights, the rates of rent tended to increase. The enlarged burden was principally assumed "by the inferior or weaker raiyats, while the upper stratum managed to obtain the lower rates in collusion with the patnidars."[22] Nor were there "any fundamental changes in the structure of land-holding at the village level."[23]

Just as decay at the core of the Mughal Empire in the eighteenth century can no longer be construed as ushering in widespread anarchy and chaos (because regional systems of power arose), the condition of estate management, as viewed from the perspective of the zamindaris, should not prompt facile generalizations regarding the collapse of any and all systems of control. The very nature of local agrarian hierarchies ensured that superordinate control could issue from many quarters, nor should the structures of support that the colonial system made available to zamindars be ignored because, together with the enormous power and influence that they intrinsically possessed over their subordinates, such advantages sited landholder raj on firmly established ground. Minor upheavals only created fissures in this edifice of control. Thus, in the aftermath of Independence, it would take all the new nation's political resources and determination to topple some of these structures by abolishing zamindaris.

About Hathwa's control there is, of course, little doubt. The decisive edge that it held over its intermediaries is clearly indicated by the ease with which it shifted from the *thikadari* system of management to a *khas* system at the turn of the twentieth century. Although the new system better integrated the chain of command between the administrative superstructure and the "man on the spot" in the outlying villages, the dynamic of control remained, as in the *thikadari* system, the village-level controller, now recruited as an agent of the estate (*sazawal*). Whether designated *thikadar* or *sazawal*, Hathwa coadjutors served as vital cogs in a machinery of control that pressed the claims of the great estate onto its hundred thousand peasants.

On a lesser scale, the "ordinary" *thikadari* or *khas* system of management of large landholders and petty *maliks* replicated the Hathwa model, except in one respect. Although less centralized, even diffuse in many cases, the basic pattern of control in most large estates was similar because they also linked up with village-level controllers. Breakdowns in this system (where intermediaries intercepted the resources of an estate), therefore, did not necessarily disrupt the claims of village-level controllers over the rest of their society.

Local and village-level controllers resorted to a wide range of tactics to gain the upper hand. Even though the state's presence in local society was highly

22. Taniguchi 1981: 58   23. Ratnalekha Ray 1979: 108.

attenuated, its institutions, such as the legal system, provided a mechanism by which indigenous controllers enhanced their power. Beyond the pale of the law also lay strategems of control centering on the manipulation of rent and illegal cesses, as well as credit networks, and each of these were juggled to reinforce and tighten the grip of local systems of control. Invariably, these systems of control bore down most heavily on the poorer raiyats; the well-to-do peasants were frequently tied into these systems of control. And, because these systems favored cleavages within village society, peasants found common cause against them difficult to sustain. The mastery of landholders over their estates in U.P. also points to the less structured ways of exercising power: a zamindar's forceful personality and influence, the use of low-caste spies, a policy of divide-and-rule that encouraged caste and factional rivalries among employees, and the recruitment of clients traditionally beholden to the landholder by virtue of ascriptive or agnatic ties.[24]

For ordinary people the Limited Raj had profound consequences. With the power and authority of the state largely refracted through local systems and strategies of control, Saran raiyats found their options severely restricted. One choice that peasants historically made in adverse conditions was flight, such movement often assuming the proportions of avoidance protest. This phenomenon commonly occurred in indigo plantations where the planters' demands on land and labor clashed fundamentally with the peasant system of agriculture. Desertions, often constituting desperate acts of evasion from harsh natural conditions and extraordinary superordinate pressures, were also frequent from the estates of zamindars. Such abscondings usually involved entire families, many of whom were drawn from the poorest peasants of the village. Flight was the only way to avoid complete ruin.

A different kind of option was seasonal migration—movement largely precipitated by push factors. Over 10 percent of the population was consistently reported outside Saran in the late nineteenth and early twentieth centuries. Most people who moved were peasants of low economic and social status inhabiting the crowded southern thanas; an overwhelming number were male. Their typical destination was the "East"—the areas in Bengal where employment prospects existed in the form of such menial jobs as harvesting, manual labor, or unskilled factory labor. A seasonal migrant netted earnings averaging Rs. 30 to 80.

Seasonal migration persisted as a major option for Saran peasants because it represented a relatively secure proposition. Prospects for gain were quite certain because wages were higher in the east than within the district, and its timing dovetailed with the slack period in the agricultural calendar (between December and May). Furthermore, the development of railways added elasticity to this choice because it enabled more members of a family to leave and to

---

24. Metcalf 1979: 271–72.

adapt the duration and location of their stay to conditions obtaining in their sending and receiving communities.

Seasonal migration, however, also highlights the constraints that limited raiyat choices. Although seasonal migration was designed to benefit migrants and their families in their home communities—thus, the predominance of peasants of low social and economic status among the annual migrants east—such movement also represented their efforts to earn supplementary income to meet the demands of landholders and moneylenders. It was not solely a mechanism for peasants to maximize their resources but stemmed from a basic imperative to eke out a minimum subsistence. Nor were these gains made without psychic costs. As the popular Bhojpuri literature of this region shows, the "pangs of separation" suffered by the wife at home while her husband was "abroad" were a favorite theme of audiences in whom it evoked a familiar sentiment.

In contrast with desertion, seasonal migration was much more of a positive step toward enhancing one's resources. Yet, as with the people who voted with their feet, the fact that the beneficiaries of seasonal migration were also local and village-level controllers suggests the extent to which seasonal exodus ultimately epitomized the Saran raiyats' inability to break out of the prevailing system of control. Both desertions and migration represented stopgap measures aimed at keeping zamindars and maliks at bay.

Peasants also manifested their grievances in routine acts of resistance and recalcitrance. Although these were expressed in individual and sporadic acts of contentiousness,[25] they rarely assumed the proportions of a peasant movement. Instead, protest was generally articulated by acts and behaviors intended to preserve threatened rights, that is, to maintain a moral economy. Gatherings of large numbers of peasants before a landholder or a government official to appeal or to plead were a common occurrence. So were petitions seeking redress. Still others employed the time-honored custom of being recalcitrant and cunning to ward off the demands of their superordinates. Some turned to a life of crime.

Although the recognition of the South Asian peasant as "subaltern" has rightly added a vital, "insurgent" dimension to his behavior, an aspect not adequately covered by his characterizations as "moral" and "rational," it represents more the extraordinary side of peasant life than the routine. Throughout the subcontinent, organized peasant violence directed at superordinates was rare. The few instances in which peasants acted collectively and beyond a momentary outburst of violence in Saran were occasions in which outside targets provided a common cause. Unity was forged out of bonds created by a mutual enmity toward the intrusions of the local representatives of the state, especially the police, or by superordinates without much local anchorage in village society.

25. Robb 1979: 119.

Indigo plantations, against which "criminal" riots and affrays frequently erupted, were another popular target. Wherever indigo plantations played a significant role in local agriculture in Bihar, such incidents were a systemic feature of the agrarian society. Such upheavals, moreover, followed on the heels of an earlier round of campaigns against indigo planters in Bengal where these plantations formerly flourished.[26] But indigo disputes were not clear-cut acts of peasant solidarity and violence directed at superordinates, but actions organized generally by local zamindars or substantial raiyats against the unpopular foreign planters. Consider, for instance, the indigo agitation known as the Champaran *Satyagraha* because of Gandhi's participation. The local raiyat who enlisted the Mahatma's assistance was no ordinary peasant. A Brahmin cultivator, Raj Kumar Shukla, was also a moneylender with business of over Rs. 1,500. His holdings included a sizable amount of land, seventeen cattle, and two houses, and he had once been the clerk of the leading landholder of the district. And the so-called "anti-factory oligarchy" was composed primarily of "high-caste peasants: Brahmans, Rajputs, Babhans [Bhumihar Brahmins], Kayasths, Muslim Sheikhs, etc. Most of these leaders were well-off or rich peasants."[27] The leaders of the previous indigo agitations in Champaran in 1866–1867, 1894–1895, and 1907–1909 were of similar economic and social backgrounds.[28] Thus, collective action and violence in indigo plantations were structured by the same framework that shaped the local configuration of control.

So were most other acts of collective violence. Averaging as many as fifty a year in the late nineteenth and early twentieth centuries, riots in Saran were highly localized and momentary affairs, usually involving a handful of people in disputes over rights and claims in relation to land and its produce. Occasionally, they represented peasant attacks on their superordinates, but more likely, as the faces in the crowd indicate, they were supported or led by men of important village standing—the village-level controllers.

In the few instances that collective action and violence endured beyond the typically brief lapses into violence and centered on issues that extended beyond village boundaries, solidarity was generated by village-level and local controllers uniting with ordinary peasants over concerns that affected them generally. Two important manifestations of the linkages that were effected between localized concerns and region-wide (and even nation-wide) issues were the Cow Protection movement of the 1890s, whose use of fundamental symbols fostered a sense of group identity among Hindu inhabitants; and the Noncooperation movement of the Indian National Congress in the early 1920s, whose nationalist message was translated by the residents of a cluster of villages into a "spirit of lawlessness" against the local government and also against the officials of their landholder—the maharaja of Hathwa. In the latter

---

26. Fisher 1976: chaps. 3–4; Palit 1975: 96–151; Kling 1977.
27. Pouchepadass 1974: 71–73.   28. Ibid., 79–81.

case, the locus of the disturbances was the locality of Bhorey, an area in which the Hathwa estate had had recurring problems beginning with the "internal rising" of the early nineteenth century and continuing in the periodic desertions that ensued in the late nineteenth and early twentieth centuries. Thus, both the Cow Protection and Noncooperation movements activated the familiar dynamics of the local agrarian society and, consequently, sought to channel localized concerns and structures into their own ideology and organization.

Mass movements in Bihar after the 1920s, both nationalist and peasant, rose on the crest of waves created largely by rich peasants and small landholders, in short, the village-level controllers. And although an active *Kisan Sabha* sprang up to champion the rights of the raiyats, even instigating a "subaltern rebellion" in 1942, the peasant movement, subordinated to the elitist-dominated nationalist movement, was ultimately mitigated by the interests of Congress.[29] Elsewhere too, in the twentieth century, "middle and rich peasants" or the "dominant peasantry," comprising an "oligarchy of rich and well-off peasants belonging to a respectable caste [sic] who hold either as owners or as tenants the bulk of the land rights in each village" were often the driving force behind the movements that erupted in different parts of the country.[30] That their emergence as a political force came in the wake of a worldwide rise of rich peasants in the late nineteenth century due to the development of markets and an international economy is probably not coincidental, although as yet little investigated for South Asia.[31]

In the aftermath of Independence, Bihar became the first state in the new nation to institute agrarian reform by a campaign of zamindari abolition. Over three decades later, however, it remains an area that typifies the continuing agrarian crisis in India. The "lords of the land" who enjoyed the supportive hand of the colonial state no longer command unlimited power and influence and the great estates have been largely broken up, but the village-level controllers, comprising the substantial raiyats and the petty landholders, have emerged as the new force in rural society. The demise of the Limited Raj set the stage for the decline of its most powerful local allies, and it also ushered in a shift in power in the countryside to the intermediate level of controllers, a process facilitated and encouraged by the political character of the new nation.[32]

This study of agrarian relations in Saran shows that the control of the colonial state tapered off sharply at the levels below the district. In its absence, landholders with close ties to the British held sway as the local controllers. They, in turn, with varying degrees of command and intensity, extended their authority and power to the fundamental level of agrarian society, also the

29. Henningham 1982: 150–51; Hauser 1961: 153–56.
30. Pouchepadass 1980b: 147; Dhanagare 1983: 218–24; Low 1977: 20–24.
31. Charlesworth 1979a: 61–95.
32. Studies that emphasize the continuities in agrarian control and conflict in contemporary Bihar are Das (1982), Jannuzi (1974), and Hauser (1983). See also Pandey (1977: 218) on the emergence of Congress as "a rich peasants' party by 1940."

immediate arena of action for any peasant, through the village-level controllers who were ultimately the key to both control and conflict. In the Limited Raj of the colonial British state—at the local level—control and conflict were thus woven into the same tapestry. It is this social fabric that continues to pattern agrarian relations today, even though the Sonepur Meet folded up its tents and disbanded long ago.

Glossary

Aghani—November–December; winter harvest or crop

amil—government official; local revenue collector or revenue farmer

amla—(estate) official or retainer; rent collector

arhar—a kind of pulse

Asarh—June–July

Aswin—September–October

athrahaoni—a form of interest collected on loans

arzee (arzi)—a petition; an address; a memorial

bakasht—land in cultivating possession

bania—moneylender; banker

barahil—peon

basta—a bundle of papers (wrapped in cloth)

Bhadoi—August–September; autumn harvest or crop

bidesh—a foreign country

birtdar—a holder of a maintenance grant for religious and charitable purposes, usually rentfree

chetra (*chhatra*)—a place of shelter for travelers; a serai

chiragi—an allowance for keeping lamps lit

choongee (*chungi*)—a handful of grain levied as a tax or a fee

cottah (*kattha*)—unit of land measurement; one-twentieth of a bigha

dam—a coin; a money of account; in Akbar's period 40 dams equaled Re. 1

darshan—to pay one's respect

Dashara—Hindu festival at beginning of the agricultural year

diara—alluvial land

ekarnamah—a deed of agreement

fard tanaza—register of rent disputes

gadi (gaddi)—throne; seat
ganga-asnan—ceremonial bathing in the Ganges River
garasa—battle ax
garh—mud-walled fort or house
gauraksha—cow protection
gomastah—steward; agent or collector
gorait—village peon
gram—a generic term for pulses

hal—wooden plow
Harihar Kshetra (Harihar chhatra)—place of Hari (Vishnu) and Har (Shiva)
hat—periodic marketplace
hukumat—rules; customs
hundi—a bill of exchange

jati—caste
jeth-raiyat—village headman; senior or principal cultivator
jotedar—an intermediate landholder; a rich farmer

kachcheri (cutcherry)—an office; a court; a hall; a place where public business is conducted
karnam—accountant; patwari
Kartik—October–November
kharhaul—land producing thatching grass
khas—direct system of rent collection
khillut—insignia and dress of honor
kothi—house; establishment

lathi—club; heavy stick
lathial—clubmen; men armed with heavy sticks

mahajani—moneylending; a specific kind of interest on loan
mauza—revenue village
mohurrir—writer
mokarrari—permanent intermediate land tenure
munsif—civil judge
musaheb—retainer

GLOSSARY 243

nankar qanungo—land or revenue assigned to a qanungo for his subsistence

panchayet—village or caste council of elders
patnidar—holder of a patni (permanent lease)
patshala—indigenous school
patta—lease
pauseri—about 7 lbs.
podar—cashier

qanungo—registrar
qazi—judge

Rabi—March–April; spring; spring harvest or crop

sabha—association
sadr—headquarters; principal; chief
sarkar—district
sattu—coarse grain; parched grain
sawai—a form of interest collected on loans
sazawal—land steward
shiqdar (*shikdar*)—a revenue officer or collector appointed by government or a zamindar
sir—see *khas*

tahrir—a fee for a written statement; a written statement
thikadar—rent collector
thikadari—system of rent collection by thikadar
tirtha-yatra—pilgrimage

ziraat—land in cultivating possession of landholder
zoolum—oppression or tyranny

Bibliography

The bibliography is designed to assist those who wish to pursue local-level studies of the British Raj. In offering brief descriptions of the sources used, my purpose is to show the nature and range of documentation available on the social history of modern South Asia. For the study of Indian society at the grassroots level, district and village records provide a wealth of indispensable information. Although many of these materials, such as those kept at the district and collectorate offices, are still consulted by local lawyers, administrators, and residents, they are only now beginning to be used by scholars. Additional information on primary sources appears in Yang (1979c: 1–23) and Hagen and Yang (1976: 75–84).

Unpublished Primary Sources
SARAN DISTRICT

(1) *Chapra: Saran District Record Room*

(a) Saran District, *Faujdari Bastas*, English Correspondence, 1860–1909. Manuscript copies of correspondence and reports submitted by district and subdistrict officers relating to judicial and criminal matters and collected together in bundles (*bastas*) wrapped with cloth.

    (b) Saran District Village Notes (SVN), 1893–1901 (3 vols.)
        Chapra thana nos. 1–136, 273–407
        Gopalganj thana nos. 127–317

    (c) SVN, 1915–1921
        Basantpur thana nos. 1–100, 101–200, 201–300, 301–400
        Chapra thana nos. 1–100, 101–200, 201–300, 301–400, 401–533
        Darauli thana nos. 1–100, 101–200, 201–300, 301–400, 401–533
        Gopalganj thana nos. 1–100, 101–200, 201–300, 301–400, 401–504
        Manjhi thana nos. 1–100, 101–200, 201–285
        Mashrak thana nos. 1–100, 101–200, 201–285
        Mirganj thana nos. 1–100, 101–200, 201–300, 301–400, 401–500, 501–600, 601–700, 701–800, 801–900, 901–1000, 1001–1064
        Parsa thana nos. 1–100, 101–200, 201–300, 301–400, 401–500, 501–561
        Siwan thana nos. 1–100, 101–200, 201–300, 301–400, 401–500, 501–588
        Sonepur thana nos. 1–100, 106–122

Compiled during the attestation period of settlement operations, the village notes are of exceptional value because of their rich data on a village-by-village basis. Topics covered are population and caste; family and village histories; land rights and rents; village economy and agriculture; and village officials. The 1893–1901 set is incomplete.

(d) Saran District *Fard Tanaza* (List of Disputes). Compiled during the revision settlement of 1915–1921, these papers offer the rent conflict history of each and every village in the district.

(2) *Chapra: Saran Collectorate Library*

Mansfield, P. T. "Rent Settlement: Being a Note on the Results of Different Methods of Rent Settlement Adopted in Different Districts in Bihar and Orissa," July 14, 1933.

(3) *Chapra: Private Holding*

"A History of the Manjha Family." MS, comp. by N. K. Roy, assistant manager and treasury officer, Manjha Estate. In possession of Hari Surendra Sahi of Manjha family, Rusi Kothi.

(4) *Hathwa: Hathwa Raj Record Room*

Hathwa Raj *Bastas*, 1870–1912. These estate records, primarily in English, are the correspondence and papers relating to the administrative functioning of the zamindari. They also include personal letters of the maharajas and their officials, communications from village-level controllers, and petitions from the estate's tenants. Zamindari records are of utmost importance in sketching the agrarian history of north India.

BIHAR STATE

(1) *Patna: Bihar State Archives*

(a) Saran Collectorate (S.C.) Records (bound volumes), 1779–1900. District collectorate records contain copious information, year by year, on local society. The Saran records are primarily copies of the official revenue and judicial correspondence between subdivisional administrators and their district-level superiors, as well as between district officers and the divisional commissioner at Patna.

(b) Patna Commissioner's Records, 1811–1900
Court of Wards, *Basta* nos. 136–176, esp. no. 136, Saran, 1854–1908; *Basta* no. 141, Wards Dept., Gen. Colltn.; *Basta* no. 144, Wards General; *Basta* no. 166, Hathwa estate
From Colltr. of Saran, 1854–1875, *Basta* nos. 102–107
General Dept., *Basta* nos. 275–321
Important bundles, Revenue and Judicial departments (catalogued alphabetically, by subject matter), *Basta* nos. 220–236.
Loose uncatalogued *bastas*, various years (no numbers)
Monthly bundles, 1854–1876
Revenue Dept., 1876–1900, *Basta* nos. 322–372

Next to the district records, the commissioner's records contain the most detailed information on local affairs. These include materials generated from the district and subdistrict levels and sent to the divisional headquarters, as well as those issuing from the commissioner to his superiors in Calcutta. Some of these records can also be found in the Bengal Proceedings volumes.

(c) Patna Commissioner's Annual Administration Reports (AGRPD), 1871–1872 to 1904–1905. Variously titled—"Annual General Report—Patna Division, 18—,"

"Annual General Administration Report of the Patna Division, 18—," and "Miscellaneous Annual Report of the Patna Division for the Year 19—"—these reports offer a great deal of valuable information on every aspect of local administration and conditions. Most annual statements were printed up in the Proceedings volumes of the General Department. The more detailed subdivisional and district annual reports (of far greater value for local-level investigations) have not all survived; those that have are in the Patna Commissioner's records.

    (d) Government of Bengal (GOB)
        Agriculture Dept. B Proceedings
        Judicial A Bundles, 1859–1901
        Judicial B Proceedings, 1859–1901
        Land Revenue B Proceedings, 1859–1909
        Political, Police Branch B Proceedings, 1875–1884
        Revenue A Bundles, 1866–1900.

These collections comprise the original "B" materials, which were briefly noted in the Procs. volume but not reprinted in them. This classification of records was retained at the divisional and provincial offices and not transmitted to higher authorities because of its supposedly local concerns. The "A" bundles, categorized by departments, contain documents largely reproduced in the Proceedings volumes. A few items in a file, however, because of their confidential nature or, on occasion, because of their "pedestrian" nature, were not printed up. The "A" bundles also include the "K.W." (Keep With) Proceedings, which generally remained in Patna or Calcutta and were not sent to London. These, primarily of a confidential or demi-official status, include the personal memoranda and intraoffice notes that often accompanied official communications.

(2) *Patna: Private Holdings*

Basu, Lal Behari. 1923. "Life of Devendra Nath Dutt." Bengali MS. In possession of Professor Bannerjee of Patna University.

ENGLAND

(1) *London: India Office Library and Records*

    (a) European Manuscripts
        Elgin Papers. The Earl of Elgin and Kincardine, Correspondence with Persons in India, commencing from Jan. 1894, MSS Eur. F 84/34, F 84/35, F 84/36. Letters from Persons in India, July–Dec. 1894, MSS Eur. F 84/65.
        Hubback Papers. John Hubback, "A Wkkehamist in the Indian Civil Service," Photo Eur. 152.
        Lansdowne Papers. Letters from the Marquess of Lansdowne, G.C.M.G. to the Right Honorable the Earl of Kimberley, K.G., Secretary of State for India, Correspondence with the Secretary of State for India. Vol. 5: Jan. 1893–Jan. 1894, MSS Eur. D 558/6.
        Risley Collection. District Reports received by the Superintendent of Census Operations for Bengal, bound and indexed, 1901–1902, MSS Eur. E 295/7.
        Temple Papers. Sir Richard Temple Papers, Letter B Famine, MSS Eur. F 86/121; Journal B Famine 1874, MSS Eur. F 86/132; Special Letters,

Bengal, 1874–1877, MSS Eur. F 86/137; Letters from Bengal Officers, 1873–1876, MSS Eur. F 86/139; Bengal Letters, semi-official, MSS Eur. F 86/161; Prince of Wales' Tour, Bengal, 1875, MSS Eur. F 86/163; Bengal Rent Law, 1876, MSS Eur. F 86/214; Minutes 1874–1875, 2 vols., MSS Eur. F 86/152 & 153.

The kinds of personal papers preserved hitherto by most repositories—of high officials or major leaders—are not especially rich in material about local history. Recent efforts to collect the papers of rank-and-file officials, as well as those of less notable people who lived and traveled in the subcontinent, promise to yield much more rewarding fruits for the social historian.

(b) Government of Bengal (GOB)
Patna Factory Records, 1743–1779
Behar and Benares Revenue Proceedings, 1816–1822
Bengal Criminal Judicial Consultations, 1795–1842
Bengal Education Proceedings, 1859–1912
Bengal General (Misc.) Proceedings, 1859–1912
Bengal Judicial Consultations, 1842–1857
Bengal Judicial Proceedings, 1859–1912
Bengal Police Proceedings, 1873–1874 to 1876, 1877–1885, 1911–1912 (other years in Judicial or Political Proceedings)
Bengal Political Proceedings, 1905–1910
Bengal Revenue Consultations, 1773–1858
Bengal Revenue Proceedings, 1859–1912
Bengal Statistics Proceedings, 1868–1897
Calcutta Revenue Committee Consultations, 1771
Native Newspaper Reports, Dec. 1874–1912

(c) Government of Bihar and Orissa (GOB&O)
Education Proceedings, 1918–1922
Education and Municipal Proceedings, 1912–1918
General Proceedings, 1912–1925
Judicial Proceedings, 1918–1922
Judicial, Police and Political Proceedings, 1913–1917
Municipal Proceedings, 1918–1921
Political Proceedings, 1918–1925
Revenue Proceedings, 1912–1925

(d) Government of India (GOI)
Economic Dept., Revenue, Collection to Despatches, 1866–1925, L/E/6/ and L/3/7/
Education Proceedings, 1866–1872
Home Proceedings (Police, Confidential [Political]), 1894, 1917–1921
Parliamentary Branch, L/Parl/, various dates
Public and Judicial, Collection to Despatches, 1866–1925, L/P&J/6/

The unpublished records of the provincial and central governments, particularly the proceedings or consultation volumes, form a major body of official information and have been widely used by recent historians. For the pre-twentieth-century period, the India

Office Library's collections compare favorably with those available at the National Archives in New Delhi or at regional archives in the states of India.

(2) *London: School of Oriental and African Studies Library*

Bengal, "Famine Narratives, 1874."

(3) *Cambridge: Centre for South Asian Studies*

P. T. Mansfield Papers

(4) *Oxford: Bodleian Library*

MacDonnell Papers. Papers of Lord A. P. MacDonnell of Swinford, 1844–1925, MSS Eng. Hist. a.11–12, b.206, c.321, 350–73, d.235–8, e.215–8: Letter book as Lieutenant-Governor.

Published Primary Sources
OFFICIAL PUBLICATIONS

A valuable source, especially on matters not covered in unpublished government materials. Also helpful in providing systematic data on a variety of subjects, from prices to wages, and from population size to caste composition. The reports of special committee, commissions, and parliamentary inquiries into specific topics are another rich source of information. To pursue intensive examinations of local-level society, official publications (district gazetteers, settlement reports, censuses, and other periodic government reports) relating to a specific area or community are the best starting point and are readily available. Outside of India, the most complete collections of official publications are in the India Office Library or the British Library in London.

(1) *Government of Bengal (GOB)*

Annual Crime Report of the Patna Division for the year 1869, 1870, 1871. 1870–1872. Calcutta.
Appointments in Bengal and their Holders from about year 1850 down to 1910. 1912. Calcutta.
Bengal Government Selections, *Papers regarding the Village and Rural Indigenous Agency employed in taking the Bengal Census of 1872.* 1873. Calcutta: Bengal Secretariat Press.
Committee on Improvement of Mofussil Police. 1838. Calcutta.
Famine, Bengal and Orissa, 1866. 1867. 3 vols. Calcutta: Government Printing.
Guide and Glossary to the Survey and Settlement Operations in the Patna and Bhagalpur Divisions. 1907. Calcutta: Bengal Secretariat Press.
Kerr, J. H. 1926. *Final Report on the Survey and Settlement Operations in the Darbhanga District, 1896 to 1903.* Patna: Government Printing.
Lister, E. 1907. *Final Report on the Survey and Settlement Operations in the Maksudpur Estate in the District of Gaya, 1900–1904.* Calcutta: Bengal Secretariat Press.
O'Malley, L. S. S. 1912. *Memorandum on the Material Condition of Bengal and Bihar and Orissa in the Years 1902–03 to 1911–12.* Darjeeling.
O'Malley, L. S. S., and Chakravarti, Monmohan. 1912. *Bengal District Gazetteers: Hooghly.* Calcutta: Bengal Secretariat Book Depot.
Report on the Administration of Bengal, 1873–74. 1875. Calcutta: Bengal Secretariat Press.
Report of Committee on Coolies and Mr. Doomsun's Minute. 1840. Calcutta.

Report of Enquiries made Regarding Food-Stocks in Bengal, 1896–97. 1897. Calcutta: Bengal Secretariat Press.
Report on the Police of the Patna Division, 1866, 1867, 1868. 1867–1872. Calcutta.
Report on Wards and Attached Estates in the Lower Provinces for the years, 1874–75. 1876. Calcutta: Bengal Secretariat Press.
Saran District Gazetteer. Statistics, 1901–02. 1905. Calcutta: Bengal Secretariat Book Depot.
Saran District Gazetteer. B Vol.: *Statistics, 1900–01 to 1910–11.* 1914. Allahabad: Government Press.
SDG, 1908. O'Malley, L. S. S. 1908. *Bengal District Gazetteers: Saran.* Calcutta: Bengal Secretariat Book Depot.
Selections from Divisional and District Annual Administration Reports, 1872–73. 1874. Calcutta: Bengal Secretariat Press.
Selections from Papers, Bengal Tenancy Act. 1920. Calcutta.
Shirres, L. P. 1920. *Memorandum on the Material Condition of the People of Bengal in the years 1892–93 to 1901–02.* Calcutta.
SR. Kerr, J. H. 1903. *Final Report on the Survey and Settlement Operations in the Saran District, 1893 to 1901.* Calcutta: Bengal Secretariat Press.
Stephenson-Moore, C. J. 1922. *Final Report on the Survey and Settlement Operations in the Muzaffarpur District, 1892 to 1899.* Patna: Government Printing.
Trial of the Basantpur Riot Case in the Court of the Sessions Judge of Saran, 1893. 1894. Calcutta.
Twenty Years' Statistics, 1883–84 to 1903–04. 1905(?). 5 vols. Calcutta.
Vas, J. A. 1911. *Eastern Bengal and Assam District Gazetteers, Rangpur.* Allahabad: Government press.

(2) *Government of Bihar and Orissa (GOB&O)*

An Account of the Tours of His Honour the Lieutenant-Governor of Bihar and Orissa (Oct. and Dec. 1912) (Sir C. S. Bayley). 1914. Patna: Government Printing.
The Bihar and Orissa Provincial Banking Enquiry Committee, 1929–30. 1930. 3 vols. Patna: Government Printing.
Report on the Administration of the Police in the Province of Bihar and Orissa for the years 1920, 1921, 1922. 1921–1923. Patna: Government Printing.
Report on Wards' Encumbered, Trust and Attached Estates in the Provinces of Bihar and Orissa for the year 1911–1912. 1912. Ranchi.
SDG, 1930. Middleton, A. P. 1930. *Bihar and Orissa District Gazetteers: Saran.* Rev. ed. Patna: Government Printing.
SRR. Gupta, Phanindra Nath. 1923. *Final Report on the Survey and Settlement Operations (Revision) in the District of Saran, 1915 to 1921.* Patna: Government Printing.
Swanzy, R. E. 1938. *Bihar and Orissa District Gazetteers: Champaran.* Rev. ed. Patna: Government Printing.

(3) *Government of Bihar*

Chaudhury, P. C. 1956. *Sarkar Saran* (based on old correspondence regarding Saran District in Bengal from 1785 to 1866). Patna: Free Press.
Datta, K. K. 1957. *History of the Freedom Movement in Bihar.* 3 vols. Patna.
Kumar, N. 1971. *Bihar District Gazetteers. Journalism in Bihar.* Patna: Government of Bihar.

Prasad, S. D. 1966. *Census 1961, Bihar, District Census Handbook*, 4, *Saran*. Patna: Government of Bihar.
SDG, 1960. Chaudhury, P. C. *Bihar District Gazetteers: Saran*. Patna: Secretariat Press.

(4) *Government of India (GOI)*

Agricultural Statistics of British India, 1890–91. 1896. Calcutta: Bengal Secretariat Press.
Beverley, H. 1872. *Census of Bengal, 1872*. Calcutta: Bengal Secretariat Press.
Bourdillon, J. A. 1883. *Census of India, 1881*. Vol. 3: *Report of the Census of Bengal, 1881*. Calcutta: Bengal Secretariat Press.
———. 1898. *Census of India, 1891, District Census Reports, Saran*. Calcutta: Bengal Secretariat Press.
Census of India, 1931, vol. 1, part 2: *Imperial Tables*. Delhi: 1933.
Gait, E. A. 1913. *Census of India, 1901*. Vol. 3: *The Lower Provinces of Bengal and their Feudatories*. Part I, *The Report*. Calcutta: Bengal Secretariat Book Depot.
Indian Statutory Commission. Vol. 15: *Extracts from Official Evidence*. 1930. London: His Majesty's Stationery Office.
O'Donnell, C. J. 1893. *Census of India, 1891*. Vol. 5: *The Lower Provinces of Bengal and their Feudatories*, Part 1: *The Report*. Calcutta: Bengal Secretariat Press.
O'Malley, L. S. S. 1913. *Census of India, 1911*. Vol. 5: *Bengal, Bihar and Orissa and Sikkim*. Part 1: *Report*. Calcutta: Bengal Secretariat Book Depot.
Prasad, S. D. 1964. *Census of India, 1961*. Vol. 4: *Bihar*. Part 7-B, *Fairs and Festivals of Bihar*. New Delhi.
Prices and Wages in India, 1921. 1923. 37th issue. Calcutta.
Report on the Working of the Indian Factories Act during the year 1898. 1899. Calcutta.
Tallents, P. C. 1923. *Census of India, 1921*. Vol. 7: *Bihar and Orissa*, Part 1: *Report*. Patna: Government Printing.

(5) *Great Britain*

Parliament, *Parliamentary Papers* (Commons), *1812–13*. Vol. 9: "Answers to Interrogatories of the Governor General; and New Systems of Revenue, and Judicial Administration (1801)."
———. *Parliamentary Papers* (Commons), *1867*. Vol. 170: "Papers relating to the Famine in Behar including Mr. F. R. Cockerell's Report."
———. *Parliamentary Papers* (Commons), *1905*. Vol. 57: Cmnd. 2478, "Report of the Indian Police Commission and Resolution of the Government of India."
Royal Commission on Labour in India. 1931. Vol. 4, part 2. London: HMSO.

(6) *Other Official Publications*

Atkinson, Edwin T., ed. 1881. *Statistical, Descriptive and Historical Account of the North-Western Provinces of India*. Vol. 6: *Gorakhpur*. By E. B. Alexander. Allahabad: Government Press.
Datta, K. L. 1914. *Report on the Enquiry into the Rise of Prices in India*, Vol. 3: *Statistics of Wages, Population, Agriculture, Rainfall, Rents, Communications and Freights*. Calcutta.
Firminger, W. K. 1962. *Historical Introduction to the Bengal Portion of the Fifth Report*. Calcutta: Bengal Past and Present.
Foley, B. 1906. *Report on Labour in Bengal*. Lucknow.

Fremantle, S. H. 1906. *Report on the Supply of Labour in the United Provinces and Bengal.* Lucknow.
Grierson, George A. 1883. *Report on Colonial Emigration from the Bengal Presidency (with "Diary").* Calcutta.
———. 1975 (reprint ed., 1885). *Bihar Peasant Life.* Delhi: Cosmo Publication.
Hunter, W. W. 1873. *Famine Aspects of Bengal Districts.* Simla.
———. 1887. *A Statistical Account of Bengal,* Vol. 11: *Districts of Patna and Saran.* London: Trubner.
MacDonnell, A. P. 1876. *Report on the Food-Grain Supply and Statistical Review of the Relief Operations in the Distressed Districts of Bihar and Bengal during the Famine of 1873–1874.* Calcutta: Bengal Secretariat Press.
McNeile, D. J. 1866. *Report on the Village Watch of the Lower Provinces of Bengal.* Calcutta.
Nevill, H. R. 1909. *District Gazetteers of the United Provinces of Agra and Oudh.* Vol. 31: *Gorakhpur.* Allahabad: Government Press.
Wilson, H. H. 1868. *A Glossary of Judicial and Revenue Terms.* 2nd ed. Delhi: Munshiram Manoharlal.
Wyatt, Alexander. 1847(?). *Statistics of the District of Sarun.* Calcutta.

CONTEMPORARY WORKS

Although fraught with personal idiosyncrasies, contemporary works (especially autobiographies, memoirs, and reminiscences) provide significant glimpses into local society. Even when written by officials, they throw light on contemporary social and economic conditions.

Abbott, Harry E. 1896. *Sonepore Reminiscences (Years 1840–1896).* Calcutta: "Star" Press.
Ashby, Lillian Luker, with Roger Whately. 1938. *My India.* London: Michael Joseph.
Beames, John. 1961. *Memoirs of a Bengal Civilian.* London: Chatto & Windus.
Bignold, Thomas Frank. 1888. *Leviora; being the rhymes of a Successful Competitor.* Calcutta: Thacker, Spink & Co.
Buchanan, Francis. 1925. *Journal of Francis Buchanan (afterwards Hamilton) kept during the Survey of the Districts of Patna and Gaya in 1811–1812.* Ed. V. H. Jackson. Patna: Government Printing.
———. 1925. *An Account of the Districts of Bihar and Patna in 1811–1812.* Patna: Bihar and Orissa Research Society.
Buckland, C. T. 1884. *Sketches of Social Life in India.* London.
Chanakya Society, Patna College. *Chanakya Society Annual Reports,* 1910–11 to 1918–19.
Chowdhary, Ramgopal Singh. 1917. *Rambles in Bihar.* Bankipur: Express Press.
———. 1920. *Selected Writings and Speeches of Babu Ramgopal Singh Chowdhary.* Patna: Bishun Prasad Sinha.
Chunder, Bholanauth. 1869. *The Travels of a Hindoo to Various Parts of Bengal and Upper India.* 2 vols. London.
[Clay, A. L.]. 1896. *Leaves from a Diary in Lower Bengal.* By C. S. (retired). London: Macmillan.
Cox, Sir Edmund C. 1911. *Police and Crime in India.* London: Stanley Paul.
Dutt, Devendra Nath. 1909. *A Brief History of the Hatwa Raj.* (Compiled and published under the authority of Her Highness the Maharani Sahiba of Hatwa) Calcutta: K. P. Mookerjee.

Dutt, Girindra Nath. 1905. *History of the Hutwa Raj.* Bankipur: La'iiri & Co. "Royal Press."
Gibbon, J. 1838. "State of Agriculture in Behar." *Transactions of the Agricultural and Horticultural Society of India* 2.
[Graham, G.]. 1878. *Life in the Moffusil or, The Civilian in Lower Bengal.* By an ex-civilian. London: C. Kegan Paul.
Harrison, F. C. 1890. "The Behar Ryot at Home." *Calcutta Review* 16: 274–305.
The Hutwa Raj Family. 1914. (An account of the services rendered to government by the Hutwa raj). Calcutta.
Khan, Shafaat Ahmad, ed. 1927. *John Marshall in India: Notes and Observations in Bengal, 1668–1672.* London: Humphrey Milford.
Macpherson, William Charles, ed. 1927. *Soldiering in India, 1764–1787.* (Extracts from journals and letters left by Lt. Col. Allan Macpherson and Lt. Col. John Macpherson of the East India Company's Service). Edinburgh.
Muddiman, Sir Alexander. 1930. *Memoirs* (For private circulation only). Allahabad: Government Press.
O'Donnell, C. J. 1860. *The Ruin of an Indian Province* (An Indian famine explained) (A letter to Marquis of Hartington, Secretary of State for India in the liberal and reforming government). London: C. Kegan Paul.
Phillips, H. A. D. 1866. *Our Administration of India* (Being a complete account of the revenue and collectorate administration in all departments with special reference to the works and duties of a district officer in Bengal). London: W. Thacker.
Prasad, Rajendra. 1957. *Autobiography.* Bombay: Asia Publishing House.
Rankine, Robert. 1839. *Notes on the Medical Topography of the District of Saran.* Calcutta: Military Orphan Press.
Tayler, William. 1881–1882. *Thirty-Eight Years in India: From Juganath to the Himalaya Mountains.* 2 vols. London: W. H. Allen.
Trevelyan, G. O. 1866. *The Competition Wallah.* London.
Wilson, Minden. 1908. *History of Behar Indigo Factories; Reminiscences of Behar; Tirhoot and Its Inhabitants of the Past; History of Bihar Light Horse Volunteers.* Calcutta: Calcutta General Printing.

Secondary Sources

Adas, Michael. 1981. "From Avoidance to Confrontation: Peasant Protest in Precolonial and Colonial Southeast Asia." *Comparative Studies in Society and History* 23: 217–47.
Ahmad, Enayet. 1961. "The Rural Population of Bihar." *Geographical Review* 51: 253–76.
Ahmad, Qeyamuddin. 1973. *Corpus of Arabic and Persian Inscriptions of Bihar (A.H. 640–1200).* Patna: K. P. Jayaswal Research Institute, 1973.
——— . 1978–1979. "Aspects of Historical Geography of Medieval Bihar." *Indian Historical Review* 5: 119–35.
Ali, M. Athar. 1975. "The Passing of Empire: The Mughal Case." *MAS* 9: 385–96.
Amin, Shahid. 1982. "Small Peasant Commodity Production and Rural Indebtedness: The Culture of Sugarcane in Eastern U.P., c. 1880–1920." In *Subaltern Studies I*, ed. Ranajit Guha. Delhi: Oxford University Press.
——— . 1984. *Sugarcane and Sugar in Gorakhpur: An Inquiry into Peasant Production for Capitalist Enterprise in Colonial India.* Delhi: Oxford University Press.

Arnold, David. 1977. "The Armed Police and Colonial Rule in South India, 1914–1947." *MAS* 11: 101–125.
———. 1979. "Rural Dacoity and Rural Crime in Madras, 1860–1940." *Journal of Peasant Studies* 6: 140–67.
Asiwaju, A. I. 1976. "Migrations as Revolt: The Example of the Ivory Coast and Upper Volta before 1945." *Journal of African History* 17: 577–94.
Bagchi, A. K. 1976a. "De-industrialization in India in the Nineteenth Century: Some Theoretical Implications." *Journal of Development Studies* 12: 135–64.
———. 1976b. "Deindustrialization in Gangetic Bihar, 1809–1901." In *Essays in Honour of Professor S. C. Sarkar*, ed. Barun De. New Delhi: People's Publishing House.
———. 1976c. "Reflections on Patterns of Regional Growth in India during the period of British Rule." *Bengal Past and Present* 45: 247–89.
———. 1979. "A Reply." *IESHR* 16: 147–61.
Baker, Christopher. 1976. "Tamilnad Estates in the Twentieth Century." *IESHR* 13: 1–44.
———. 1979. "Madras Headmen," in *Economy and Society*, eds. K. N. Chaudhuri and C. J. Dewey. Delhi: Oxford University Press.
Barat, Amiya. 1962. *The Bengal Native Infantry: Its Organisation and Discipline, 1796–1852*. Calcutta: KLM.
Barnett, Richard B. 1980. *North India between Empires: Awadh, the Mughals, and the British, 1720–1801*. Berkeley and Los Angeles: University of California Press.
Barrier, N. Gerald. 1981. "The British Raj in India: The Process and Politics of Imperial Rule." In *British Imperial Policy in India and Sri Lanka*, eds. Robert I. Crane and N. Gerald Barrier. Columbia, Mo.: South Asia Books.
Bastien, Joseph W., and Bromley, David G. 1980. "Metaphor in the Rituals of Restorative and Transformative Groups." In *Rituals and Ceremonies in Popular Culture*, ed. Ray B. Browne. Ohio: Bowling Green University Popular Press.
Bayly, C. A. 1971. "Local Control in Indian Towns—the case of Allahabad, 1880–1920." *MAS* 5: 289–311.
———. 1979. "English-Language Historiography on British Expansion in India and Indian Reactions since 1945." In *Reappraisals in Overseas History*, eds. P. C. Emmer and H. L. Wesseling. Leiden: Leiden University Press.
———. 1983a. "Political and Economic Networks in Eighteenth Century India." Paper presented for the Association for Asian Studies meeting, San Francisco, March 25–27.
———. 1983b. *Rulers, Townsmen, and Bazaars: North Indian Society in the Age of British Expansion, 1770–1870*. Cambridge: Cambridge University Press.
Beals, Ralph E., and Menezes, Carmen F. 1970. "Migrant Labour and Agricultural Output in Ghana." *Oxford Economic Papers* 22: 109–127.
Beames, John. 1885. "On the Geography of India in the Reign of Akbar, Part II (No. II—Subah Bihar)." *Journal of the Asiatic Society of Bengal* 54: 162–82.
Bell, Colin, and Newby, Howard. 1972. *Community Studies: An Introduction to the Sociology of the Local Community*. New York: Praeger Publishers.
Beteille, Andre. 1974. *Studies in Agrarian Social Structure*. Delhi: Oxford University Press.
Bhardwaj, Surinder Mohan. 1973. *Hindu Places of Pilgrimages in India*. Berkeley and Los Angeles: University of California Press.
Blair, Harry W. 1979. *Voting, Caste, Community, Society: Explorations in Aggregated Data Analysis in India and Bangladesh*. Delhi: Young Asia Publications.

Blyn, George. 1966. *Agricultural Trends in India, 1891–1947: Output, Availability, and Productivity.* Philadelphia: University of Pennsylvania Press.

Boserup, Ester. 1965. *The Conditions of Agricultural Growth: The Economics of Agrarian Change under Population Pressure.* Chicago: Aldine.

Brasted, Howard. 1980. "Indian Nationalist Development and the Influence of Irish Home Rule, 1870–1886." *MAS* 14: 37–63.

Brenner, Robert. 1976. "Agrarian Class Structure and Economic Development in Pre-Industrial Europe." *Past and Present* 70: 30–75.

———. 1982. "The Agrarian Roots of European Capitalism." *Past and Present* 97: 16–113.

Brown, Judith M. 1972. *Gandhi's Rise to Power: Indian Politics, 1915–1922.* Cambridge: Cambridge University Press.

Browne, Ray B., ed. 1980. *Rituals and Ceremonies in Popular Culture.* Bowling Green, Ohio: Bowling Green University Popular Press.

Carroll, Lucy. 1975. "Caste, Social Change, and the Social Scientist: A Note on the Ahistorical Approach to Indian Social History." *JAS* 35: 63–84.

Catanach, I. J. 1970. *Rural Credit in Western India.* Berkeley and Los Angeles: University of California Press.

Chakrabarty, Dipesh. 1981. "Communal Riots and Labour: Bengal's Jute Mill-hands in the 1890s." *Past and Present* 91: 140–69.

Chandra, Bipan. 1966. *The Rise and Growth of Economic Nationalism in India: Economic Policies of Indian National Leadership, 1880–1905.* New Delhi: People's Publishing House.

———. 1979. *Nationalism and Colonialism in Modern India.* New Delhi: People's Publishing House.

Charlesworth, Neil. 1972. "The Myth of the Deccan Riots of 1875." *MAS* 6: 401–21.

———. 1979a. "The Russian Stratification Debate and India." *MAS* 13: 61–95.

———. 1979b. "Trends in Agricultural Performance of an Indian Province: The Bombay Presidency." In *Economy and Society,* eds. K. N. Chaudhuri and C. J. Dewey. Delhi: Oxford University Press.

———. 1982. *British Rule and the Indian Economy, 1800–1914.* London: Macmillan Press.

Chatterji, Basudev. 1981. "The Darogah and the Countryside: The Imposition of Police Control in Bengal and its Impact (1793–1837)." *IESHR* 18: 19–42.

Chattopadhyay, Basudeb. 1985. "The Penetration of Authority in the Interior: A Case-study of the Zamindari of Nakashipara, 1850–1860." *Peasant Studies* 12: 151–69.

Chaudhuri, Binay Bhushan. 1969a. "Agricultural Production in Bengal, 1850–1900: Co-existence of Decline and Growth." *Bengal Past and Present* 88: 152–205.

———. 1969b. "Rural Credit Relations in Bengal, 1859–1885." *IESHR* 6: 203–257.

———. 1976a. "The Agrarian Question in Bengal and the Government, 1850–1900." *Calcutta Historical Journal* 1: 51–62.

———. 1976b. "Agricultural Growth in Bengal and Bihar, 1770–1870: Growth of Cultivation Since the Famine of 1770." *Bengal Past and Present* 95: 290–340.

———. 1977. "Movement of Rent in Eastern India, 1793–1930." *Indian Historical Review* 3: 308–90.

———. 1984. "Eastern India." In *The Cambridge Economic History of India,* Vol. 1: *c. 1200–c. 1750,* eds. Tapan Raychaudhuri and Irfan Habib. Delhi: Orient Longman.

Chaudhuri, K. N., and Dewey, C. J. 1979. *Economy and Society: Essays in Indian Economic and Social History.* Delhi: Oxford University Press.

Chaudhuri, S. B. 1957. *Civil Rebellion in the Indian Mutinies*. Calcutta: World Press.
Choudhury, P. C. Roy. 1965. *Temples and Legends of Bihar*. Patna.
Chowdhury, Benoy. 1964. *Growth of Commercial Agriculture in Bengal (1757–1900)*. Calcutta: Indian Studies: Past and Present.
Claessen, J. M., and Skalnik, Peter, eds. 1981. *The Study of the State*. The Hague: Mouton.
Cohn, Bernard S. 1960. "The Initial British Impact in India: A Case Study of the Benares Region." *JAS* 19: 418–31.
———. 1962. "Political Systems in Eighteenth Century India: The Banaras Region." *Journal of American Oriental Society* 82: 312–20.
———. 1965. "Anthropological Notes on Disputes and Law in India." *American Anthropologist* 67: 82–122.
———. 1969. "Structural Change in Indian Rural Society." In *Land Control and Social Structure in Indian History*, ed. Robert Eric Frykenberg. Madison: University of Wisconsin Press.
———. 1979. "Rituals of Authority in a Colonial Society: The Imperial Assemblage at Delhi in 1877." Paper presented at Social Science Research Council Conference on Intermediate Political Linkages in South Asia, University of California, Berkeley, March 16–18.
Connell, John, Dasgupta, Biplab, Laishley, Roy, and Lipton, Michael. 1976. *Migration from Rural Areas: The Evidence from Village Studies*. Delhi: Oxford University Press.
Coser, Lewis A. 1982. "The Notion of Control in Sociological Theory." In *Social Control*, ed. Jack P. Gibbs. Beverly Hills, Calif.: Sage Press.
Crane, Robert I., and Barrier, N. Gerald, eds. 1981. *British Imperial Policy in India and Sri Lanka*. Columbia, Mo.: South Asia Books.
Cunningham, Hugh. 1977. "The Metropolitan Fairs: A Case Study of the Social Control of Leisure." In *Social Control in Britain*, ed. A. P. Donajgrodzki. Totowa, N.J.: Rowman & Littlefield.
Das, Arvind N., ed. 1982. "Agrarian Movements in India: Studies on 20th Century Bihar." *Journal of Peasant Studies* 9 (special issue): 1–152.
Datta, K. K. 1957. *Biography of Kunwar Singh and Amar Singh*. Patna: K. P. Jayaswal Research Institute.
———. 1970. *Anti-British Plots and Movements before 1857*. Meerut: Meenakshi.
De, Barun, ed. 1976. *Essays in Honour of Professor S. C. Sarkar*. New Delhi: People's Publishing House.
Desai, Meghnad, Rudolph, Susanne Hoeber, and Rudra, Ashok, eds. 1985. *Agrarian Power and Agricultural Productivity in South Asia*. Berkeley and Los Angeles: University of California Press.
Dewey, C. J. 1978. "*Patwari* and *Chaukidar*: Subordinate Officials and Reliability of India's Agricultural Statistics." In *The Imperial Impact*, ed. C. J. Dewey and A. J. Hopkins. London: Athlone Press.
Dewey, C. J., and Hopkins, A. J., eds. 1978. *The Imperial Impact: Studies in the Economic History of Africa and India*. London: Athlone Press.
Dhanagare, D. N. 1983. *Peasant Movements in India, 1920–1950*. Delhi: Oxford University Press.
Diehl, Katherine Smith, comp. 1971. *Primary Sources for 16th–19th Century Studies in Bengal, Orissa and Bihar*. Calcutta: American Institute of Indian Studies.
Dirks, Nicholas B. 1979. "The Structure and Meaning of Political Relations in a South Indian Little Kingdom." *Contributions to Indian Sociology* 13: 169–206.

Diwakar, R. R. 1959. *Bihar Through the Ages*. Calcutta: Orient Longmans.
Donajgrodzki, A. P., ed. 1977. *Social Control in Nineteenth Century Britain*. Totowa, N.J.: Rowman & Littlefield.
Dumont, Louis. 1970. *Homo Hierarchicus: An Essay on the Caste System*. Trans. by Mark Sainsbury. Chicago: University of Chicago Press.
Dutt, R. C. 1960. *The Economic History of India under Early British Rule*. 1901. Reprint, Delhi.
Emmer, P. C., and Wesseling, H. L., eds. 1979. *Reappraisals in Overseas History*. Leiden: Leiden University Press.
Firth, Raymond, and Yamey, B. S. 1963. *Capital, Saving and Credit in Peasant Societies*. Chicago: Aldine.
Fisher, C. M. 1976. "Indigo Plantations and Agrarian Society in North Bihar in the Nineteenth and Early Twentieth Centuries." Ph.D. dissertation, University of Cambridge.
Fox, Richard G. 1969. *From Zamindar to Ballot Box: Community Change in a North Indian Market Town*. Ithaca: Cornell University Press.
―――. 1971. *Kin, Clan, Raja and Rule: State-Hinterland Relations in Pre-Industrial India*. Berkeley and Los Angeles: University of California Press.
Fraser, Hugh. 1883. "Folklore from Eastern Gorakhpur." *Journal of Asiatic Society of Bengal* 52: 7–8.
Freitag, Sandria. 1978. " 'Natural Leaders,' Administrators and Social Control: Communal Riots in the United Provinces, 1870–1925." *South Asia*, n.s., 1: 27–41.
―――. 1979. "Religious Rites and Riots: From Community Identity to Communalism in U.P." Ph.D. dissertation. University of California, Berkeley.
―――. 1980. "Sacred Symbol as Mobilizing Ideology: The North Indian Search for a 'Hindu' Community." *Comparative Studies in Society and History* 22: 597–625.
Frykenberg, Robert Eric. 1965. *Guntur District, 1788–1848: History of Localizing Influence and Central Authority in South India*. London: Oxford University Press.
Frykenberg, Robert Eric, ed. 1969. *Land Control and Social Structure in Indian History*. Madison: University of Wisconsin Press.
Gallagher, John. 1973. "Congress in Decline: Bengal 1930 to 1939." *MAS* 7: 589–645.
Gibbs, Jack P., ed. 1982. *Social Control: Views from the Social Sciences*. Beverly Hills, Calif.: Sage Publications.
Glass, D. V., and Revelle, Roger, eds. 1972. *Population and Social Change*. London: Edwin Arnold.
Gough, Kathleen. 1974. "Indian Peasant Uprisings." *EPW* 9 (special issue): 1391–1412.
―――. 1978. "Agrarian Relations in Southeast India, 1750–1976." *Review* 2: 25–53.
Graves, Nancy B., and Graves, Theodore D. 1974. "Adaptive Strategies in Urban Migration." *Annual Review of Anthropology*, vol. 3, eds. Bernard J. Siegel et al. Palo Alto.
Guha, Ranajit. 1963. *A Rule of Property for Bengal: An Essay on the Idea of Permanent Settlement*. Paris: Mouton.
―――. 1983. *Elementary Aspects of Peasant Insurgency in Colonial India*. Delhi: Oxford University Press.
Guha, Ranajit, ed. 1982a. *Subaltern Studies I: Writings on South Asian History and Society*. Delhi: Oxford University Press.
―――, ed. 1982b. *Subaltern Studies II: Writings on South Asian History and Society*. Delhi: Oxford University Press.

———, ed. 1984. *Subaltern Studies III: Writings on South Asian History and Society*. Delhi: Oxford University Press.
Gupta, Ajit Das. 1972. "Study of the Historical Demography of India." In *Population and Social Change*, eds. D. V. Glass and Roger Revelle. London: Edwin Arnold.
Gupta, Ranajit Das. 1976. "Factory Labour in Eastern India: Sources of Supply, 1855–1946—Some Preliminary Findings." *IESHR* 13: 277–329.
Gustafson, W. Eric, and Jones, Kenneth W., eds. 1975. *Sources on Punjab History*. Delhi: Manohar.
Habib, Irfan. 1963. *The Agrarian System of Mughal India, 1556–1707*. London: Asia Publishing House.
———. 1969. "Potentialities of Capitalistic Development in the Economy of Mughal India." *Journal of Economic History* 29: 32–78.
———. 1982. *An Atlas of the Mughal Empire*. Delhi: Oxford University Press.
Hagen, James Ray. 1981. "Indigenous Society, the Political Economy, and Colonial Education in Patna District: A History of Social Change from 1811 to 1951 in Gangetic North India." Ph.D. dissertation, University of Virginia.
Hagen, James R., and Yang, Anand A. 1976. "Local Sources for the Study of Rural India: The 'Village Notes' of Bihar." *IESHR* 13: 75–84.
Hand, J. Reginald. 1894. *Early English Administration of Bihar, 1781–1785*. Calcutta: Bengal Secretariat Press.
Hauser, Walter. 1961. "The Bihar Provincial Kisan Sabha, 1929–1942: A Study of an Indian Peasant Movement." Ph.D. dissertation, University of Chicago.
———. 1963. "The Indian National Congress and Land Policy in the Twentieth Century." *IESHR* 1: 57–65.
———. 1983. "Patterns of Control and Mobilization in Gangetic North India." Paper presented at the Association for Asian Studies meeting, San Francisco, March 25–27.
Hauser, Walter, and Manor, James, eds. Forthcoming. *Two Faces of India: Social and Political Change in Bihar and Karnataka*.
Heesterman, J. C. 1978. "Was there an Indian Reaction? Western Expansion in Indian Perspective." In *Expansion and Reaction*, ed. H. L. Wesseling. Leiden: Leiden University Press.
Henningham, Stephen. 1979. "Contributions of Limited Violence to the Bihar Civil Disobedience Movement." *South Asia*, n.s., 2: 60–77.
———. 1982a. *Peasant Movements in Colonial India: North Bihar, 1917–1942*. Australian National University Monographs on South Asia no. 9. Canberra: Australian National University.
———. 1982b. "Quit India in Bihar and the Eastern United Provinces: The Dual Revolt." In *Subaltern Studies II*, ed. Ranajit Guha. Delhi: Oxford University Press.
———. 1983. "Bureaucracy and Control in India's Great Landed Estates: The Raj Darbhanga of Bihar, 1879 to 1950." *MAS* 17: 35–57.
Hill, John L. 1981. "A. P. MacDonnell and the Changing Nature of British Rule in India, 1885–1901." In *British Imperial Policy in India*, eds. Robert I. Crane and N. Gerald Barrier. Columbia, Mo.: South Asia Books.
Irschick, Eugene F. 1969. *Politics and Social Conflict in South India: The Non-Brahman Movement and Tamil Separatism, 1916–1929*. Berkeley and Los Angeles: University of California Press.

Islam, M. M. 1978. *Bengal Agriculture, 1920–1946: A Quantitative Study*. Cambridge: Cambridge University Press.
Jackson, J. A., ed. 1969. *Migration.* Cambridge: Cambridge University Press.
Jannuzi, F. Tomasson. 1974. *Agrarian Crisis in India: The Case of Bihar*. Austin: University of Texas Press.
Janowitz, Morris. 1978. *The Last Half-Century: Societal Change and Politics in America*. Chicago: University of Chicago Press.
Jha, Jata Shanker. 1962. "History of Darbhanga Raj." *Journal of Bihar Research Society* 48: 1–91.
———. 1972. *Biography of an Indian Patriot: Maharaja Lakshmishwar Singh of Darbhanga*. Patna: K. P. Jayaswal Institute.
Jones, Gareth Stedman. 1976. "From Historical Sociology to Theoretical History." *British Journal of Sociology* 27: 295–305.
———. 1977. "Class Expression versus Social Control? A Critique of Recent Trends in the Social History of 'Leisure'." *History Workshop* 4: 162–70.
Jones, Kenneth W. 1966. "The Bengali Elite in Post-Annexation Punjab: An Example of Inter-Regional Influence in 19th Century India." *IESHR* 3 (1966): 376–95.
Kaye, Harvey J. 1982. "Another Way of Seeing Peasants: The Work of John Berger." *Peasant Studies* 9: 85–105.
Kessinger, Tom G. 1974. *Vilyatpur, 1848–1968: Social and Economic Change in a North Indian Village*. Berkeley and Los Angeles: University of California Press.
Keyes, Charles F. 1983. "Introduction" to "Peasant Strategies in Asian Societies: Moral and Rational Economic Approaches—A Symposium." *JAS* 42: 753–68.
Klein, Ira. 1972. "Malaria and Mortality in Bengal, 1840–1921." *IESHR* 9: 132–60.
———. 1973. "Death in India, 1871–1921." *JAS* 32: 639–59.
Kling, Blair B. 1977. *The Blue Mutiny: The Indigo Disturbances in Bengal, 1859–1862*. Calcutta: Firma KLM.
Kosinski, Leszek A., and Prothero, R. Mansell, eds. 1975. *People on the Move: Studies on Internal Migration*. London: Methuen.
Krishnaswamy, S. 1966. "A Riot in Bombay, August 11, 1893: A Study in Hindu-Muslim Relations in Western India during the Late Nineteenth Century." Ph.D. dissertation, University of Chicago.
Kumar, Dharma. 1965. *Land and Caste in South India: Agricultural Labour in Madras Presidency in the Nineteenth Century*. Cambridge: Cambridge University Press.
Kumar, Dharma, ed. 1984. *The Cambridge Economic History of India*. Volume 2: *c. 1757–c. 1970*. Delhi: Orient Longman.
Kumar, Ravinder. 1968. *Western India in the Nineteenth Century*. London: Routledge & Kegan Paul.
Lambert, Richard D. 1952. "Hindu-Muslim Riots in India." Ph.D. dissertation, University of Pennsylvania.
Leach, E. R., ed. 1960. *Aspects of Caste in South India, Ceylon and North-West Pakistan*. Cambridge: Cambridge University Press.
Lee, Everett. 1969. "A Theory of Migration." In *Migration*, ed. J. A. Jackson. Cambridge: Cambridge University Press.
Leonard, Karen Isaksen. 1978. *Social History of an Indian Caste: The Kayasths of Hyderabad*. Berkeley and Los Angeles: University of California Press.
Libbee, M. J., and Sopher, D. E. 1975. "Marriage Migration in Rural India." In *People*

on the Move, eds. Leszek A. Kosinski and R. Mansell Prothero. London: Methuen.
Louis, Wm. Roger, ed. 1976. *Imperialism: The Robinson and Gallagher Controversy*. New York: New Viewpoints.
Low, D. A. 1973. *Lion Rampant: Essays in the Study of British Imperialism*. London: Frank Cass.
Low, D. A., ed. 1977. *Congress and the Raj*. Columbia, Mo.: South Asia Books.
Ludden, David. 1985. "Productive Power in Agriculture: A Survey of Work on the Local History of British India." In *Agrarian Power and Agricultural Productivity in South Asia*, eds. Meghnad Desai, Susanne Hoeber Rudolph, and Ashok Rudra. Berkeley and Los Angeles: University of California Press.
McAlpin, Michelle Burge. 1975. "The Effects of Expansion of Markets on Rural Income Distribution in Nineteenth Century India." *Explorations in Economic History* 12: 289–302.
MacDougall, John. 1980. "Two Models of Power in Contemporary Rural India." *Contributions to Indian Sociology*, n.s., 14: 77–94.
Macfarlane, Alan. 1977. *Reconstructing Historical Communities*. Cambridge: Cambridge University Press.
McLane, John R. 1963. "Peasants, Money-Lenders and Nationalists at the End of the Nineteenth Century." *IESHR* 1: 66–73.
———. 1977. *Indian Nationalism and the Early Congress*. Princeton: Princeton University Press.
Marriott, McKim, ed. 1955. *Village India: Studies in the Little Community*. Chicago: University of Chicago Press.
Marshall, P. J. 1976. *East Indian Fortunes: The British in Bengal in the Eighteenth Century*. Oxford: Clarendon Press.
Marx, K., and Engels, F. N.d. *The First Indian War of Independence, 1857–1859*. Reprint. Moscow: Foreign Languages Publishing House.
Mathur, J. C. 1964. *Drama in Rural India*. New York: Asia Publishing House.
Mauss, Marcel. 1974. *The Gift; Form and Functions of Exchanges in Archaic Societies*. Reprint. London: Routledge & Kegan Paul.
Metcalf, Thomas. 1979. *Land, Landlords, and the British Raj: Northern India in the Nineteenth Century*. Berkeley and Los Angeles: University of California Press.
Mintz, Sidney W. 1973. "A Note on the Definition of Peasantries." *Journal of Peasant Studies* 1: 91–106.
Mishra, Girish. 1966. "Indigo Plantation and the Agrarian Relations in Champaran during the Nineteenth Century." *IESHR* 3: 332–57.
———. 1978. *Agrarian Problems of Permanent Settlement: A Case Study of Champaran*. New Delhi: People's Publishing House.
Misra, Baniprasana. 1975. "Factory Labour during the Early Years of Industrialization: An Appraisal in the Light of the Indian Factory Commission, 1890." *IESHR* 12: 203–228.
Misra, Bankey Bihari. 1959. *The Central Administration of the East India Company, 1773–1834*. Manchester: Manchester University Press.
Misra, Shree Govind. 1970. *History of Bihar*. New Delhi: Munshiram Manoharlal.
Mitra, K. P. 1944. "The Office of the Qanungo in Bihar." *Indian History Records Proceedings* 21: 17–19.
Moore, Barrington, Jr. 1966. *Social Origins of Dictatorship and Democracy. Lord and Peasant in the Making of the Modern World*. Boston: Beacon.

Moorhouse, H. F. 1978. "The Marxist Theory of the Labour Aristocracy." *Social History* 3: 61–82.
———. 1979. "History, Sociology and the Quiescence of the British Working Class: A Reply to Reid." *Social History* 4: 481–90.
Morris, Morris D. 1965. *The Emergence of an Industrial Labor Force in India: A Study of the Bombay Cotton Mills, 1854–1947.* Berkeley and Los Angeles: University of California Press.
———. 1974. "The Population of All-India, 1800–1951." *IESHR* 11: 303–13.
Morris, Morris D., et al. 1969. *Indian Economy in the Nineteenth-Century: A Symposium.* Delhi: Indian Economic and Social History Association.
Mukherjee, Nilmani. 1975. *A Bengal Zamindar: Jayakrishna Mukherjee of Uttarpara and His Times, 1808–1888.* Calcutta: Firma K. L. Mukhopadhyay.
Munholland, J. Kim. 1981. " 'Collaboration Strategy' and the French Pacification of Tonkin, 1885–1897." *The Historical Journal* 24: 629–50.
Muraskin, William A. 1976. "The Social-Control Theory in American History: A Critique." *Journal of Social History* 9: 559–69.
Musgrave, P. J. 1972. "Landlords and Lords of the Land: Estate Management and Social Control in Uttar Pradesh, 1860–1920." *MAS* 6: 257–75.
———. 1978. "Rural Credit and Rural Society in the United Provinces, 1860–1920." In *The Imperial Impact,* eds. C. J. Dewey and A. J. Hopkins. London: Athlone Press.
———. 1983. "A Reply." *MAS* 17: 56–57.
Nairn, Tom. 1964. "The British Political Elite." *New Left Review* 23: 19–25.
Ness, Gayle D., and Stahl, William. 1977. "Western Imperialist Armies in Asia." *Comparative Studies in Society and History* 19: 2–29.
Omvedt, Gail. 1980. "Migration in Colonial India: The Articulation of Feudalism and Capitalism by the Colonial State." *Journal of Peasant Studies* 7: 185–212.
Ostor, Akos. 1980. *The Play of the Gods: Locality, Ideology, Structure, and Time in the Festivals of a Bengali Town.* Chicago: University of Chicago Press.
Palit, Chittabrata. 1975. *Tensions in Bengal Rural Society: Landlords, Planters and Colonial Rule, 1830–1860.* Calcutta: Progressive Publishers.
Pandey, Gyanendra. 1977. "A Rural Base for Congress: the United Provinces, 1920–40." In *Congress and the Raj,* ed. D. A. Low. Columbia, Mo.: South Asia Books.
Perlin, Frank. 1978. "Of White Whale and Countrymen in the Eighteenth Century Maratha Deccan: Extended Class Relations, Rights, and the Problem of Rural Autonomy under the Old Regime." *Journal of Peasant Studies* 5: 172–237.
———. 1980. "Precolonial South Asia and Western Penetration in the Seventeenth to Nineteenth Centuries: A Problem of Epistemological Status." *Review* 4: 267–306.
———. 1981. "The Precolonial Indian State in History and Epistemology: A Reconstruction of Societal Formation in the Western Deccan from the Fifteenth to the Early Nineteenth Century." In *The Study of the State,* ed. Henri J. M. Claessen and Peter Skalnik. Hague: Mouton.
———. 1983. "Proto-Industrialization and Pre-Colonial South Asia." *Past and Present* 98: 30–95.
Phillips, C. H., ed. 1961. *Historians of India, Pakistan and Ceylon.* London: Oxford University Press.
Popkin, Samuel L. 1979. *The Rational Peasant: The Political Economy of Rural Society in Vietnam.* Berkeley and Los Angeles: University of California Press.

Pouchepadass, Jacques. 1974. "Local Leaders and the Intelligentsia in the Champaran Satyagraha (1917): A Study in Peasant Mobilization." *Contributions to Indian Sociology*, n.s., 8: 67–87.

———. 1980a. "L'endettement paysan dans le Bihar Colonial." *Purusartha* 4: 165–205.

———. 1980b. "Peasant Classes in Twentieth Century Agrarian Movements in India." In *Peasants in History: Essays in Honour of Daniel Thorner*. Calcutta: Oxford University Press.

Prasad, Leela. 1981. *Opposition to British Supremacy in Bihar—1757–1803*. Patna: Janaki Prakashan.

Prasad, Pradhan H. 1979. "Caste and Class in Bihar." *EPW* 14: 481–84.

Prasad, Satyanarain. 1979. "Munshi Pearey Lal and Social Reform Movement in Bihar." *Journal of Historical Research* 12: 71–80.

Price, Pamela G. 1979. "Rajadharma in 19th Century South India: Land, Litigation and Largess in Ramnad Zamindari." *Contributions to Indian Sociology* 13: 207–39.

Pryor, Robin J. 1975. "Migration and the Process of Modernization." In *People on the Move*, ed. Leszek A. Kosinski and R. Mansell Prothero. London: Methuen.

——— 1977. "The Migrant to the City in Southeast Asia—Can, and Should We Generalise?" *Asian Profile* 5: 63–89.

Quereshi, Ishtiaq Husain. 1966. *The Administration of the Mughal Empire*. Karachi: University of Karachi Press.

Ray, Rajat. 1973. "The Crisis of Bengal Agriculture, 1870–1927—The Dynamics of Immobility." *IESHR* 10: 244–79.

Ray, Ratnalekha. 1979. *Change in Bengal Agrarian Society, c 1760–1850*. New Delhi: Manohar.

———. 1984. "Landlords and Peasants: A Historiographical View of Rural Bengal from Precolonial to Colonial Times." *Peasant Studies* 11: 236–47.

Raychaudhuri, Tapan. 1969. "Permanent Settlement in Operation: Bakaraganj District, East Bengal." In *Land Control in Indian History*, ed. Robert Eric Frykenberg. Madison: University of Wisconsin Press.

Raychaudhuri, Tapan, and Habib, Irfan. 1984. *The Cambridge Economic History of India*. Vol. I: *c. 1200–c. 1750*. Delhi: Orient Longman.

Raye, N. N. 1927. *The Annals of the Early English Settlement in Bihar*. Calcutta: Kamala Book Depot.

Reid, Alastair. 1978. "Politics and Economics in the Formation of the British Working Class: A Response to H. F. Moorhouse." *Social History* 3: 347–61.

Richards, J. F. 1981. "Mughal State Finance and the Pre-Modern World Economy." *Comparative Studies in Society and History* 23: 285–308.

Richards, J. F., Hagen, James R., and Haynes, Edward S. 1985. "Changing Land Use in Bihar, Punjab and Haryana, 1850–1970." *MAS* 19: 699–732.

Robb, Peter. 1979. "Hierarchy and Resources: Peasant Stratification in Late Nineteenth Century Bihar." *MAS* 13: 97–126.

Robinson, David J., ed. 1979. *Social Fabric and Spatial Structure in Colonial Latin America*. Syracuse: Syracuse University Press.

Robinson, F. C. R. 1971. "Consultation and Control: the United Provinces' Government and its Allies, 1860–1906." *MAS* 5: 313–36.

———. 1973. "Municipal Government and Muslim Separatism in the United Provinces, 1883 to 1916." *MAS* 7: 389–441.

Robinson, Ronald. 1978. "European Imperialism and Indigenous Reactions in British West Africa." In *Expansion and Reaction*, ed. H. L. Wesseling. Leiden: Leiden University Press.

Rothermund, Dietmar. 1977. "A Survey of Rural Migration and Land Reclamation in India, 1885." *Journal of Peasant Studies* 4: 230–42.

———. 1978. *Government, Landlord, and Peasant in India: Agrarian Relations under British Rule, 1865–1935*. Wiesbaden: Franz Steiner Verlag.

Rudolph, Susanne Hoeber, and Rudolph, Lloyd I. R. with Singh, Mohan. 1975. "A Bureaucratic Lineage in Princely India: Elite Formation and Conflict in a Patrimonial System." *JAS* 34: 717–53.

Saha, Panchanan. 1970. *Emigration of Indian Labour, 1834–1900*. Delhi: People's Publishing House.

Sahlins, Marshall. 1972. *Stone Age Economics*. Chicago: Aldine.

Saran, P. 1972. *The Provincial Government of the Mughals, 1526–1658*. Bombay: Asia Publishing House.

Sarkar, Jadunath. 1963. *Mughal Administration*. 5th ed. Calcutta: Sarkar.

Scott, James C. 1976. *The Moral Economy of the Peasant: Rebellion and Subsistence in Southeast Asia*. New Haven: Yale University Press.

Seal, Anil. 1973. "Imperialism and Nationalism in India." *MAS* 7: 321–47.

Shanin, Teodor. 1971. "Peasantry: Delineation of Sociological Concept and a Field of Study." *European Journal of Sociology* 12: 289–300.

———. 1979. "Defining Peasants: Conceptualizations and De-conceptualizations Old and New in a Marxist Debate." *Peasant Studies* 8: 38–60.

Siddiqi, M. H. 1978. *Agrarian Unrest in North India: The United Provinces (1918–1922)*. Delhi: Vikas.

Siddiqi, Noman Ahmad. 1970. *Land Revenue Administration under the Mughals (1700–1750)*. Bombay: Asia Publishing House.

Singer, Milton. 1972. *When a Great Tradition Modernizes: An Anthropological Approach to Indian Civilization*. New York: Praeger.

Singh, Rana P. B. 1977. *Clan Settlements in the Saran Plain (Middle Ganga Valley): A Study in Cultural Geography*. Varanasi: National Geographic Society of India, Research Publications Series, no. 18.

Sinha, B. K. 1961. "The Office of the Qanungo in Bihar—Its Abolition and Restoration following the Permanent Settlement." *Bengal Past and Present* 86: 10–16.

Sinha, Bindeshwari Prasad, ed. 1974. *Comprehensive History of Bihar*, vol. I, part I. Patna: Kashi Prasad Jayaswal Research Institute.

Skinner, G. William. 1964. "Marketing and Social Structure in Rural China." (Part I) *JAS* 24: 3–43.

———. 1971. "Chinese Peasants and the Closed Community: An Open and Shut Case." *Comparative Studies in Society and History* 13: 270–81.

Srinivas, M. N. 1959. "The Dominant Caste in Rampura." *American Anthropologist* 61: 1–15.

———. 1962. *Caste in Modern India*. Bombay: Asia Publishing House.

Standing, Guy. 1981. "Migration and Modes of Exploitation: Social Origins of Immobility and Mobility." *Journal of Peasant Studies* 8: 173–211.

Stevenson, John. 1977. "Social Control and the Prevention of Riots in England, 1789–1829." In *Social Control in Britain*, ed. A. P. Donajgrodzki. Totowa, N.J.: Rowman & Littlefield.

Stokes, Eric. 1959. *The English Utilitarians and India*. Oxford: Clarendon Press.
———. 1978. *The Peasant and the Raj: Studies in Agrarian Society and Peasant Rebellion in Colonial India*. Cambridge: Cambridge University Press.
Taniguchi, Shinkichi. 1981. "The Patni System—A Modern Origin of the 'Sub-Infeudation' of Bengal in the Nineteenth Century." *Hitotsubashi Journal of Economics* 22: 32–60.
Tea District Labour Association, Calcutta. 1924. *Hand-Book of Castes and Tribes Employed on Tea Estates in North-East India*. Calcutta.
Tinker, Hugh. 1974. *A New System of Slavery: The Export of Indian Labour Overseas, 1830–1920*. London: Oxford University Press.
Tiwari, Udai Narain. 1960. *The Origin and Development of Bhojpur*. Calcutta: Asiatic Society.
Turner, Victor. 1974. *Drama, Fields and Metaphors: Symbolic Action in Human Society*. Ithaca: Cornell University Press.
Turner, Victor, and Turner, Edith. 1978. *Image and Pilgrimage in Christian Culture: Anthropological Perspectives*. Oxford: Basil Blackwell.
Varady, Robert Gabriel. 1979. "North Indian Banjaras: Their Evolution as Transporters." *South Asia*, n.s., 2 & 3: 1–18.
Vicziany, Marika. 1979. "The Deindustrialization of India in the Nineteenth Century: A Methodological Critique of Amiya Kumar Bagchi." *IESHR* 16: 105–46.
Wallerstein, Immanuel. 1974. *The Modern World System: Capitalist Agriculture and the Origins of the European World-Economy in the Sixteenth Century*. New York: Academic Press.
———. 1979. *The Capitalist World-Economy*. Cambridge: Cambridge University Press.
Washbrook, D. A. 1976. *The Emergence of Provincial Politics: The Madras Presidency, 1870–1920*. Cambridge: Cambridge University Press.
———. 1981. "Law, State and Society in Colonial India." *MAS* 15: 649–721.
Watkins, C. Ken. 1975. *Social Control*. London: Longman.
Weiner, Myron. 1978. *Sons of the Soil: Migration and Ethnic Conflict in India*. Princeton: Princeton University Press.
Wesseling, H. L., ed. 1978. *Expansion and Reaction*. Leiden: Leiden University Press.
Whitcombe, Elizabeth. 1971. *Agrarian Conditions in Northern India*. Vol. I: *The United Provinces under British Rule, 1860–1900*. Berkeley and Los Angeles: University of California Press.
Wolf, Eric R. 1971. *Peasant Wars of the Twentieth Century*. London: Faber and Faber.
Yang, Anand A. 1979a. "An Institutional Shelter: The Court of Wards in Late Nineteenth-Century Bihar." *MAS* 13: 247–64.
———. 1979b. "Peasants on the Move: A Study of Internal Migration in India." *Journal of Interdisciplinary History* 10: 38–45.
———. 1979c. "Social History and Local Records: Sources for the Study of Modern Bihar." *Indian Archives* 28: 1–23.
———. 1980. "Sacred Symbol and Sacred Space in Rural India: Community Mobilization in the 'Anti-Cow Killing' Riot of 1893." *Comparative Studies in Society and History* 22: 576–96.
———. 1987. "A Conversation of Rumors: The Language of Popular *Mentalités* in Late Nineteenth Century Colonial India." *Journal of Social History* 20: 485–505.
———. Forthcoming. "Guardians of the Raj: The Police in Colonial India, Saran District, 1765–1922." In *Two Faces of India*, ed. Walter Hauser and James Manor.

Yang, Anand A., ed. 1985. *Crime and Criminality in British India*. Tucson: University of Arizona Press.
Zachariah, K. C. 1964. *A Historical Study of Internal Migration in the Indian Sub-Continent, 1901-1931*. New York: Asia Publishing House.

VERNACULAR SOURCES

Vernacular sources have yet to be tapped in a significant way by historians of modern India. Both the India Office Library and the British Library have rich collections of nineteenth- and early twentieth-century materials.

Abha (Abha Sahitya Parisad, Sonepur Ka Sandeshbahak Patr), *Sonepur Ankh* [Special issue on Sonepur], May 1956.
Aggarwala, B. P. 1922. *Aggarwala Vyapar Darpan, Bihar aur Orissa* [The Aggarwala Trade Guide, Bihar and Orissa]. Muzaffarpur: Vijaya Press.
Gosain, Bhikhari. 1983(?). *Bidesia Natak* [Bidesia Play]. Banaras: Guluprasad Kedarnath Booksellers.
Harihar Kshetra Mahatamya [The Greatness of Harihar Kshetra]. 1924. Gaya: Prabhu Narayan Misra.
Husain Khan, Ghulam. 1902. *A Translation of the Seir Mutaqherin; or View of Modern Times, being an History of India*. Trans. Nota-Manus. 4 vols. Calcutta: T. D. Chatterjee.
Jagopakarak. 1871. (Published at the behest of Maharajadhiraj Sriyut Radha Prasad Singh Bahadur of Dumraon). Patna.
Lala, Sangama. 1894. *Banshvali Chainpur ke Babuon ki* [Genealogy of Chainpur babus]. Kashi: Bharatijivan Yantralaya.
Majhauli, Lalkhadg Bahadur Mal. 1881. "Bishen Kshatri ki Utpati aur os bansh ke rajao ke kuch itihas [The Origins of the Bishen Rajputs and Some History of its Rajas]." *Kshatriyapatrika* 1.
Thakur, Bhikhari. 1931(?). *Asli Bhikhari ka Bidesia Natak* [Bidesia Play of the Real Bhikhari]. Patna: Kanahiya Lal Bookseller.
———. 1931. *Asli Bhikhari ka Bidesia Natak*. Gaya: Ramchandra Chandradev Bookseller.
Upadhyya, Krishnadev. 1960. *Bhojpur Lok Sahitya ka Addhyan* [A Study of Bhojpuri Folk Literature]. Varanasi: Hindi Pracharaka Pustukalya.
'Vinod', Baijnath Singh. 1958. *Bhojpuri Lok Sahitya: Ek Addhyan* [Bhojpuri Folk Literature: A Study]. Patna: Gyanpati.

INTERVIEWS

Ansorge, Sir Eric Cecil. Assistant magistrate and collector, Saran, Dec. 1911–Jan. 1913. Gerards' Cross, Bucks, England, May 20, 1973.
Askari, Syed Hasad. Professor of History, Patna University, and descendant of Kujhwa zamindari. Patna, May 20–21, 1974.
Davies, V. E. Ex-Bihar civil servant. London, England, May 8, 1973.
Jain, Prasoon Dutt. Great-grandson of Rai Bahadur Gulab Chand, Chapra, May 19, 1974.
Kemp, Arthur Hugh. District magistrate of Saran, March 1938–Oct. 1940. Boars Hill, Oxford, England, June 3, 1973.
Mansfield, P. T. Assistant Settlement officer, north Bihar, Oct. 20, 1916–March 1917. Witham, Essex, England, July 31, 1973.

Sahi, Bishwanath Pratap. Descendant of cadet line of Hathwa. Hathwa village, June 22, 1974.
Sahi, Gouri Shanker Prasad. Descendant of one branch of the Chainpur family. Chainpur Kothi, Patna, June 10, 1974.
Sahi, Hari Surendra. Descendant of the Manjha family. Rusi Kothi, Chapra, May 1974.
Sahi, Maharaja Kumar Brajeshwar Prasad. Uncle of the present Hathwa maharaja. Hathwa Kothi, Patna, Dec. 1973.
Sahi, S. P. Descendant of the Bagoura family. Patna, May 22, 1974.
Sinha, Rajandhari. Hathwa estate manager, Sept. 1938–Dec. 1944. Patna, May 23, 1974.

Index

Abwabs. *See* Cesses
Agriculture, 31–52; commercialization of, 37–40; extension of cultivation in, 34–42; and population, 34–42; subsistence, 48–52; technology of, 40. *See also* Harvest calendar
Ahirs, 45–47; as chaukidars, 104; as deserters, 187; as migrants, 195–96; occupations of, 47; as rioters, 217; as tenants, 45
Amla, 157; in Hathwa raj, 130–32, 153, 168
Amnour estate, 46, 73, 159; history of, 57
Awadh, 61, 63, 64; taluqdars of, 231

Bagoura estate, 56, 68, 73, 75, 156, 226; history of, 60–61
Banaras, 57, 64, 67; Raja of, 76. *See also* Chait Singh
Banias, 44–47; as landholders, 44, 172; as moneylenders, 171; occupations of, 47
Barharia estate, 56, 59, 63, 73, 226
Basantpur: Cow Riots in, 220–21; migrants from, thana, 194
Bengal: estate management in, 231; landholding system in, 230, 233–34; as migration destination, 192–94, 195–99, 200–203, 235
Bengalis: and Court of Wards, 88, 124–25; and Hathwa estate, 119, 124–25
Béteille, André, 7
Bettiah estate, 26, 62, 73, 76, 143; contrast with Hathwa estate, 152, 233; estate management, 233; relations with Hathwa estate, 143–44
Bhars, 56–57
Bhikhari Thakur, 198–99
Bhojpur and Bhojpuri culture, 198–99, 205, 236
Bhorey, 141; Brahmins of, 141, 233; desertions from, 184; riots in, 222–23
Bhumihar Brahmins, 44–46, 55–61, 119; as landholders, 44, 46, 61, 74–75; as migrants, 195; as moneylenders, 171; occupations of, 46; settlement patterns of, 57; as tenants, 45, 46, 50
Bihar Landholders Association, 27, 72
Birtdars, 141–43, 219
Boserup, Ester, 42
Brahmins, 44–46; of Bhorey, 141, 223; as deserters, 188; as landholders, 44; as migrants, 195; as moneylenders, 170–71; as tenants, 45, 50
Brenner, Robert, 42
Bujahawan Misra, 141–46, 219

Calcutta, 21; as migration destination, 197, 198–99, 201
Caste: as analytical unit, 7, 43–44; dominant, 171; and landholding, 43–48. See also *specific caste names*
Cesses: illegal, 165–68
Chainpur: estate, 46, 56, 68, 72–73, 157, 158–59, 226; history of, 59–61, 74–76; population of, 34
Chait Singh, 64, 67–69; rebellion of, 67–68; and Hathwa, 64, 68; and other district landholders, 68
Chamars, 48, 50; as chaukidars, 104; and differential rent rates, 166; as migrants, 195
Champaran district, 9, 31, 32, 68, 71, 110; chaukidars in, 105; desertions to, 187; Hathwa interests in, 151; migration to, 192–93, 197, 200; Permanent Settlement in, 227; rice cultivation in, 37; Satyagraha, 237
Chapra, 13, 91, 95; chaukidars in, 105; indigo in, 211; market, 47; population of, 34–35, 40–41; rent rates in, subdivision, 49; subdivision, 31, 96; town, 22; landholders of, 73
Charity, 2; and landholders, 122–23
Chatterdhari Sahi, 69, 73–74, 83, 119, 142, 145–46, 203. *See also* Hathwa estate: maharaja of

Chaudhuri, B. B., 175
Chaukidars, 48, 90, 103-11, 207, 230; and crime, 106; and police, 103-6, 110; and riots, 217; socioeconomic backgrounds of, 104, 107, 109-10; wages of, 104-5. *See also* Panchayets: chaukidari
Cheros, 56-57
Chirand estate. *See* Goolera estate
Class: as analytical unit, 1-2, 7, 43-44
Cohn, Bernard, 27, 72-73
Collaboration and Collaborators. *See* Control: local-level
Control: colonial, 6, 70-89, 90-111, 225-39; definition of, 1-2; and hegemony, 2; local-level, 3-4, 6, 215-21, 223-24, 225-39; metaphors of, 13; and moneylending, 170-71; social, 1-2; strategies of local, 161-77; village-level, 7, 129-31, 152-53, 215-21, 223-24, 230-35
Cow Protection: Movement, 18, 219-21, 224, 237-38; Riots, 71-72, 86, 91, 108, 219-21
Credit: Manipulation, 169-76; System, 7, 173-75. *See also* Moneylenders
Crime: and chaukidars, 106; and migration, 208-9; and protest, 208-9, 236; statistics, 212-13
Cropping patterns, 36-42 and landholders, 168; nonfood, 37-42
Crowds. *See* Riots
Cultivation. *See* Agriculture

Dacoits, 209
Dalrymple, F. A. E., 143-46
Dampier, W., 143-46
Darbhanga: chaukidars in, 110; and Court of Wards, 83-84, 85-86, 88; estate, 26-27, 83-84, 231; migrants to, 192, 197, 200; rice cultivation in, 37
Dashara, 105; as a festival of landholders, 72, 115-17, 122-23, 137, 160
Deccan Riots of 1875, 172, 217
Decennial Settlement. *See* Permanent Settlement
Desertions: definition of, 181; of 1879, 146-51, 153, 185-90, 204; and famines, 182-83, 189, 204; and floods, 182-83; from Hathwa estate, 182-90, 204; and indigo cultivation, 183-84, 204, 235; and migration, 181, 188, 204-5, 235; and moneylending, 184; as peasant option, 181-90, 204-5, 235; and population, 182-83; and rent rates, 183-84,

188-90, 204, 235; socioeconomic backgrounds of people involved in, 183, 184, 186-88
Development Cycle of estates, 59-61
Diara lands, 36; in Gopalganj subdivision, 34
Dumont, Louis, 43
Dumraon estate, 26; and Cow Riots, 86
Durbar, 27, 73
Dusadhs, 48, 50; as chaukidars, 104, 110
Dutt family, 88, 124-25

Estate, definition of, 6
Estate management: of Bettiah estate, 152, 233; direct system (khas) of, 135-38, 159, 233-35; of estates in other regions, 233-35; of Hathwa estate, 126-38, 232-35; intermediary system of, 126-34, 137-38; of large estates, 155-77, 159; of small estates, 155-77. *See also* Thikadars

Fairs, 18-19, 20, 29-30. *See also* Sonepur Mela
Famine: and crime, 209; and desertions, 182-83, 189, 204; of 1769-1770, 31, 34; of 1866, 93-94, 182-83, 207; of 1873-74, 40, 86, 183, 189, 207
Fateh Sahi, 62-69, 75, 80, 119, 142-44, 145, 152, 226; and birtdars, 142-43; and desertions, 182; Rebellion of, 62-69, 226, 229, 231. *See also* Huseypur
Festivals, 14-21, 72, 105. *See also* Dashara; Fairs
Fisher, C., 39
Fox, Richard, 59, 60, 156
Frykenberg, R. E., 9, 230-31

Gallagher, J. A., 3
Gandak river, 9, 14, 17, 47, 56, 57, 193
Gandhi, Mahatma, 211, 222-23, 237
Ganges river, 9, 14, 56, 193
Gaurakshini Sabha. *See* Cow Protection
Gaya district: chaukidars in, 110; migration to, 192
Gogra river, 9, 56
Gomastahs, 135-37; in Hathwa estate, 135-37
Goolera estate, 56, 73, 77-78, 81, 226; and Court of Wards, 81
Gopalganj: expansion of cultivation in, subdivision, 35; market, 47; population of, subdivision, 34, 35, 96, 176; rents in, subdivision, 49; subdivision, 31, 34
Goraits, 161

INDEX

Gorakhpur district, 9, 22, 34, 58, 63–66; and Bhojpuri culture, 198; birtdars of, 143, 145; collective violence in, 222; desertions to, 146, 184, 187; Hathwa interests in, 151; migration to, 192–93
Grierson, George A., 202, 203
Guntur district, 9, 95, 230–31

Habib, Irfan, 5–6, 182
Hajipur, 14, 15
Harihar Kshetra Mela. *See* Sonepur: Mela
Harvest calendar, 36–37, 199–200; and cesses, 168; and migration, 42, 199–200, 235
Hathwa: Market, 121–22; Village, 95–96, 119
Hathwa Estate, 49, 117–18, 151; and Banaras, 122; and Bengalis, 119, 124–25; cadet line of, 73–74, 151; and charity, 122–23, 124; and Court of Wards, 80–82, 123–24, 146; desertions from, 146–51, 182–90; and education, 120, 122–23; estate management system of, 80, 85, 119–20, 123–38, 139–41, 149–51, 151–54, 232–35; history of, 55–69, 73–75, 141–46, 229, 231; and indigo, 132–34, 138, 141, 219; legal system of, 151; maharaja of, 6, 19, 43, 46, 72–73, 220 (*see also* Chatterdhari Sahi; Krishna Pratap Sahi); and rent rates, 149, 153–54, 165–66; and temples, 120, 122; tenant rights in, 151–54
Hauser, Walter, 18
Huseypur: history of, 55–69, 74–75, 119, 226; Rebellion, 62–69, 226, 229, 231. *See also* Fateh Sahi; Hathwa

Indebtedness. *See* Credit; Moneylenders
Indian National Congress, 18, 211, 222–24, 237–38
Indigo, 36–40; in Champaran district, 237; and desertions, 183–84, 204, 235; in Hathwa estate, 132–34, 138, 141, 219; labor demands of, 200; and landholders, 211; peasant attitudes toward, 40, 183–84, 208; planters, 19; planters and dispute settlements, 162; planters and thikadars, 132–34, 138, 141; riots, 217–19
Interest, rates of. *See* Credit; Moneylenders
Irrigation, 40

Jeth-raiyats, 7, 140; in Hathwa, 116; and thikadars, 140, 159–61. *See also* Thikadars

Kayasths, 44–46, 119; as landholders, 44, 46, 159; as legal agents of landholders, 158; as moneylenders, 171; occupations of, 46; as patwaris, 101; as tenants, 45
Kessinger, Tom G., 9
Khaira estate, 46, 75; history of, 60
Khajhua estate, 73
Khas system. *See* Estate management: direct system
Kisan Sabha, Bihar Provincial, 18, 223, 238
Koeris, 45–47; as deserters, 187; and differential rent rates, 166; as migrants, 196; as moneylenders, 171; as tenants, 45, 47, 187
Krishna Pratap Sahi, 115–16, 122, 125, 139, 187–88; attitudes toward thikadars, 133, 139; religious outlook of, 122. *See also* Hathwa estate: maharaja of
Kurmis, 45–47; as deserters, 187; and differential rent rates, 166; as migrants, 196; as patwaris, 101; as tenants, 45, 47, 187

Land: holdings and caste, 44–48; revenue in Mughal period, 57; revenue and rent, 52, 165; revenue at time of Permanent Settlement, 55–56; sales and transfers, 174–76
Landless laborers, 48–52
Law, 91, 162–65; as strategy of control, 162–65
Livestock: and melas, 28–29; at Mirganj market, 122

MacDonnell, A. P., 41, 103, 148–49, 181–82, 185, 186, 189, 209
Mahajans. *See* Moneylenders
Majhauli estate: 55, 58–59, 65, 68–69, 73; history of, 58–59
Maksudpur estate, 76
Maliks: British attitudes toward, 155; definition of, 6, 7; as moneylenders, 169–76; as rioters, 215–21; in Sonepur thana, 156–57; and thikadars, 158–61. *See also* Thikadars
Manjha estate, 56, 73, 76, 157, 158, 226; history of, 59–61, 76
Manjhi: estate, 56, 73, 157, 158–59, 226; history of, 76–77; population of, thana, 34; Rajput settlement pattern in, thana, 57
Markets: and marketing network, 7, 15, 47; and thikadars, 129–30
Mashrak: indigo in, thana, 211; landholder of, 73, market, 47; migrants from, thana, 194–95; moneylenders of, thana, 171–72; population of, 34–35
Migration: to Bengal, 192–94, 195–99, 200–203, 235; and crime, 208–9; definition

of, 181; and desertions, 181, 188, 204–5, 235; destinations, India, 191–99, 235; destinations, overseas, 191, 194, 205; female, 191, 193–94, 201; and harvest calendar, 42, 199–200, 235; incomes from, 196–99, 204–5; and indigo, 200; internal, 33, 52, 204–5, 235; landholder attitudes toward, 203–4; marriage, 193; as peasant option, 194–205, 235–36; and population, 33; and prices, 52; socioeconomic backgrounds of people involved in, 195–96; and transportation, 199; volume of, 190–94, 235
Military, 62, 65–66, 68, 91, 226, 229–30; recruits from district, 191; role in suppressing 1844 riots, 145
Mirganj: expansion of cultivation in, thana, 36; market, 47, 121–22; moneylenders in, thana, 171; population of, 34–35; thana, 36
Mohurrirs, 85, 152
Moneylenders, 169–76; and agriculture, 39–40; in Bengal, 172; in Deccan, 172; in Muzaffarpur district, 170; and rates of interest, 172–74; socioeconomic backgrounds of, 169–72, 175–76; and thikadars, 139–40, 160–61, 169–76; in U.P., 172, 176; as village-level controllers, 171
Mughal Empire, 5–6, 15, 55, 57, 60, 61, 95, 182, 234
Mukhtars, 151
Musgrave, P. J., 118–19, 129–30
Muslims, 18, 44–45, 48, 119; as landholders, 44, 61; as moneylenders, 170–71; as patwaris, 101; settlement patterns of, 57–58; as tenants, 45–46
Mutiny/Rebellion of 1857, 3–4, 30, 71, 75, 91, 93, 119, 157, 172
Muzaffarpur district, 9, 14, 15, 25, 34, 110; chaukidars in, 110; Hathwa interests in, 151; indigo in, 218; migration to, 192–93, 197, 200; rice cultivation in, 37

Narrowney zamindars, 64, 67
Nationalism, 30, 222–24, 237–39
Nuniyas, 47, 50; as migrants, 195–96

O'Donnell, Charles James, 86, 146–51, 186, 207
Opium, 38–39

Panchayets: caste, 161; chaukidari, 106, 108–9; definition of, 106; village, 161
Parsa: estate, 46, 72–73, 75, 156, 157, 158; history of, estate, 59–60; market, 47; migrants from, thana, 194–95; population of, 34–35
Patna: city, 17, 21, 22, 25; district, 9; Hathwa interests in, city, 151; migration to, district, 192–93, 197
Patwaris, 7, 90, 97–103, 110–11, 167–68, 230; duties of, 97, 101–2; in Hathwa estate, 135–37, 222; and landholders, 100–103, 168–69; in Mughal period, 98; and qanungos, 97–102; socioeconomic backgrounds of, 101; and thikadars, 161; wages of, 101
Pawsey, R. H., 147, 151, 187, 197
Perlin, Frank, 5, 60
Permanent Settlement, 22, 52, 55–56, 70–71, 155–56, 226–28; comparison with other settlements, 228; effects of, in different districts, 226–27
Petitions: to Hathwa estate, 207–8; peasant, 142–43, 207–8, 236; regarding indigo, 207–8
Pilgrims and pilgrimage, 14–15, 17, 18–19, 30; and crime, 208–9
Police, 2, 22, 94–95, 103–4, 212, 229–30
Population, 31–36; and agriculture, 34–42; destiny, 34–46; and desertions, 181–82; and famines, 31–32, 33
Prasad, Rajendra, 124
Prices, agricultural, 50–52
Primogeniture, 73–75, 151, 229
Proprietors, petty. *See* Maliks
Protest, 206–24, 235–39; by assembling, 206–7, 236; "avoidance," 181–90, 204–5; and crime, 208–9, 236; in Hathwa estate, 209–10; and indigo, 207, 211, 237; and petitions, 207–8, 236; and recalcitrance, 206–12, 236; and riots, 212–24

Qanungos, 90, 97–103, 110–11, 230; duties of, 97; in Mughal period, 98; socioeconomic backgrounds of, 99; and patwaris, 97–102, 230

Railways, 22, 26, 41; and migration, 200–201, 203, 205, 235–36
Rajendra Pratap Sahi, 74, 82. *See also* Hathwa estate: maharaja of
Rajputs, 44–46; as landholders, 44; as migrants, 195; as moneylenders, 170–72; occupations of, 46; settlement patterns of, 57–61; as tenants, 45, 46, 50
Religion: and nationalism, 30; popular, 14–18, 27–30. *See also* Festivals; Pilgrims and Pilgrimage; Sonepur: mela

INDEX

Rent, 49–52; in cash, 39; and cesses, 165–68; definition of, 165; and desertions, 183–84, 188–90, 204, 235; differential rates of, 140, 165–66; disputes, 50, 210–11; enhancements, 141, 153–54, 165–66, 189–90; in Hathwa estate, 116, 149, 153–54, 165–66; kists (instalments), 116; and land: revenue, 52, 165
Rentfree holdings. *See* Birtdars
Revelganj town: history of, 92; population of, 34
Rice, 37–42; prices of, 51
Riots, 212–24, 237–38; and agriculture, 213–15; causes of, 212–24; and crime, 212; of 1844, 141–46, 219, 221; in Hathwa estate, 141–46, 219; incidence of, 212–15; numbers of participants in, 215; and police, 217; socioeconomic backgrounds of people involved in, 215–24
Roads, 22. *See also* Transportation
Robinson, Ronald E., 3
Rusi estate, 46, 75, 76, 158; history of, 60, 76

Sarishtadar, 85
Sazawals, 135–37, 138, 234; socioeconomic backgrounds of Hathwa, 136
Scheduled castes, 45, 48, 49; as tenants, 46
Scott, James C., 8, 189
Seal, Anil, 94
Sahahabad district, 9, 110; chaukidars in, 110; Hathwa interests in, 117, 119, 151; migration to, 192–93
Sir system. *See* Estate management: direct
Siwan: cultivation in, thana, 36; Hathwa interests in, 151; landholder of, 56, 63, 68, 73, 226; market, 47; Muslims in, 58; population of, town, 34; population of, thana, 35, 40–41; subdivision, 31, 96
Sonepur, 13–15, 17, 22–26; cultivation in, thana, 36; durbar, 27, 73; landholding patterns in, thana, 156–57; market, 15, 28–29; Meet, 13–14, 19–30, 225–26, 239; Mela, 13–18, 20–30, 225–26; migrants from, thana, 194–95
Stokes, Eric, 3, 71
Subaltern Studies, 2, 236
Sugarcane, 37–40
Survey and Settlement: of 1840s, 142–43; of 1893–1901, 153–54, 209–10; of 1915–1921 (revision), 210, 211–12

Tahsildars, 127–28; socioeconomic backgrounds of Hathwa estate, 128–29
Tamkuhi estate, 63, 69
Telis, 47; as deserters, 187; and illegal cesses, 168; as migrants, 195; occupations of, 47
Temples, 15, 29–30, 120, 122
Tenancy legislation, 164–65
Tenants and Tenancy, 48–49; in Hathwa estate, 151–54
Thana, definition of, 31
Thikadars, 48, 126–34, 138, 168–69, 232–35; and disputes with tenants, 140–41, 162; and estate management: direct system of, 126–27, 139–41, 232–34; Hathwa's amla, 131–32, 138; Hathwa's European, 132–34, 138, 141; Hathwa's Indian, 129–32, 138, 139–41; in Hathwa estate, 126–38, 139–41, 148–51, 232–34; and indigo planters, 132–34; in large estates, 158–59, 176; methods of coercion used by, 149–51, 234–35; and moneylending, 170–71; and riots, 215–21; socioeconomic backgrounds of, 129–34, 139–40, 158–61; in U.P., 129–30
Trade and Traders, 41–42, 47; in Mirganj market, 122; and thikadars, 130
Transportation: improvements in, 221, 235–36; and migration, 200–201; 202–3, 205, 235–36. *See also* Railways; Roads

U.P. (Uttar Pradesh), 9, 22, 57; Court of Wards in, 229; estate management in, 231–32, 235; landholding patterns in, 227–28; migration to, 191–93; thikadars in, 129–30

Village, relation to estates, 158–59
Village headmen. *See* Jeth-raiyats

Wages, 52, 196–97; in agriculture, 196–97, 201–2; in Bengal, 196–97, 201–2; in Bihar, 196–97; of chaukidars, 104–5; in industry, 196–97, 201–2; of patwaris, 101; and prices, 52
Wards, Court of, 6, 78–89, 229; appointed personnel, 80, 85–86; and Bengalis, 88; and development of estate resources, 81–84; and education, 86–88; and Hathwa estate, 80–82, 123–24, 146; as normative institution, 86–89; in U.P., 229